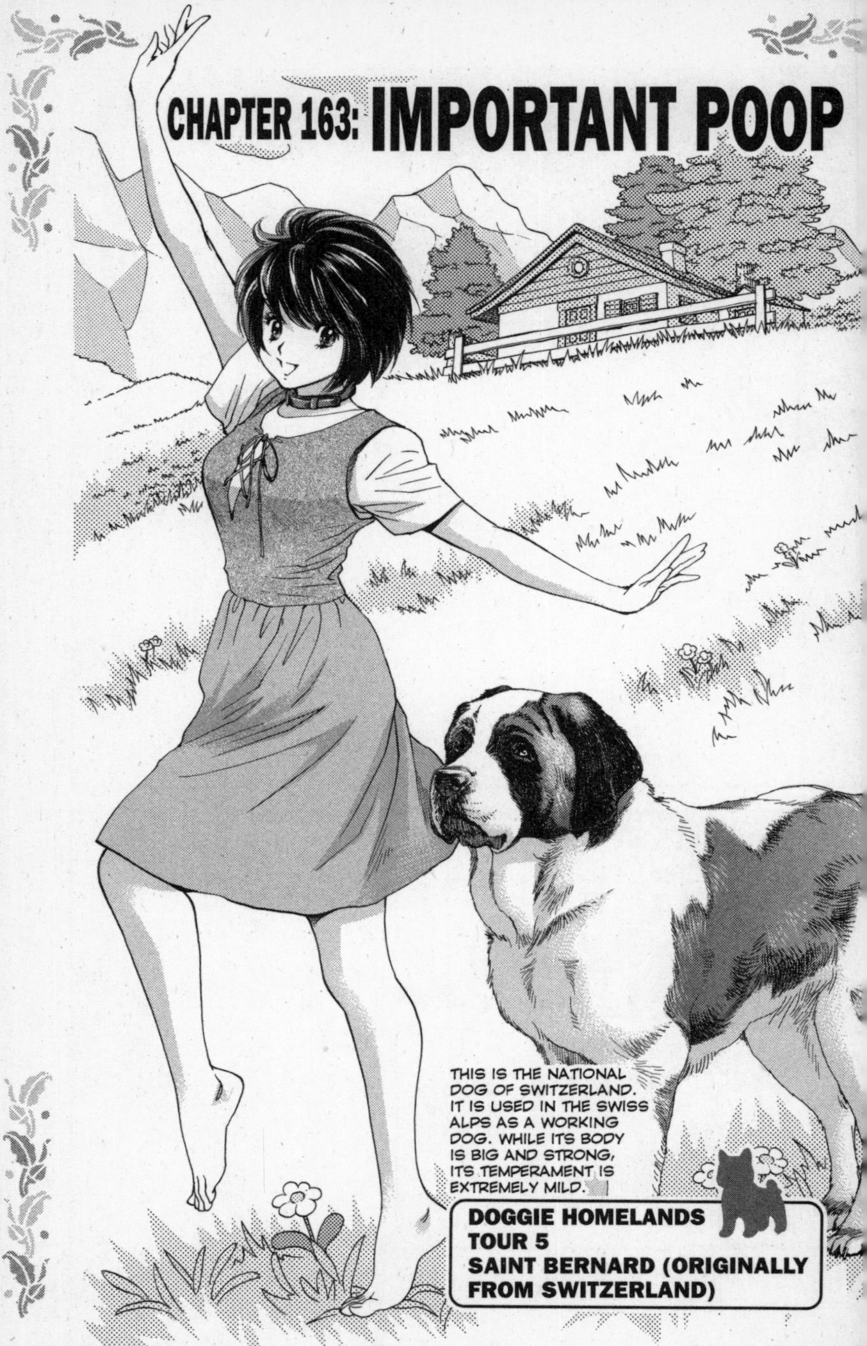
CHAPTER 163: IMPORTANT POOP
THIS IS THE NATIONAL DOG OF SWITZERLAND. IT IS USED IN THE SWISS ALPS AS A WORKING DOG. WHILE ITS BODY IS BIG AND STRONG, ITS TEMPERAMENT IS EXTREMELY MILD.
DOGGIE HOMELANDS TOUR 5 SAINT BERNARD (ORIGINALLY FROM SWITZERLAND)

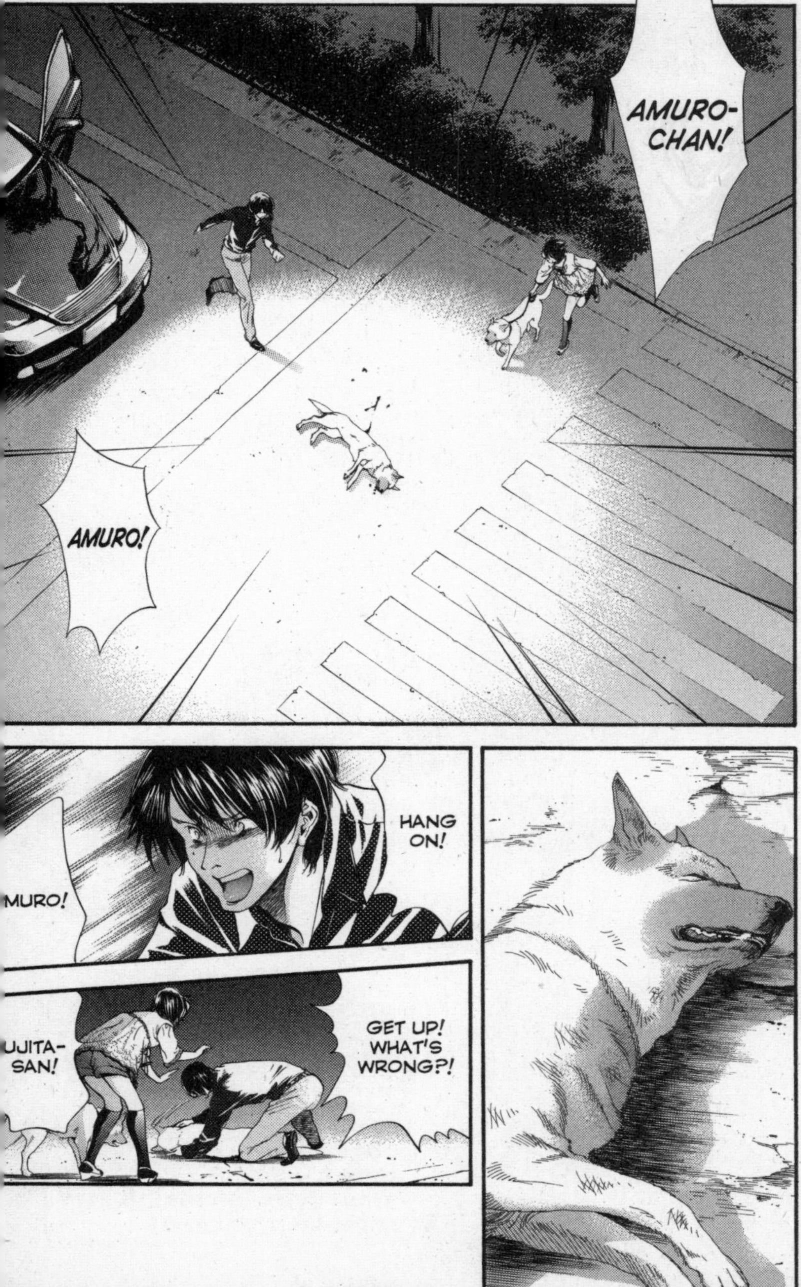
AMURO-CHAN!
AMURO!
HANG ON!
MURO!
GET UP! WHAT'S WRONG?!
UJITA-SAN!

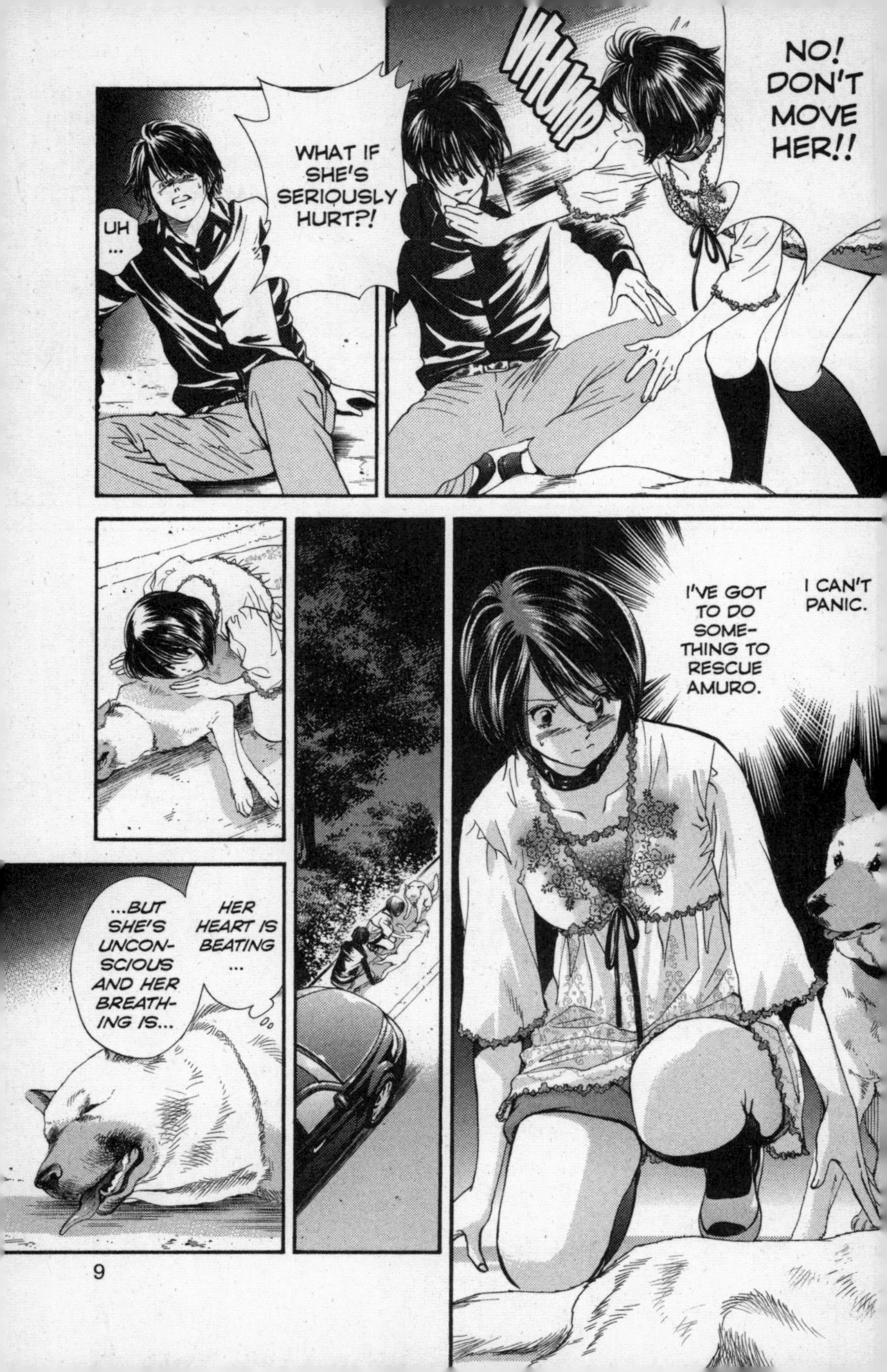
NO! DON'T MOVE HER!!
WHUMP
WHAT IF SHE'S SERIOUSLY HURT?!
UH ...
I CAN'T PANIC.
I'VE GOT TO DO SOMETHING TO RESCUE AMURO.
HER HEART IS BEATING ...
...BUT SHE'S UNCONSCIOUS AND HER BREATHING IS...

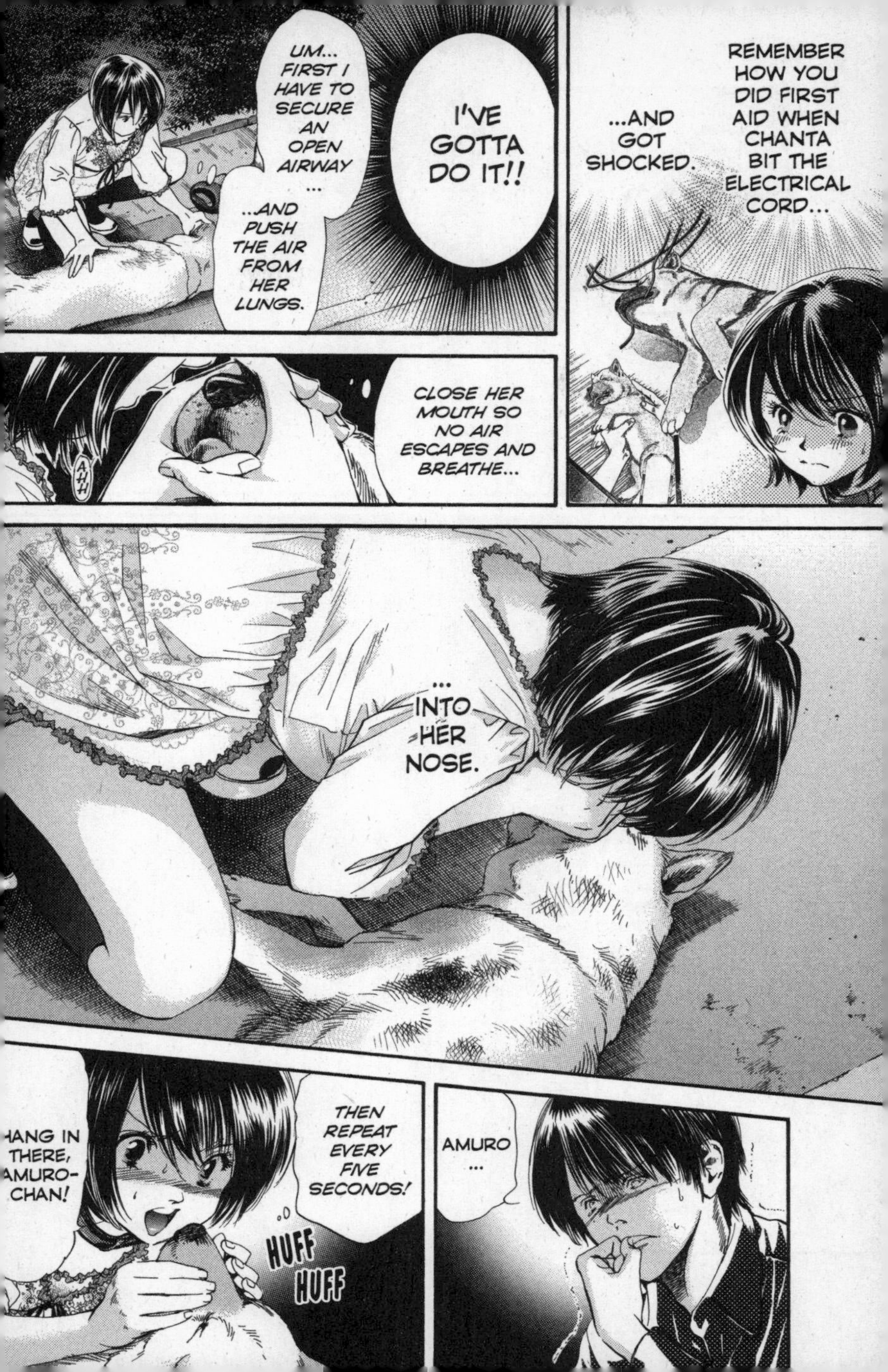
REMEMBER HOW YOU DID FIRST AID WHEN CHANTA BIT THE ELECTRICAL CORD...
...AND GOT SHOCKED.
I'VE GOTTA DO IT!!
UM... FIRST I HAVE TO SECURE AN OPEN AIRWAY...
...AND PUSH THE AIR FROM HER LUNGS.
CLOSE HER MOUTH SO NO AIR ESCAPES AND BREATHE...
AHH
...INTO HER NOSE.
AMURO...
THEN REPEAT EVERY FIVE SECONDS!
HANG IN THERE, AMURO-CHAN!
HUFF
HUFF

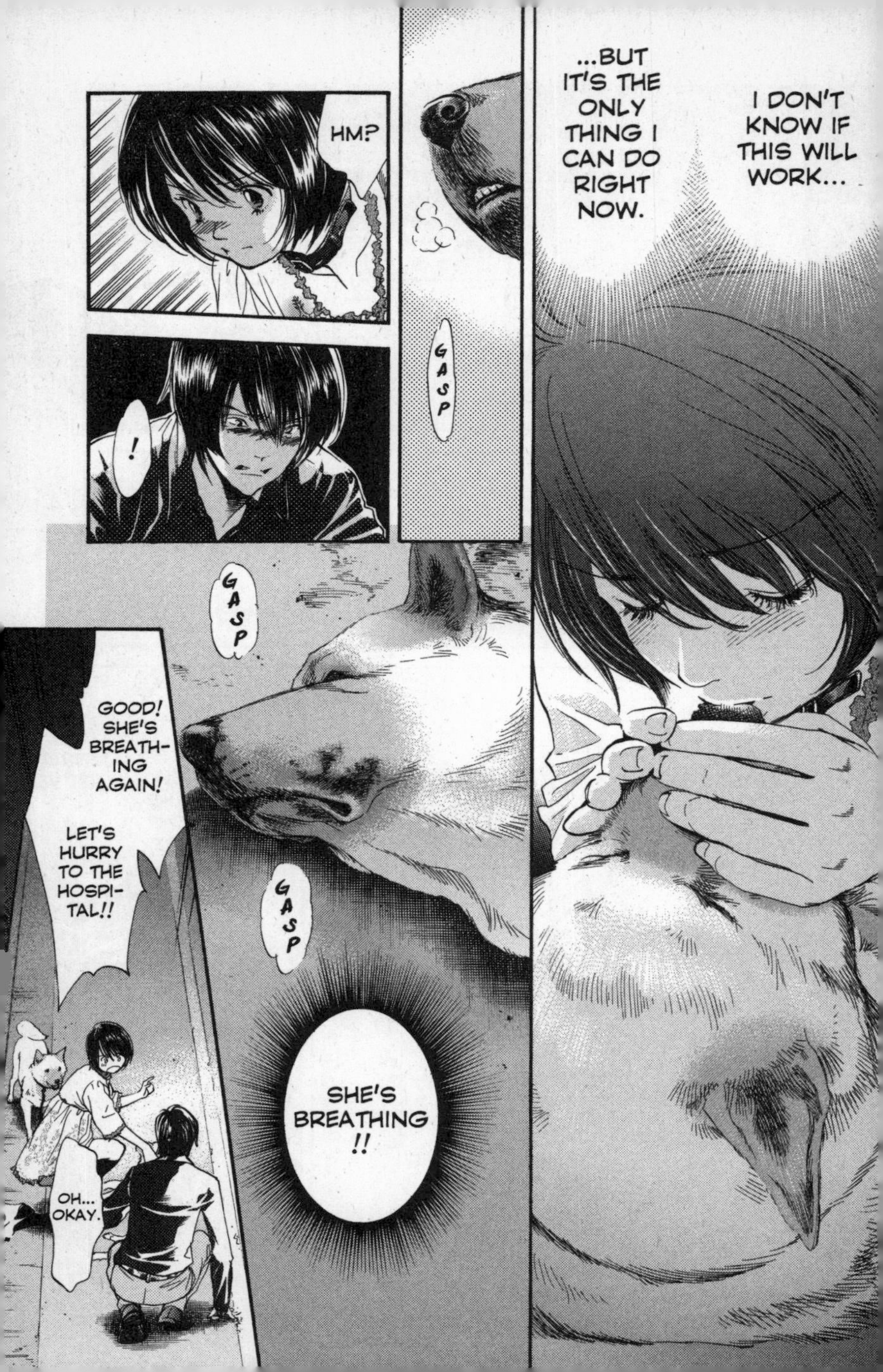
I DON'T KNOW IF THIS WILL WORK...
...BUT IT'S THE ONLY THING I CAN DO RIGHT NOW.
GASP
HM?
!
GASP
GASP
SHE'S BREATHING!!
GOOD! SHE'S BREATH-ING AGAIN!
LET'S HURRY TO THE HOSPI-TAL!!
OH... OKAY.

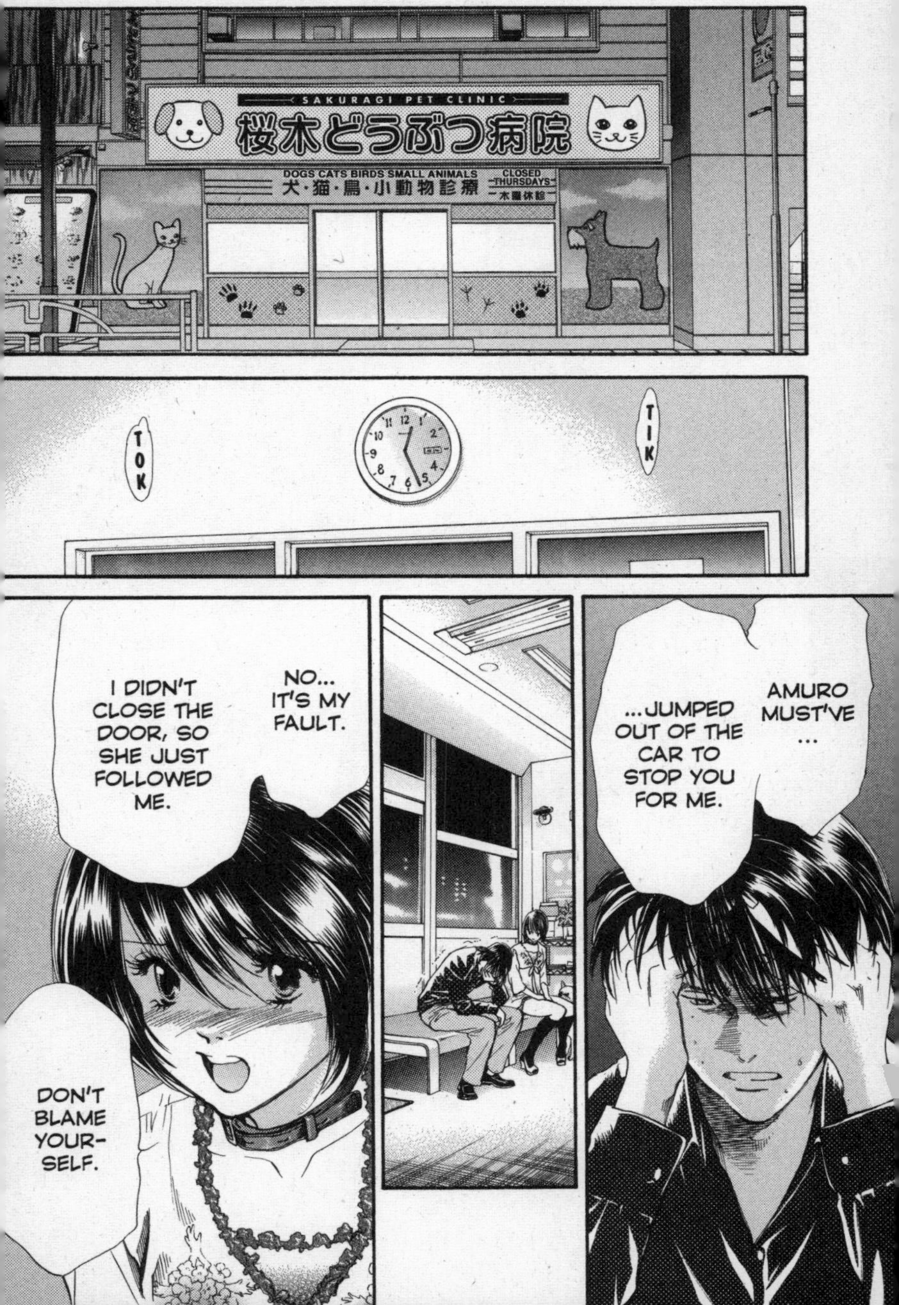
SAKURAGI PET CLINIC
桜木どうぶつ病院
DOGS CATS BIRDS SMALL ANIMALS
犬・猫・鳥・小動物診療
CLOSED THURSDAYS
木曜休診
TIK
TOK
AMURO MUST'VE ...
...JUMPED OUT OF THE CAR TO STOP YOU FOR ME.
NO... IT'S MY FAULT.
I DIDN'T CLOSE THE DOOR, SO SHE JUST FOLLOWED ME.
DON'T BLAME YOUR-SELF.

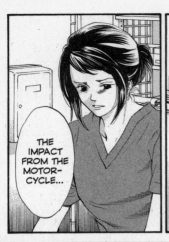

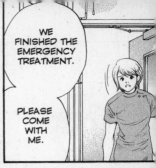

WE FINISHED THE EMERGENCY TREATMENT.

PLEASE COME WITH ME.

THE IMPACT FROM THE MOTOR-CYCLE...

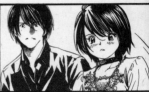

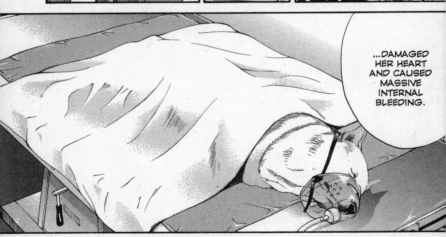

...DAMAGED HER HEART AND CAUSED MASSIVE INTERNAL BLEEDING.

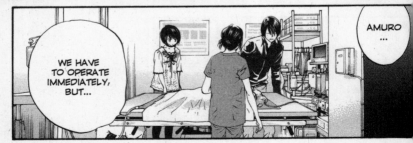

WE HAVE TO OPERATE IMMEDIATELY, BUT...

AMURO...

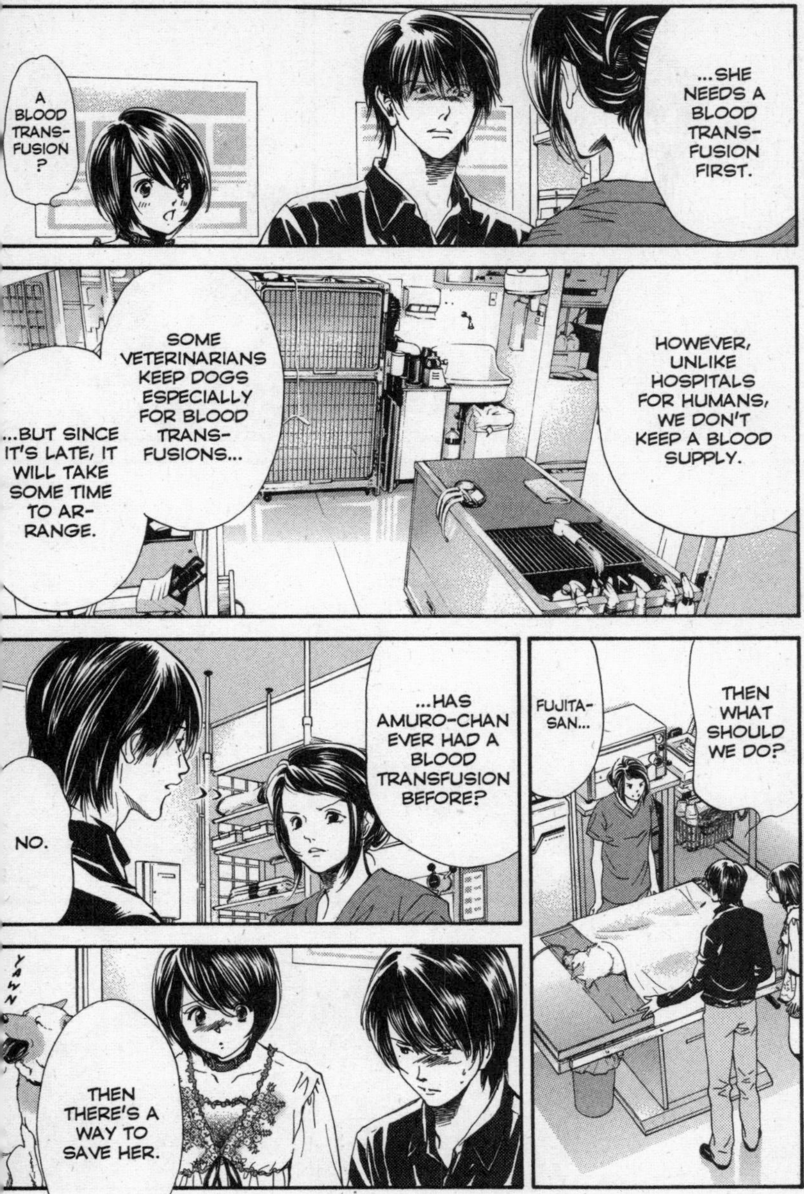
...SHE NEEDS A BLOOD TRANSFUSION FIRST.
A BLOOD TRANSFUSION?
HOWEVER, UNLIKE HOSPITALS FOR HUMANS, WE DON'T KEEP A BLOOD SUPPLY.
SOME VETERINARIANS KEEP DOGS ESPECIALLY FOR BLOOD TRANSFUSIONS...
...BUT SINCE IT'S LATE, IT WILL TAKE SOME TIME TO ARRANGE.
THEN WHAT SHOULD WE DO?
FUJITA-SAN...
...HAS AMURO-CHAN EVER HAD A BLOOD TRANSFUSION BEFORE?
NO.
YAWN
THEN THERE'S A WAY TO SAVE HER.

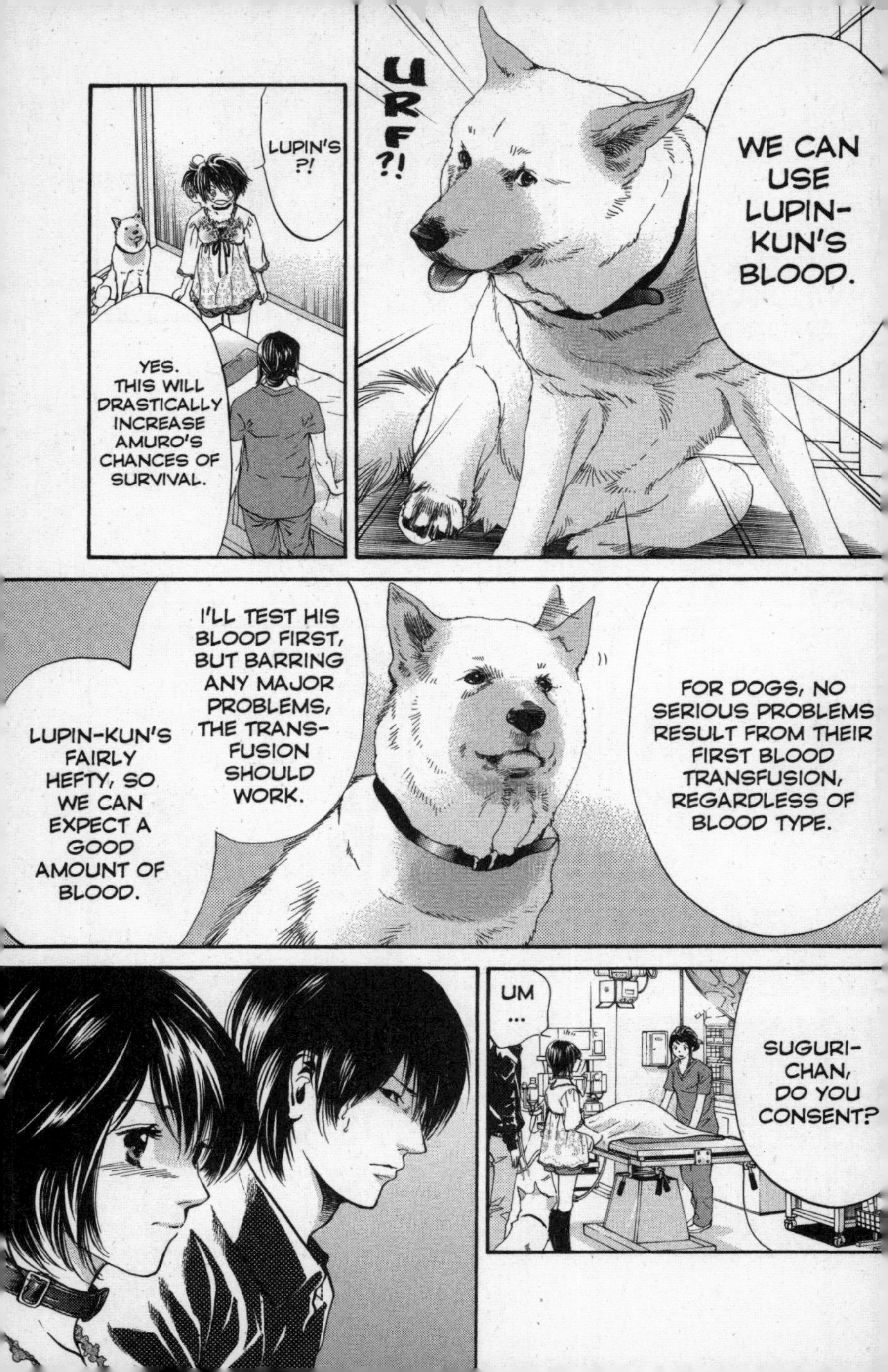
WE CAN USE LUPIN-KUN'S BLOOD.
URF ?!
LUPIN'S ?!
YES. THIS WILL DRASTICALLY INCREASE AMURO'S CHANCES OF SURVIVAL.
FOR DOGS, NO SERIOUS PROBLEMS RESULT FROM THEIR FIRST BLOOD TRANSFUSION, REGARDLESS OF BLOOD TYPE.
I'LL TEST HIS BLOOD FIRST, BUT BARRING ANY MAJOR PROBLEMS, THE TRANS-FUSION SHOULD WORK.
LUPIN-KUN'S FAIRLY HEFTY, SO WE CAN EXPECT A GOOD AMOUNT OF BLOOD.
SUGURI-CHAN, DO YOU CONSENT?
UM ...

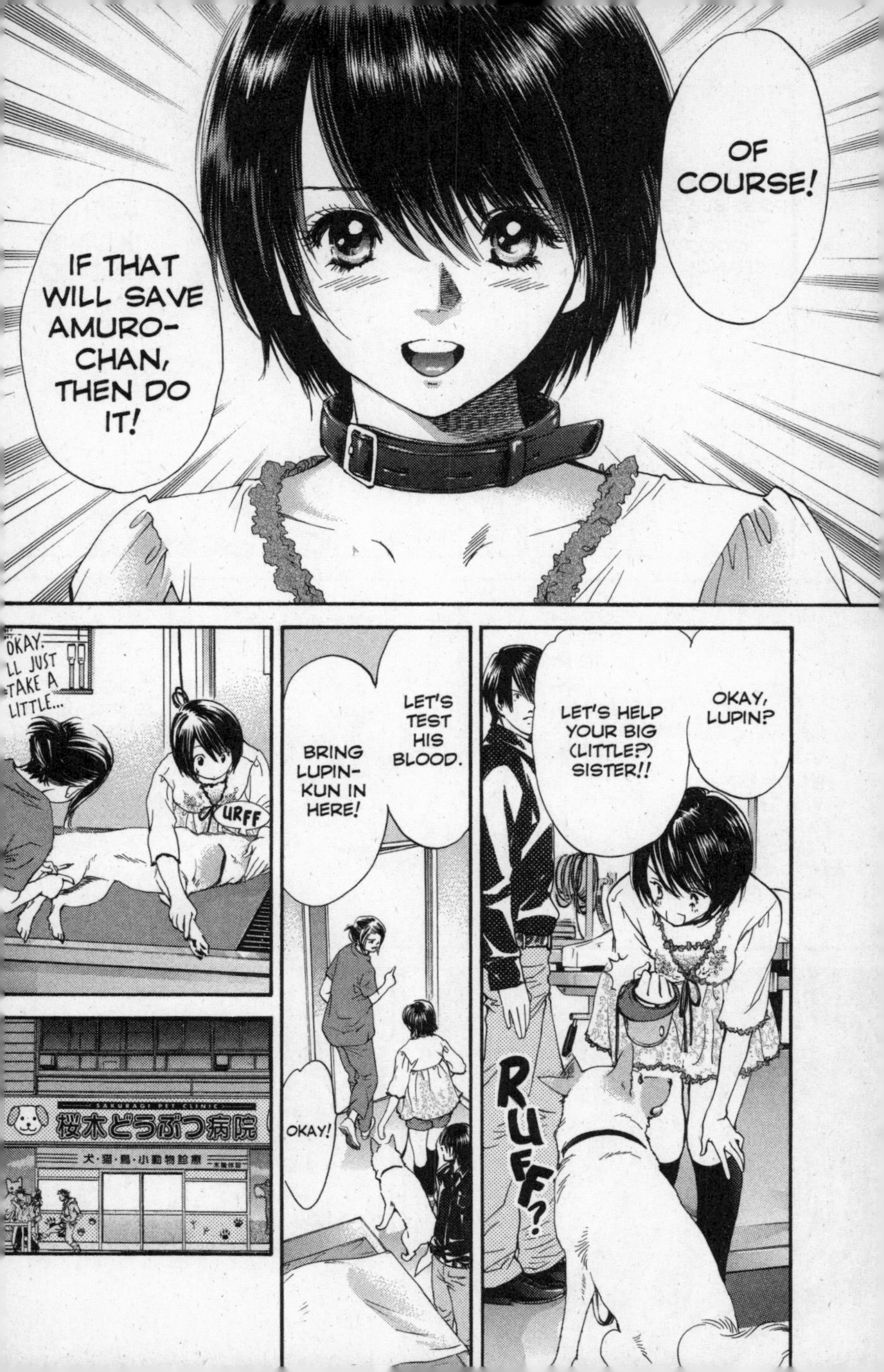
OF COURSE!
IF THAT WILL SAVE AMURO-CHAN, THEN DO IT!
OKAY, LUPIN?
LET'S HELP YOUR BIG (LITTLE?) SISTER!!
RUFF?
LET'S TEST HIS BLOOD.
BRING LUPIN-KUN IN HERE!
OKAY!
OKAY. LL JUST TAKE A LITTLE...
URFF
SAKURAGI PET CLINIC
桜木どうぶつ病院
犬・猫・鳥・小動物診療

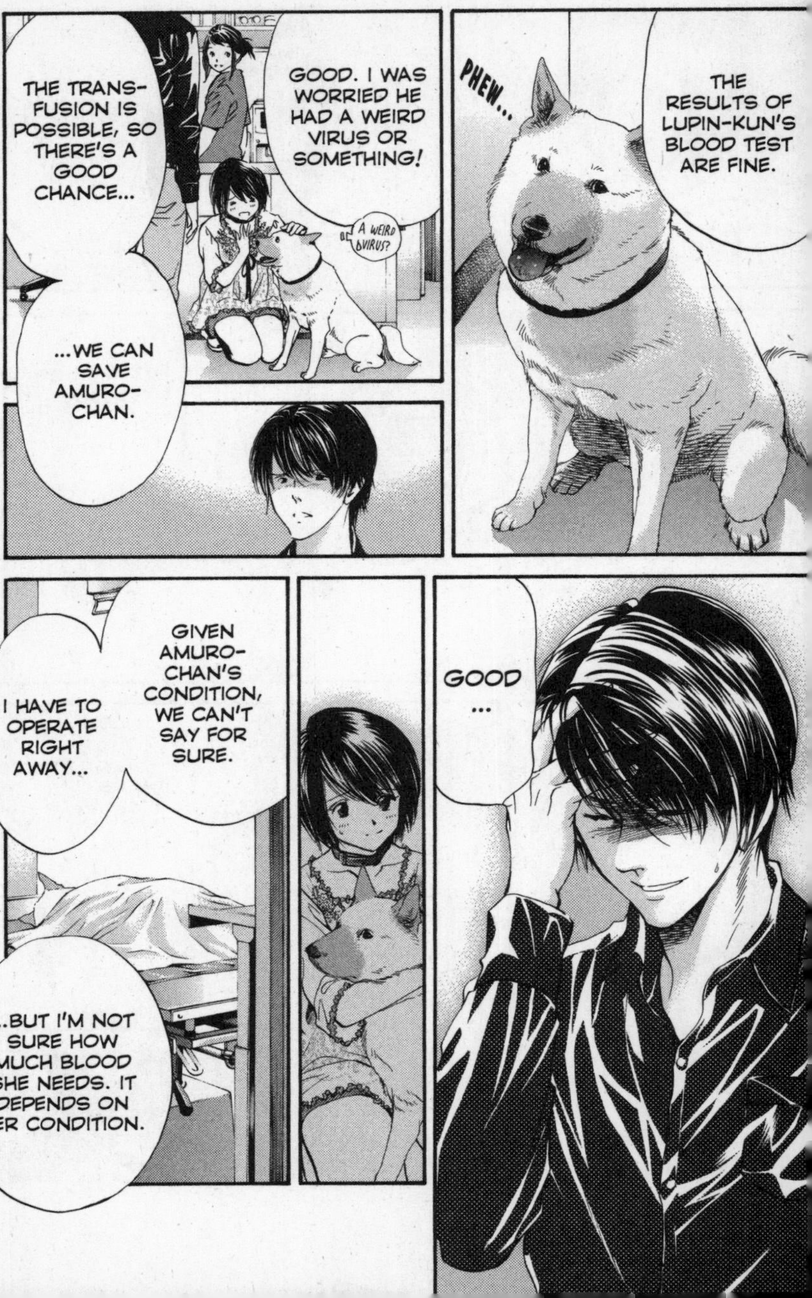
THE RESULTS OF LUPIN-KUN'S BLOOD TEST ARE FINE.
PHEW...
GOOD. I WAS WORRIED HE HAD A WEIRD VIRUS OR SOMETHING!
A WEIRD VIRUS?
THE TRANS-FUSION IS POSSIBLE, SO THERE'S A GOOD CHANCE...
...WE CAN SAVE AMURO-CHAN.
GOOD ...
GIVEN AMURO-CHAN'S CONDITION, WE CAN'T SAY FOR SURE.
I HAVE TO OPERATE RIGHT AWAY...
...BUT I'M NOT SURE HOW MUCH BLOOD SHE NEEDS. IT DEPENDS ON HER CONDITION.

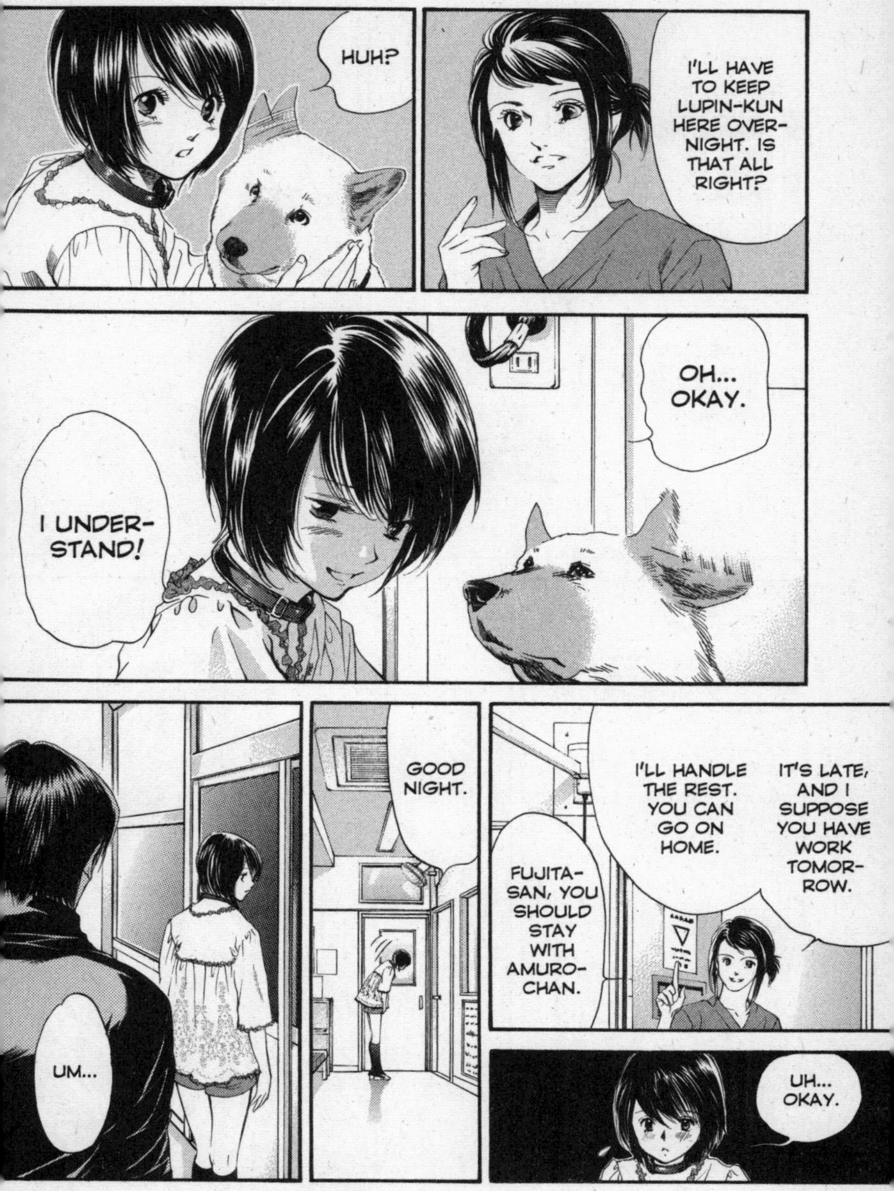
I'LL HAVE TO KEEP LUPIN-KUN HERE OVER-NIGHT. IS THAT ALL RIGHT?
HUH?
OH... OKAY.
I UNDER-STAND!
IT'S LATE, AND I SUPPOSE YOU HAVE WORK TOMOR-ROW.
I'LL HANDLE THE REST. YOU CAN GO ON HOME.
FUJITA-SAN, YOU SHOULD STAY WITH AMURO-CHAN.
UH... OKAY.
GOOD NIGHT.
UM...

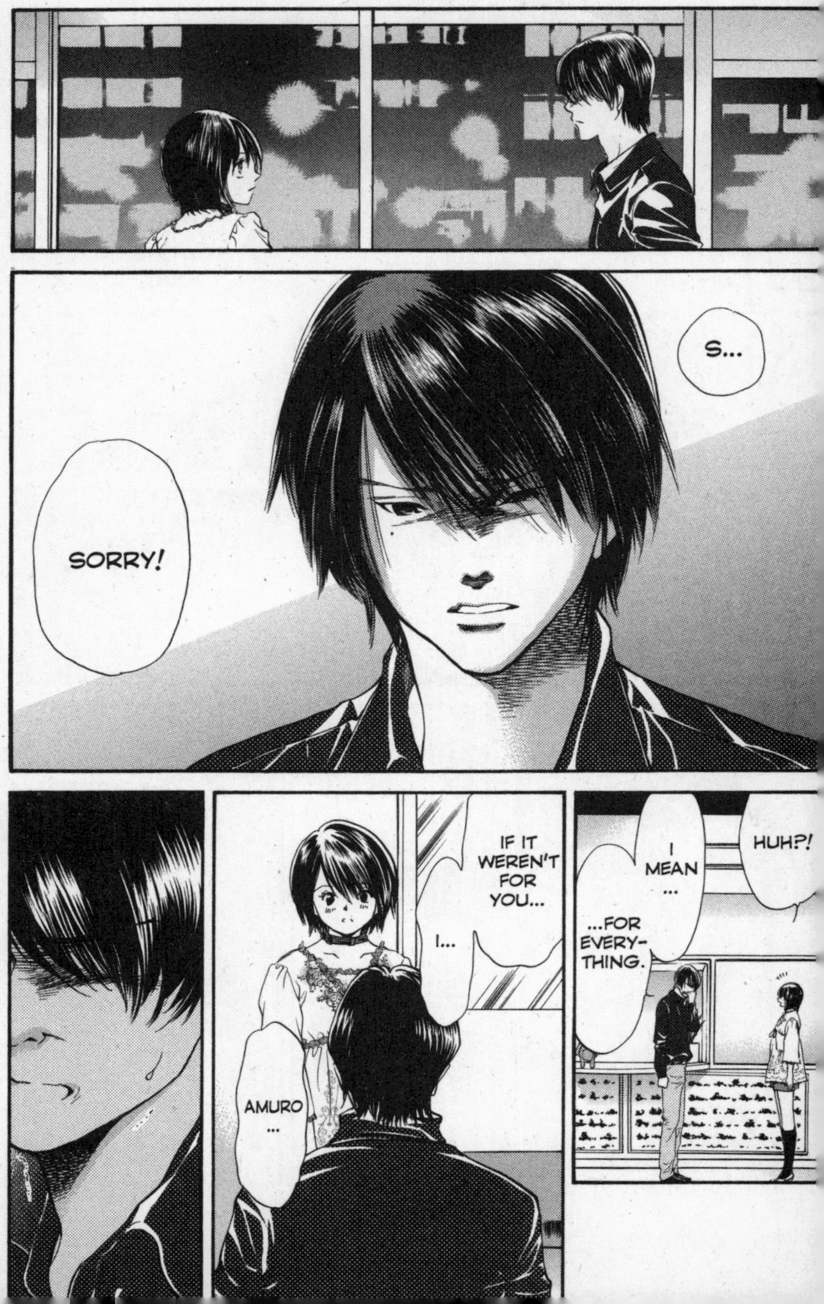
S...
SORRY!
HUH?!
I MEAN ...
...FOR EVERY-THING.
IF IT WEREN'T FOR YOU...
I...
AMURO ...

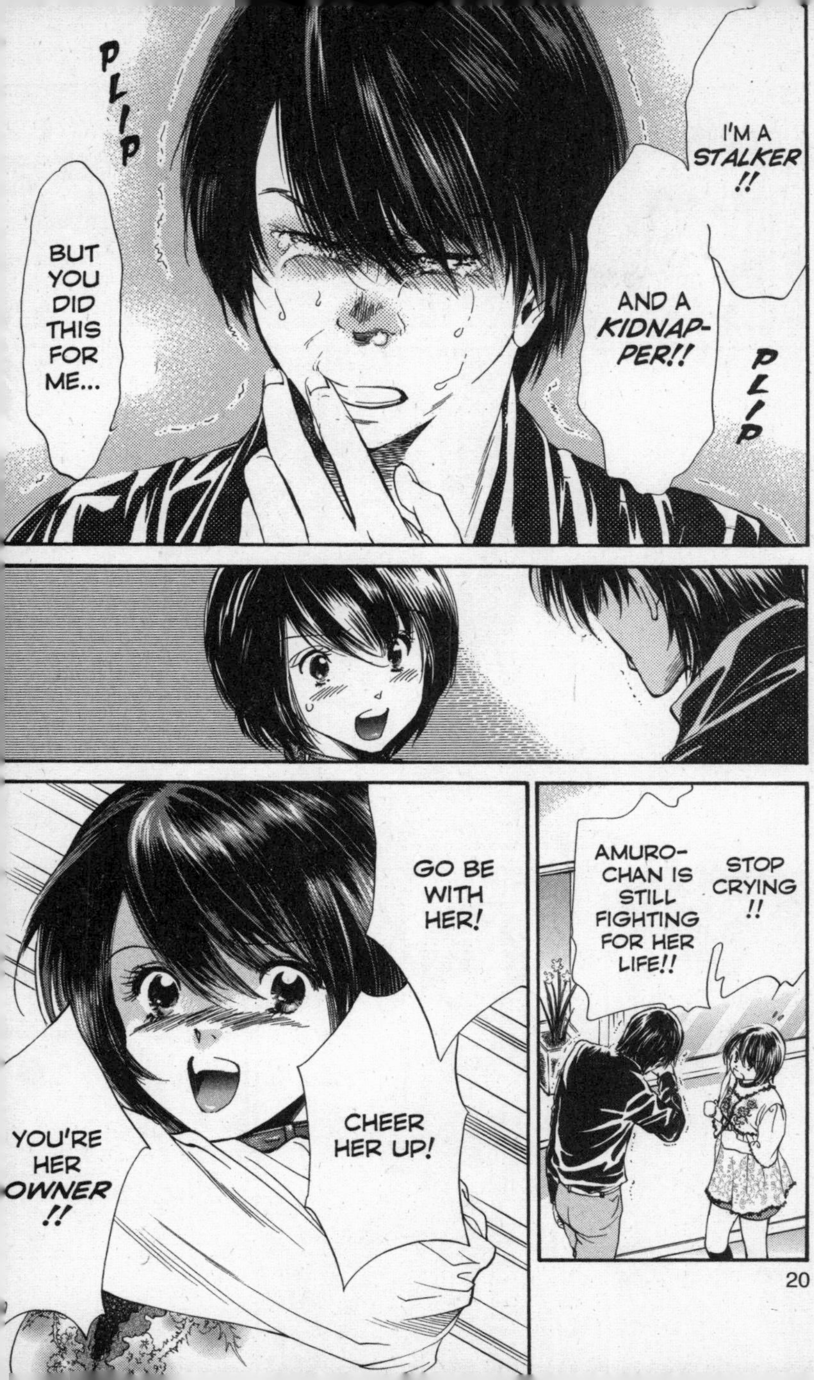
I'M A STALKER!!
AND A KIDNAPPER!!
PLIP
BUT YOU DID THIS FOR ME...
PLIP
STOP CRYING!!
AMURO-CHAN IS STILL FIGHTING FOR HER LIFE!!
GO BE WITH HER!
CHEER HER UP!
YOU'RE HER OWNER!!

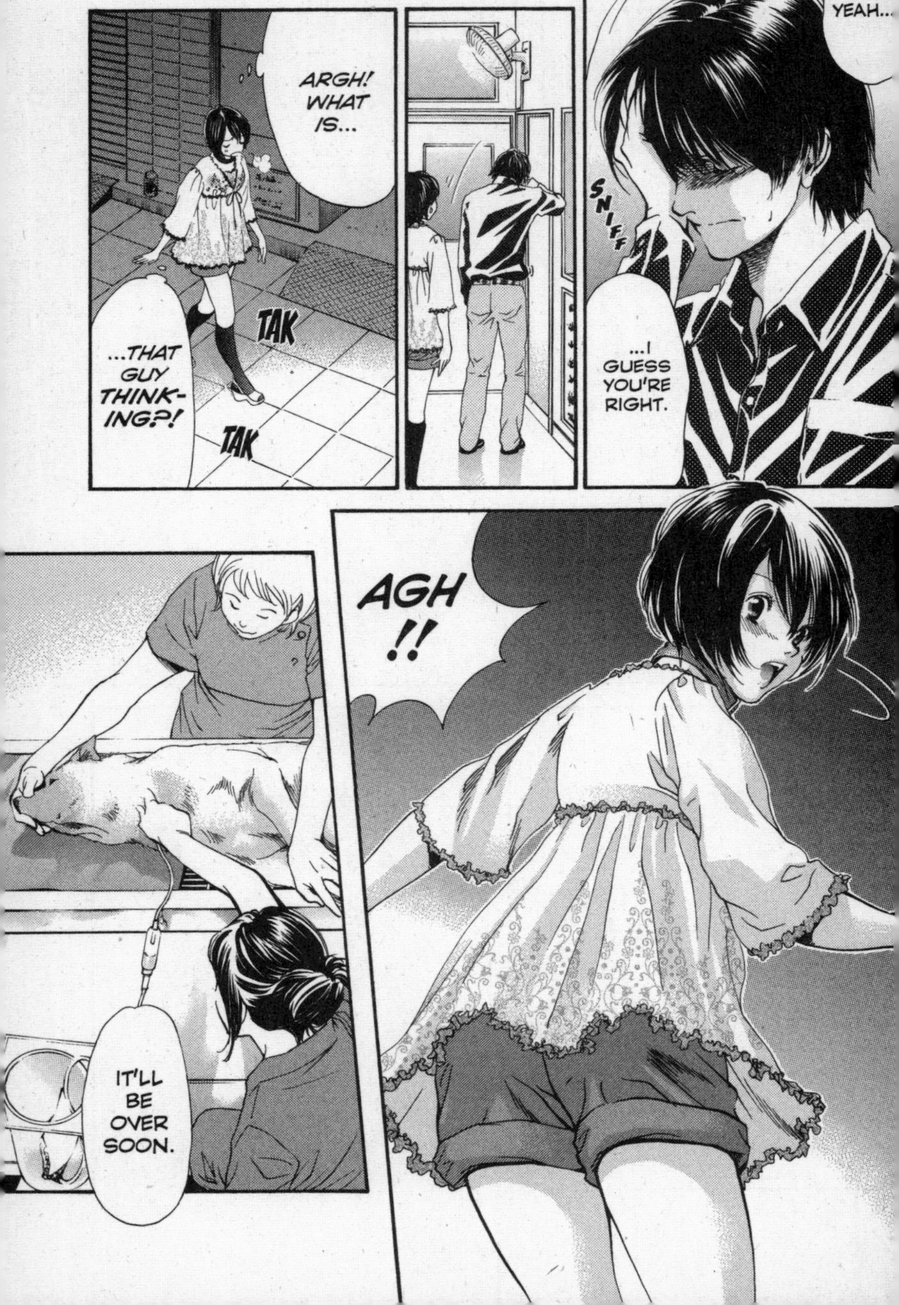
YEAH...
SNIFF
...I GUESS YOU'RE RIGHT.
ARGH! WHAT IS...
TAK
...THAT GUY THINKING?!
TAK
AGH!!
IT'LL BE OVER SOON.

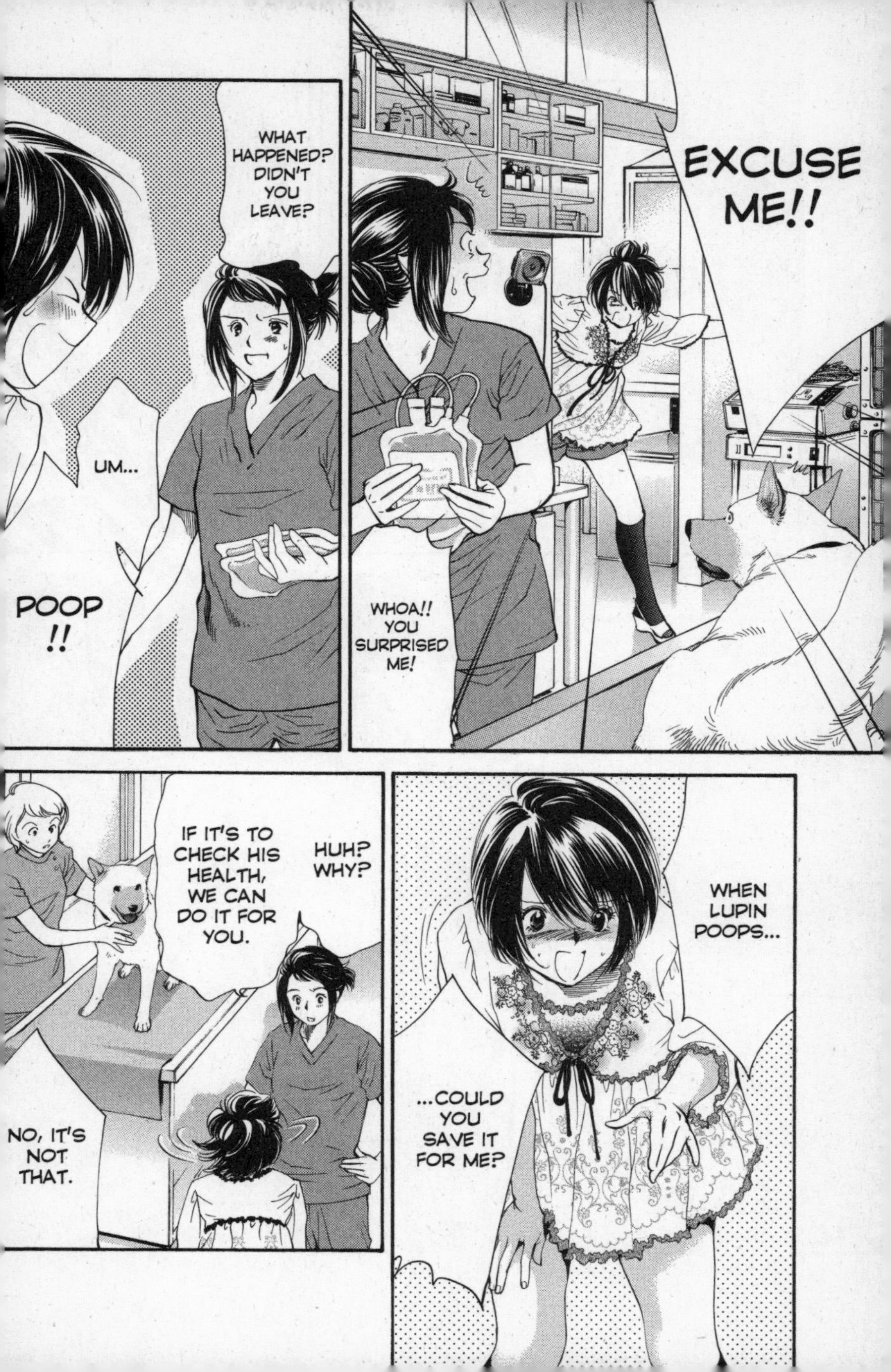
EXCUSE ME!!
WHOA!! YOU SURPRISED ME!
WHAT HAPPENED? DIDN'T YOU LEAVE?
UM...
POOP !!
WHEN LUPIN POOPS...
...COULD YOU SAVE IT FOR ME?
HUH? WHY?
IF IT'S TO CHECK HIS HEALTH, WE CAN DO IT FOR YOU.
NO, IT'S NOT THAT.

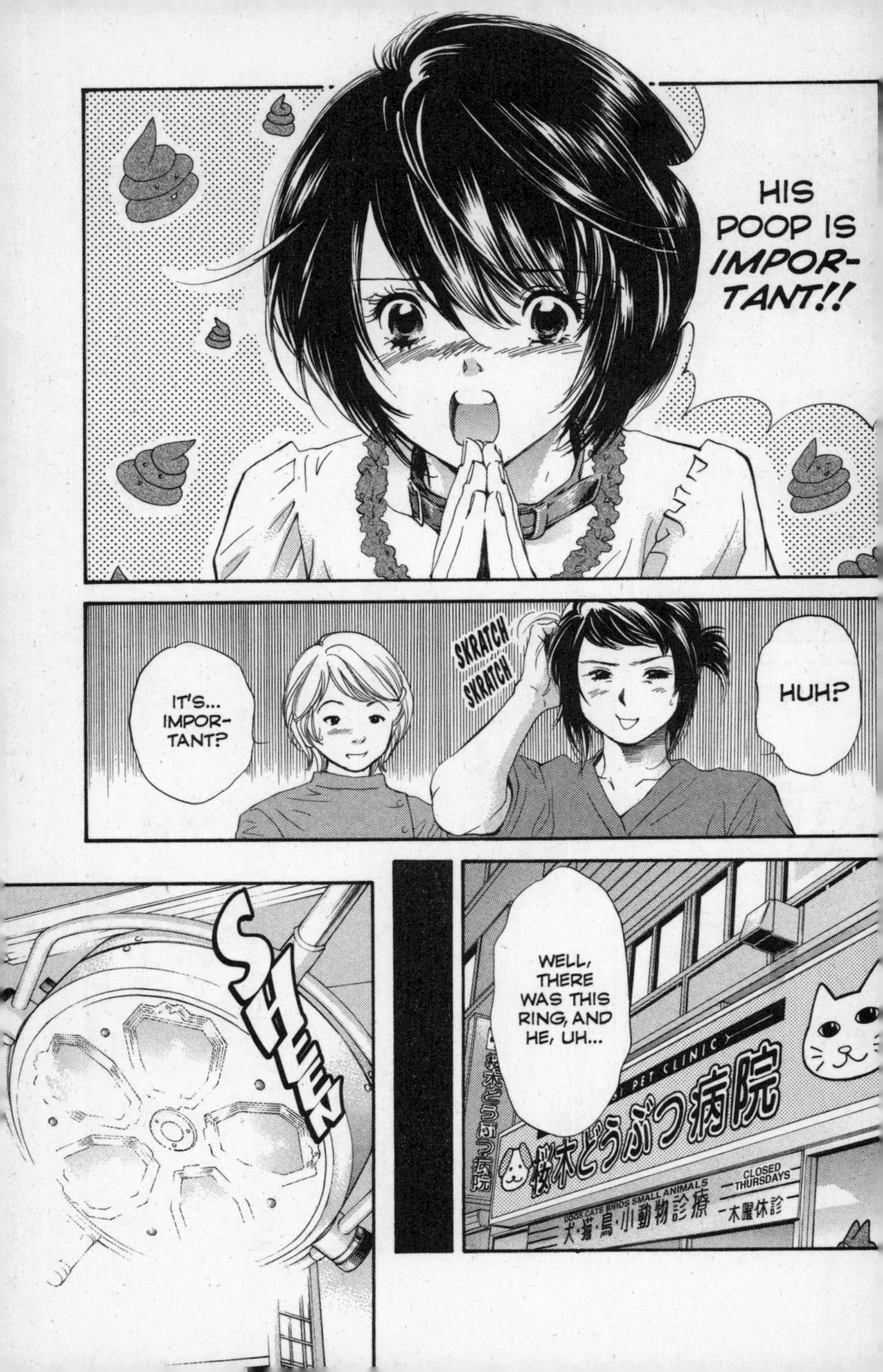
HIS POOP IS IMPORTANT!!
HUH?
SKRATCH SKRATCH
IT'S... IMPORTANT?
WELL, THERE WAS THIS RING, AND HE, UH...
桜木どうぶつ病院
桜木どうぶつ病院
DOGS CATS BIRDS SMALL ANIMALS
犬·猫·鳥·小動物診療
CLOSED THURSDAYS
木曜休診
SHEEN

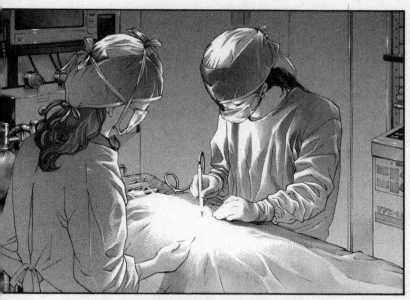

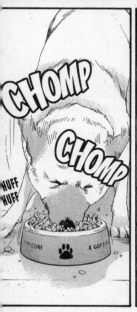

CHOMP

CHOMP

HUFF
HUFF

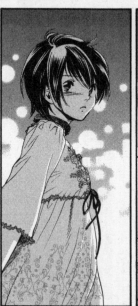

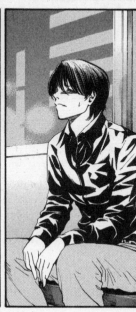

24

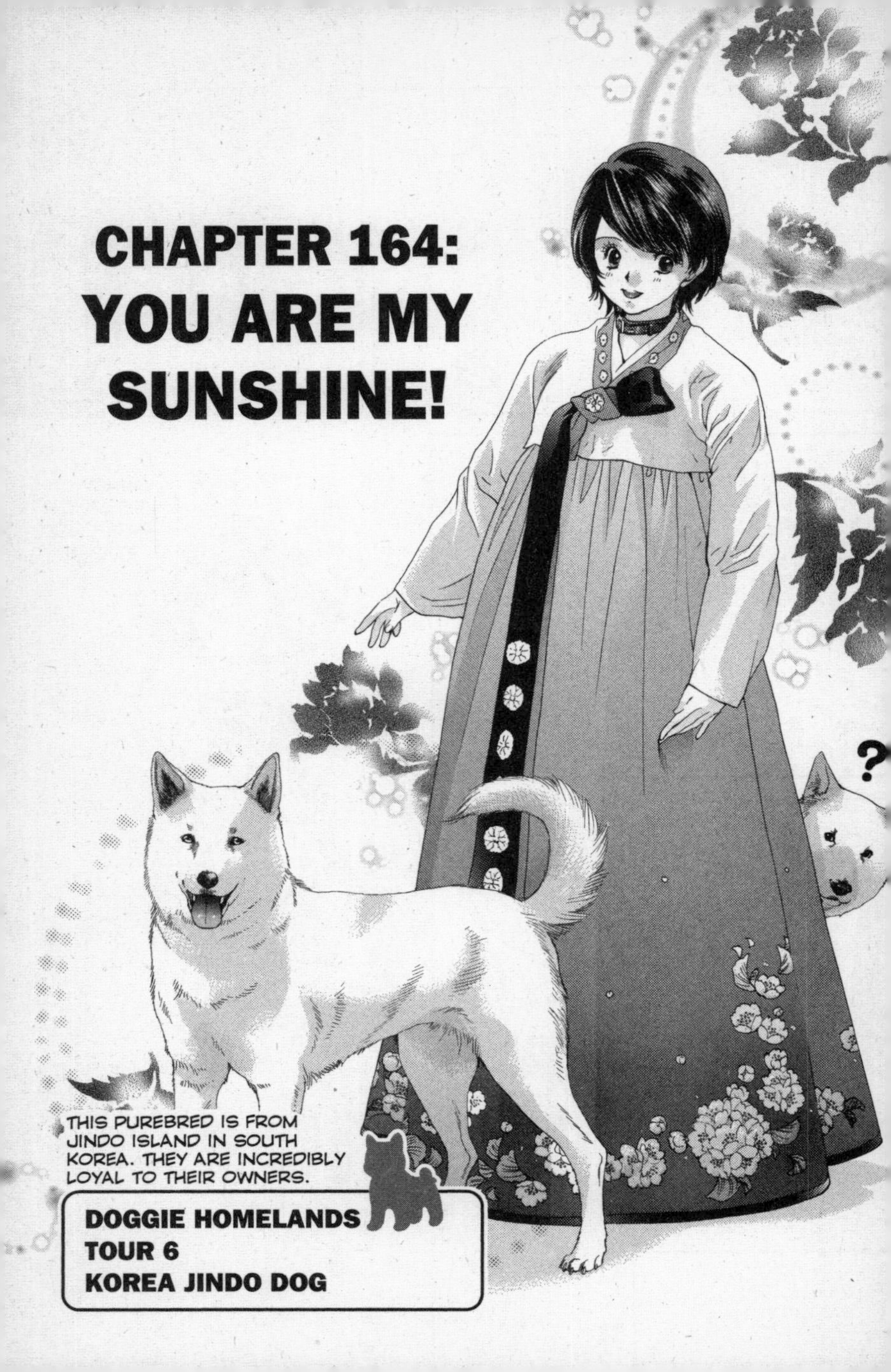
CHAPTER 164: YOU ARE MY SUNSHINE!
?
THIS PUREBRED IS FROM JINDO ISLAND IN SOUTH KOREA. THEY ARE INCREDIBLY LOYAL TO THEIR OWNERS.
DOGGIE HOMELANDS TOUR 6 KOREA JINDO DOG

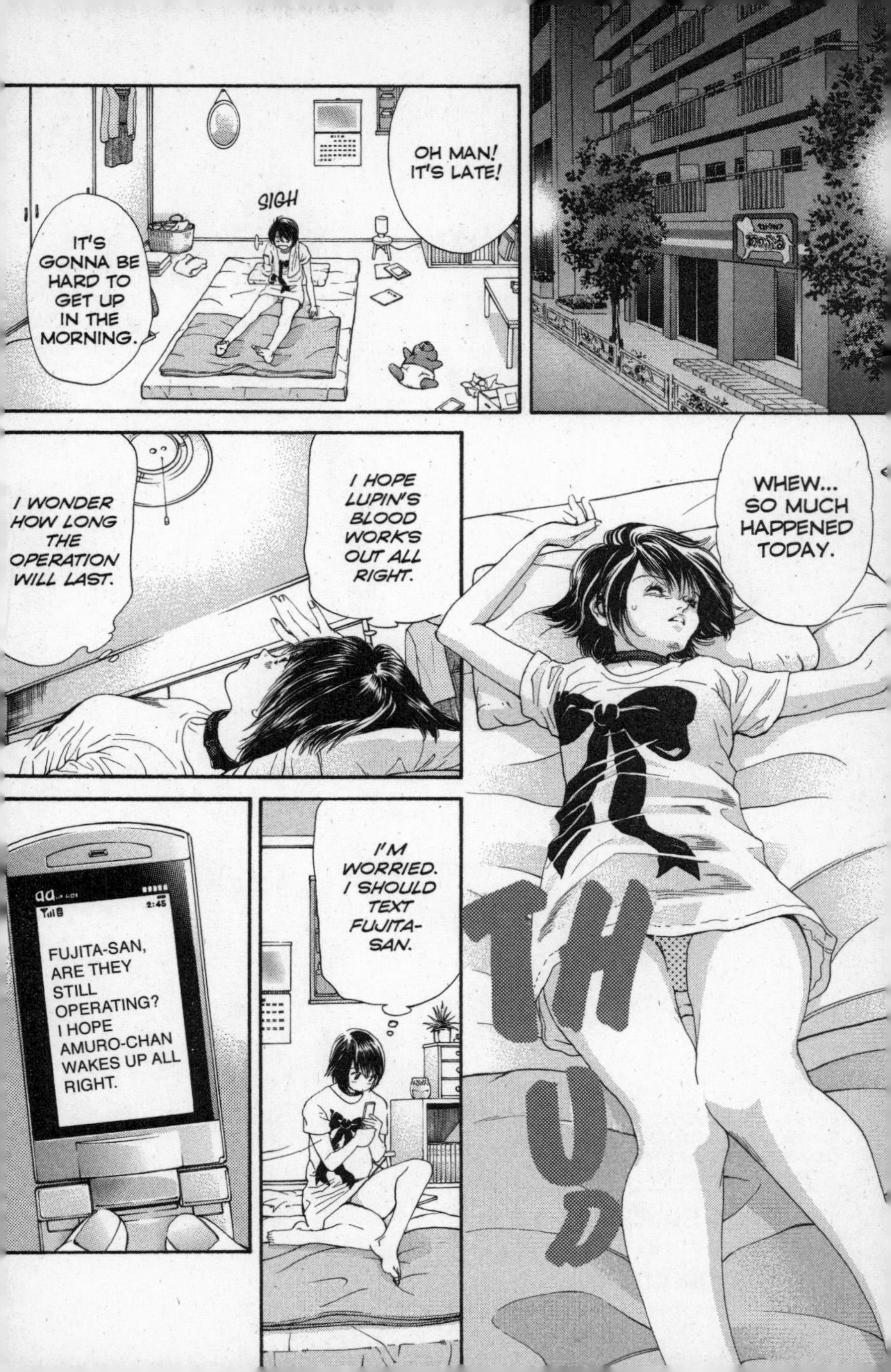

OH MAN! IT'S LATE!
SIGH
IT'S GONNA BE HARD TO GET UP IN THE MORNING.
WHEW... SO MUCH HAPPENED TODAY.
THUD
I HOPE LUPIN'S BLOOD WORKS OUT ALL RIGHT.
I WONDER HOW LONG THE OPERATION WILL LAST.
I'M WORRIED. I SHOULD TEXT FUJITA-SAN.
2:45
FUJITA-SAN, ARE THEY STILL OPERATING? I HOPE AMURO-CHAN WAKES UP ALL RIGHT.

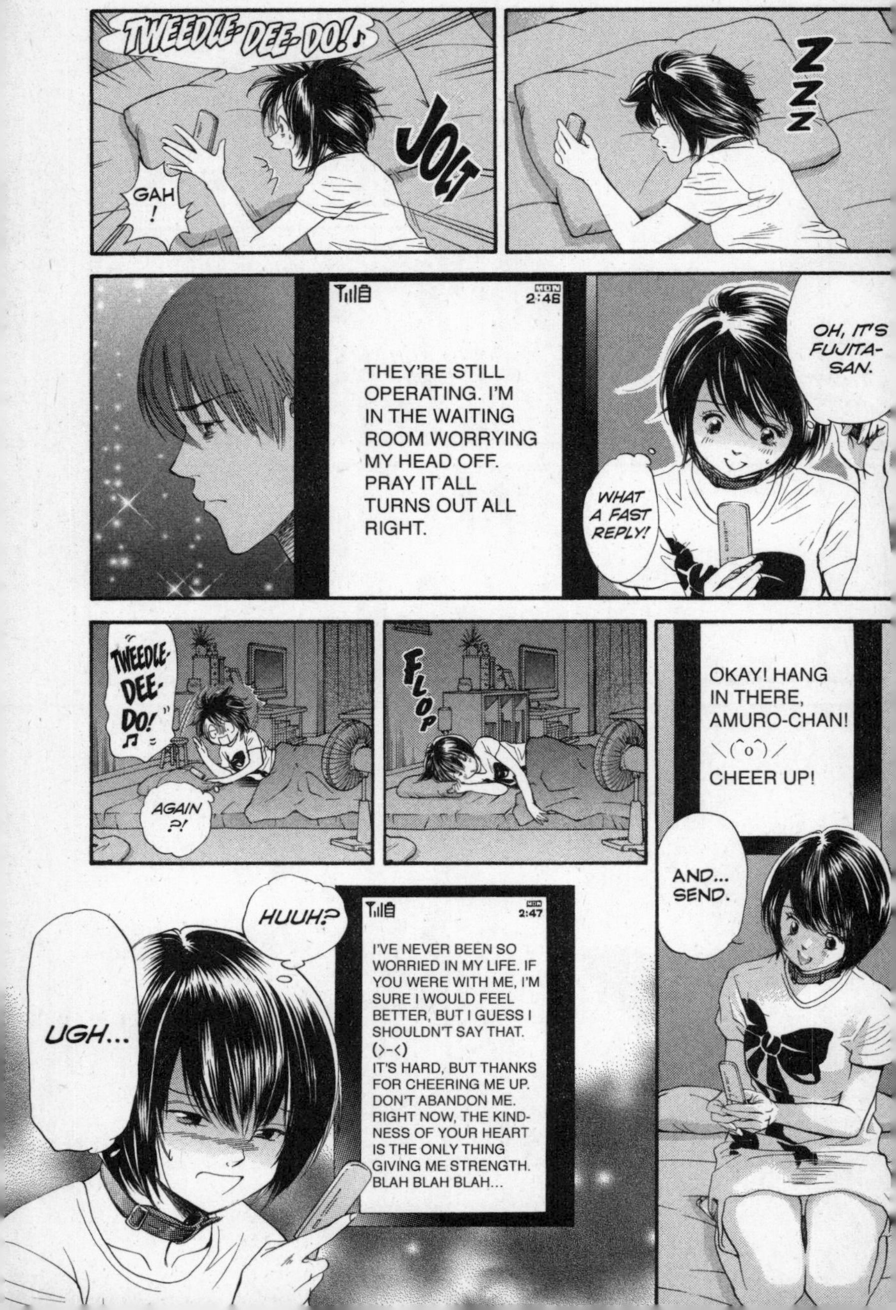
ZZZ
TWEEDLE-DEE-DO! ♪
JOLT
GAH!
OH, IT'S FUJITA-SAN.
WHAT A FAST REPLY!
MON
2:46
THEY'RE STILL OPERATING. I'M IN THE WAITING ROOM WORRYING MY HEAD OFF. PRAY IT ALL TURNS OUT ALL RIGHT.
OKAY! HANG IN THERE, AMURO-CHAN!
＼(^o^)／
CHEER UP!
FLOP
TWEEDLE-DEE-DO! ♫
AGAIN?!
AND... SEND.
MON
2:47
I'VE NEVER BEEN SO WORRIED IN MY LIFE. IF YOU WERE WITH ME, I'M SURE I WOULD FEEL BETTER, BUT I GUESS I SHOULDN'T SAY THAT.
(>-<)
IT'S HARD, BUT THANKS FOR CHEERING ME UP. DON'T ABANDON ME. RIGHT NOW, THE KINDNESS OF YOUR HEART IS THE ONLY THING GIVING ME STRENGTH. BLAH BLAH BLAH...
HUUH?
UGH...

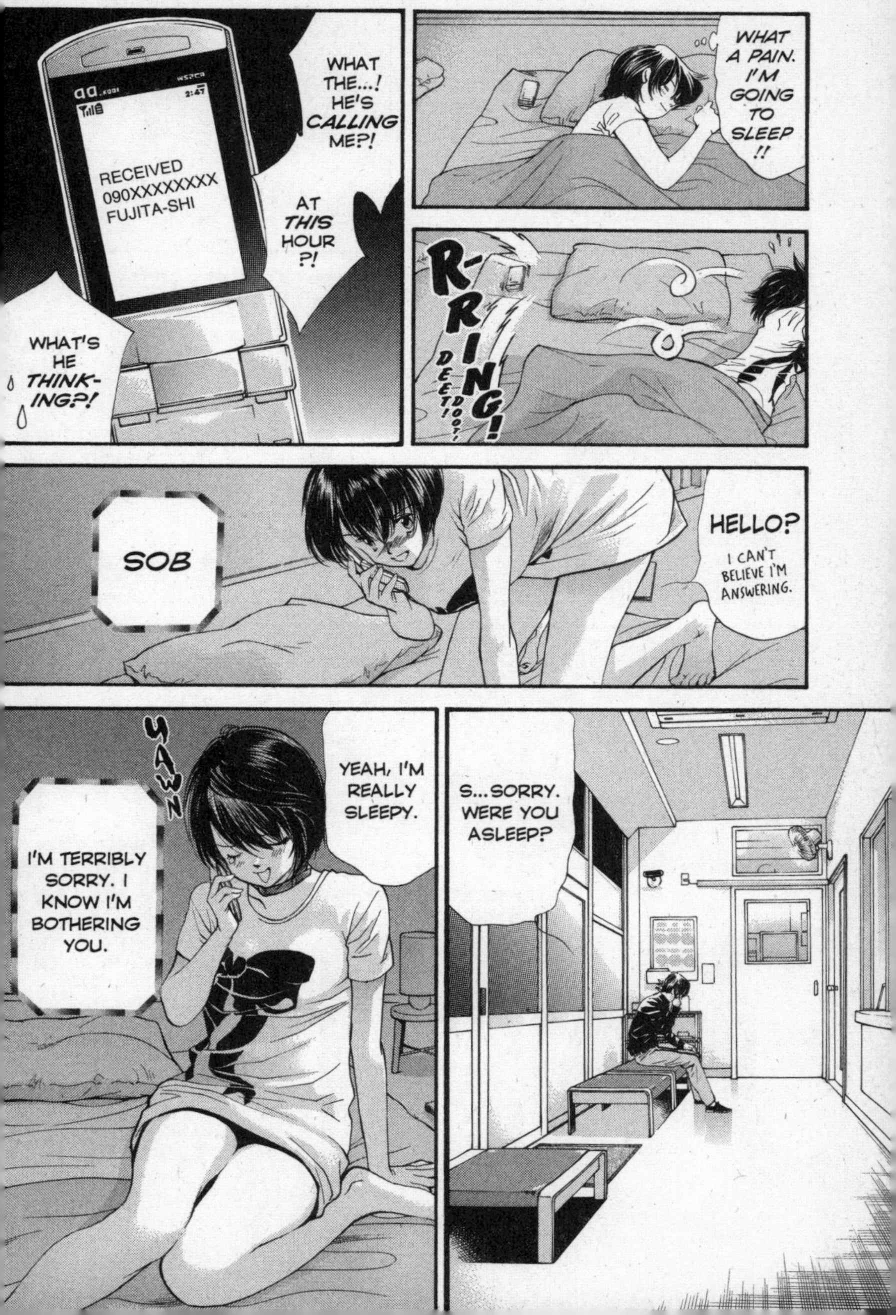
WHAT A PAIN. I'M GOING TO SLEEP !!
R-RING!
DEET! DOOT!
aa
2:47
RECEIVED
090XXXXXXXX
FUJITA-SHI
WHAT THE...! HE'S CALLING ME?!
AT THIS HOUR ?!
WHAT'S HE THINKING?!
HELLO?
I CAN'T BELIEVE I'M ANSWERING.
SOB
S...SORRY. WERE YOU ASLEEP?
YEAH, I'M REALLY SLEEPY.
YAWN
I'M TERRIBLY SORRY. I KNOW I'M BOTHERING YOU.

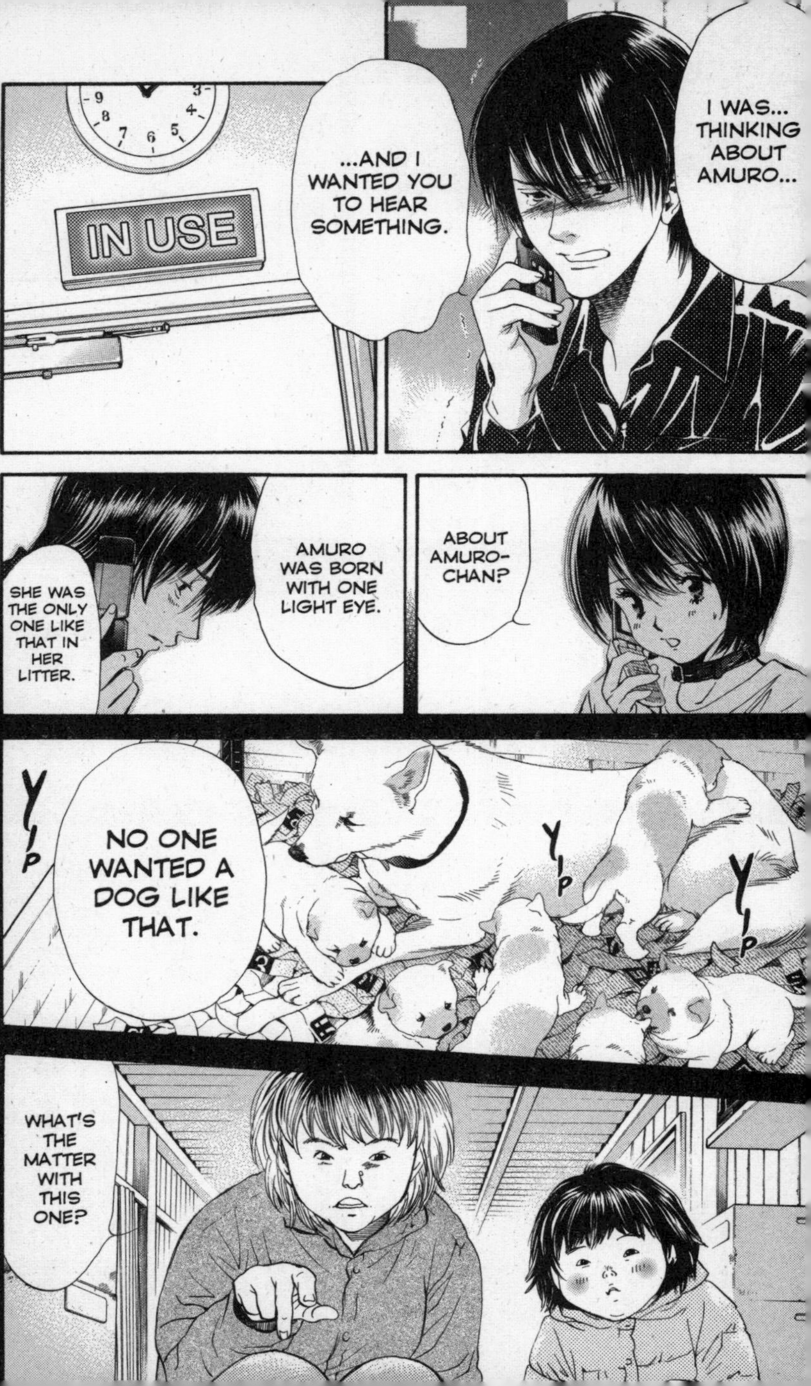
I WAS... THINKING ABOUT AMURO...
...AND I WANTED YOU TO HEAR SOMETHING.
IN USE
ABOUT AMURO-CHAN?
AMURO WAS BORN WITH ONE LIGHT EYE.
SHE WAS THE ONLY ONE LIKE THAT IN HER LITTER.
YIP
YIP
YIP
NO ONE WANTED A DOG LIKE THAT.
YIP
WHAT'S THE MATTER WITH THIS ONE?

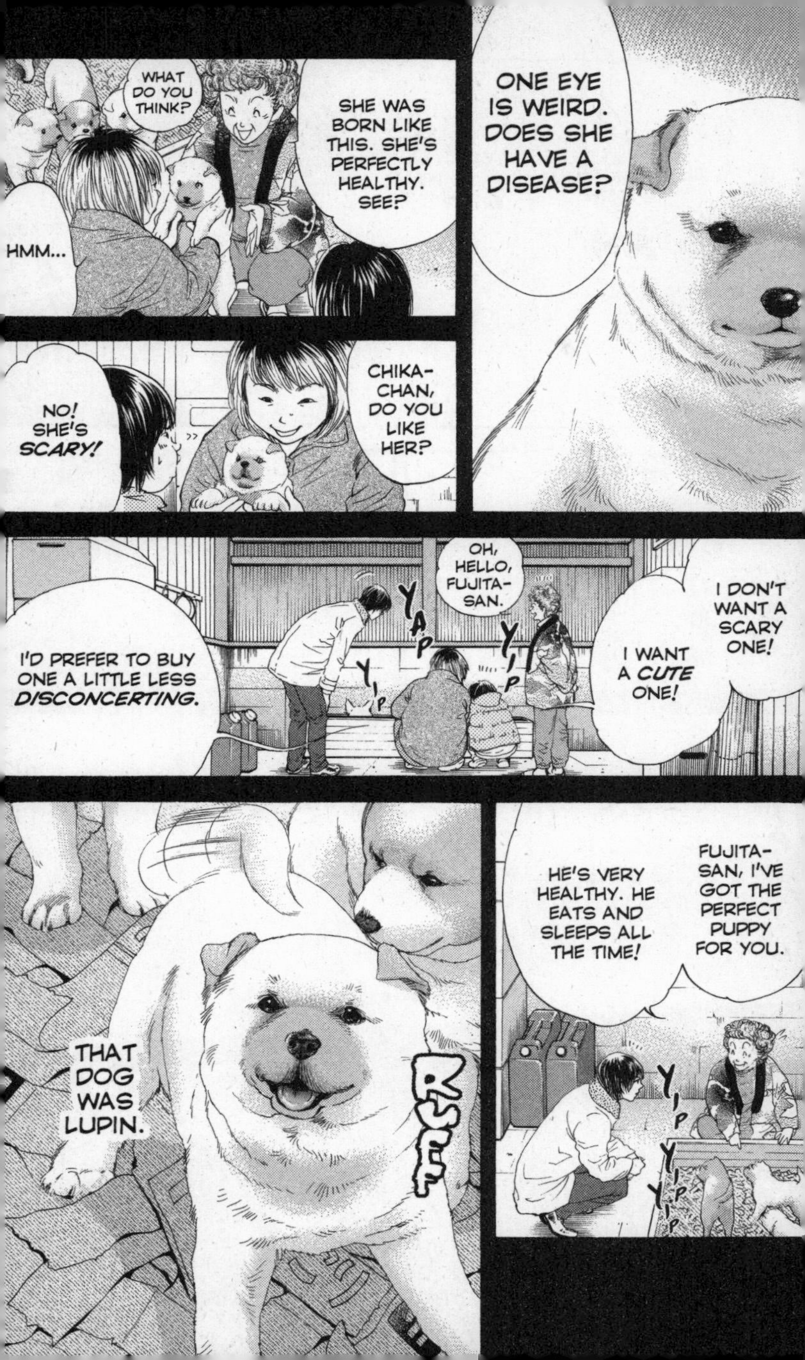
ONE EYE IS WEIRD. DOES SHE HAVE A DISEASE?
SHE WAS BORN LIKE THIS. SHE'S PERFECTLY HEALTHY. SEE?
WHAT DO YOU THINK?
HMM...
CHIKA-CHAN, DO YOU LIKE HER?
NO! SHE'S *SCARY!*
I DON'T WANT A SCARY ONE!
I WANT A *CUTE* ONE!
OH, HELLO, FUJITA-SAN.
YIP
YAP
YIP
I'D PREFER TO BUY ONE A LITTLE LESS *DISCONCERTING.*
FUJITA-SAN, I'VE GOT THE PERFECT PUPPY FOR YOU.
HE'S VERY HEALTHY. HE EATS AND SLEEPS ALL THE TIME!
YIP
YIP
YIP
THAT DOG WAS LUPIN.

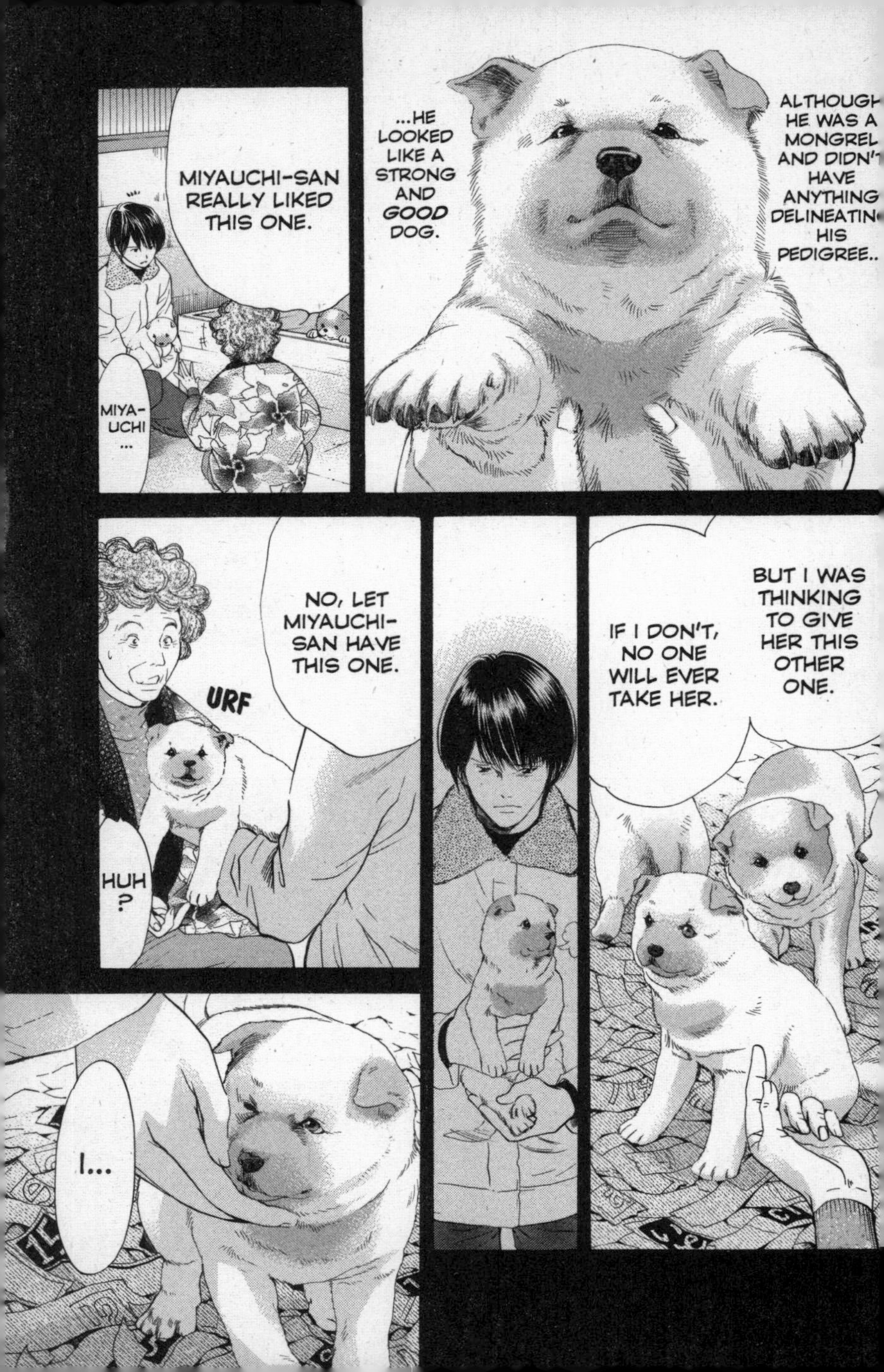
ALTHOUGH HE WAS A MONGREL AND DIDN'T HAVE ANYTHING DELINEATING HIS PEDIGREE..
...HE LOOKED LIKE A STRONG AND *GOOD* DOG.
MIYAUCHI-SAN REALLY LIKED THIS ONE.
MIYA-UCHI ...
BUT I WAS THINKING TO GIVE HER THIS OTHER ONE.
IF I DON'T, NO ONE WILL EVER TAKE HER.
NO, LET MIYAUCHI-SAN HAVE THIS ONE.
URF
HUH ?
I...

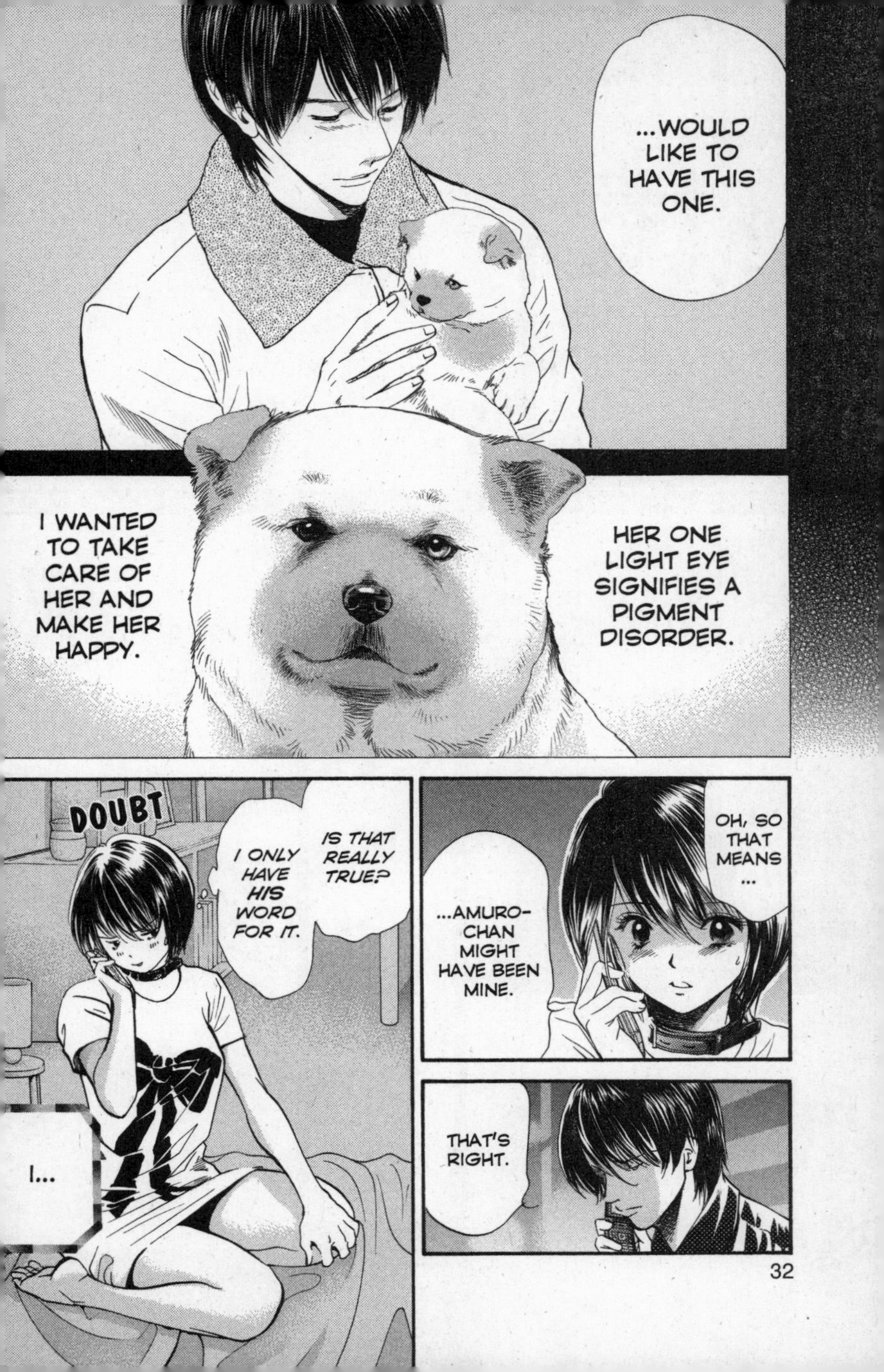
...WOULD LIKE TO HAVE THIS ONE.
HER ONE LIGHT EYE SIGNIFIES A PIGMENT DISORDER.
I WANTED TO TAKE CARE OF HER AND MAKE HER HAPPY.
OH, SO THAT MEANS ...
...AMURO-CHAN MIGHT HAVE BEEN MINE.
THAT'S RIGHT.
DOUBT
IS THAT REALLY TRUE?
I ONLY HAVE HIS WORD FOR IT.
I...

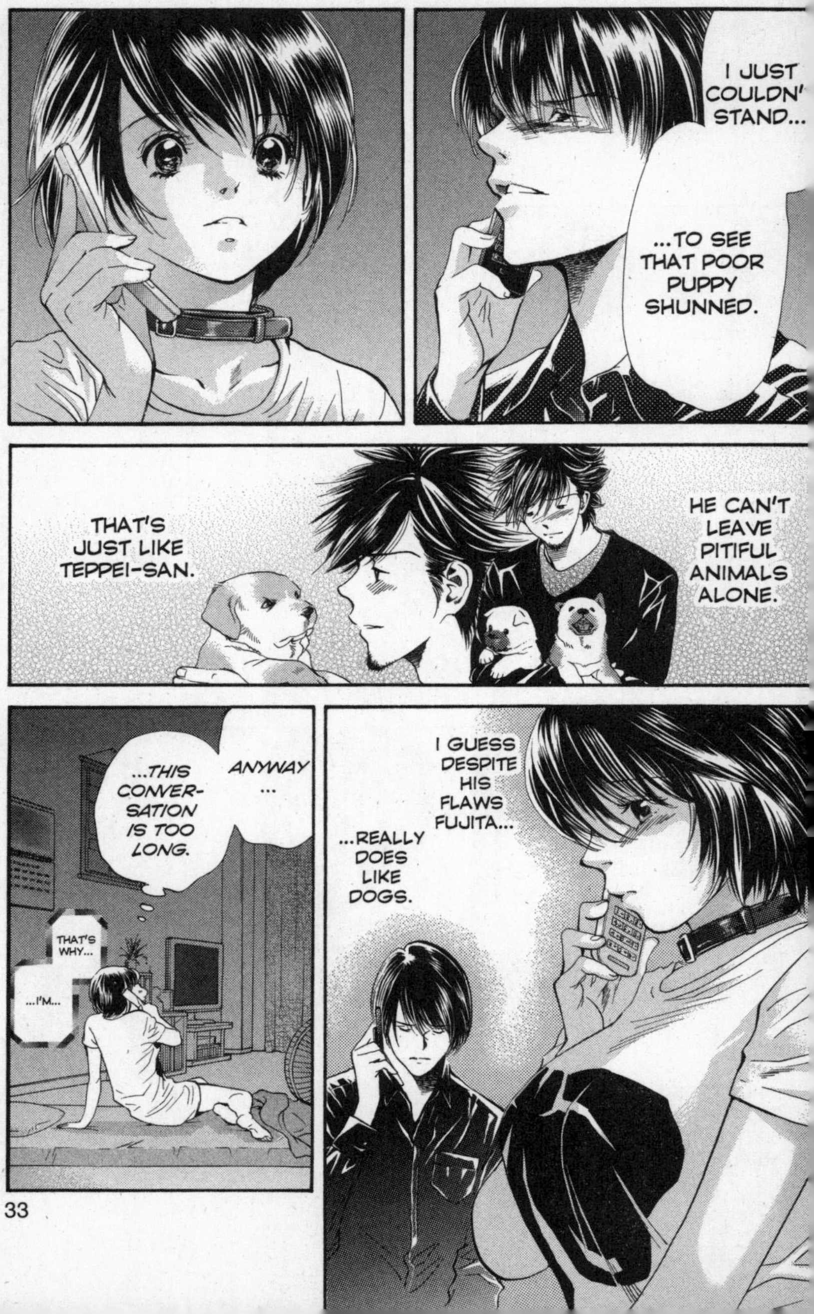
I JUST COULDN' STAND...
...TO SEE THAT POOR PUPPY SHUNNED.
HE CAN'T LEAVE PITIFUL ANIMALS ALONE.
THAT'S JUST LIKE TEPPEI-SAN.
I GUESS DESPITE HIS FLAWS FUJITA...
...REALLY DOES LIKE DOGS.
ANYWAY ...
...THIS CONVER-SATION IS TOO LONG.
THAT'S WHY...
...I'M...

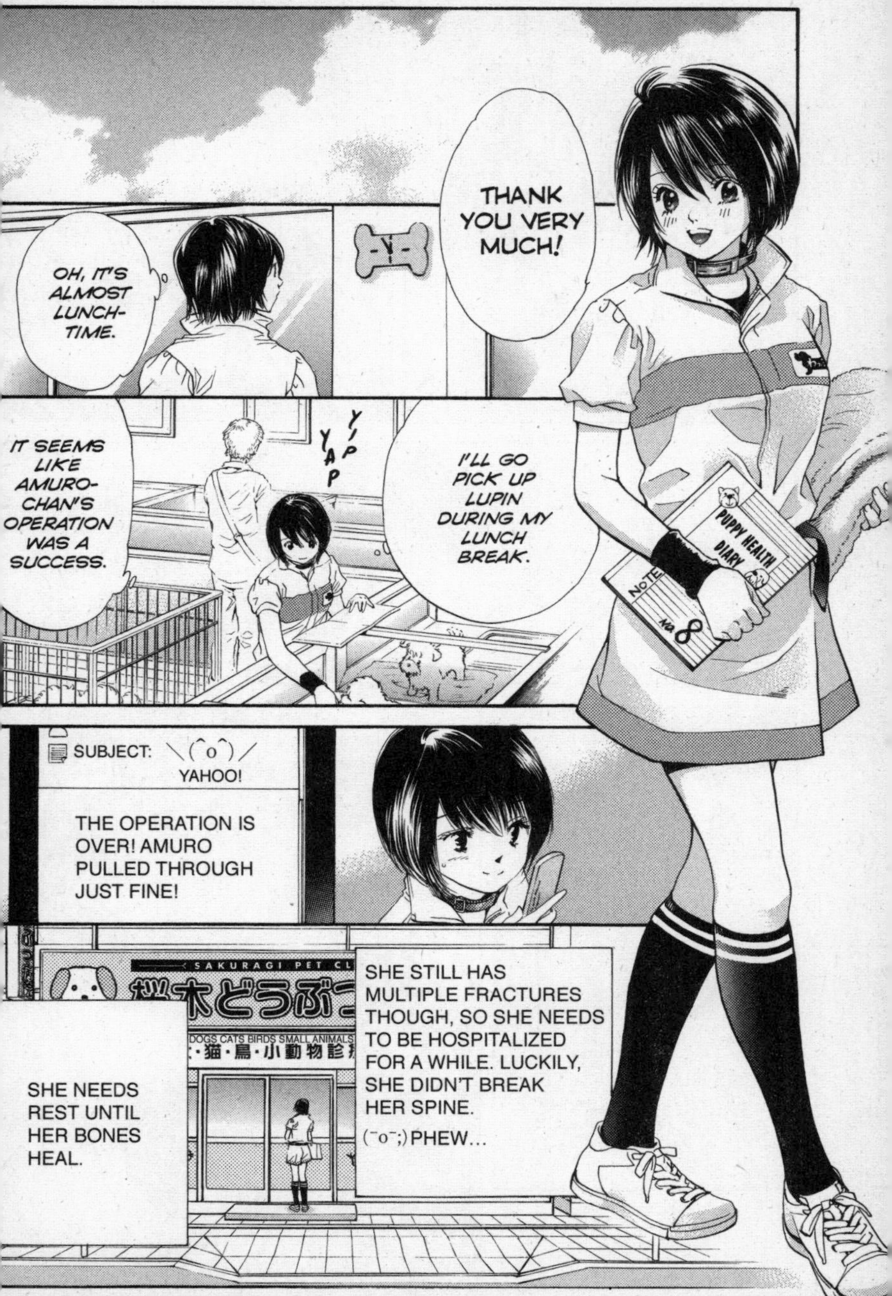
THANK YOU VERY MUCH!
PUPPY HEALTH DIARY
NOTE No. 8
OH, IT'S ALMOST LUNCH-TIME.
I'LL GO PICK UP LUPIN DURING MY LUNCH BREAK.
YIP YAP
IT SEEMS LIKE AMURO-CHAN'S OPERATION WAS A SUCCESS.
SUBJECT: \(^o^)/ YAHOO!
THE OPERATION IS OVER! AMURO PULLED THROUGH JUST FINE!
DOGS CATS BIRDS SMALL ANIMALS
SHE STILL HAS MULTIPLE FRACTURES THOUGH, SO SHE NEEDS TO BE HOSPITALIZED FOR A WHILE. LUCKILY, SHE DIDN'T BREAK HER SPINE.
(¯o¯;) PHEW…
SHE NEEDS REST UNTIL HER BONES HEAL.

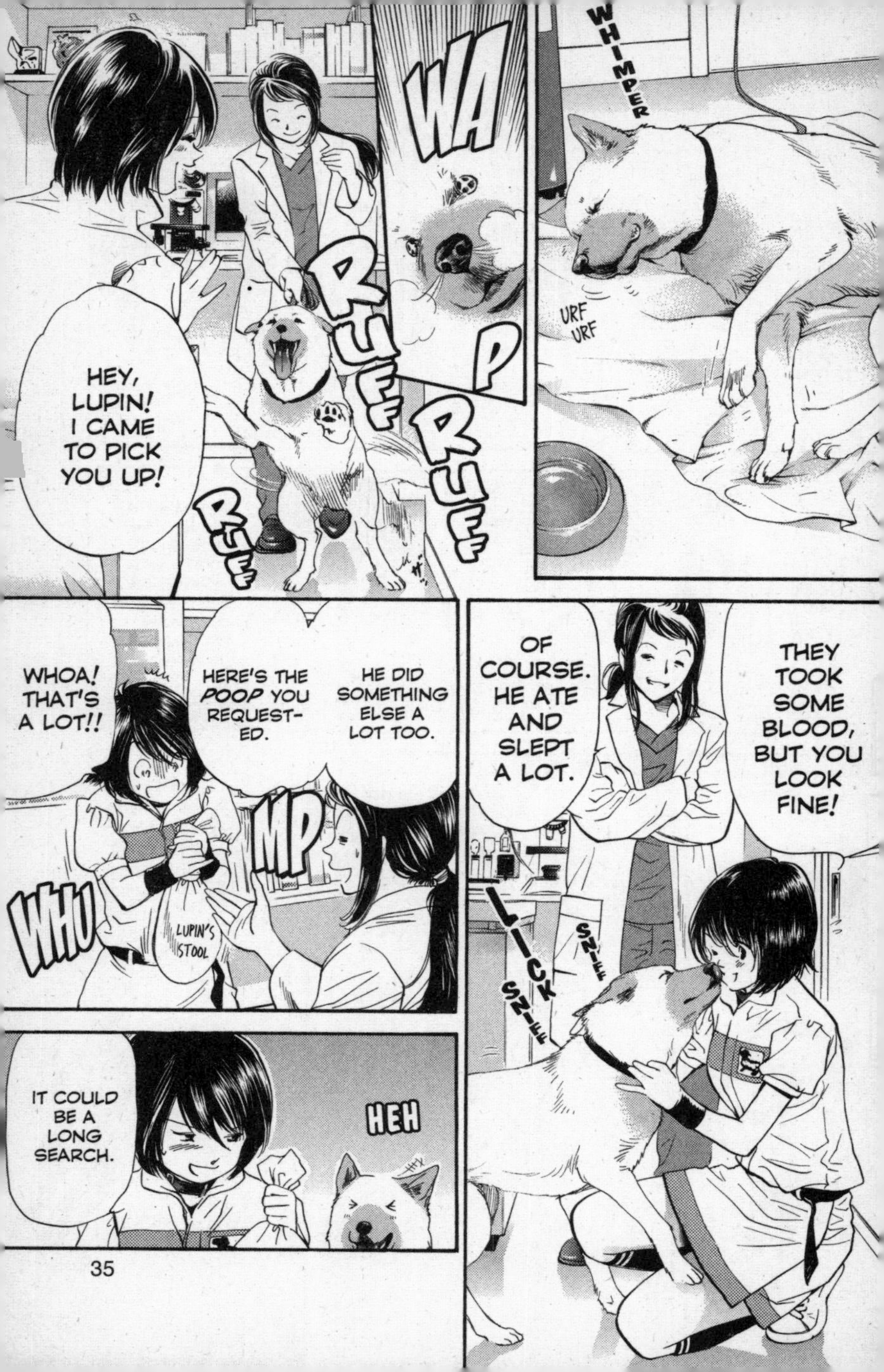
WHIMPER
URF URF
WA
P
HEY, LUPIN! I CAME TO PICK YOU UP!
RUFF
RUFF
RUFF
THEY TOOK SOME BLOOD, BUT YOU LOOK FINE!
OF COURSE. HE ATE AND SLEPT A LOT.
SNIFF
LICK
SNIFF
HE DID SOMETHING ELSE A LOT TOO.
HERE'S THE *POOP* YOU REQUEST-ED.
WHOA! THAT'S A LOT!!
WHU
MP
LUPIN'S STOOL
HEH
IT COULD BE A LONG SEARCH.

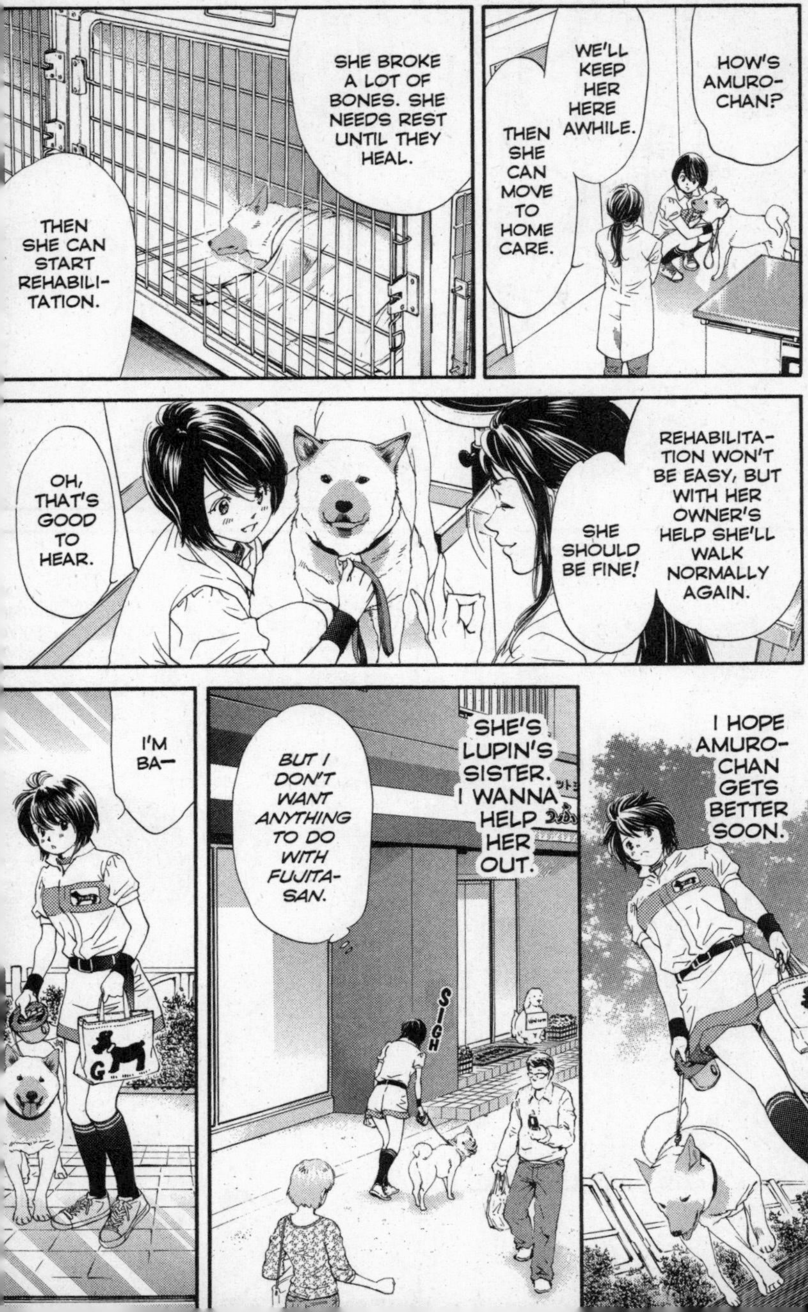
HOW'S AMURO-CHAN?
WE'LL KEEP HER HERE AWHILE.
THEN SHE CAN MOVE TO HOME CARE.
SHE BROKE A LOT OF BONES. SHE NEEDS REST UNTIL THEY HEAL.
THEN SHE CAN START REHABILITATION.
REHABILITATION WON'T BE EASY, BUT WITH HER OWNER'S HELP SHE'LL WALK NORMALLY AGAIN.
SHE SHOULD BE FINE!
OH, THAT'S GOOD TO HEAR.
I HOPE AMURO-CHAN GETS BETTER SOON.
SHE'S LUPIN'S SISTER. I WANNA HELP HER OUT.
BUT I DON'T WANT ANYTHING TO DO WITH FUJITA-SAN.
SIGH
I'M BA—

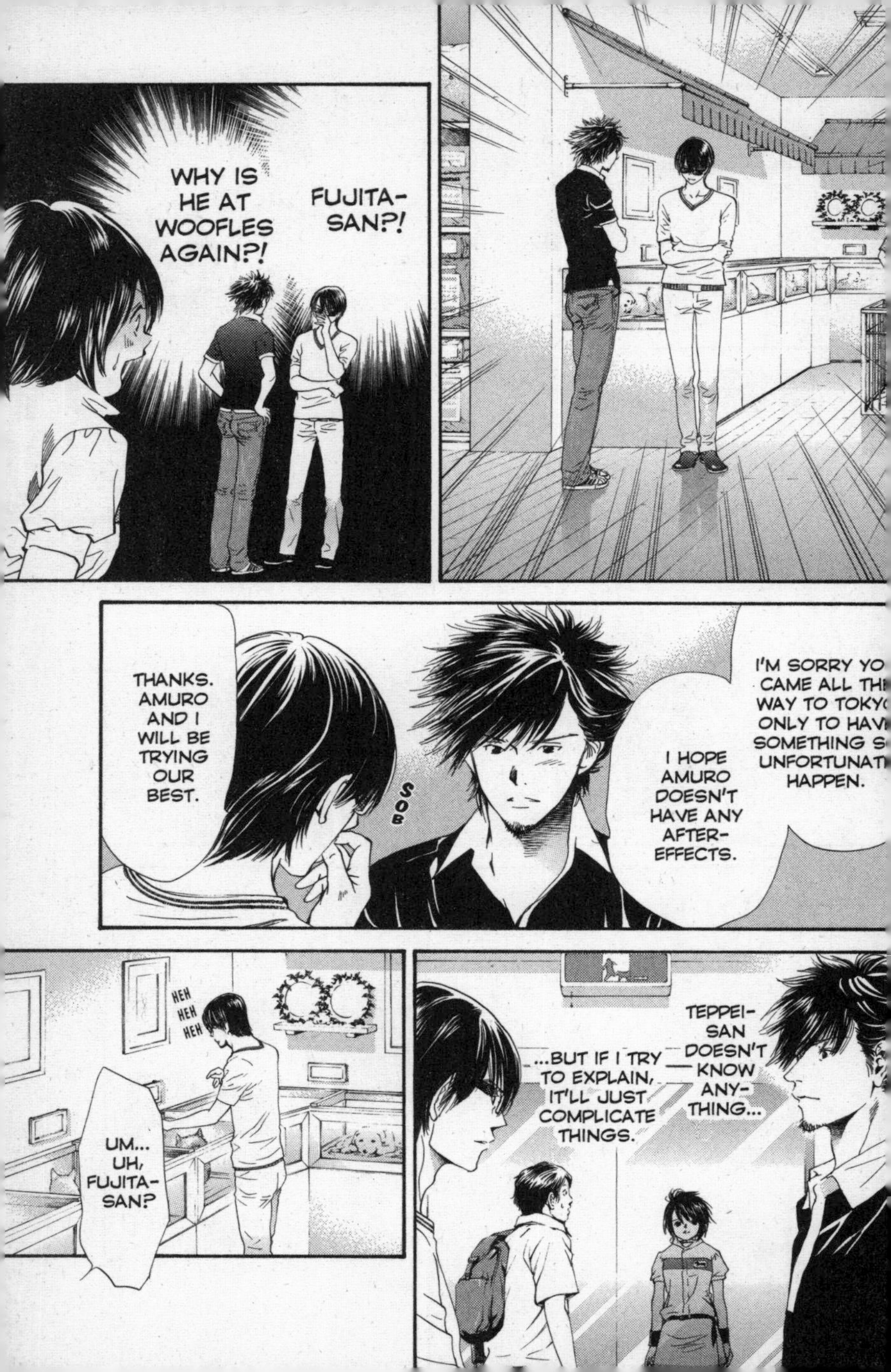
FUJITA-SAN?!
WHY IS HE AT WOOFLES AGAIN?!
I'M SORRY YO CAME ALL TH WAY TO TOKY ONLY TO HAV SOMETHING S UNFORTUNAT HAPPEN.
I HOPE AMURO DOESN'T HAVE ANY AFTER-EFFECTS.
SOB
THANKS. AMURO AND I WILL BE TRYING OUR BEST.
TEPPEI-SAN DOESN'T KNOW ANY-THING...
...BUT IF I TRY TO EXPLAIN, IT'LL JUST COMPLICATE THINGS.
HEH HEH HEH
UM... UH, FUJITA-SAN?

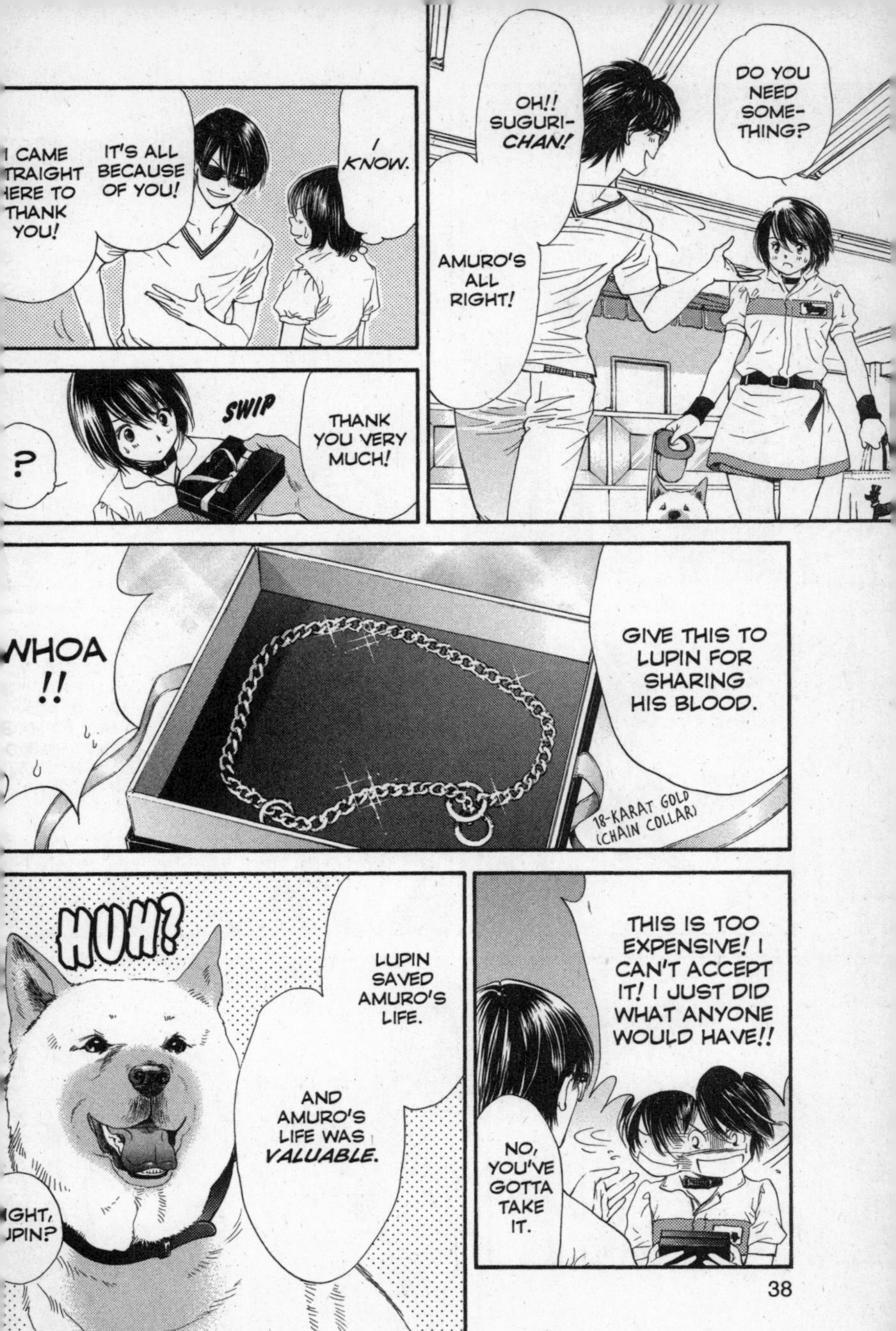
DO YOU NEED SOMETHING?
OH!! SUGURI-*CHAN!*
AMURO'S ALL RIGHT!
I KNOW.
IT'S ALL BECAUSE OF YOU!
I CAME TRAIGHT HERE TO THANK YOU!
THANK YOU VERY MUCH!
SWIP
?
GIVE THIS TO LUPIN FOR SHARING HIS BLOOD.
18-KARAT GOLD (CHAIN COLLAR)
WHOA !!
THIS IS TOO EXPENSIVE! I CAN'T ACCEPT IT! I JUST DID WHAT ANYONE WOULD HAVE!!
NO, YOU'VE GOTTA TAKE IT.
LUPIN SAVED AMURO'S LIFE.
AND AMURO'S LIFE WAS *VALUABLE.*
HUH?
IGHT, UPIN?

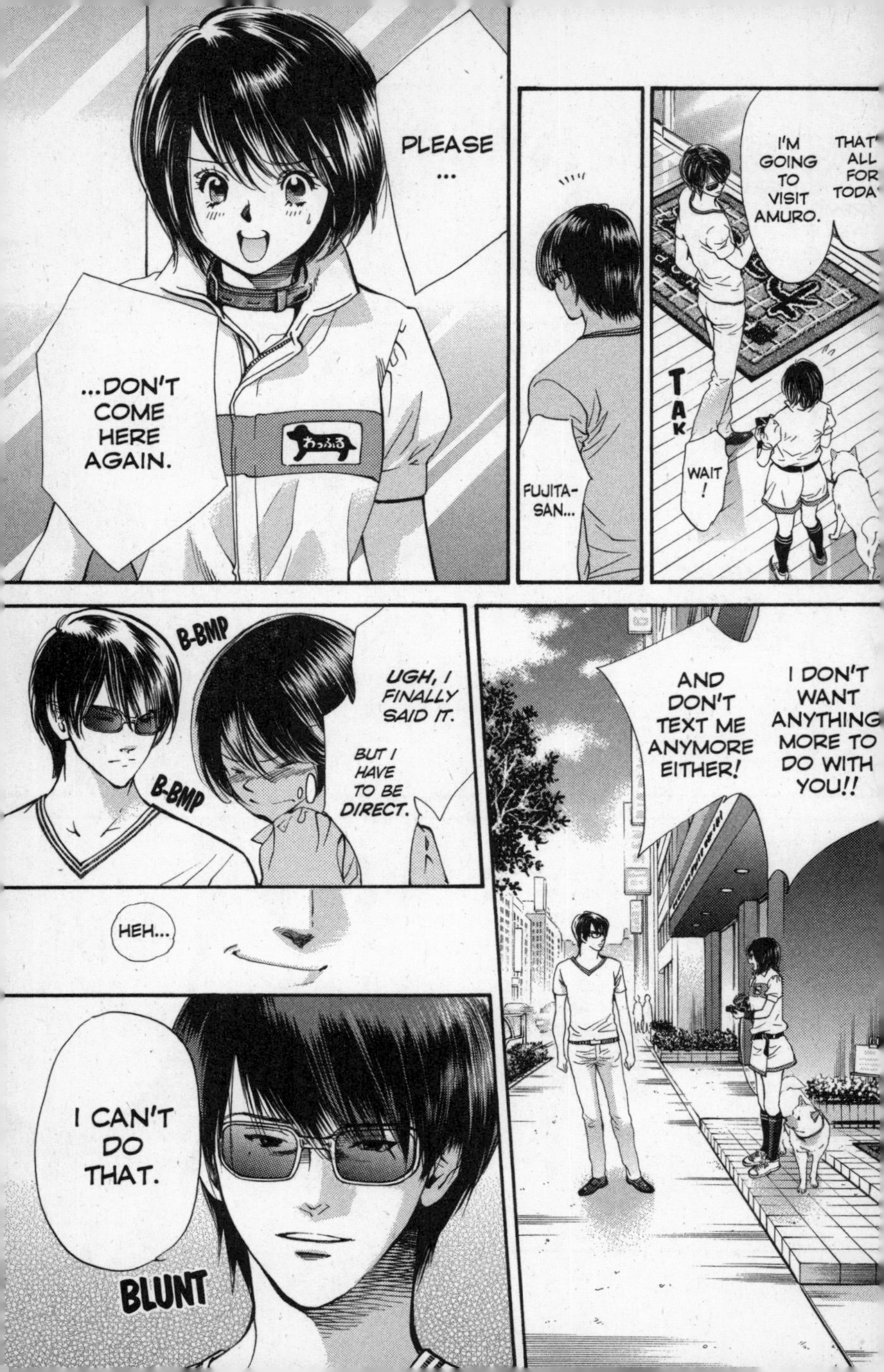
THAT' ALL FOR TODA
I'M GOING TO VISIT AMURO.
TAK
WAIT!
FUJITA-SAN...
PLEASE...
...DON'T COME HERE AGAIN.
I DON'T WANT ANYTHING MORE TO DO WITH YOU!!
AND DON'T TEXT ME ANYMORE EITHER!
UGH, I FINALLY SAID IT.
BUT I HAVE TO BE DIRECT.
B-BMP
B-BMP
HEH...
I CAN'T DO THAT.
BLUNT

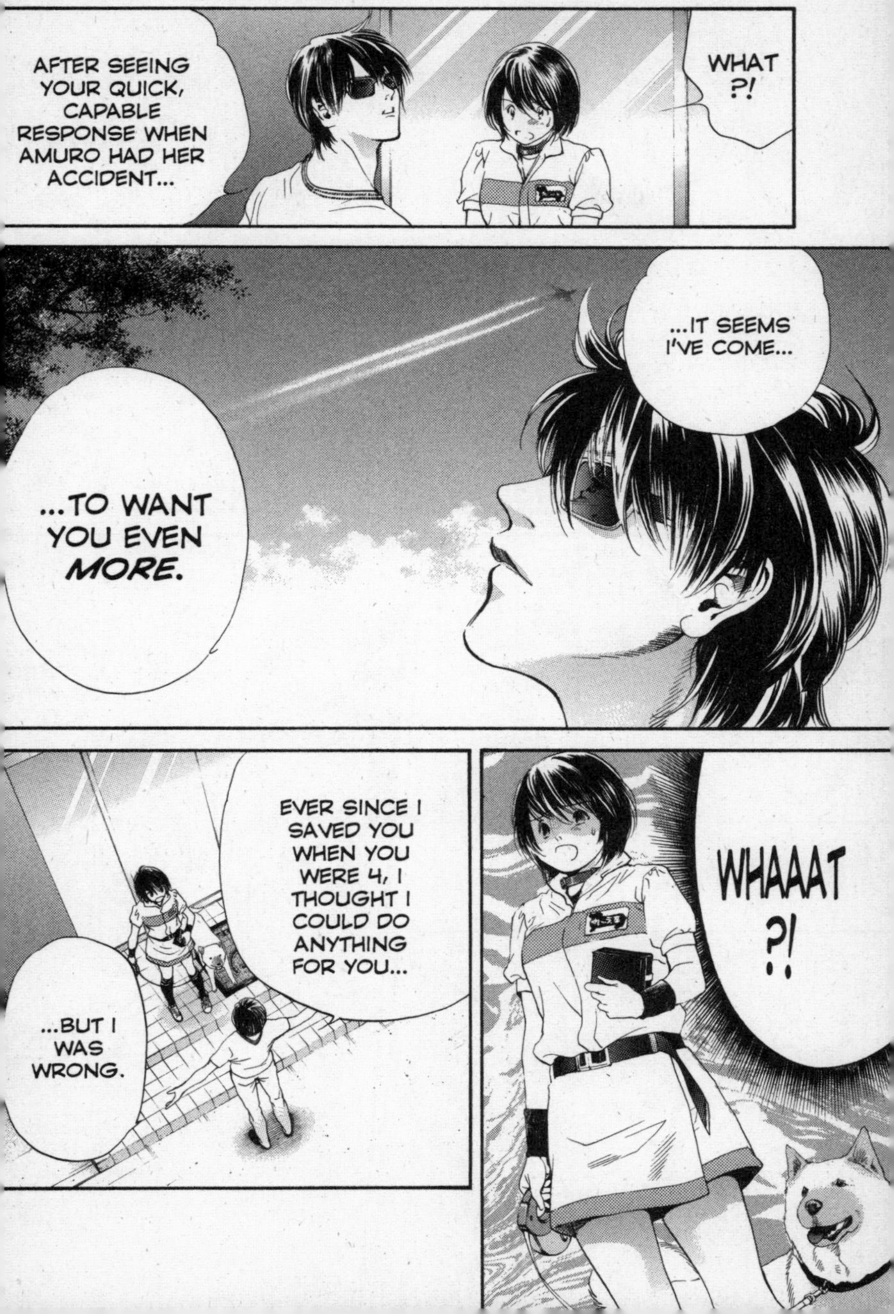
WHAT ?!
AFTER SEEING YOUR QUICK, CAPABLE RESPONSE WHEN AMURO HAD HER ACCIDENT...
...IT SEEMS I'VE COME...
...TO WANT YOU EVEN *MORE.*
WHAAAT ?!
EVER SINCE I SAVED YOU WHEN YOU WERE 4, I THOUGHT I COULD DO ANYTHING FOR YOU...
...BUT I WAS WRONG.

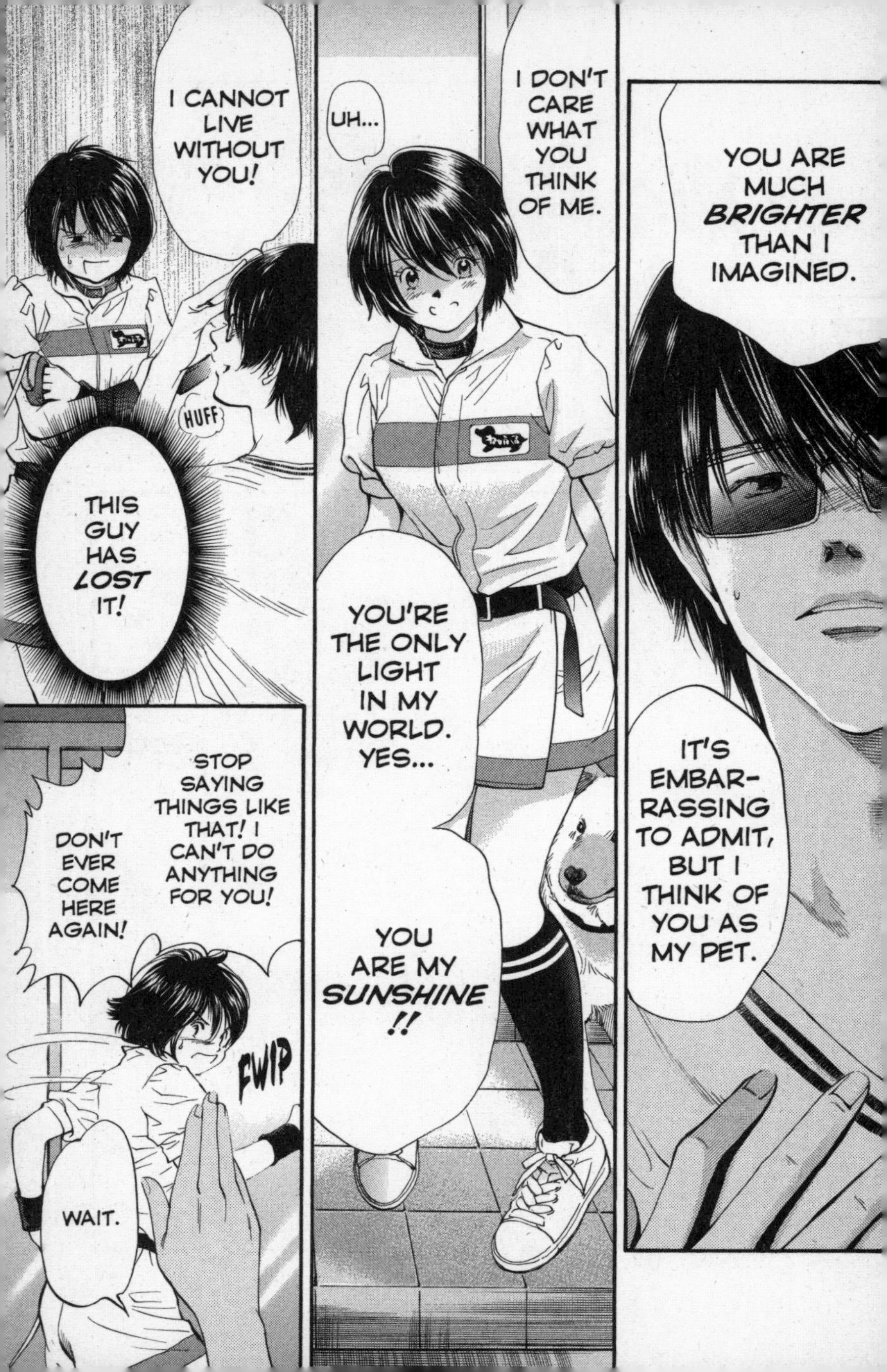
YOU ARE MUCH BRIGHTER THAN I IMAGINED.
IT'S EMBARRASSING TO ADMIT, BUT I THINK OF YOU AS MY PET.
I DON'T CARE WHAT YOU THINK OF ME.
UH...
YOU'RE THE ONLY LIGHT IN MY WORLD. YES...
YOU ARE MY SUNSHINE!!
I CANNOT LIVE WITHOUT YOU!
HUFF
THIS GUY HAS LOST IT!
STOP SAYING THINGS LIKE THAT! I CAN'T DO ANYTHING FOR YOU!
DON'T EVER COME HERE AGAIN!
FWIP
WAIT.

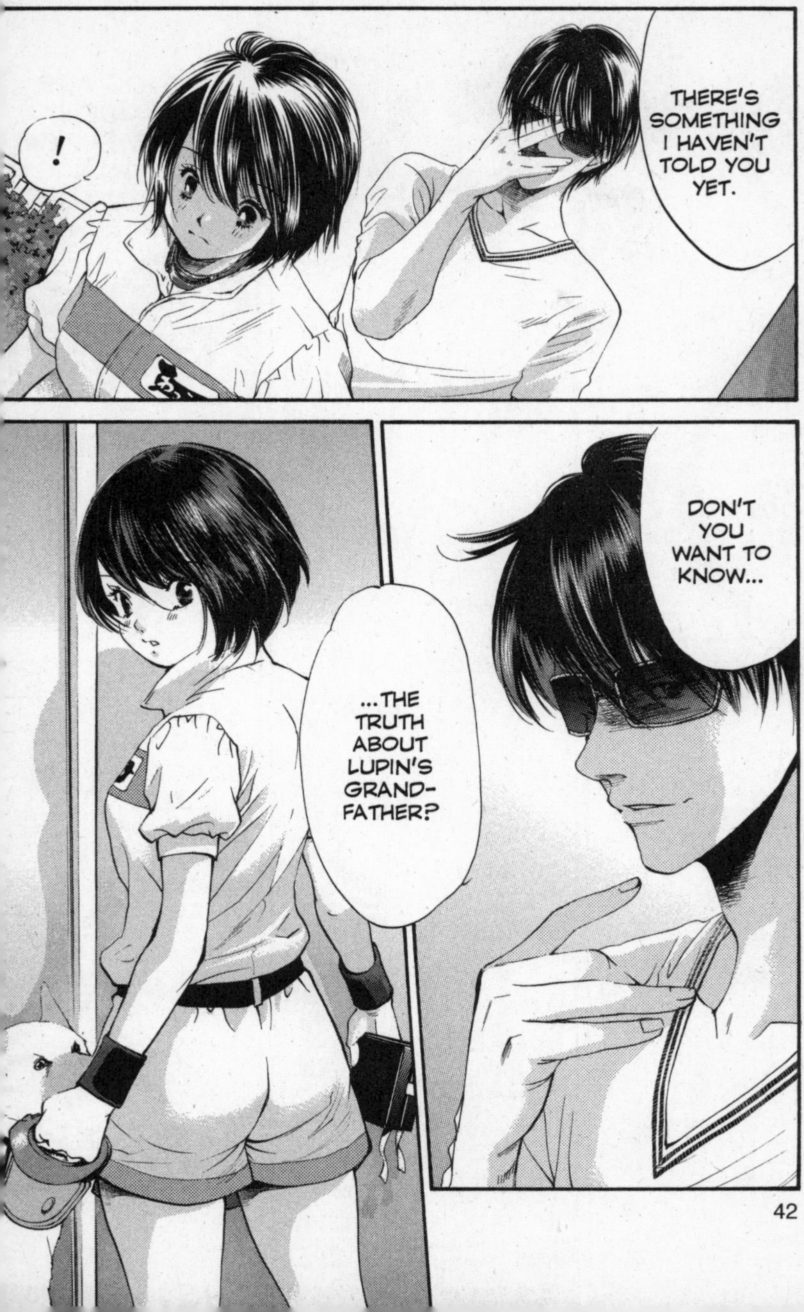
THERE'S SOMETHING I HAVEN'T TOLD YOU YET.
!
DON'T YOU WANT TO KNOW...
...THE TRUTH ABOUT LUPIN'S GRAND-FATHER?

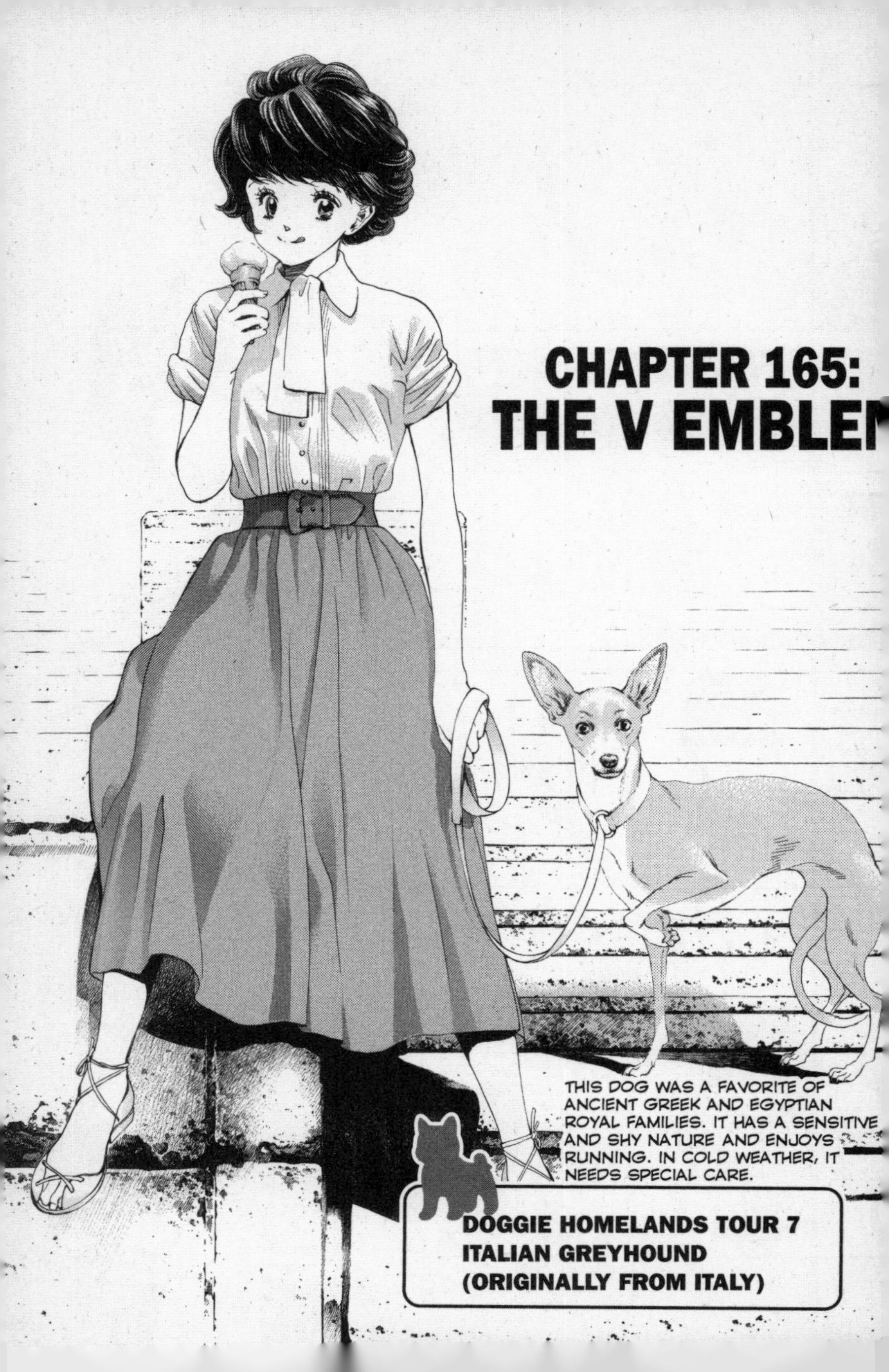
CHAPTER 165:
THE V EMBLEM
THIS DOG WAS A FAVORITE OF ANCIENT GREEK AND EGYPTIAN ROYAL FAMILIES. IT HAS A SENSITIVE AND SHY NATURE AND ENJOYS RUNNING. IN COLD WEATHER, IT NEEDS SPECIAL CARE.
DOGGIE HOMELANDS TOUR 7
ITALIAN GREYHOUND
(ORIGINALLY FROM ITALY)

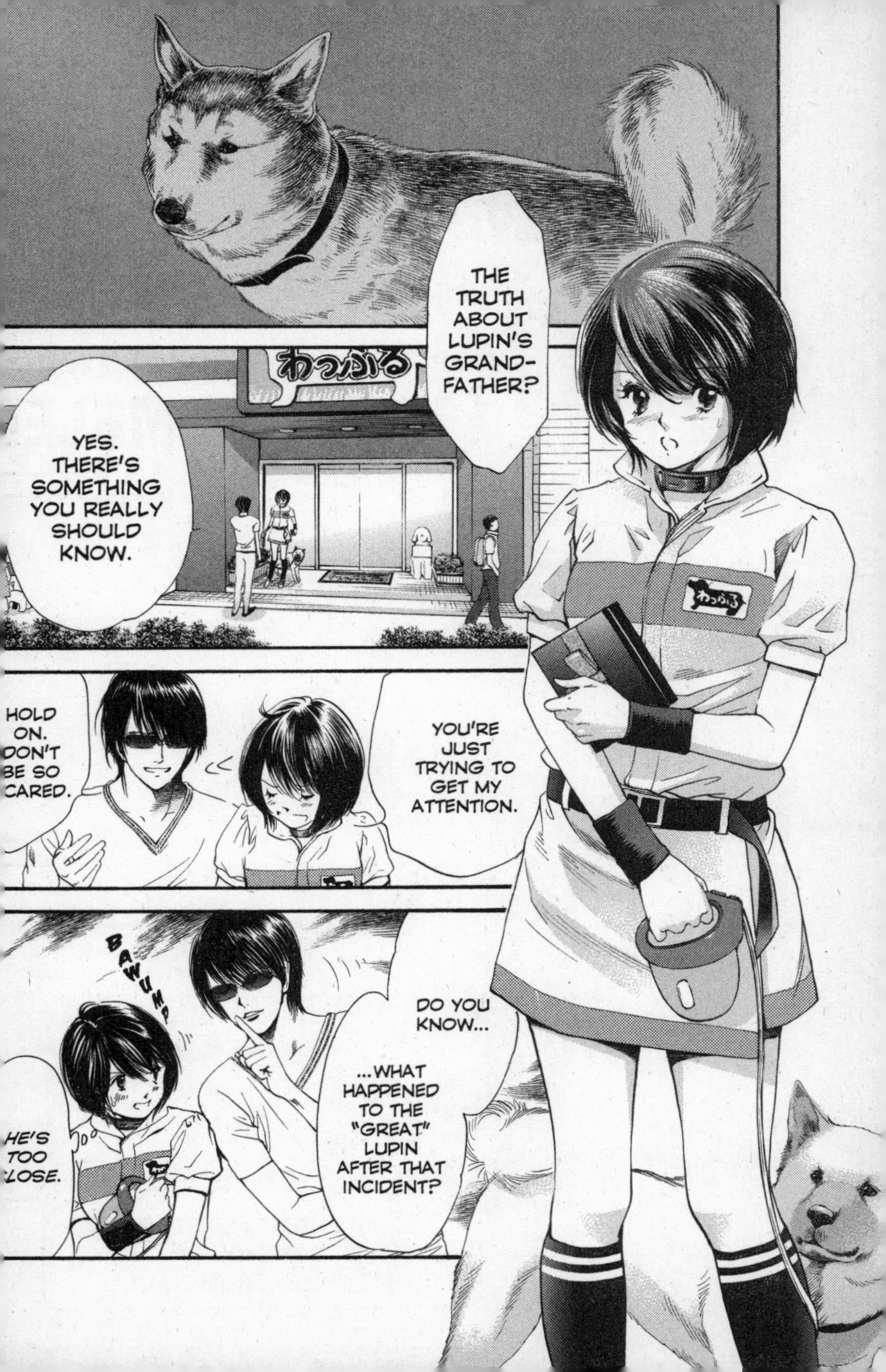
THE TRUTH ABOUT LUPIN'S GRAND-FATHER?
わっぷる
YES. THERE'S SOMETHING YOU REALLY SHOULD KNOW.
YOU'RE JUST TRYING TO GET MY ATTENTION.
HOLD ON. DON'T BE SO SCARED.
DO YOU KNOW...
...WHAT HAPPENED TO THE "GREAT" LUPIN AFTER THAT INCIDENT?
BAWUMP
HE'S TOO CLOSE.

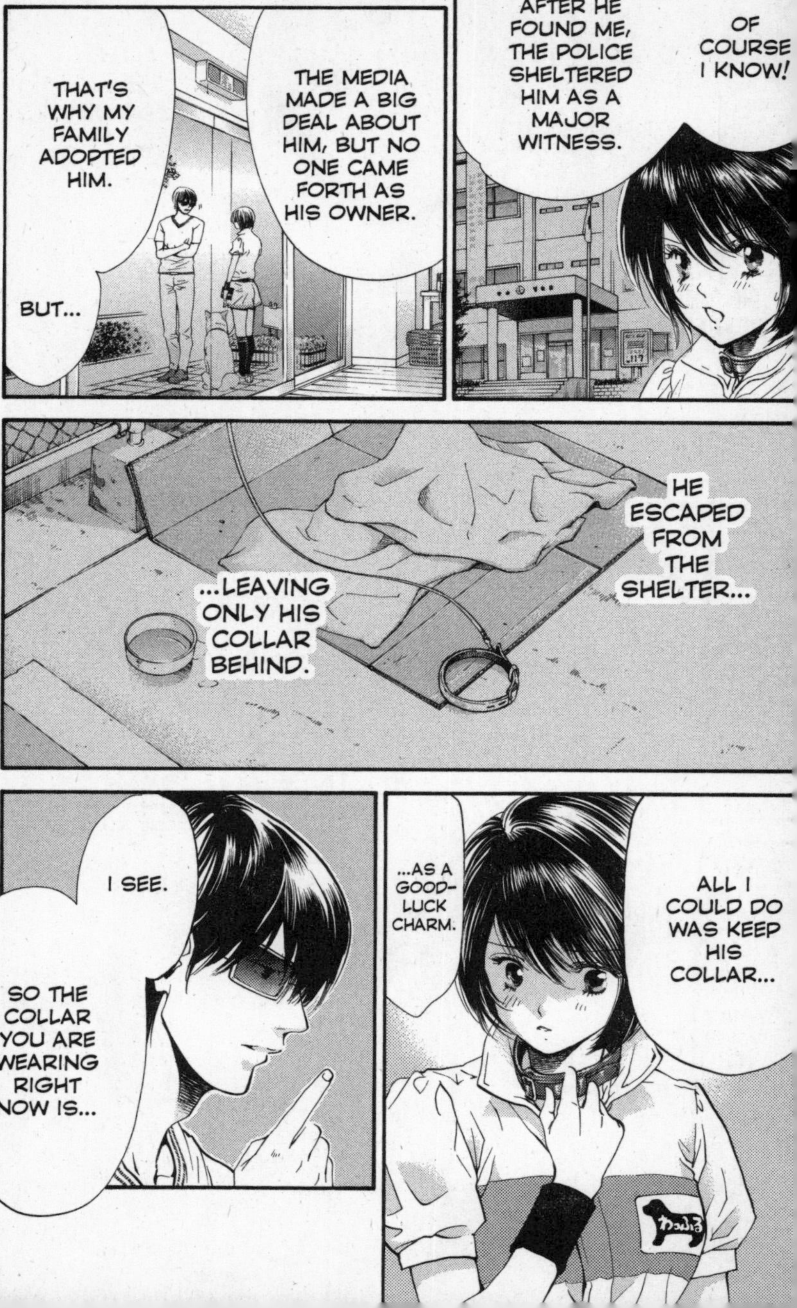
OF COURSE I KNOW!
AFTER HE FOUND ME, THE POLICE SHELTERED HIM AS A MAJOR WITNESS.
THE MEDIA MADE A BIG DEAL ABOUT HIM, BUT NO ONE CAME FORTH AS HIS OWNER.
THAT'S WHY MY FAMILY ADOPTED HIM.
BUT...
HE ESCAPED FROM THE SHELTER...
...LEAVING ONLY HIS COLLAR BEHIND.
ALL I COULD DO WAS KEEP HIS COLLAR...
...AS A GOOD-LUCK CHARM.
I SEE.
SO THE COLLAR YOU ARE WEARING RIGHT NOW IS...

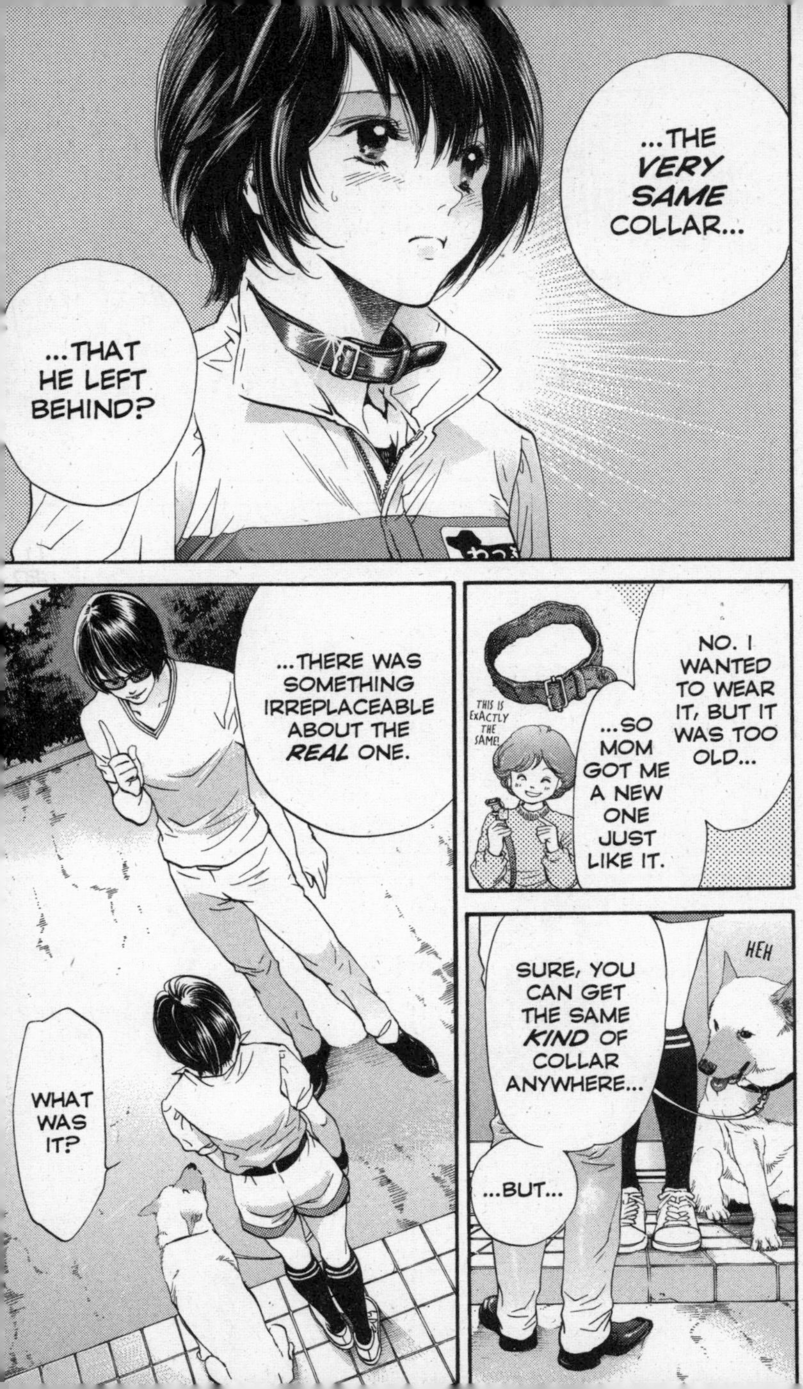
...THE VERY SAME COLLAR...
...THAT HE LEFT BEHIND?
NO. I WANTED TO WEAR IT, BUT IT WAS TOO OLD...
...SO MOM GOT ME A NEW ONE JUST LIKE IT.
THIS IS EXACTLY THE SAME!
HEH
SURE, YOU CAN GET THE SAME KIND OF COLLAR ANYWHERE...
...BUT...
...THERE WAS SOMETHING IRREPLACEABLE ABOUT THE REAL ONE.
WHAT WAS IT?

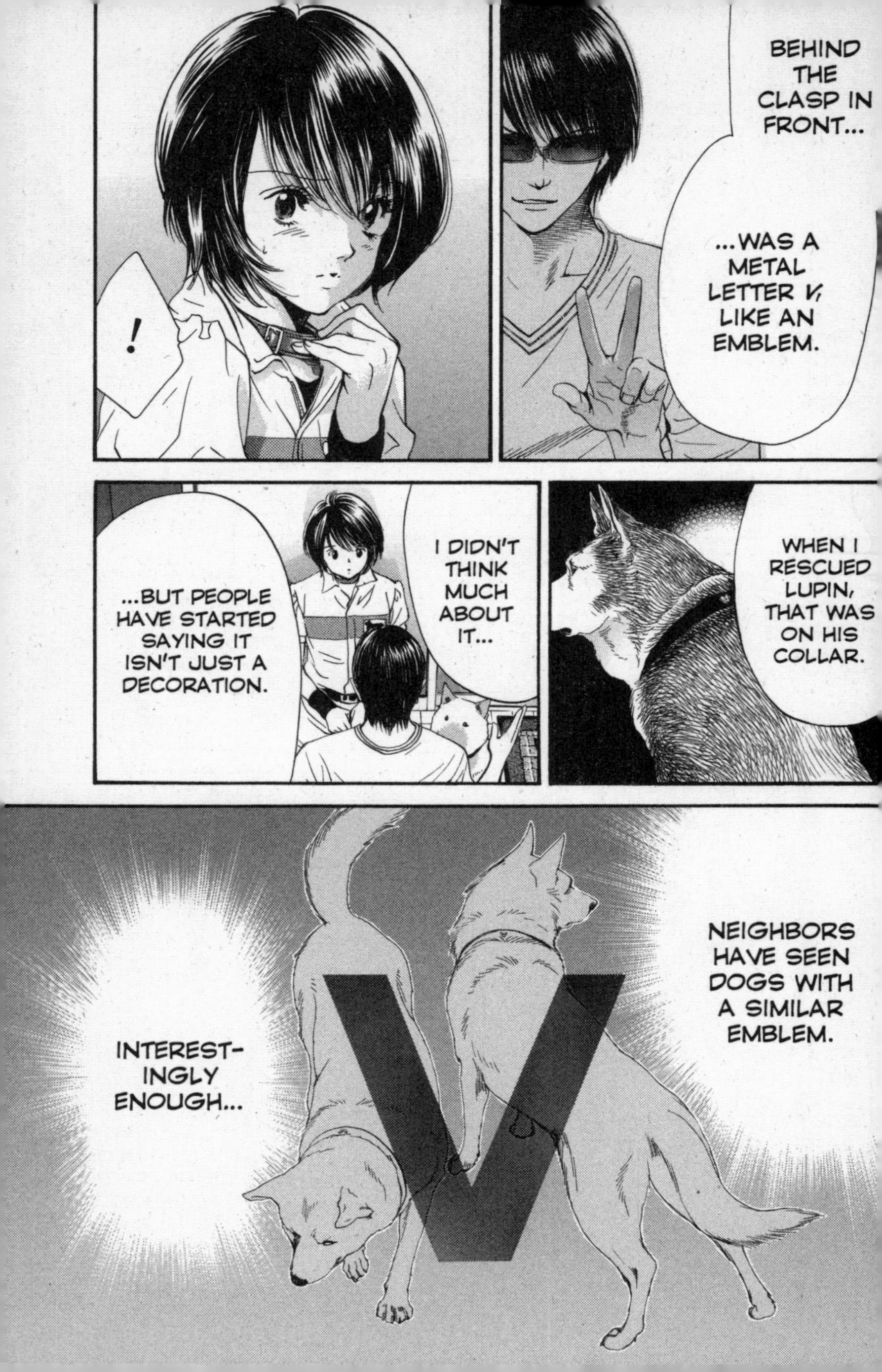
BEHIND THE CLASP IN FRONT...
...WAS A METAL LETTER V, LIKE AN EMBLEM.
!
WHEN I RESCUED LUPIN, THAT WAS ON HIS COLLAR.
I DIDN'T THINK MUCH ABOUT IT...
...BUT PEOPLE HAVE STARTED SAYING IT ISN'T JUST A DECORATION.
NEIGHBORS HAVE SEEN DOGS WITH A SIMILAR EMBLEM.
INTEREST-INGLY ENOUGH...

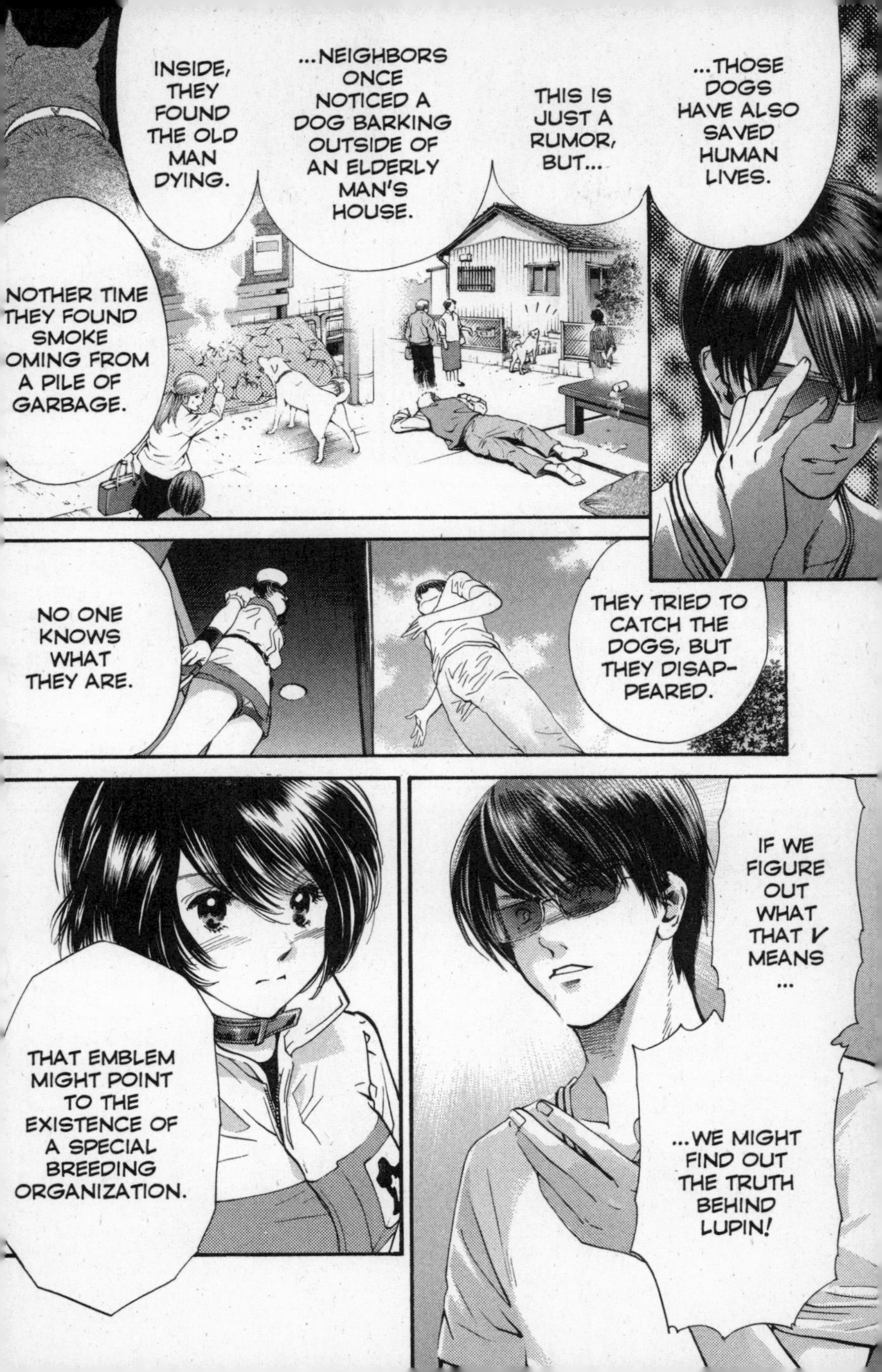
...THOSE DOGS HAVE ALSO SAVED HUMAN LIVES.
THIS IS JUST A RUMOR, BUT...
...NEIGHBORS ONCE NOTICED A DOG BARKING OUTSIDE OF AN ELDERLY MAN'S HOUSE.
INSIDE, THEY FOUND THE OLD MAN DYING.
NOTHER TIME THEY FOUND SMOKE OMING FROM A PILE OF GARBAGE.
THEY TRIED TO CATCH THE DOGS, BUT THEY DISAP-PEARED.
NO ONE KNOWS WHAT THEY ARE.
IF WE FIGURE OUT WHAT THAT V MEANS ...
...WE MIGHT FIND OUT THE TRUTH BEHIND LUPIN!
THAT EMBLEM MIGHT POINT TO THE EXISTENCE OF A SPECIAL BREEDING ORGANIZATION.

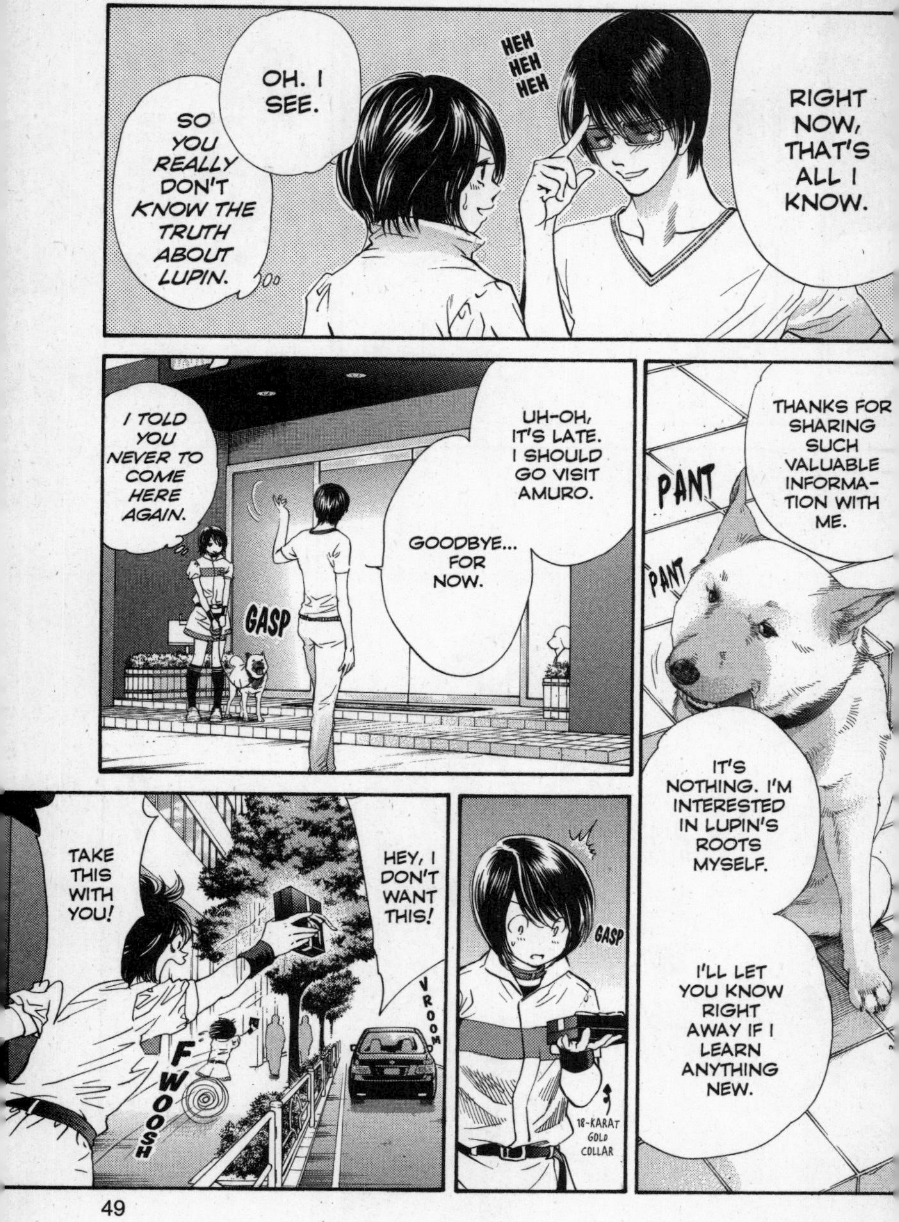
RIGHT NOW, THAT'S ALL I KNOW.
HEH HEH HEH
OH. I SEE.
SO YOU REALLY DON'T KNOW THE TRUTH ABOUT LUPIN.
THANKS FOR SHARING SUCH VALUABLE INFORMATION WITH ME.
PANT
PANT
IT'S NOTHING. I'M INTERESTED IN LUPIN'S ROOTS MYSELF.
I'LL LET YOU KNOW RIGHT AWAY IF I LEARN ANYTHING NEW.
UH-OH, IT'S LATE. I SHOULD GO VISIT AMURO.
GOODBYE... FOR NOW.
GASP
I TOLD YOU NEVER TO COME HERE AGAIN.
GASP
18-KARAT GOLD COLLAR
HEY, I DON'T WANT THIS!
VROOM
TAKE THIS WITH YOU!
FWOOSH

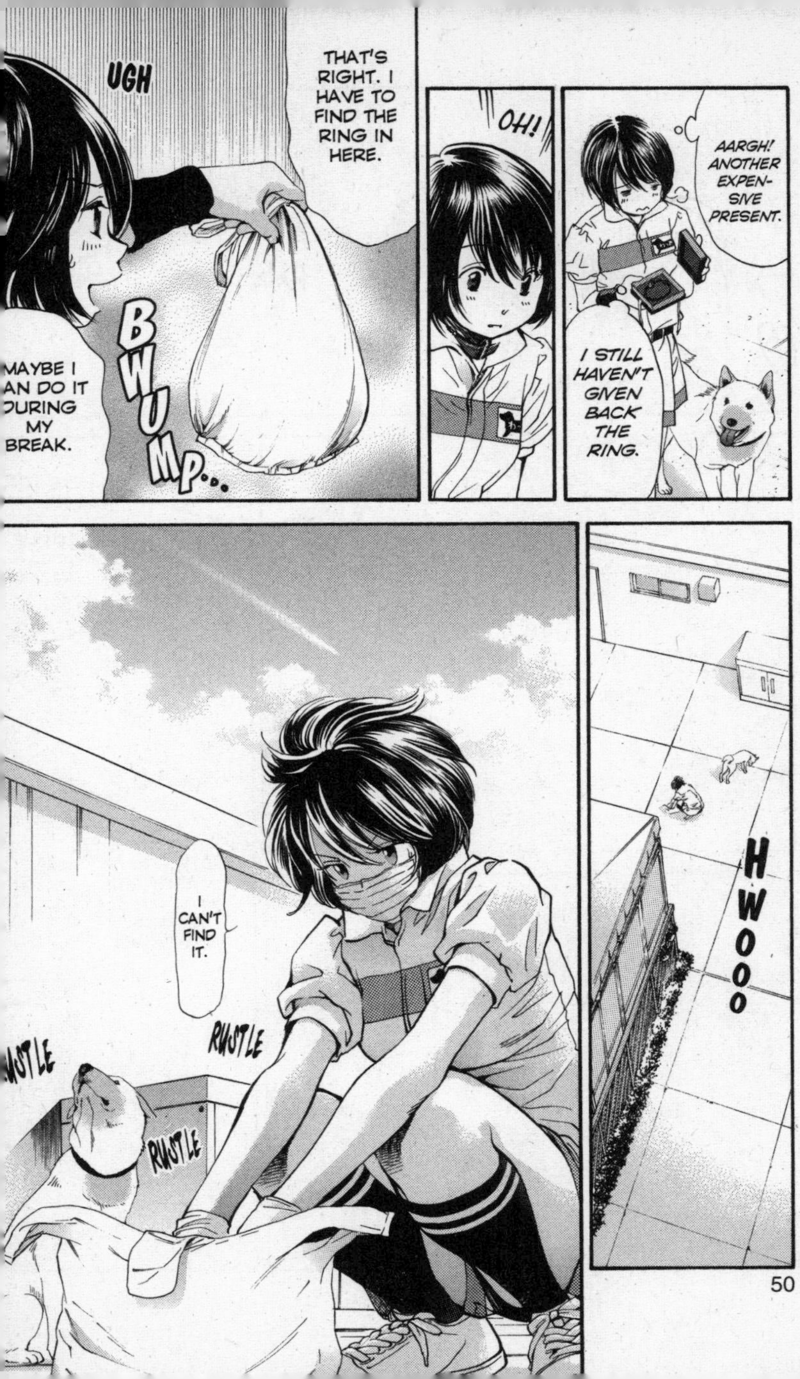
AARGH! ANOTHER EXPEN-SIVE PRESENT.
I STILL HAVEN'T GIVEN BACK THE RING.
OH!
THAT'S RIGHT. I HAVE TO FIND THE RING IN HERE.
UGH
BWUMP...
MAYBE I AN DO IT URING MY BREAK.
HWOOOO
I CAN'T FIND IT.
RUSTLE
RUSTLE
USTLE

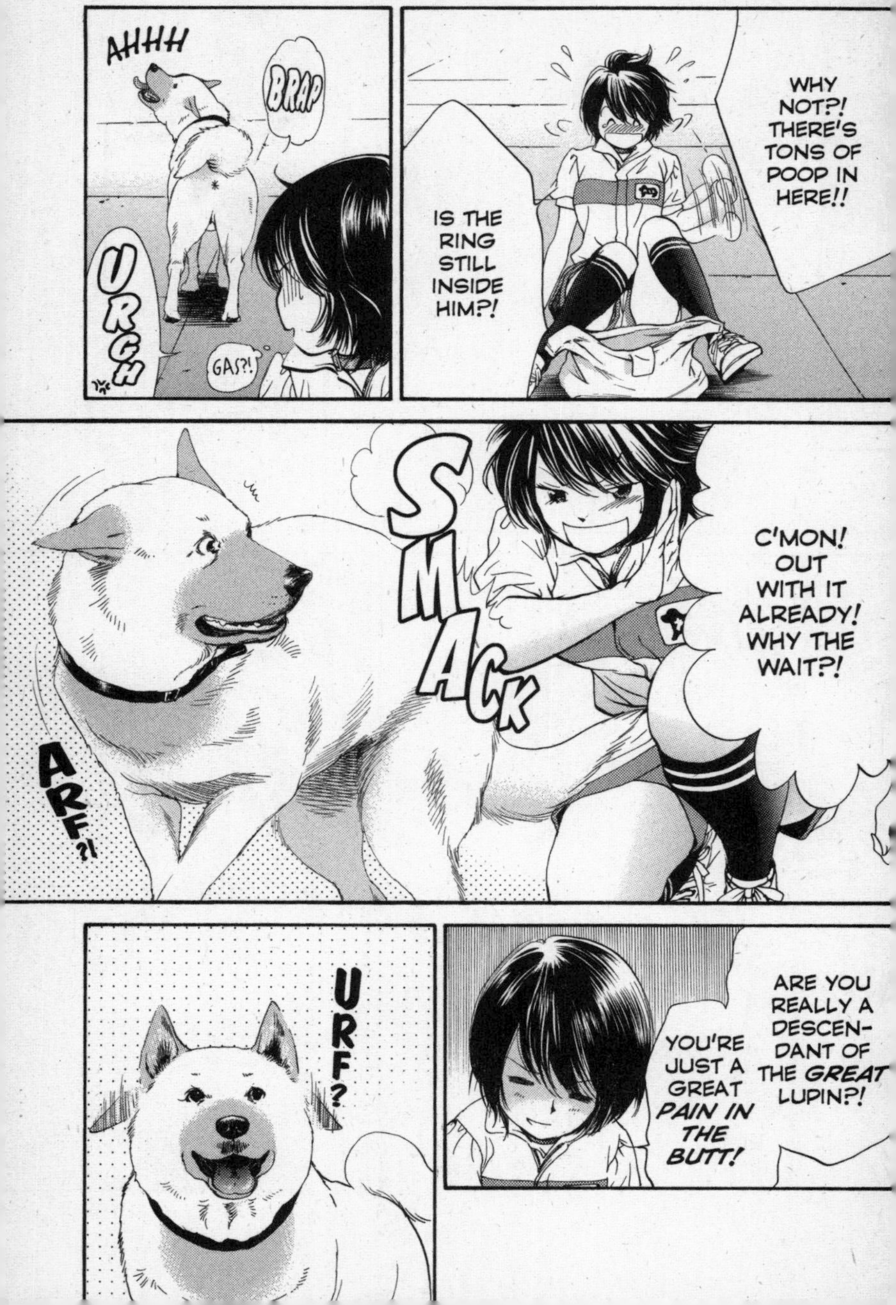
WHY NOT?! THERE'S TONS OF POOP IN HERE!!
IS THE RING STILL INSIDE HIM?!
BRAP
AHHH
GAS?!
URGH
C'MON! OUT WITH IT ALREADY! WHY THE WAIT?!
SMACK
ARF?!
ARE YOU REALLY A DESCEN-DANT OF THE *GREAT* LUPIN?!
YOU'RE JUST A GREAT *PAIN IN THE BUTT!*
URF?

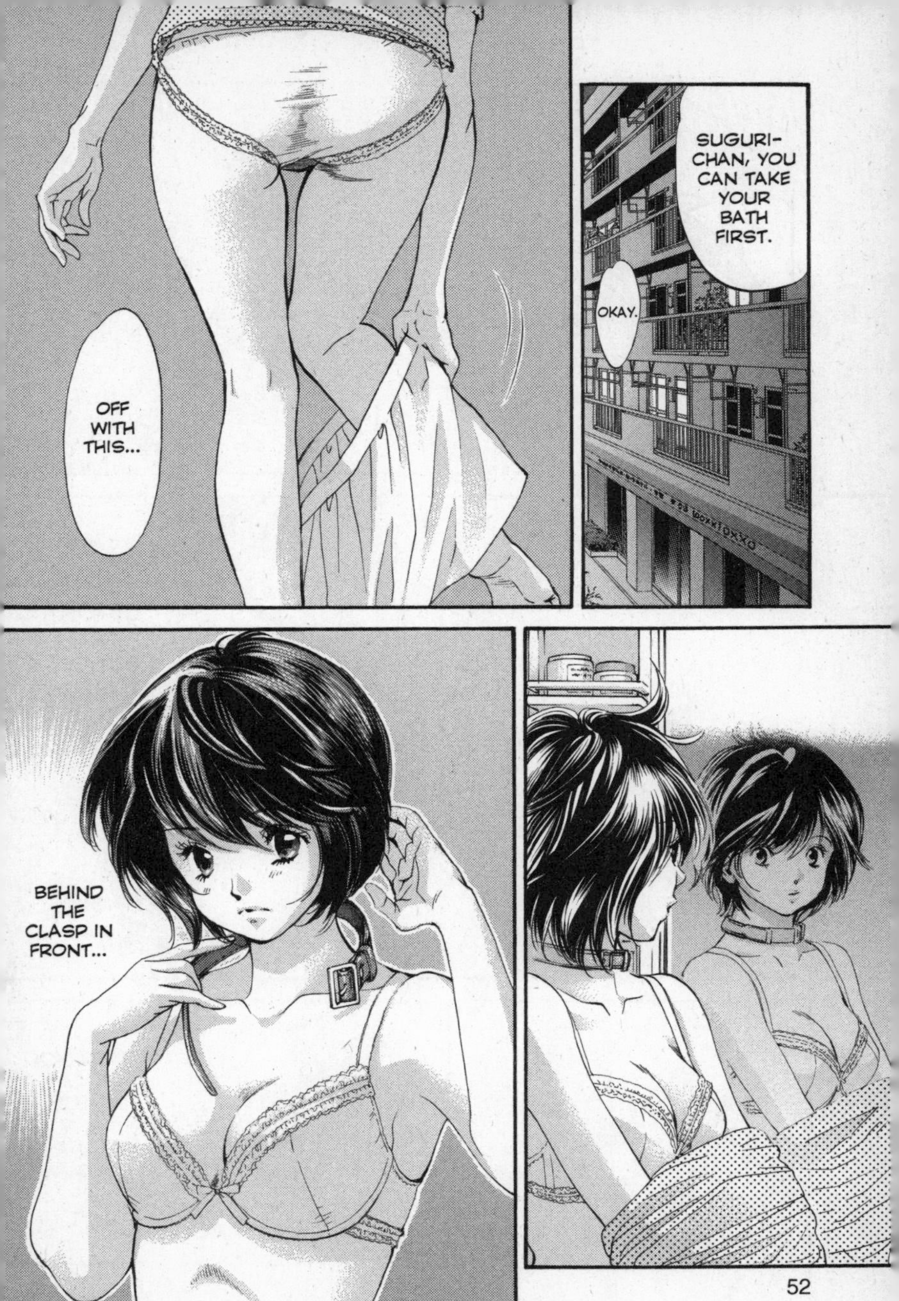
SUGURI-CHAN, YOU CAN TAKE YOUR BATH FIRST.
OKAY.
OFF WITH THIS...
BEHIND THE CLASP IN FRONT...

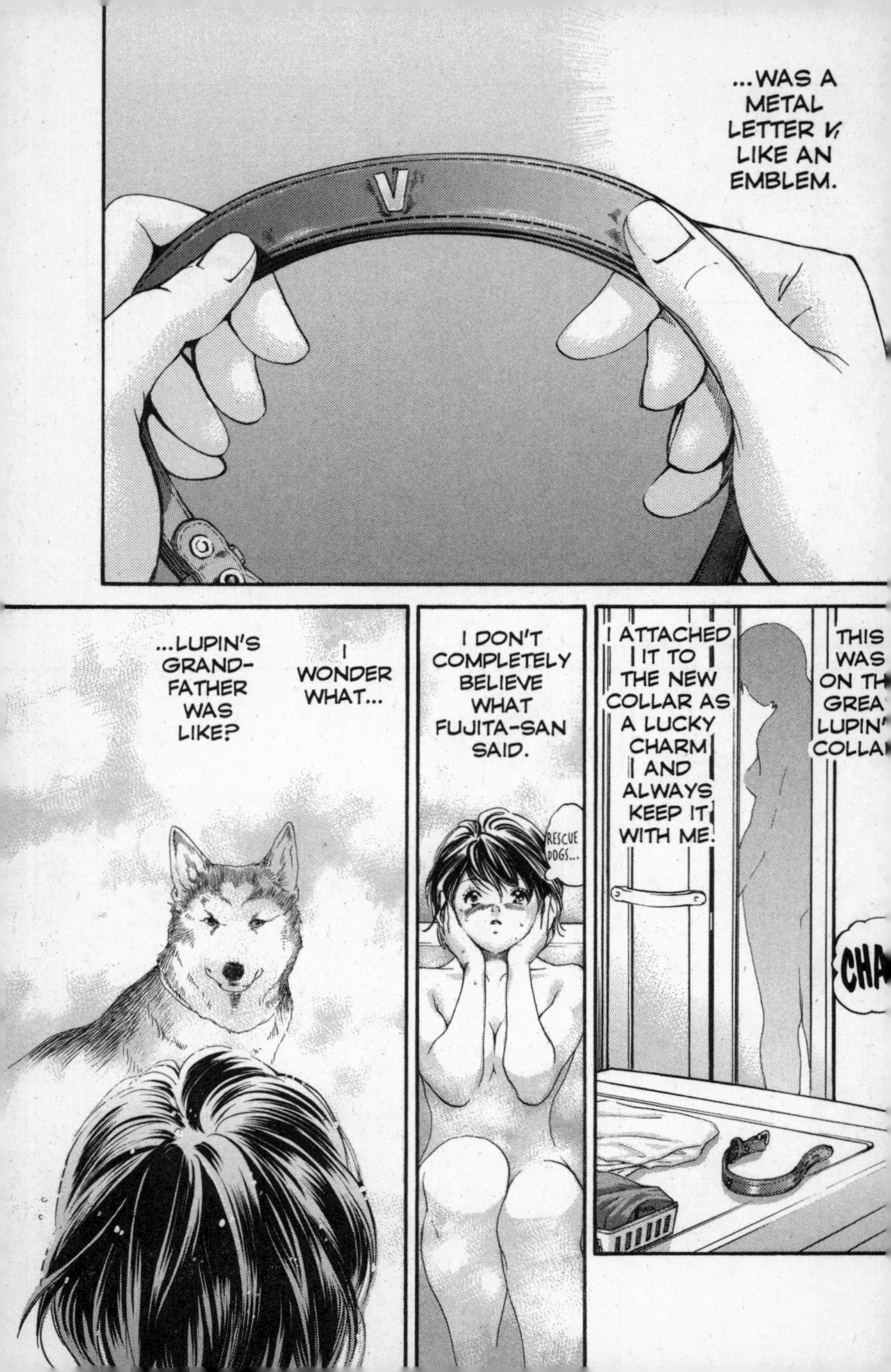
...WAS A METAL LETTER V, LIKE AN EMBLEM.
THIS WAS ON TH GREA LUPIN' COLLA
I ATTACHED IT TO THE NEW COLLAR AS A LUCKY CHARM AND ALWAYS KEEP IT WITH ME.
CHA
I DON'T COMPLETELY BELIEVE WHAT FUJITA-SAN SAID.
RESCUE DOGS...
I WONDER WHAT...
...LUPIN'S GRAND-FATHER WAS LIKE?

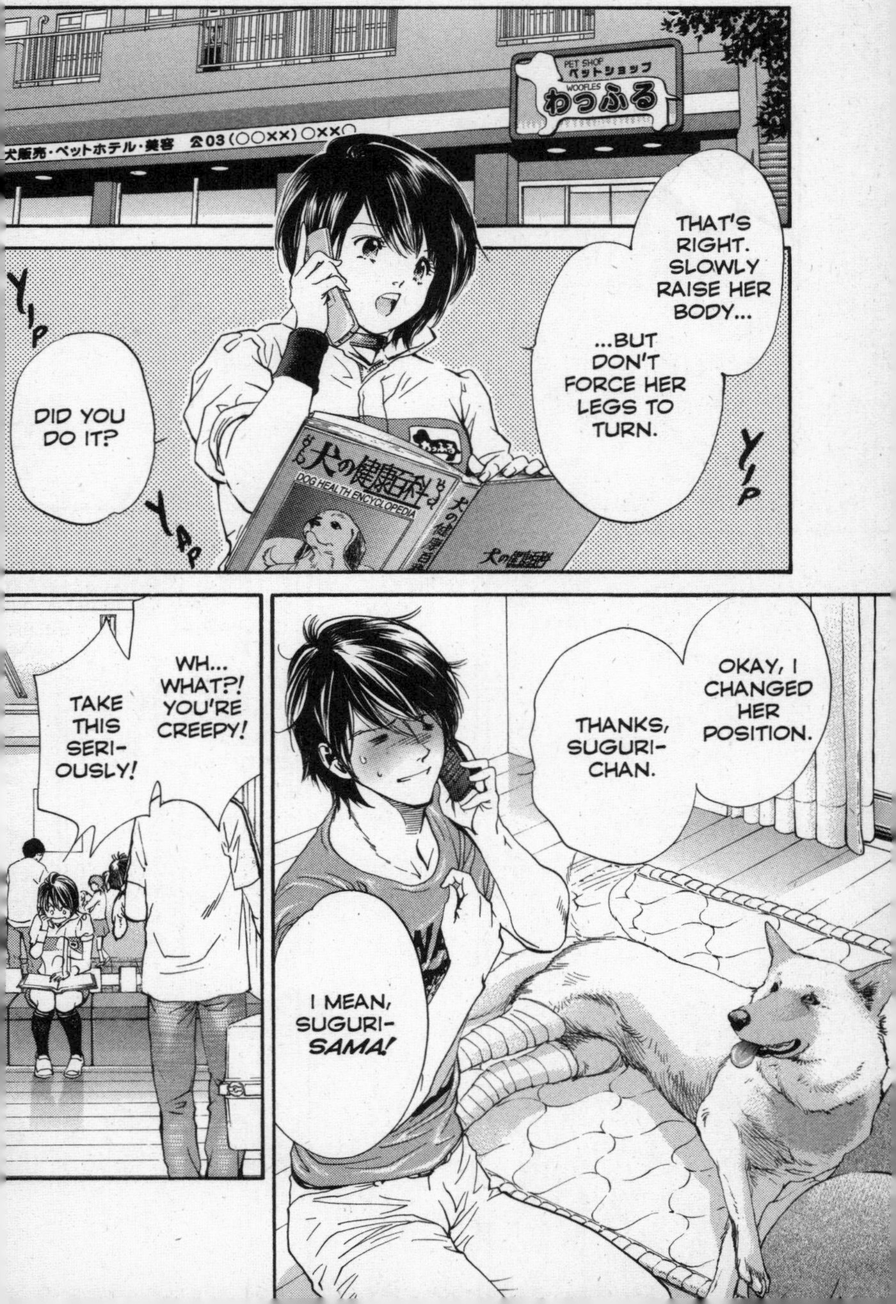
PET SHOP ペットショップ
WOOFLES わっふる
犬販売・ペットホテル・美容 ☎03 (○○××) ○××○
THAT'S RIGHT. SLOWLY RAISE HER BODY...
...BUT DON'T FORCE HER LEGS TO TURN.
YIP
DID YOU DO IT?
YIP
YAP
犬の健康百科
DOG HEALTH ENCYCLOPEDIA
OKAY, I CHANGED HER POSITION.
THANKS, SUGURI-CHAN.
I MEAN, SUGURI-*SAMA!*
WH... WHAT?! YOU'RE CREEPY!
TAKE THIS SERI-OUSLY!

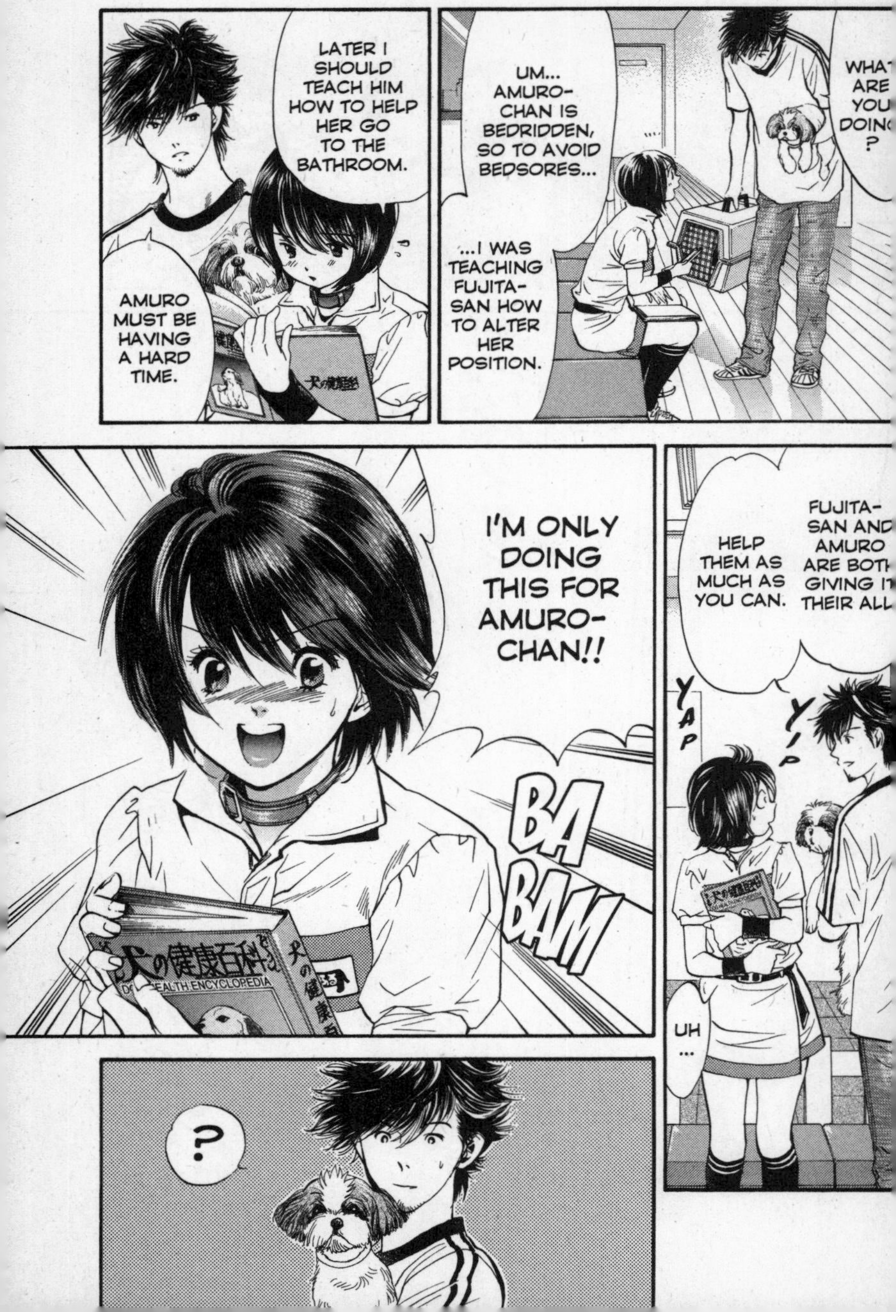
WHAT ARE YOU DOIN ?
...
UM... AMURO-CHAN IS BEDRIDDEN, SO TO AVOID BEDSORES...
...I WAS TEACHING FUJITA-SAN HOW TO ALTER HER POSITION.
LATER I SHOULD TEACH HIM HOW TO HELP HER GO TO THE BATHROOM.
AMURO MUST BE HAVING A HARD TIME.
FUJITA-SAN AND AMURO ARE BOTH GIVING IT THEIR ALL
HELP THEM AS MUCH AS YOU CAN.
YAP
YIP
UH...
I'M ONLY DOING THIS FOR AMURO-CHAN!!
BA BAM
犬の健康百科
?

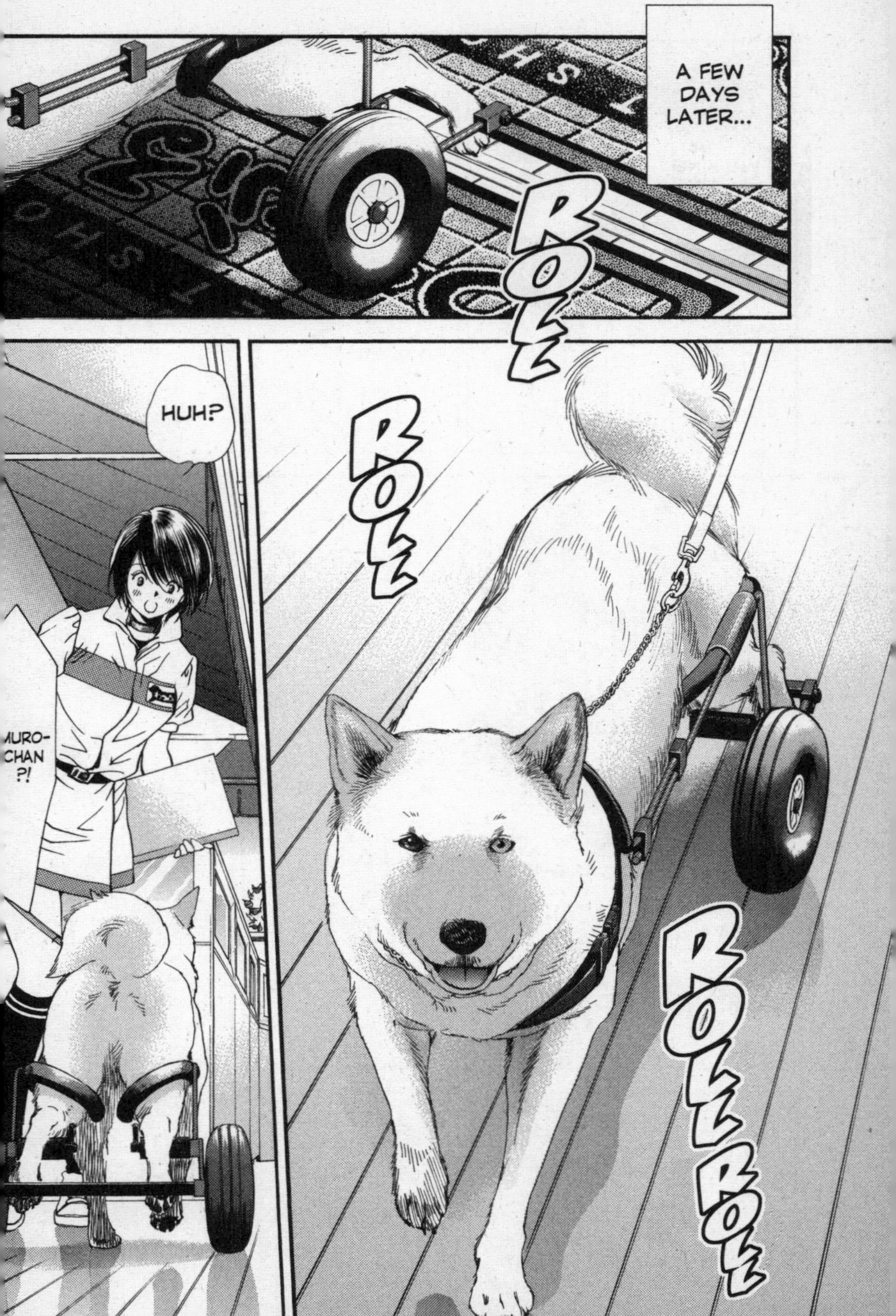
A FEW DAYS LATER...
ROLL
ROLL
ROLLROLL
HUH?
MURO-CHAN?!

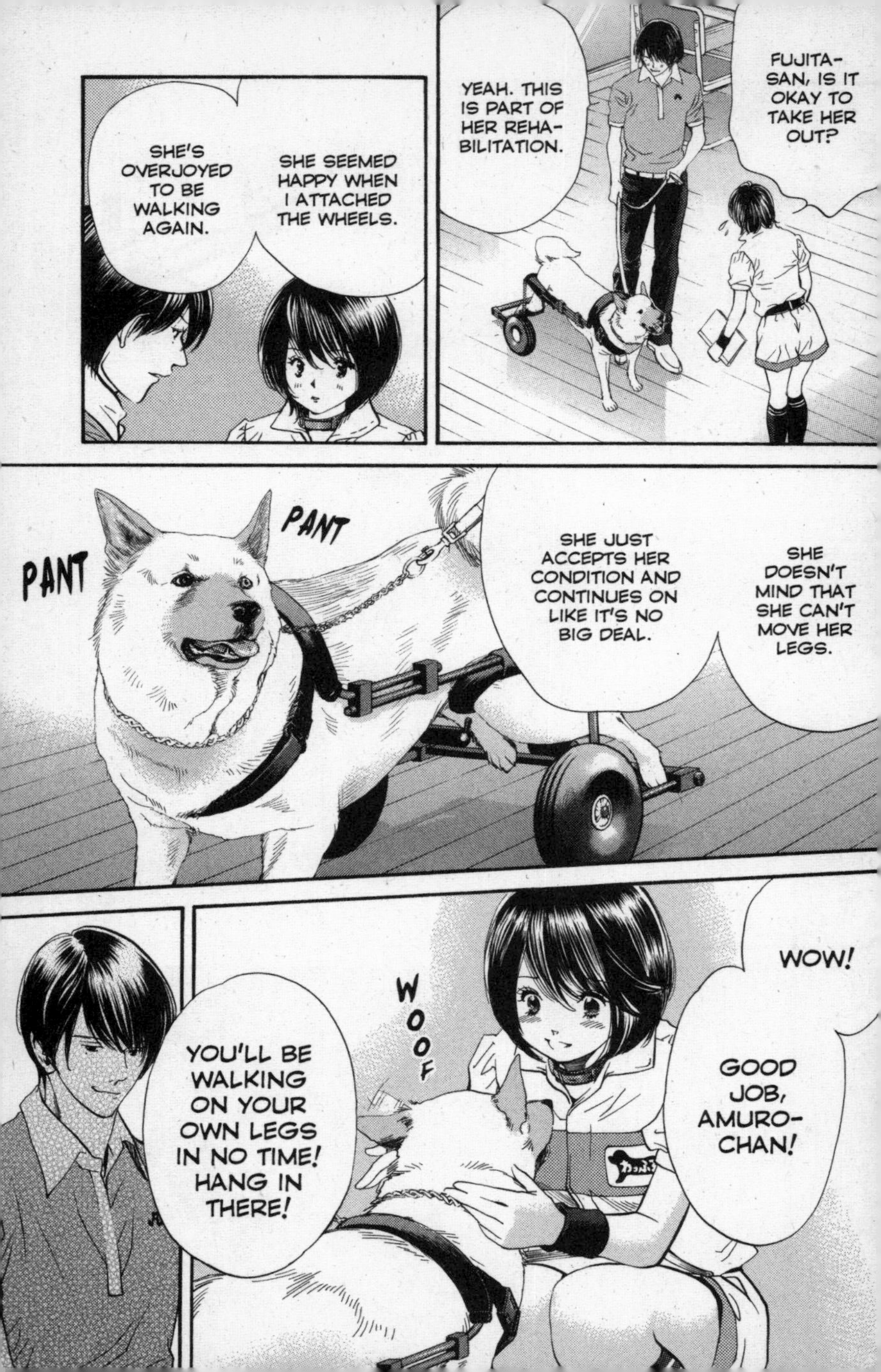
FUJITA-SAN, IS IT OKAY TO TAKE HER OUT?
YEAH. THIS IS PART OF HER REHABILITATION.
SHE SEEMED HAPPY WHEN I ATTACHED THE WHEELS.
SHE'S OVERJOYED TO BE WALKING AGAIN.
SHE DOESN'T MIND THAT SHE CAN'T MOVE HER LEGS.
SHE JUST ACCEPTS HER CONDITION AND CONTINUES ON LIKE IT'S NO BIG DEAL.
PANT
PANT
WOW!
GOOD JOB, AMURO-CHAN!
WOOF
YOU'LL BE WALKING ON YOUR OWN LEGS IN NO TIME! HANG IN THERE!

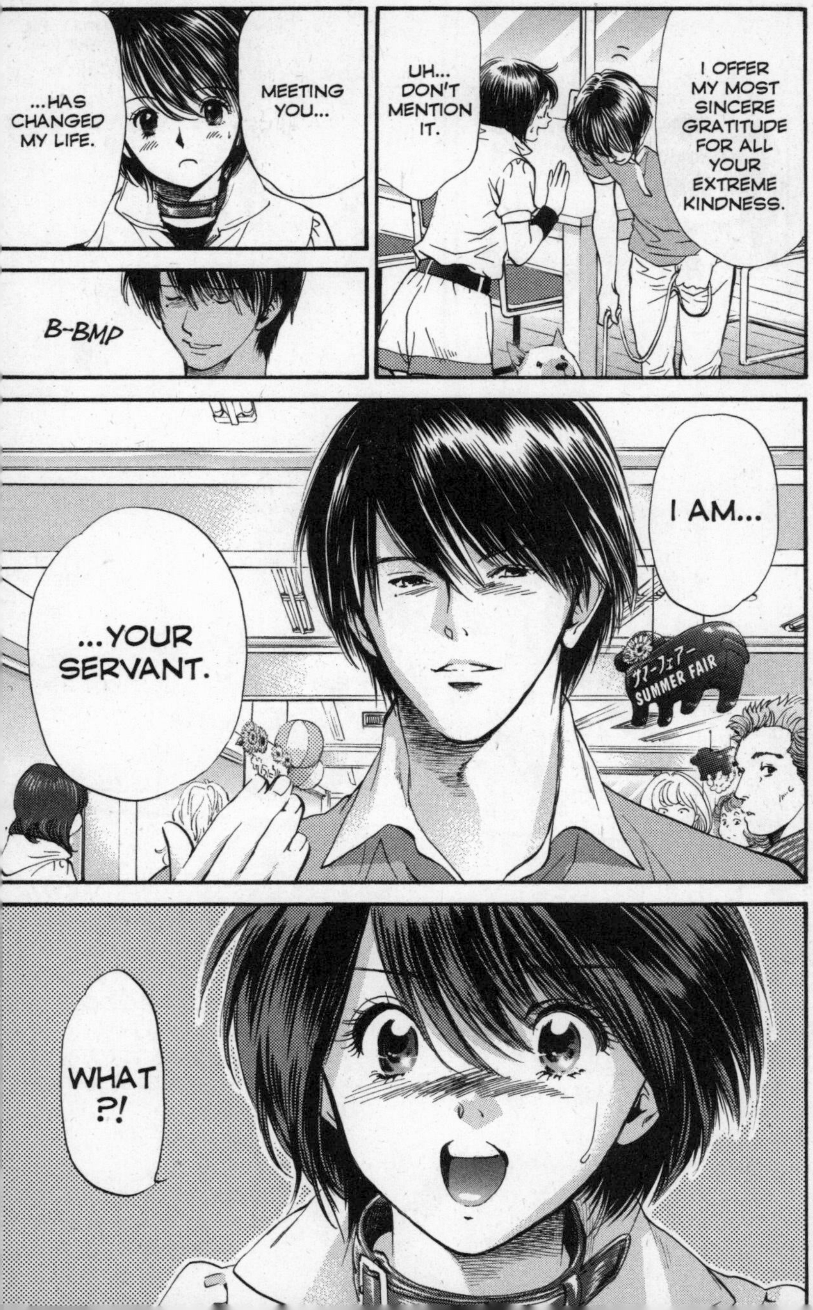
I OFFER MY MOST SINCERE GRATITUDE FOR ALL YOUR EXTREME KINDNESS.
UH... DON'T MENTION IT.
MEETING YOU...
...HAS CHANGED MY LIFE.
B-BMP
I AM...
...YOUR SERVANT.
サマーフェアー SUMMER FAIR
WHAT?!

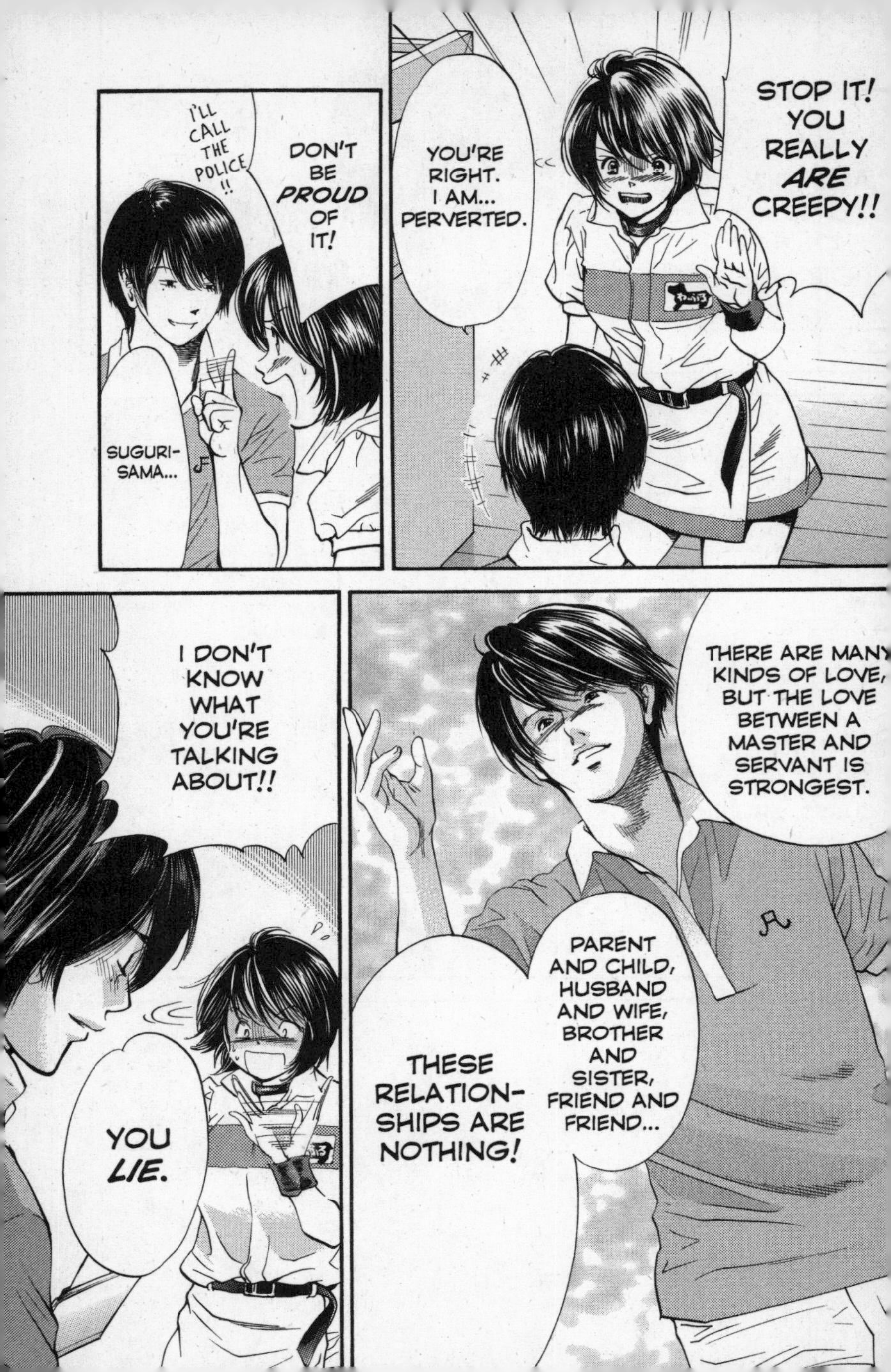
STOP IT! YOU REALLY ARE CREEPY!!
YOU'RE RIGHT. I AM... PERVERTED.
DON'T BE PROUD OF IT!
I'LL CALL THE POLICE!!
SUGURI-SAMA...
THERE ARE MANY KINDS OF LOVE, BUT THE LOVE BETWEEN A MASTER AND SERVANT IS STRONGEST.
PARENT AND CHILD, HUSBAND AND WIFE, BROTHER AND SISTER, FRIEND AND FRIEND...
THESE RELATION-SHIPS ARE NOTHING!
I DON'T KNOW WHAT YOU'RE TALKING ABOUT!!
YOU LIE.

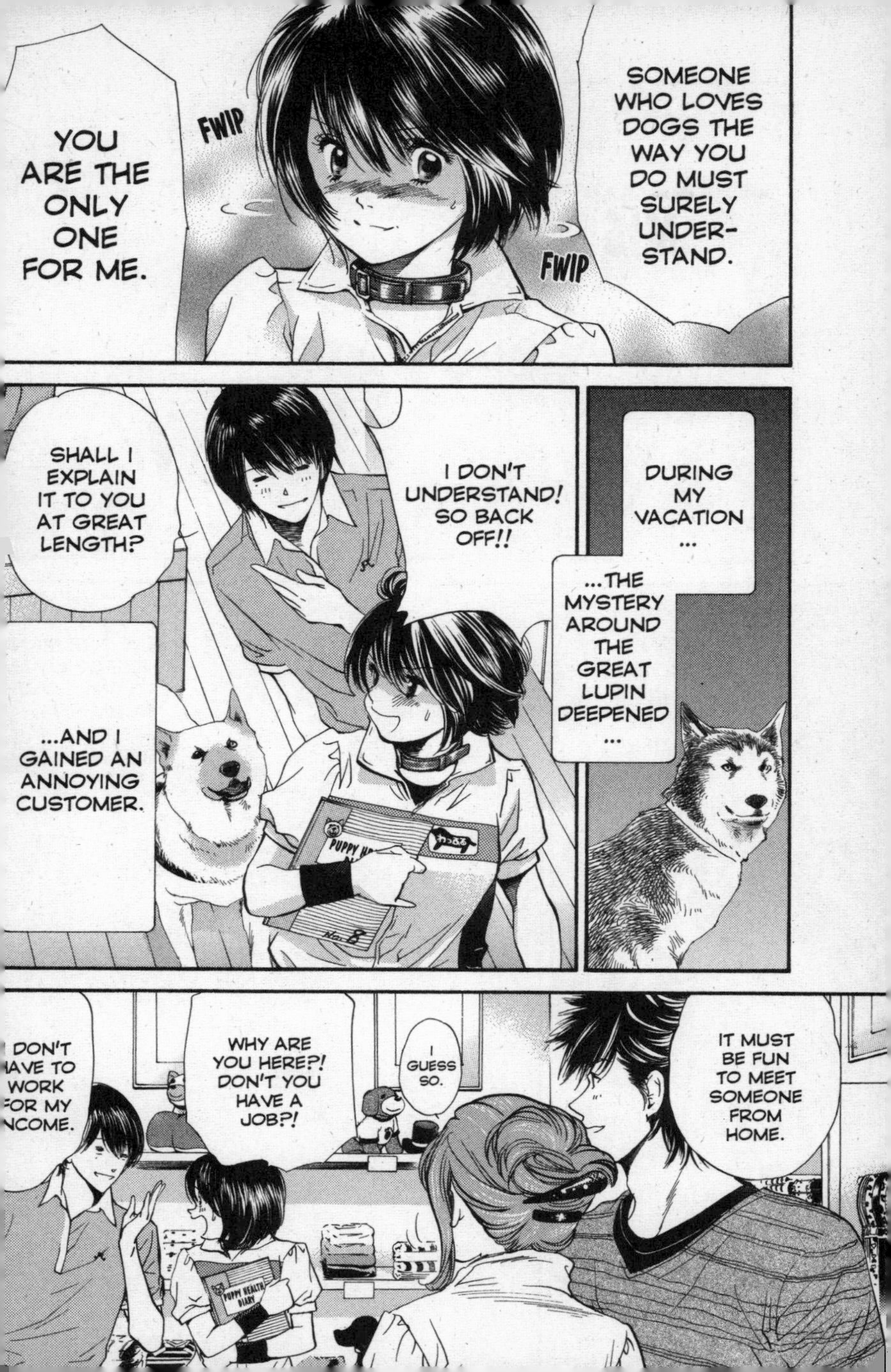
SOMEONE WHO LOVES DOGS THE WAY YOU DO MUST SURELY UNDER-STAND.
FWIP
FWIP
YOU ARE THE ONLY ONE FOR ME.
DURING MY VACATION ...
...THE MYSTERY AROUND THE GREAT LUPIN DEEPENED ...
I DON'T UNDERSTAND! SO BACK OFF!!
SHALL I EXPLAIN IT TO YOU AT GREAT LENGTH?
...AND I GAINED AN ANNOYING CUSTOMER.
IT MUST BE FUN TO MEET SOMEONE FROM HOME.
I GUESS SO.
WHY ARE YOU HERE?! DON'T YOU HAVE A JOB?!
DON'T HAVE TO WORK FOR MY NCOME.

CHAPTER 166: A LITTLE SOMETHING MISSING

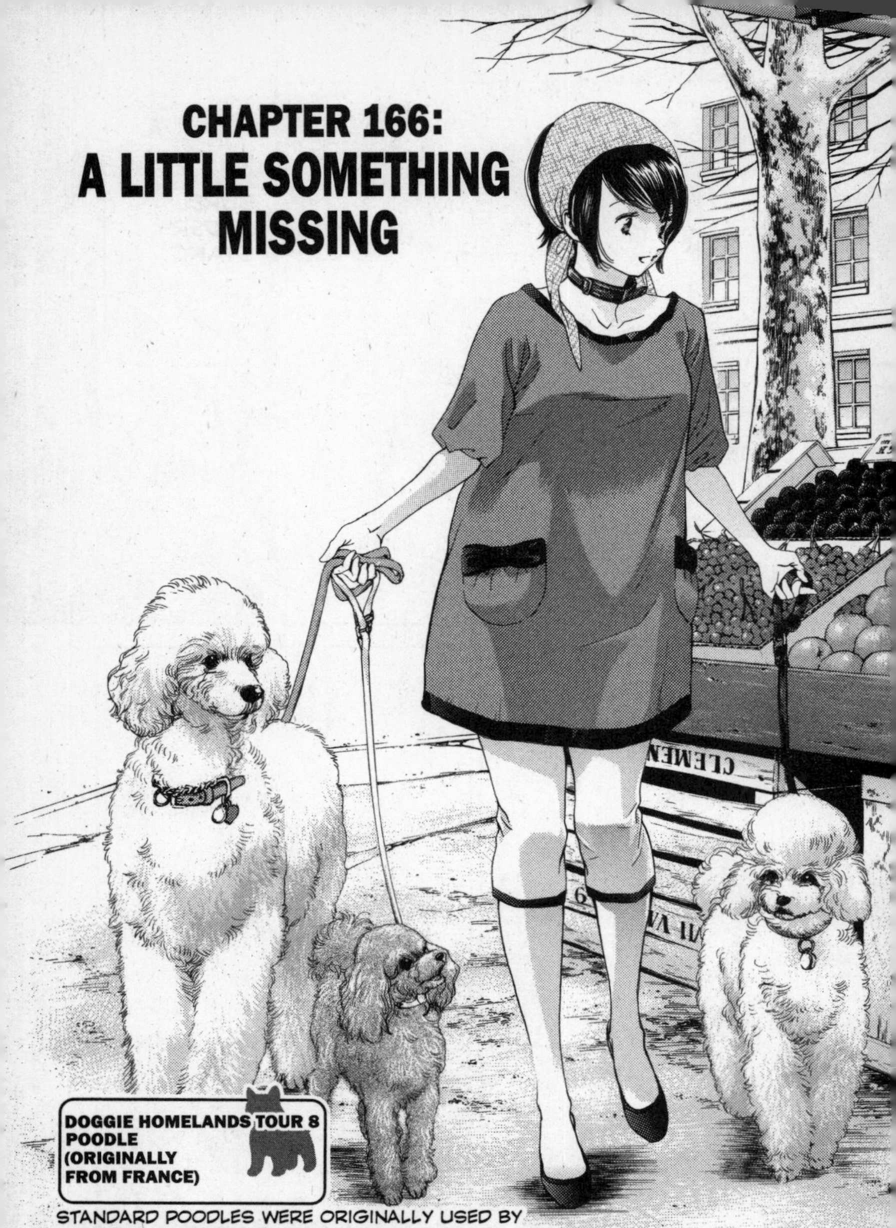
CLEMEN

DOGGIE HOMELANDS TOUR 8
POODLE
(ORIGINALLY FROM FRANCE)

STANDARD POODLES WERE ORIGINALLY USED BY HUNTERS TO RETRIEVE BIRDS THAT HAD FALLEN INTO RIVERS AND PONDS. MINIATURE POODLES AND TOY POODLES HAVE BEEN BRED TO A SMALLER SIZE. ALL POODLES ARE FAST LEARNERS, INTELLIGENT AND ACTIVE. REGULAR TRIMMING IS NECESSARY TO KEEP THEIR FUR CLEAN.

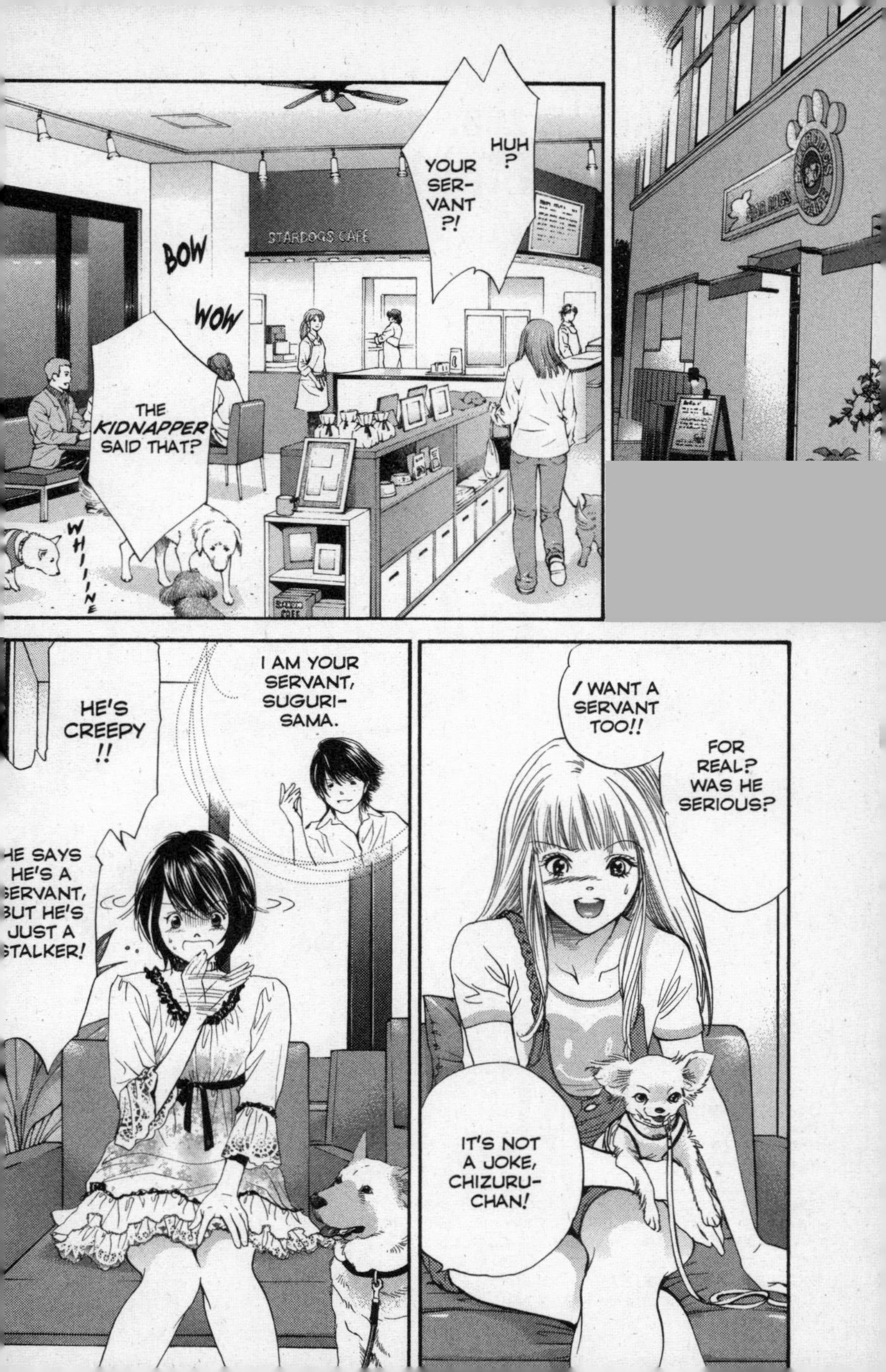
HUH?
YOUR SERVANT?!
BOW
WOW
THE KIDNAPPER SAID THAT?
WHIIINE
STARDOGS CAFE
I WANT A SERVANT TOO!!
FOR REAL? WAS HE SERIOUS?
IT'S NOT A JOKE, CHIZURU-CHAN!
I AM YOUR SERVANT, SUGURI-SAMA.
HE'S CREEPY!!
HE SAYS HE'S A SERVANT, BUT HE'S JUST A STALKER!

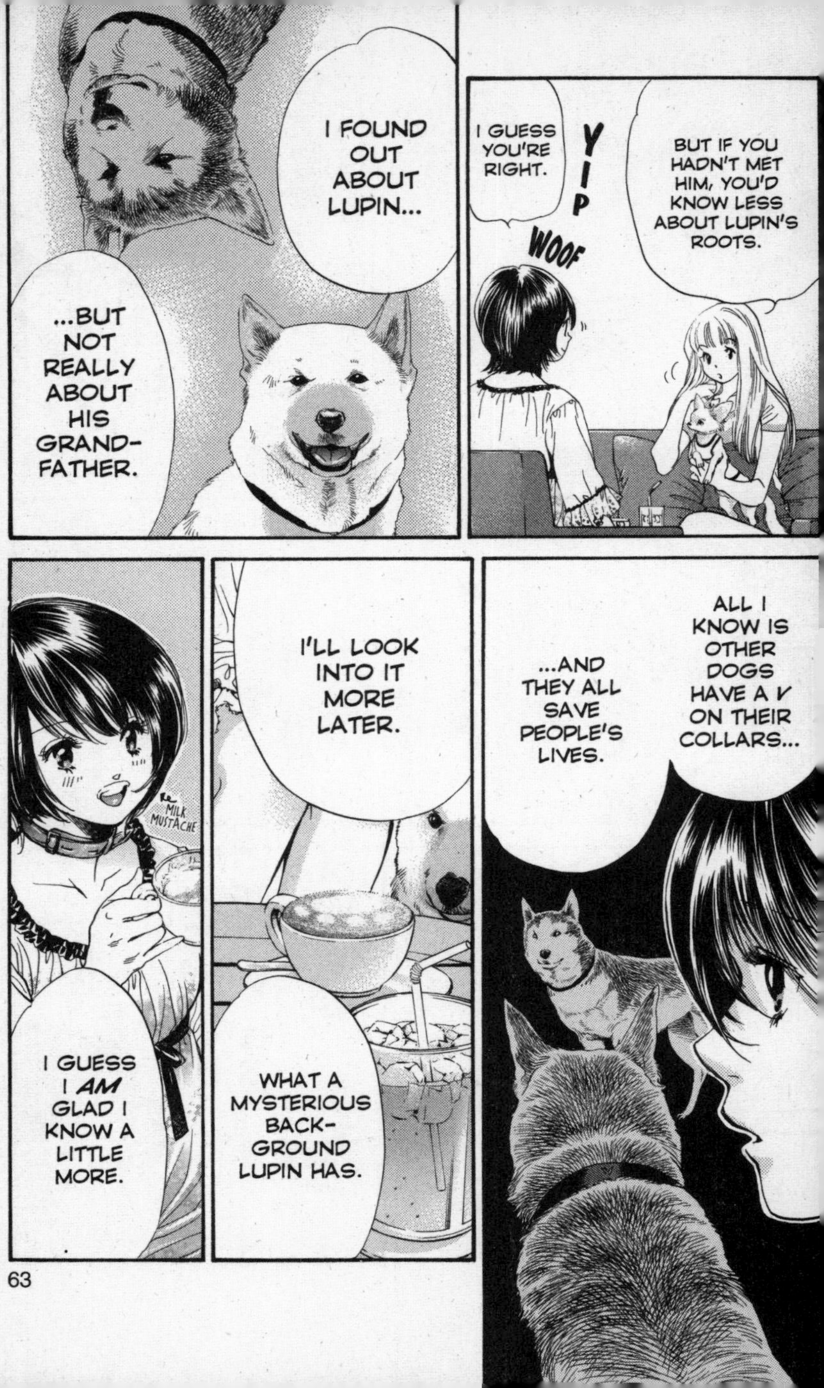
BUT IF YOU HADN'T MET HIM, YOU'D KNOW LESS ABOUT LUPIN'S ROOTS.
I GUESS YOU'RE RIGHT.
YIP
WOOF
I FOUND OUT ABOUT LUPIN...
...BUT NOT REALLY ABOUT HIS GRAND-FATHER.
ALL I KNOW IS OTHER DOGS HAVE A V ON THEIR COLLARS...
...AND THEY ALL SAVE PEOPLE'S LIVES.
I'LL LOOK INTO IT MORE LATER.
WHAT A MYSTERIOUS BACK-GROUND LUPIN HAS.
MILK MUSTACHE
I GUESS I *AM* GLAD I KNOW A LITTLE MORE.

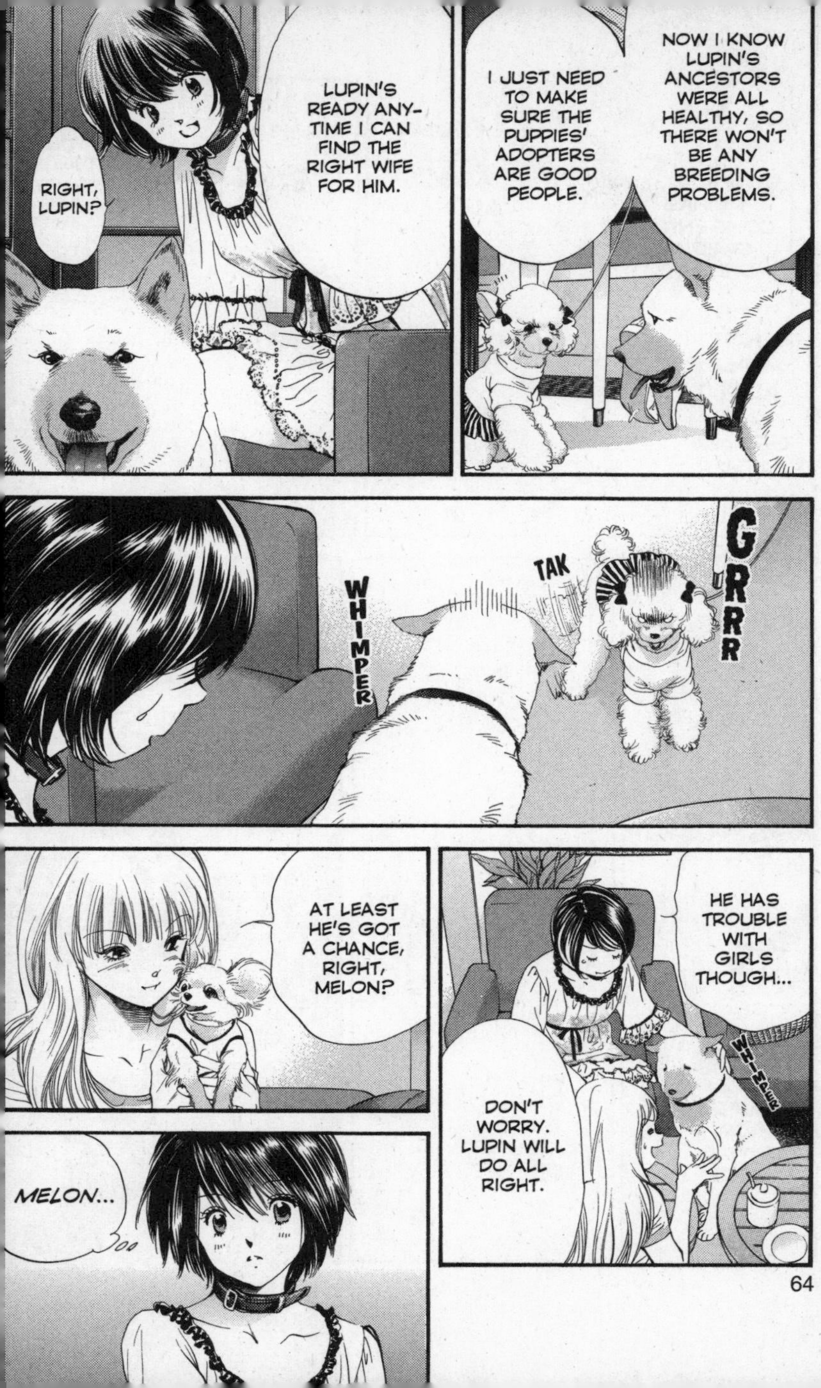
NOW I KNOW LUPIN'S ANCESTORS WERE ALL HEALTHY, SO THERE WON'T BE ANY BREEDING PROBLEMS.
I JUST NEED TO MAKE SURE THE PUPPIES' ADOPTERS ARE GOOD PEOPLE.
LUPIN'S READY ANY-TIME I CAN FIND THE RIGHT WIFE FOR HIM.
RIGHT, LUPIN?
GRRR
TAK
WHIMPER
HE HAS TROUBLE WITH GIRLS THOUGH...
WHIMPER
DON'T WORRY. LUPIN WILL DO ALL RIGHT.
AT LEAST HE'S GOT A CHANCE, RIGHT, MELON?
MELON...

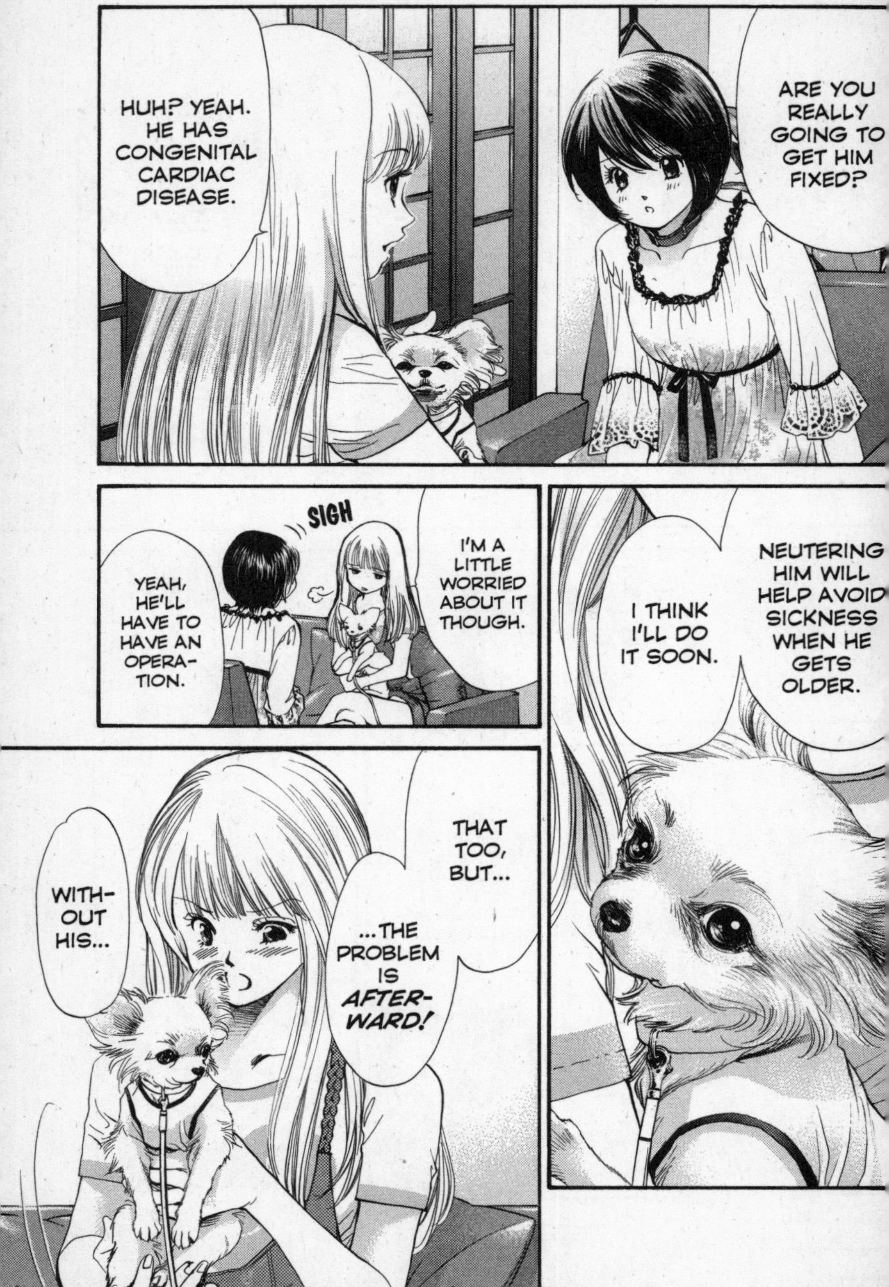
ARE YOU REALLY GOING TO GET HIM FIXED?
HUH? YEAH. HE HAS CONGENITAL CARDIAC DISEASE.
NEUTERING HIM WILL HELP AVOID SICKNESS WHEN HE GETS OLDER.
I THINK I'LL DO IT SOON.
SIGH
I'M A LITTLE WORRIED ABOUT IT THOUGH.
YEAH, HE'LL HAVE TO HAVE AN OPERA-TION.
THAT TOO, BUT...
...THE PROBLEM IS *AFTER-WARD!*
WITH-OUT HIS...

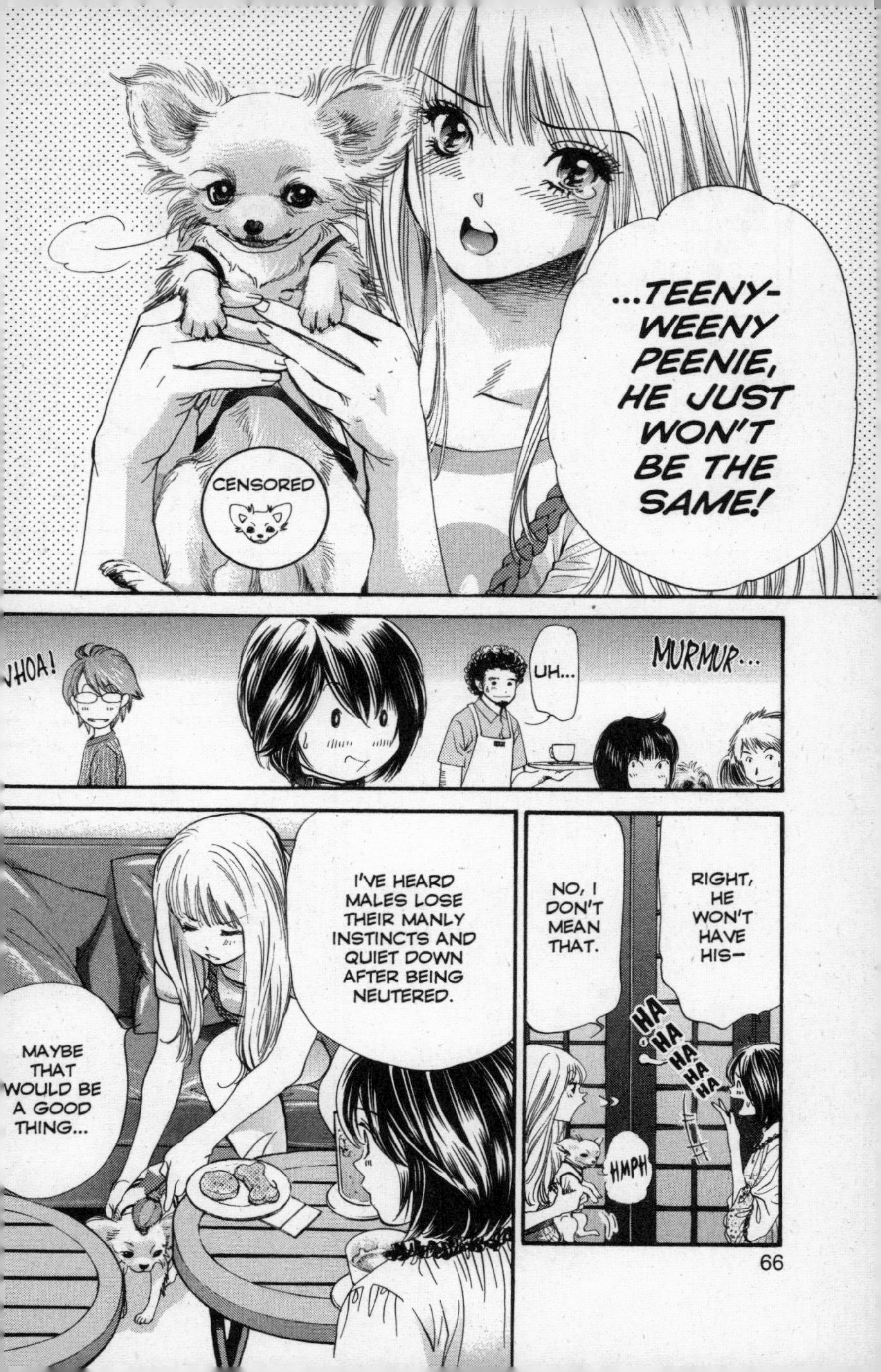
...TEENY-WEENY PEENIE, HE JUST WON'T BE THE SAME!
CENSORED
MURMUR...
UH...
WHOA!
RIGHT, HE WON'T HAVE HIS—
NO, I DON'T MEAN THAT.
HA HA HA HA HA
HMPH!
I'VE HEARD MALES LOSE THEIR MANLY INSTINCTS AND QUIET DOWN AFTER BEING NEUTERED.
MAYBE THAT WOULD BE A GOOD THING...

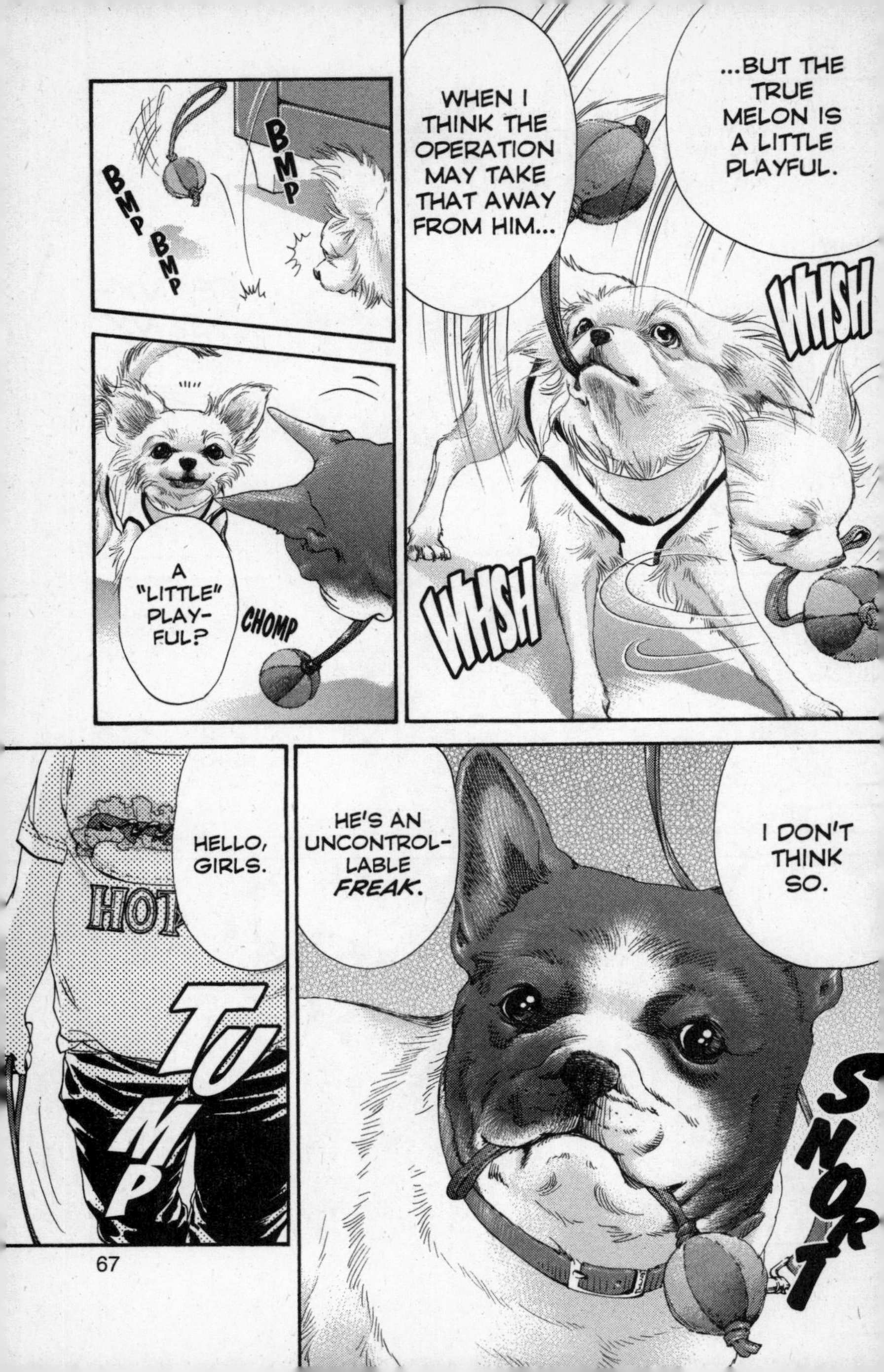
WHEN I THINK THE OPERATION MAY TAKE THAT AWAY FROM HIM...
...BUT THE TRUE MELON IS A LITTLE PLAYFUL.
WHSH
WHSH
BMP
BMP
BMP
A "LITTLE" PLAY-FUL?
CHOMP
I DON'T THINK SO.
HE'S AN UNCONTROL-LABLE *FREAK*.
SNORT
HELLO, GIRLS.
HOT
TUMP

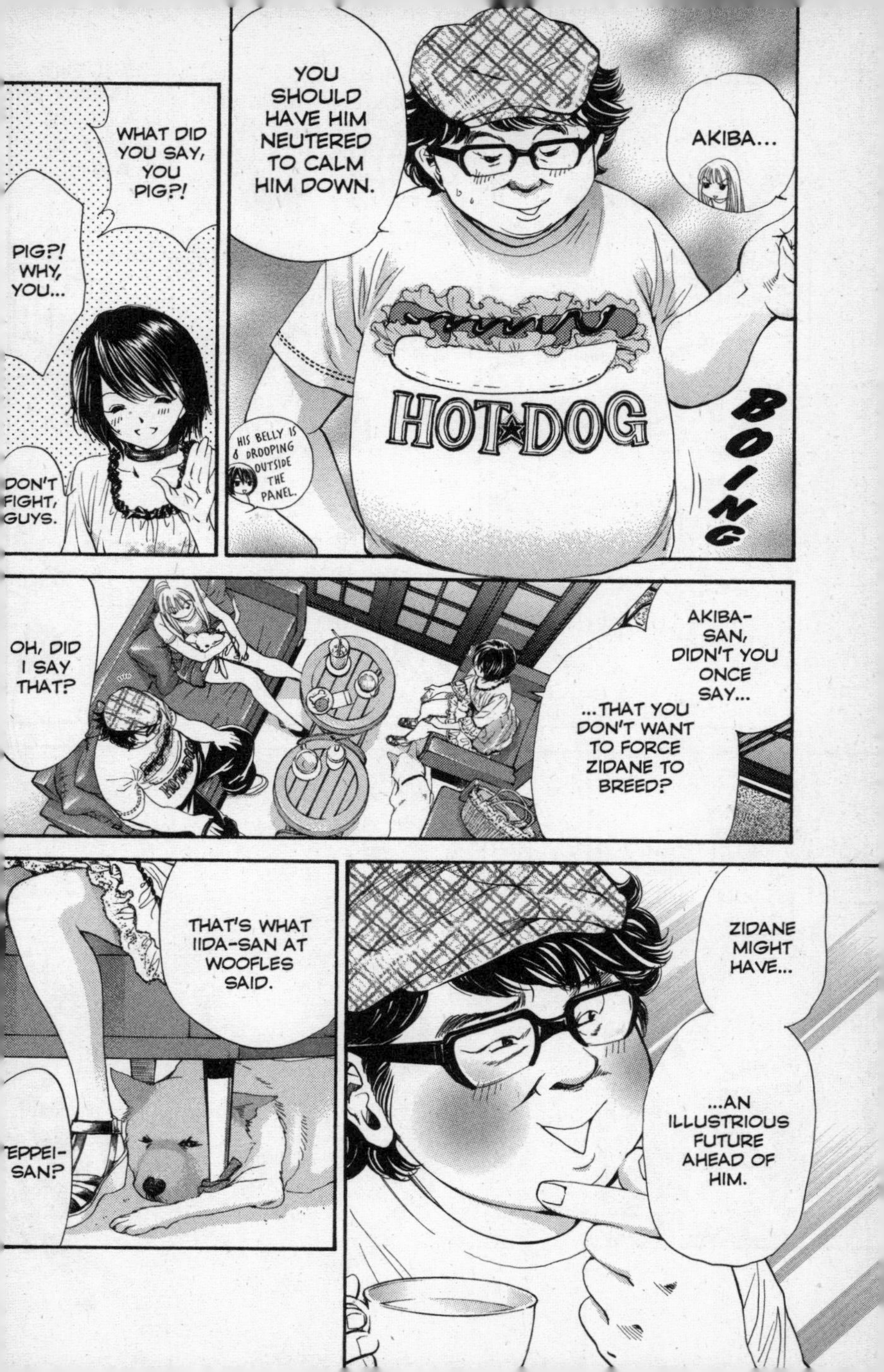
AKIBA...
YOU SHOULD HAVE HIM NEUTERED TO CALM HIM DOWN.
HOT★DOG
BOING
HIS BELLY IS DROOPING OUTSIDE THE PANEL.
WHAT DID YOU SAY, YOU PIG?!
PIG?! WHY, YOU...
DON'T FIGHT, GUYS.
AKIBA-SAN, DIDN'T YOU ONCE SAY...
...THAT YOU DON'T WANT TO FORCE ZIDANE TO BREED?
OH, DID I SAY THAT?
ZIDANE MIGHT HAVE...
...AN ILLUSTRIOUS FUTURE AHEAD OF HIM.
THAT'S WHAT IIDA-SAN AT WOOFLES SAID.
EPPEI-SAN?

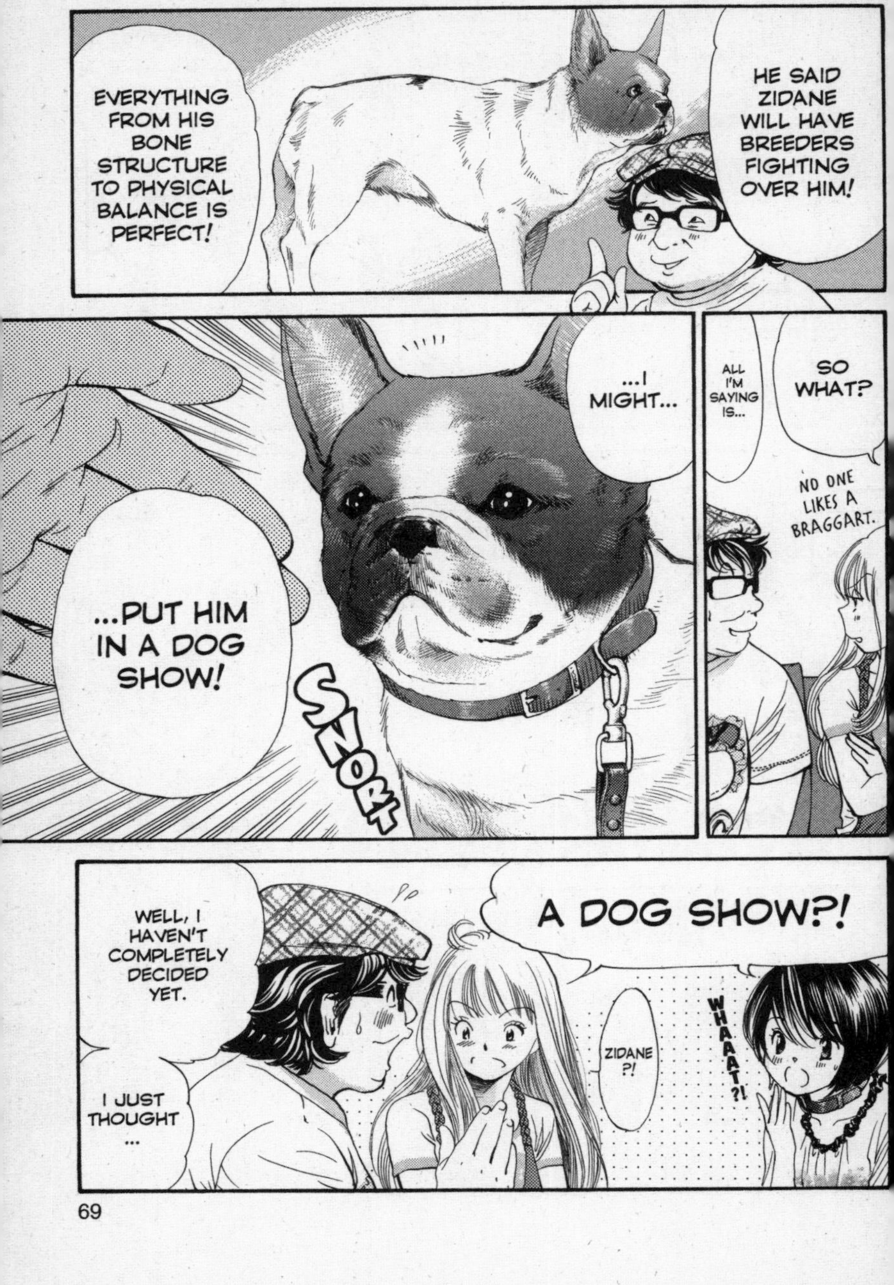
HE SAID ZIDANE WILL HAVE BREEDERS FIGHTING OVER HIM!
EVERYTHING FROM HIS BONE STRUCTURE TO PHYSICAL BALANCE IS PERFECT!
SO WHAT?
ALL I'M SAYING IS...
NO ONE LIKES A BRAGGART.
...I MIGHT...
...PUT HIM IN A DOG SHOW!
SNORT
A DOG SHOW?!
WHAAAT?!
ZIDANE ?!
WELL, I HAVEN'T COMPLETELY DECIDED YET.
I JUST THOUGHT ...

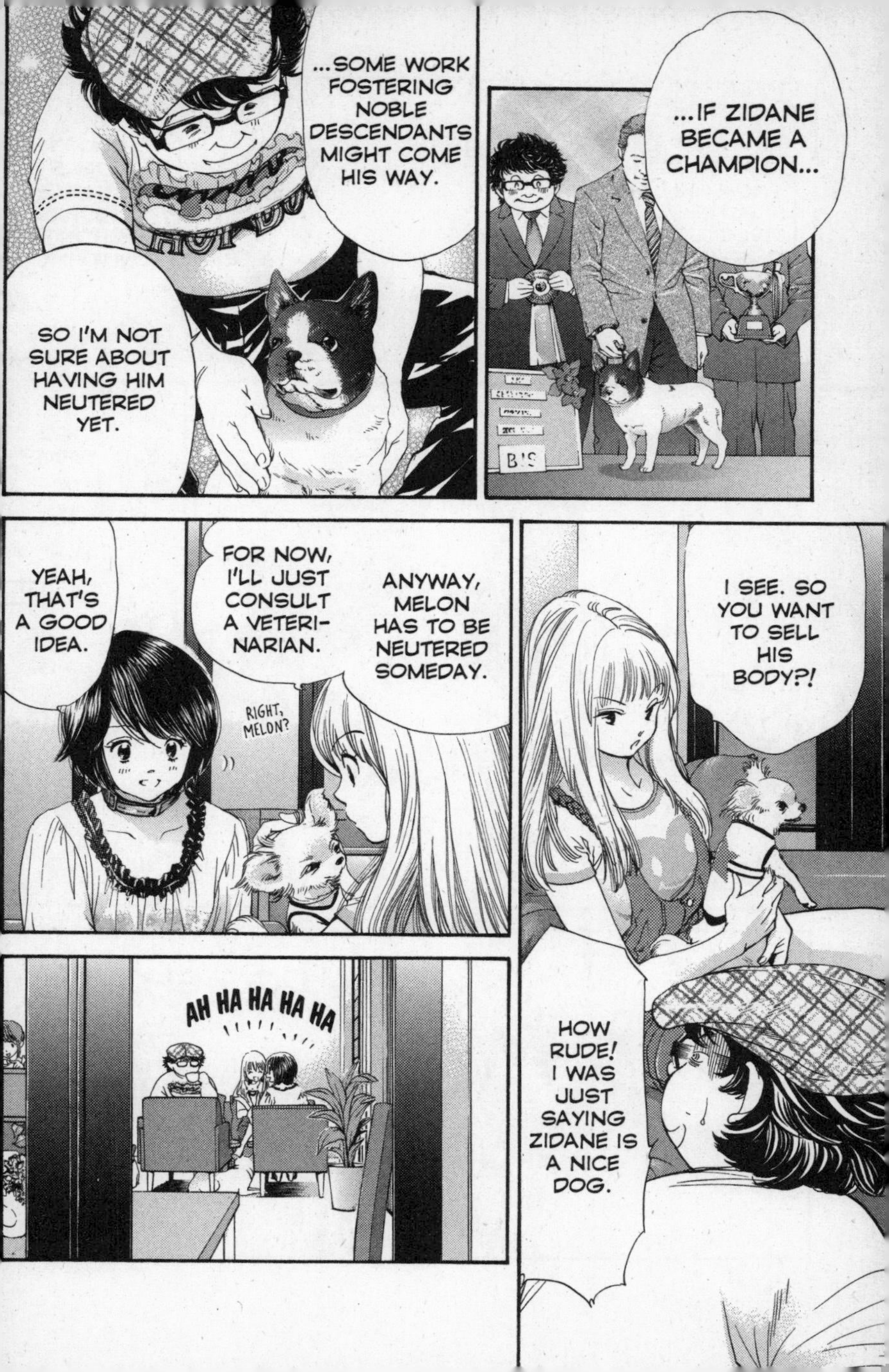
...IF ZIDANE BECAME A CHAMPION...
...SOME WORK FOSTERING NOBLE DESCENDANTS MIGHT COME HIS WAY.
SO I'M NOT SURE ABOUT HAVING HIM NEUTERED YET.
I SEE. SO YOU WANT TO SELL HIS BODY?!
HOW RUDE! I WAS JUST SAYING ZIDANE IS A NICE DOG.
ANYWAY, MELON HAS TO BE NEUTERED SOMEDAY.
FOR NOW, I'LL JUST CONSULT A VETERI-NARIAN.
RIGHT, MELON?
YEAH, THAT'S A GOOD IDEA.
AH HA HA HA HA

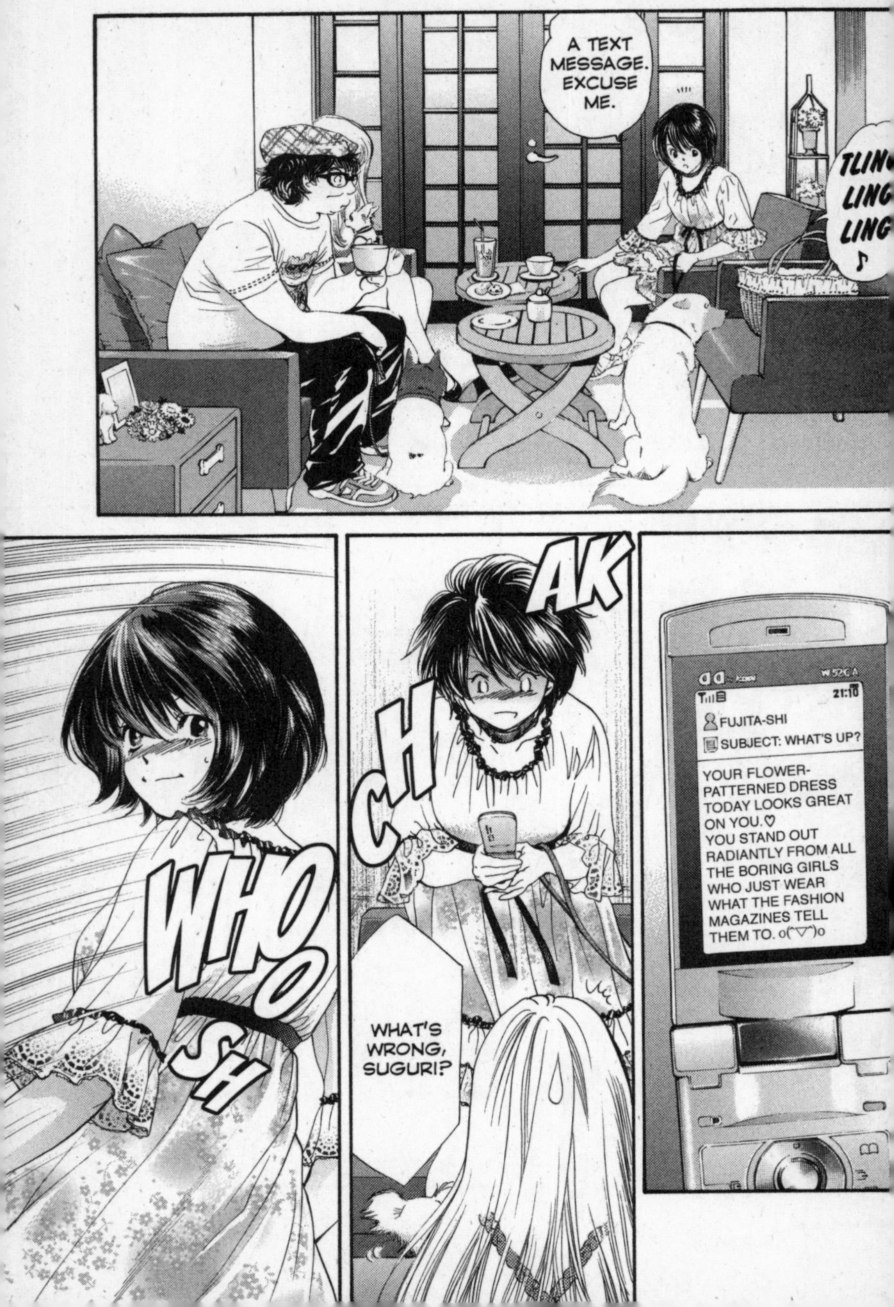
TLING LING LING ♪
A TEXT MESSAGE. EXCUSE ME.
21:10
FUJITA-SHI
SUBJECT: WHAT'S UP?
YOUR FLOWER-PATTERNED DRESS TODAY LOOKS GREAT ON YOU.♡ YOU STAND OUT RADIANTLY FROM ALL THE BORING GIRLS WHO JUST WEAR WHAT THE FASHION MAGAZINES TELL THEM TO. o(^▽^)o
CHAK
WHAT'S WRONG, SUGURI?
WHOOSH

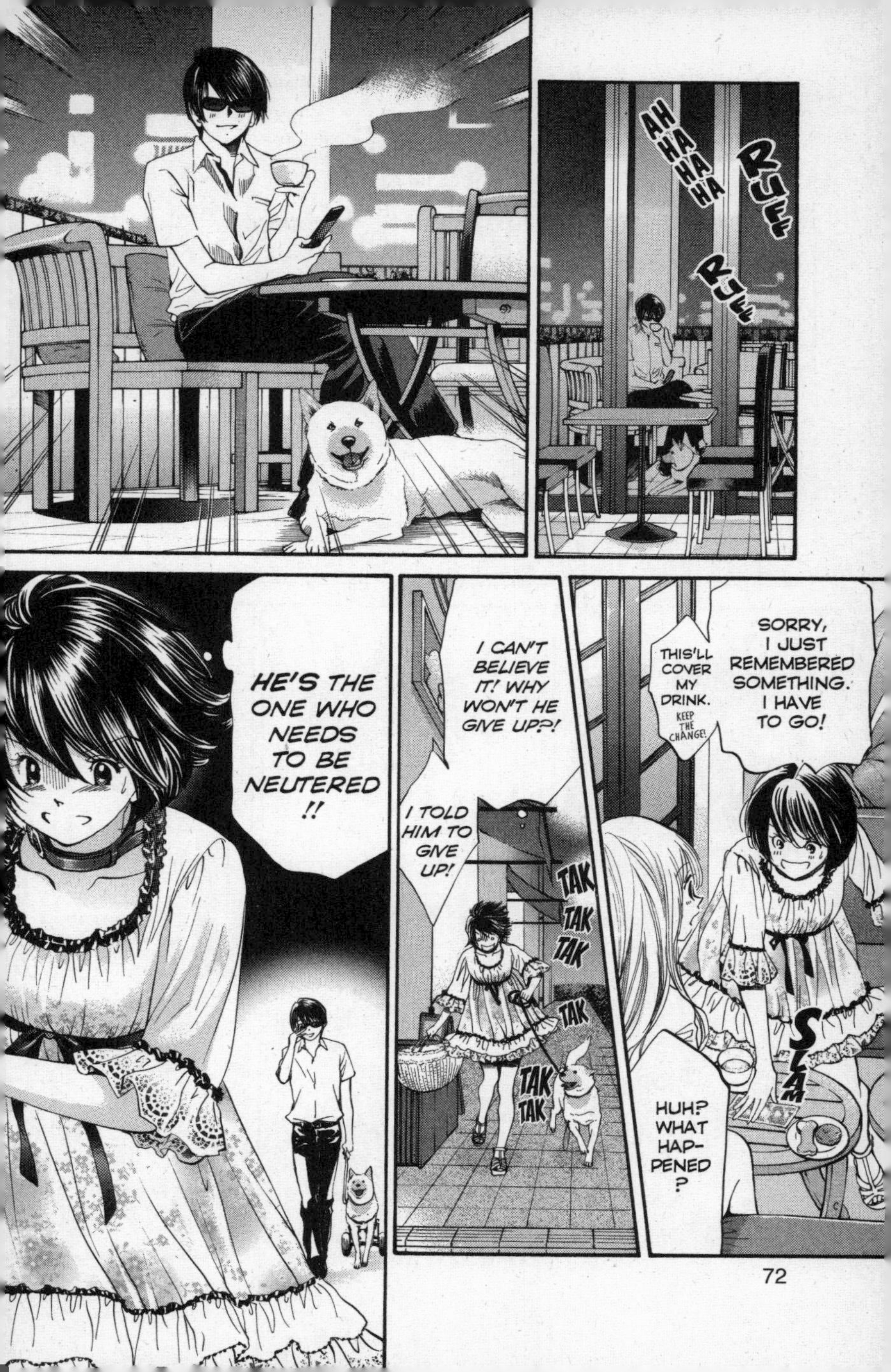
AH HA HA HA
RUFF
RUFF
SORRY, I JUST REMEMBERED SOMETHING. I HAVE TO GO!
THIS'LL COVER MY DRINK.
KEEP THE CHANGE!
SLAM
HUH? WHAT HAP-PENED?
I CAN'T BELIEVE IT! WHY WON'T HE GIVE UP?!
I TOLD HIM TO GIVE UP!
TAK TAK TAK
TAK
TAK TAK
HE'S THE ONE WHO NEEDS TO BE NEUTERED!!

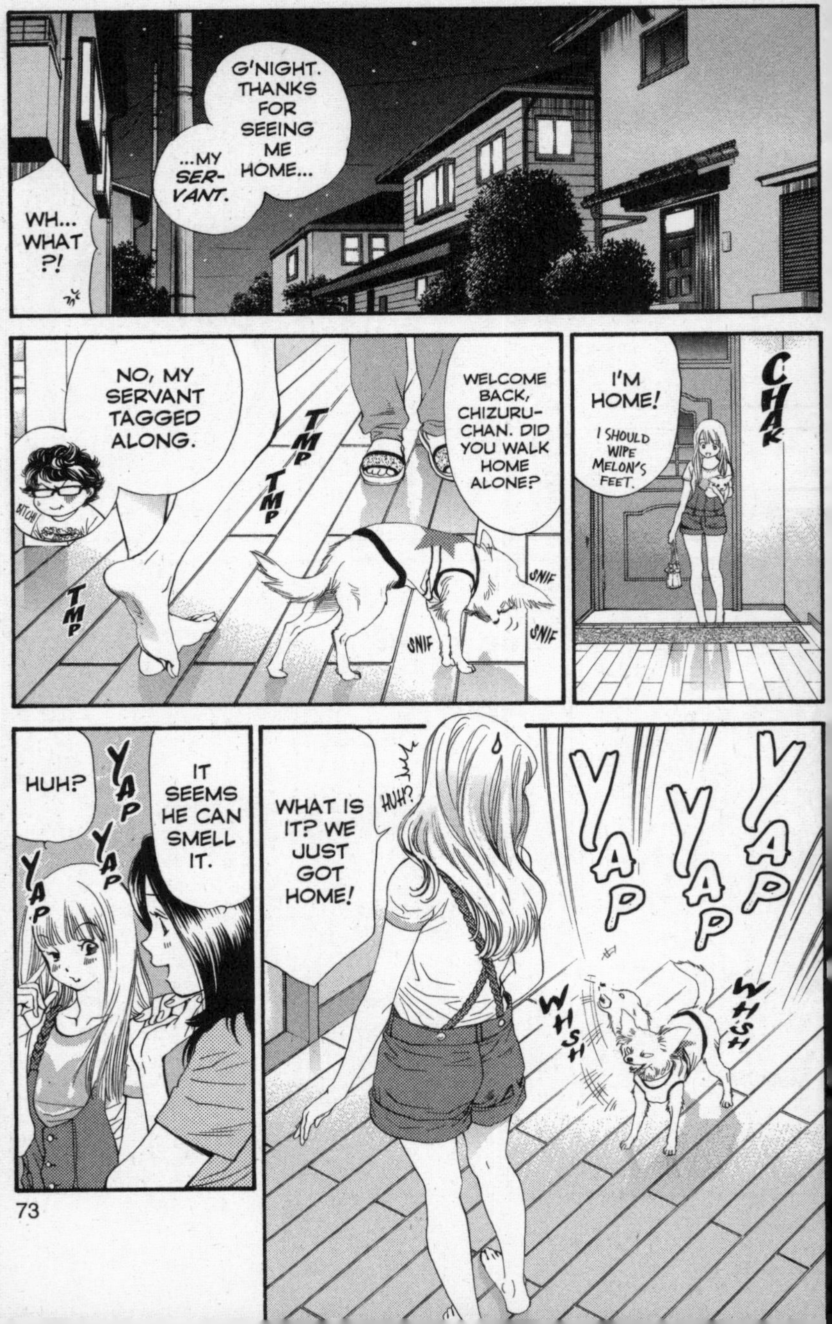
G'NIGHT. THANKS FOR SEEING ME HOME...
...MY SERVANT.
WH... WHAT?!
CHAK
I'M HOME!
I SHOULD WIPE MELON'S FEET.
WELCOME BACK, CHIZURU-CHAN. DID YOU WALK HOME ALONE?
TMP TMP
NO, MY SERVANT TAGGED ALONG.
BITCH!
TMP
SNIF
SNIF
SNIF
YAP YAP YAP
YAP YAP YAP
HUH?
WHAT IS IT? WE JUST GOT HOME!
WHSH
WHSH
IT SEEMS HE CAN SMELL IT.
YAP YAP
YAP YAP
HUH?

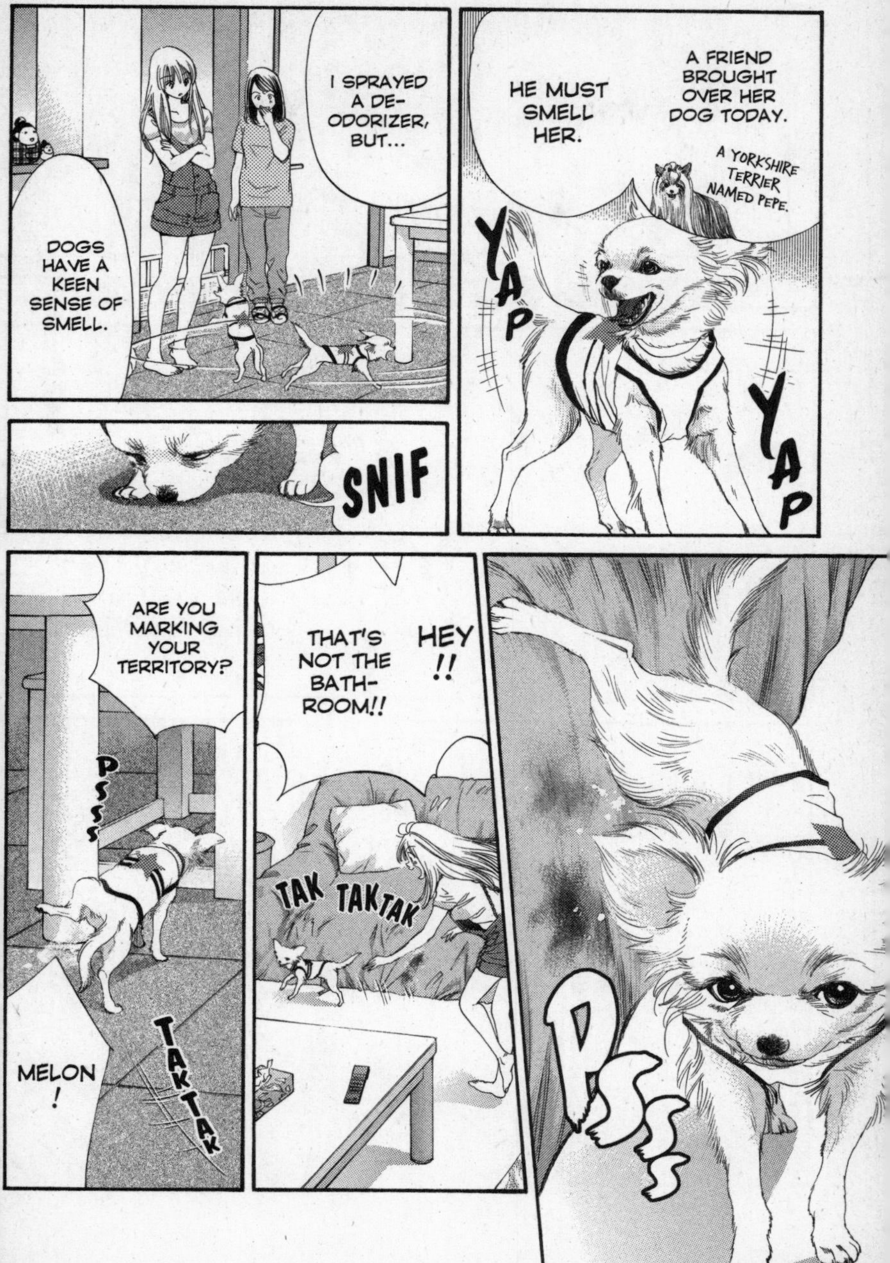
A FRIEND BROUGHT OVER HER DOG TODAY.
A YORKSHIRE TERRIER NAMED PEPE.
HE MUST SMELL HER.
YAP YAP
YAP YAP
I SPRAYED A DE-ODORIZER, BUT...
DOGS HAVE A KEEN SENSE OF SMELL.
SNIF
PSSS
HEY!!
THAT'S NOT THE BATH-ROOM!!
TAK TAKTAK
ARE YOU MARKING YOUR TERRITORY?
PSSS
TAK TAK
MELON!

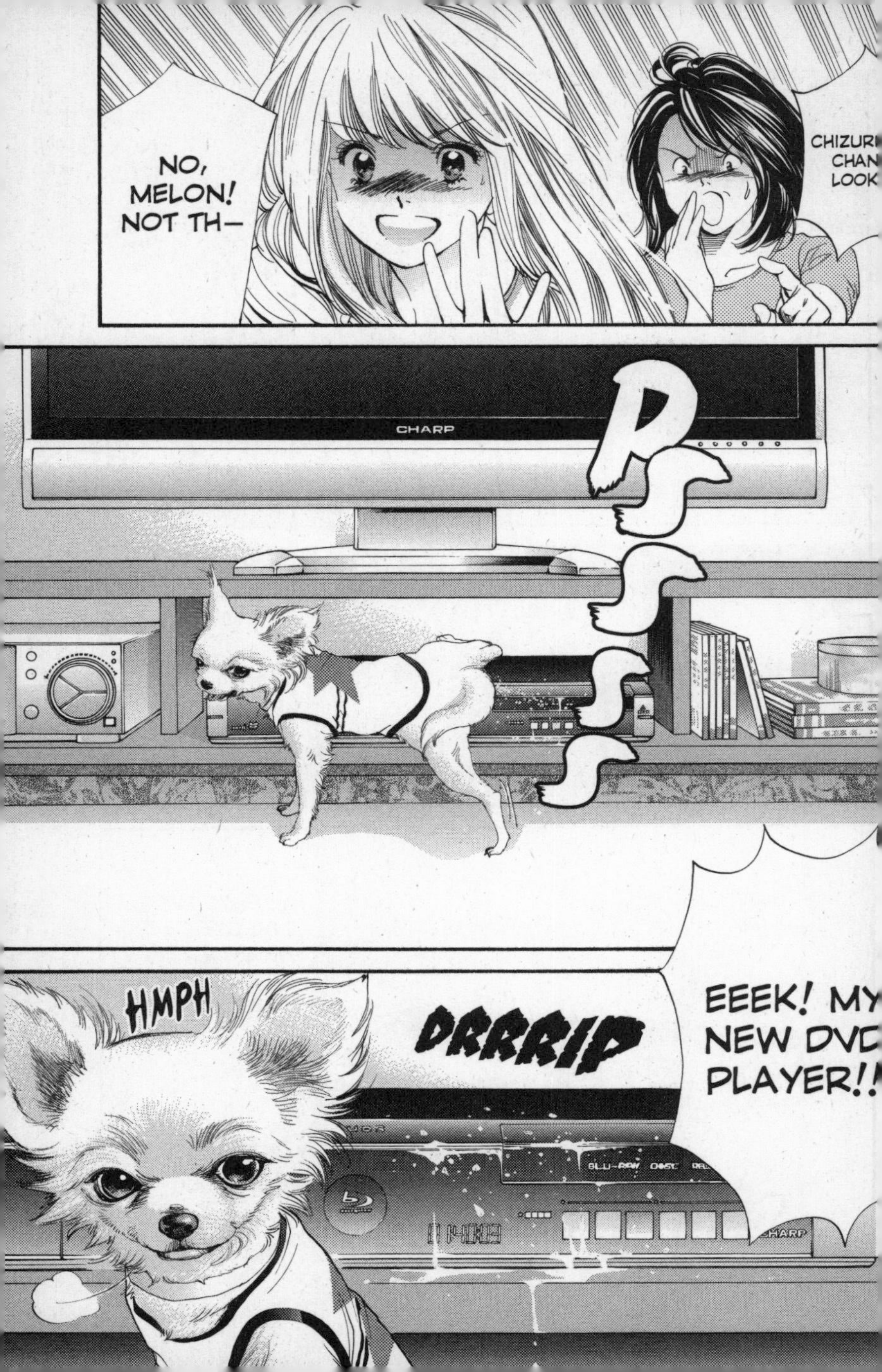
CHIZUR CHAN LOOK
NO, MELON! NOT TH—
PSSSS
CHARP
EEEK! MY NEW DVD PLAYER!!
DRRRIP
HMPH

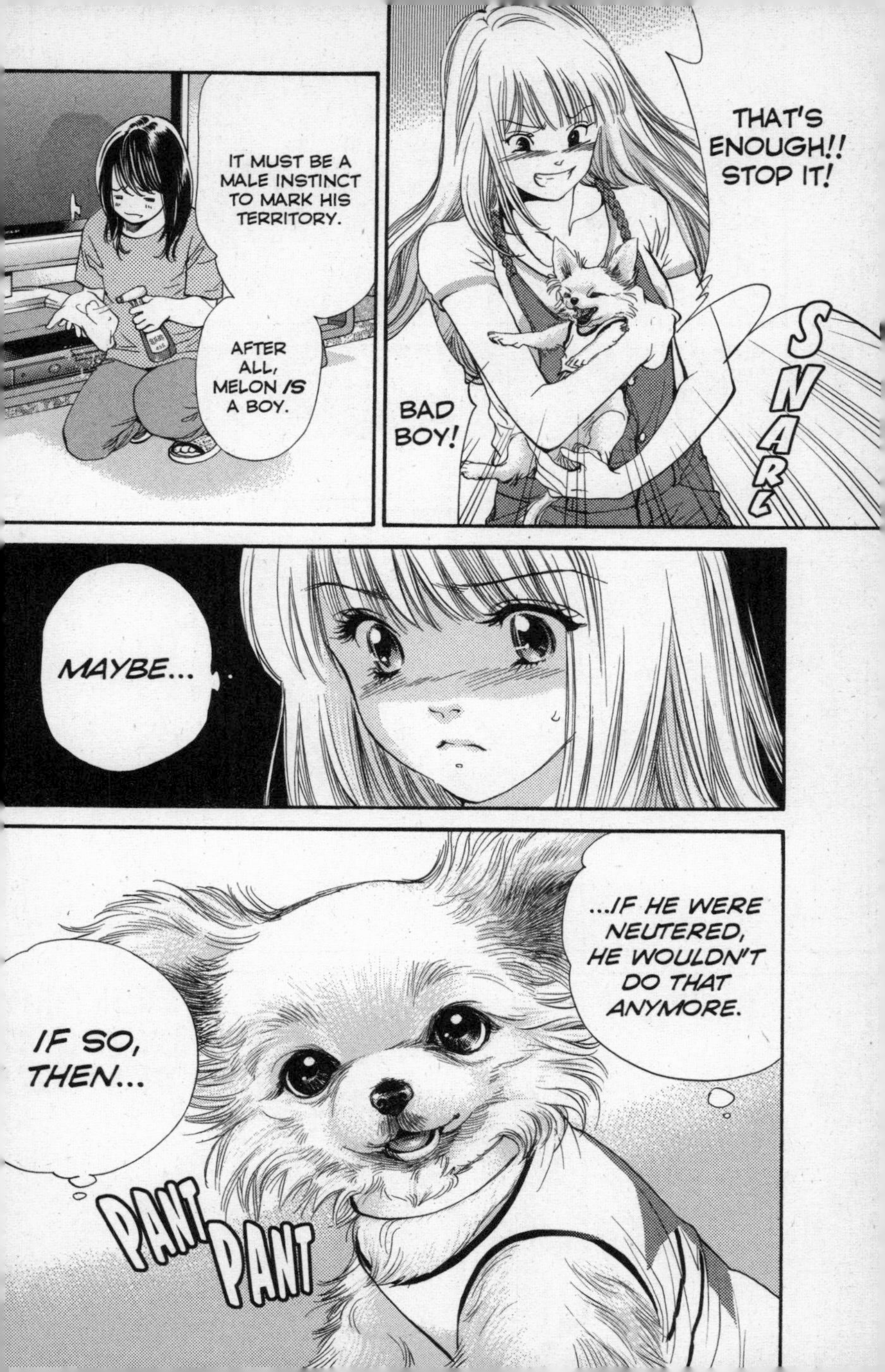
THAT'S ENOUGH!! STOP IT!
BAD BOY!
SNARL
IT MUST BE A MALE INSTINCT TO MARK HIS TERRITORY.
AFTER ALL, MELON *IS* A BOY.
MAYBE...
...IF HE WERE NEUTERED, HE WOULDN'T DO THAT ANYMORE.
IF SO, THEN...
PANT PANT

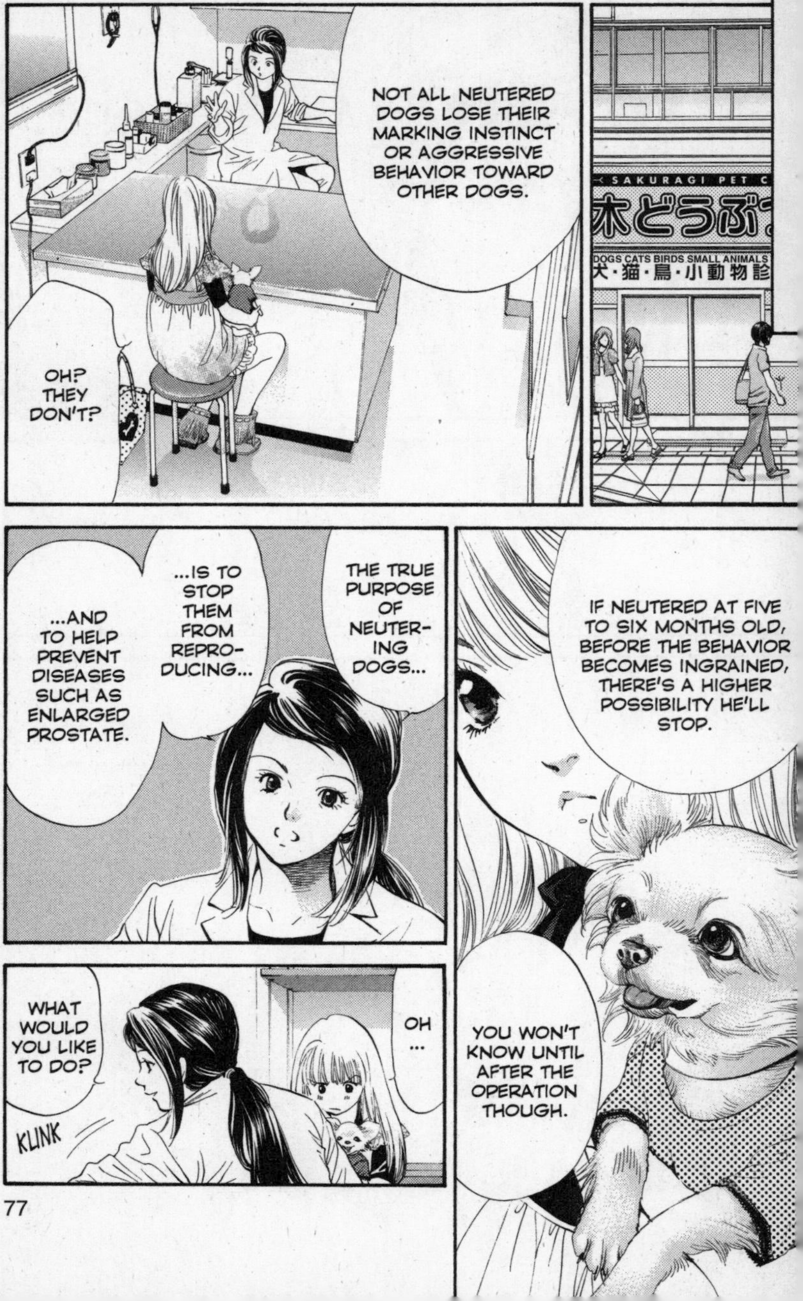
DOGS CATS BIRDS SMALL ANIMALS
NOT ALL NEUTERED DOGS LOSE THEIR MARKING INSTINCT OR AGGRESSIVE BEHAVIOR TOWARD OTHER DOGS.
OH? THEY DON'T?
IF NEUTERED AT FIVE TO SIX MONTHS OLD, BEFORE THE BEHAVIOR BECOMES INGRAINED, THERE'S A HIGHER POSSIBILITY HE'LL STOP.
YOU WON'T KNOW UNTIL AFTER THE OPERATION THOUGH.
THE TRUE PURPOSE OF NEUTER-ING DOGS...
...IS TO STOP THEM FROM REPRO-DUCING...
...AND TO HELP PREVENT DISEASES SUCH AS ENLARGED PROSTATE.
OH ...
WHAT WOULD YOU LIKE TO DO?
KLINK

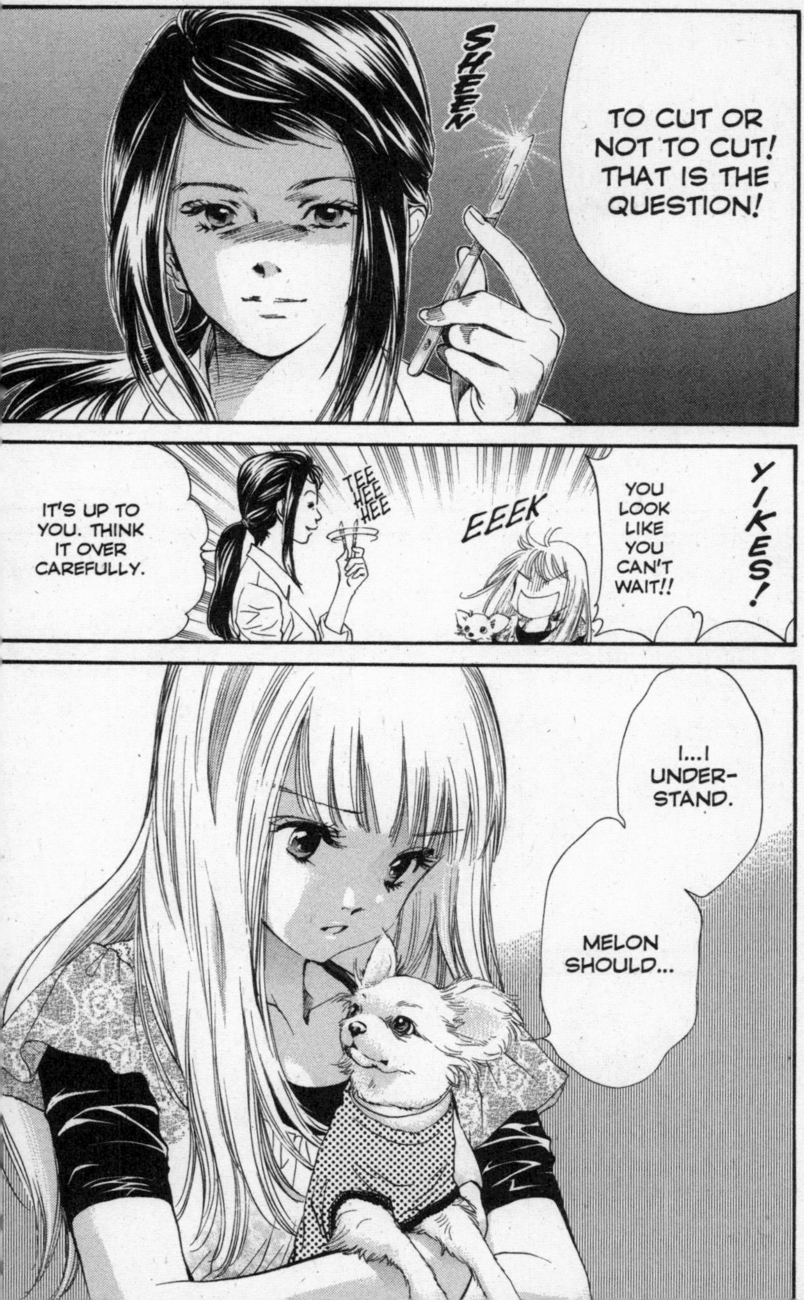
TO CUT OR NOT TO CUT! THAT IS THE QUESTION!
SHEEN
YIKES!
YOU LOOK LIKE YOU CAN'T WAIT!!
EEEK
TEE HEE HEE
IT'S UP TO YOU. THINK IT OVER CAREFULLY.
I...I UNDER-STAND.
MELON SHOULD...

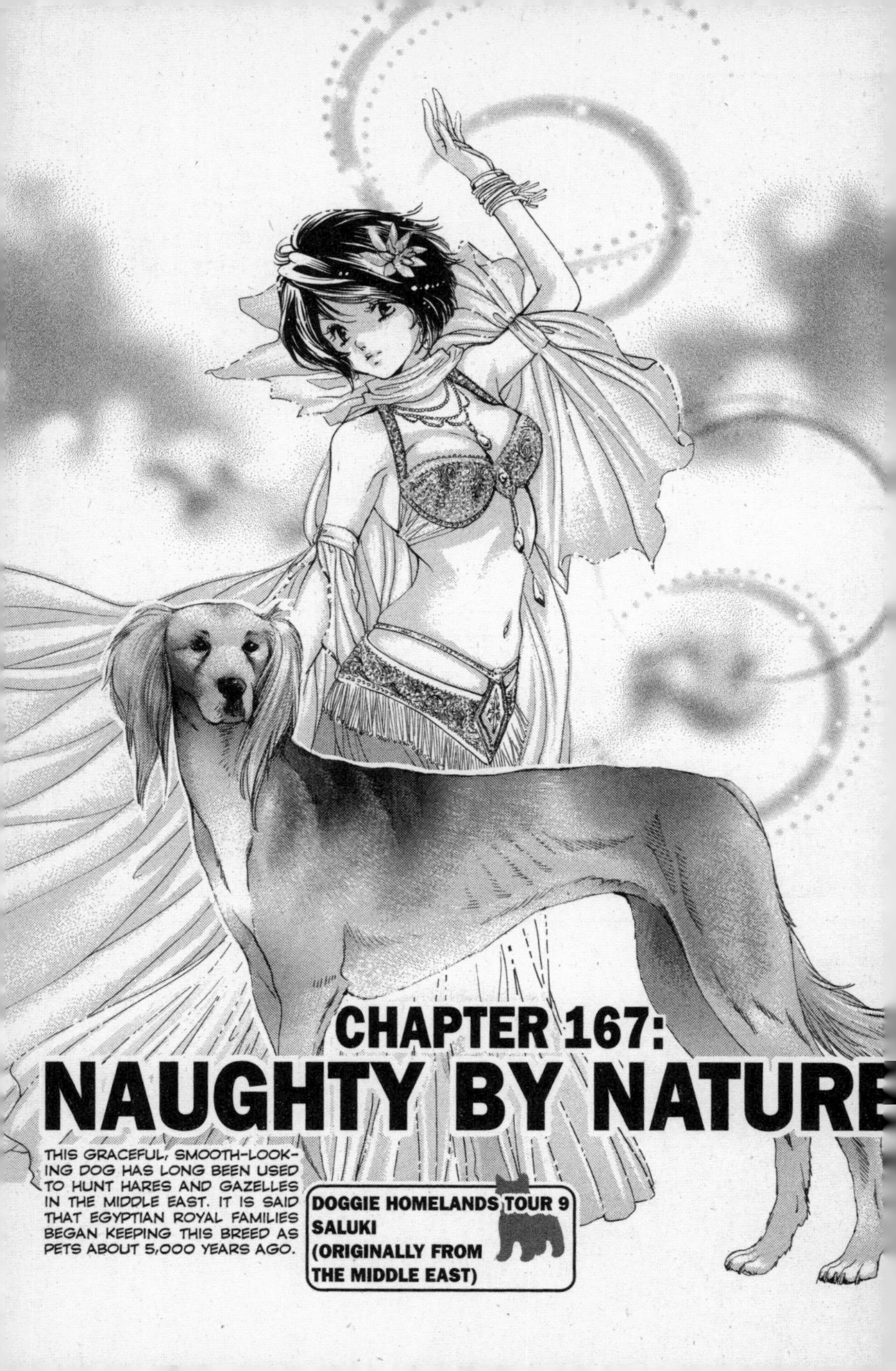
CHAPTER 167:
NAUGHTY BY NATURE
DOGGIE HOMELANDS TOUR 9
SALUKI
(ORIGINALLY FROM THE MIDDLE EAST)
THIS GRACEFUL, SMOOTH-LOOKING DOG HAS LONG BEEN USED TO HUNT HARES AND GAZELLES IN THE MIDDLE EAST. IT IS SAID THAT EGYPTIAN ROYAL FAMILIES BEGAN KEEPING THIS BREED AS PETS ABOUT 5,000 YEARS AGO.

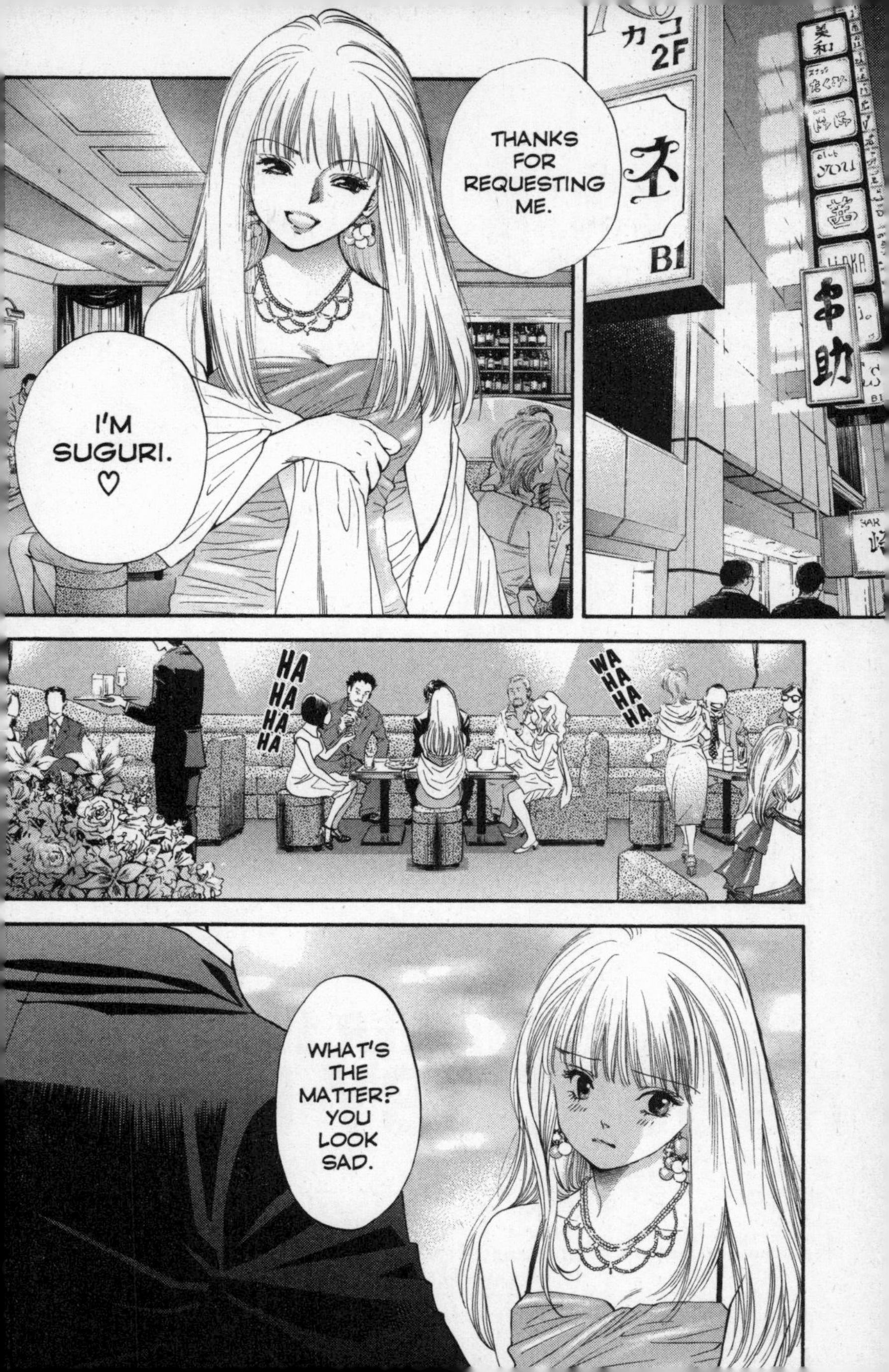
カコ
2F
B1
club YOU
串助
THANKS FOR REQUESTING ME.
I'M SUGURI. ♡
WAHAHAHA
HAHAHAHAHA
WHAT'S THE MATTER? YOU LOOK SAD.

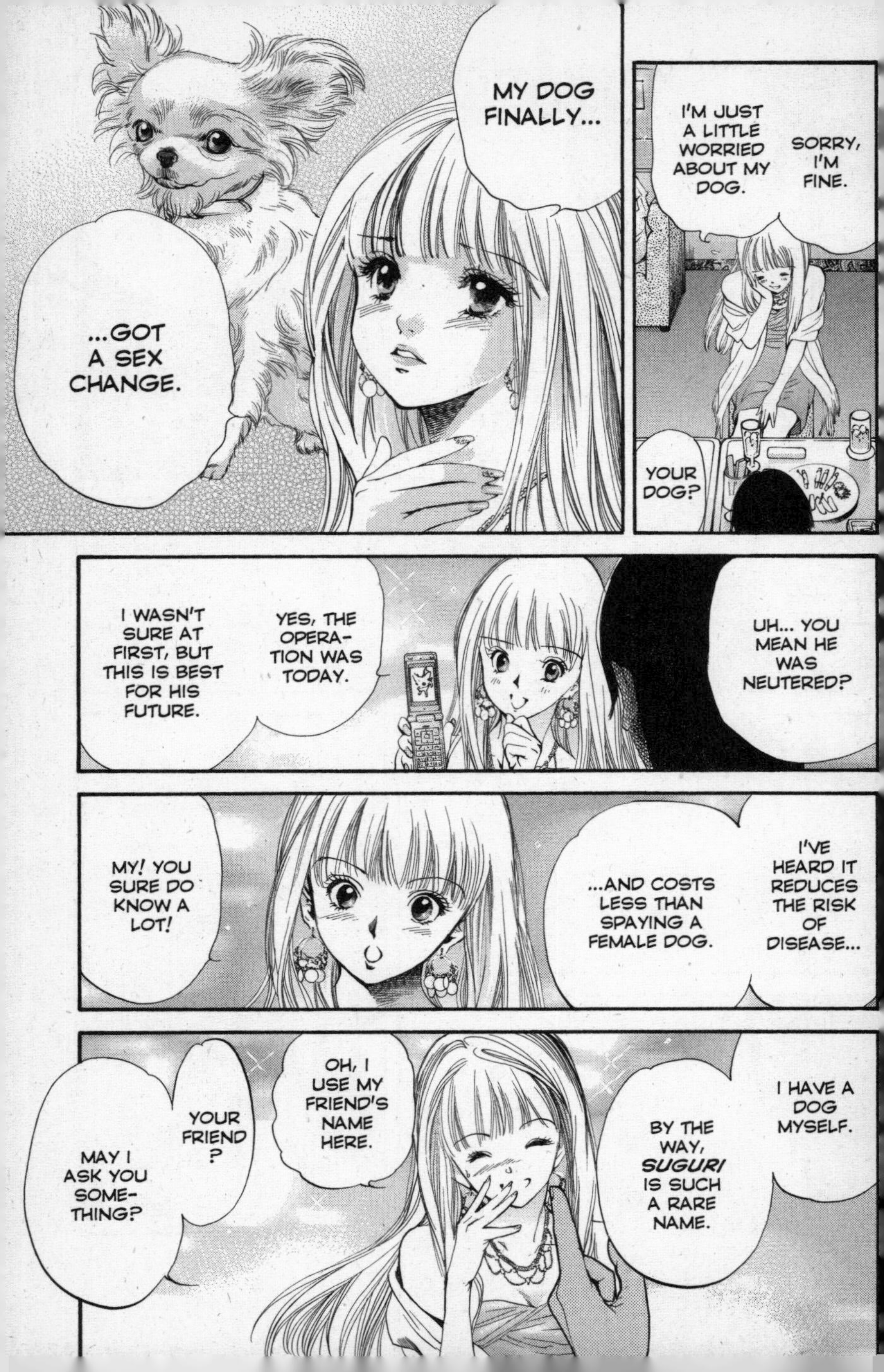
SORRY, I'M FINE.
I'M JUST A LITTLE WORRIED ABOUT MY DOG.
YOUR DOG?
MY DOG FINALLY...
...GOT A SEX CHANGE.
UH... YOU MEAN HE WAS NEUTERED?
YES, THE OPERA-TION WAS TODAY.
I WASN'T SURE AT FIRST, BUT THIS IS BEST FOR HIS FUTURE.
I'VE HEARD IT REDUCES THE RISK OF DISEASE...
...AND COSTS LESS THAN SPAYING A FEMALE DOG.
MY! YOU SURE DO KNOW A LOT!
I HAVE A DOG MYSELF.
BY THE WAY, *SUGURI* IS SUCH A RARE NAME.
OH, I USE MY FRIEND'S NAME HERE.
YOUR FRIEND?
MAY I ASK YOU SOME-THING?

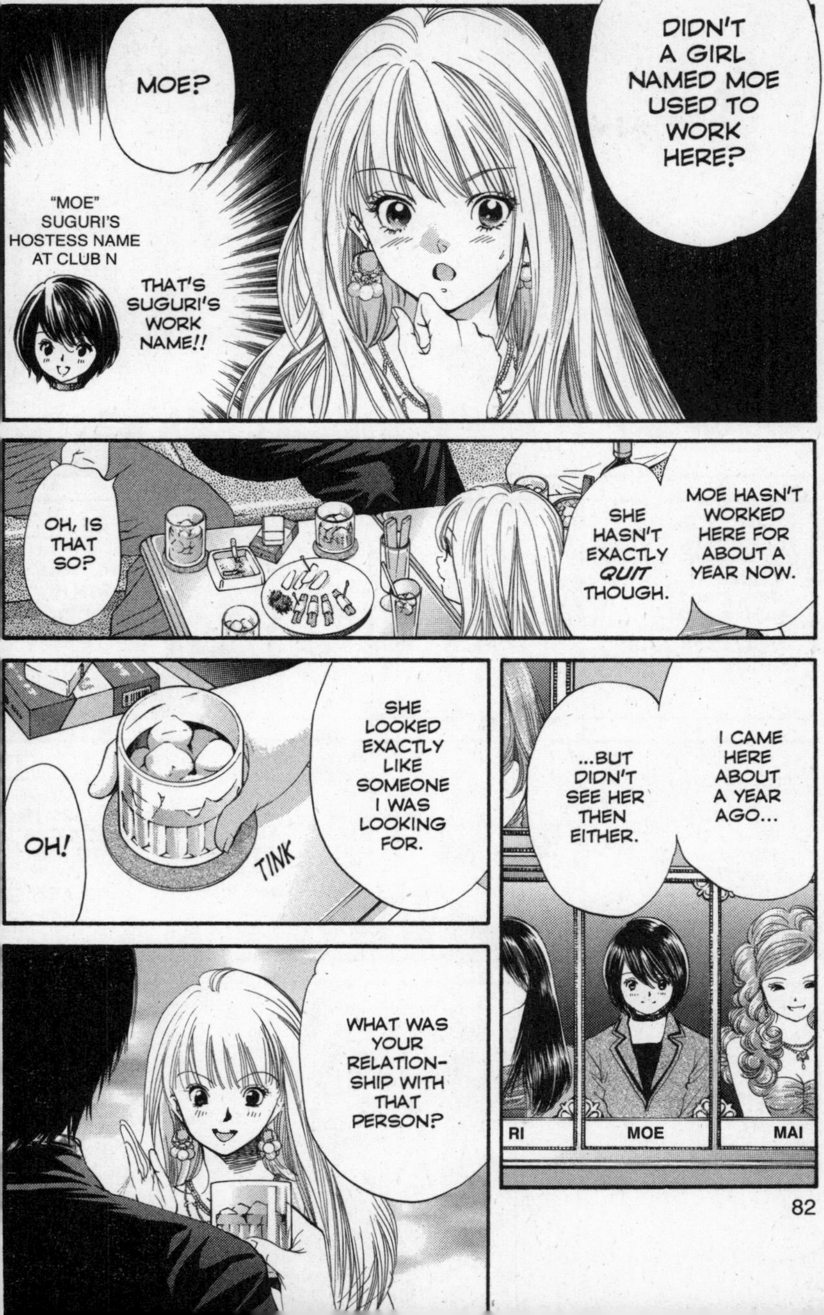
DIDN'T A GIRL NAMED MOE USED TO WORK HERE?
MOE?
"MOE" SUGURI'S HOSTESS NAME AT CLUB N
THAT'S SUGURI'S WORK NAME!!
MOE HASN'T WORKED HERE FOR ABOUT A YEAR NOW.
SHE HASN'T EXACTLY *QUIT* THOUGH.
OH, IS THAT SO?
I CAME HERE ABOUT A YEAR AGO...
...BUT DIDN'T SEE HER THEN EITHER.
RI
MOE
MAI
SHE LOOKED EXACTLY LIKE SOMEONE I WAS LOOKING FOR.
TINK
OH!
WHAT WAS YOUR RELATION-SHIP WITH THAT PERSON?

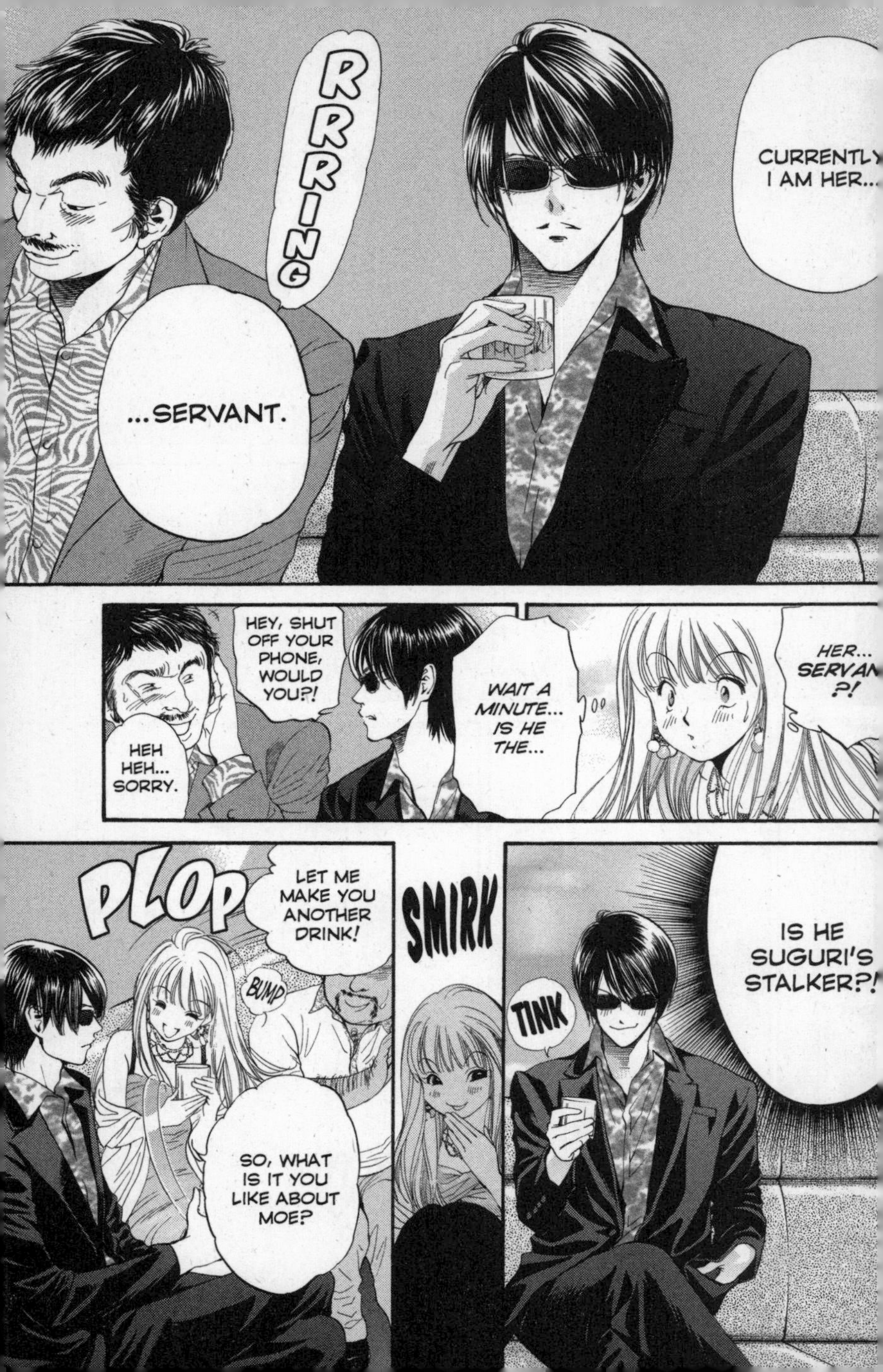
CURRENTLY I AM HER...
RRRING
...SERVANT.
HER... SERVAN ?!
WAIT A MINUTE... IS HE THE...
HEY, SHUT OFF YOUR PHONE, WOULD YOU?!
HEH HEH... SORRY.
IS HE SUGURI'S STALKER?!
TINK
SMIRK
LET ME MAKE YOU ANOTHER DRINK!
PLOP
BUMP
SO, WHAT IS IT YOU LIKE ABOUT MOE?

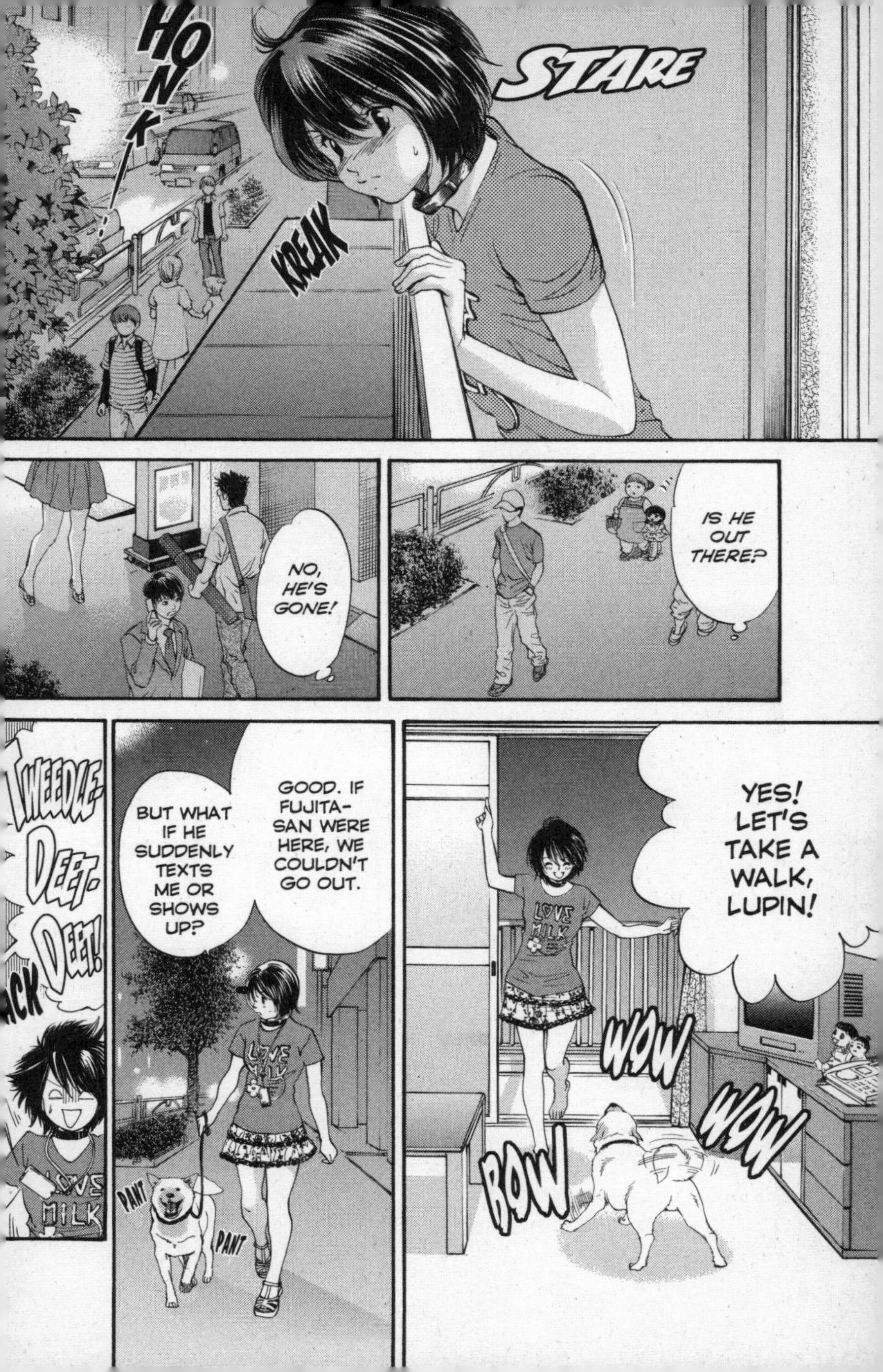

STARE
HONK!
KREAK
IS HE OUT THERE?
NO, HE'S GONE!
YES! LET'S TAKE A WALK, LUPIN!
WOW
WOW
BOW
GOOD. IF FUJITA-SAN WERE HERE, WE COULDN'T GO OUT.
BUT WHAT IF HE SUDDENLY TEXTS ME OR SHOWS UP?
PANT
PANT
TWEEDLE-DEET.
DEET!
ACK

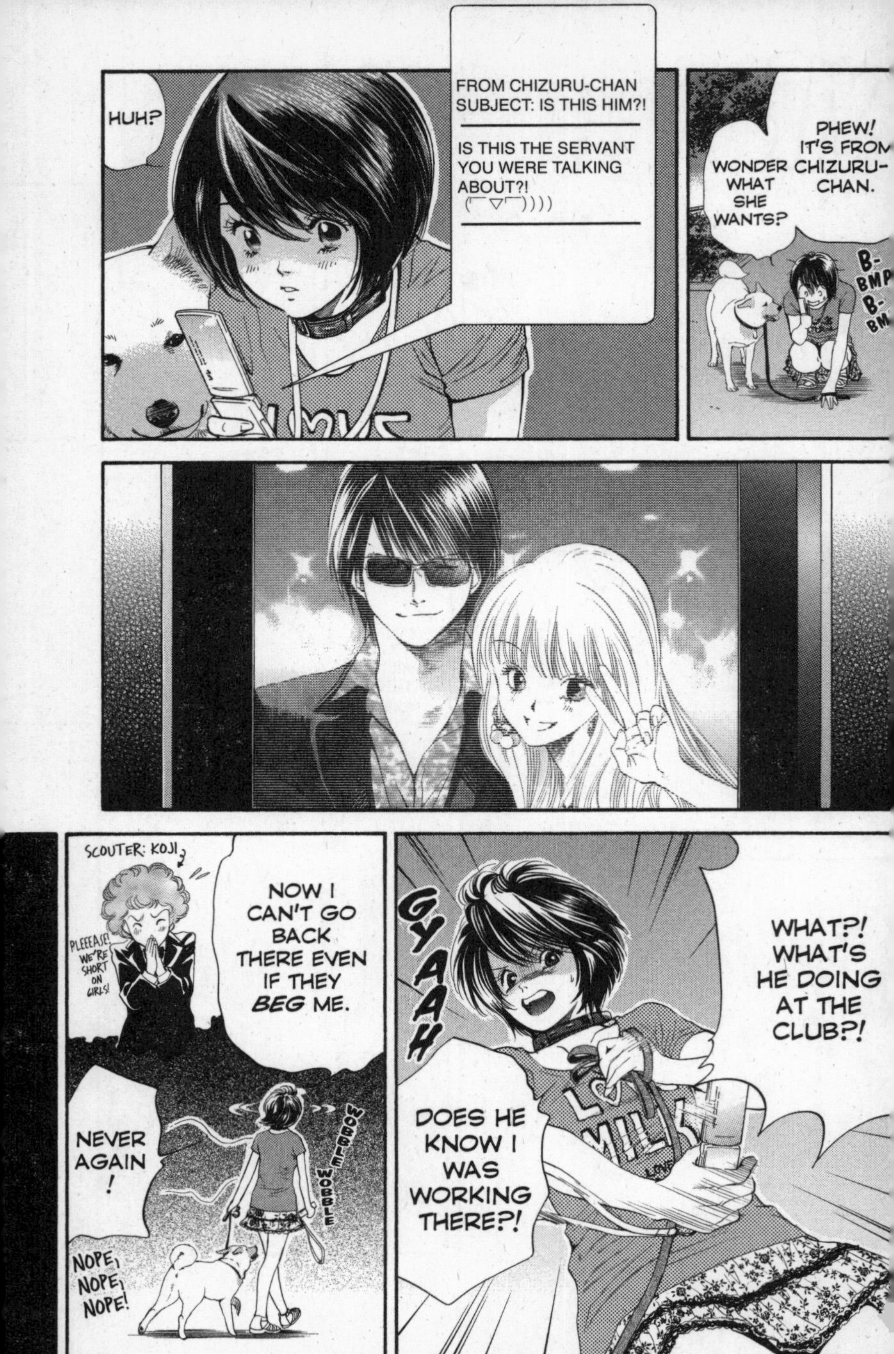
PHEW! IT'S FROM CHIZURU-CHAN.
WONDER WHAT SHE WANTS?
B-BMP B-BM
HUH?
FROM CHIZURU-CHAN
SUBJECT: IS THIS HIM?!
IS THIS THE SERVANT YOU WERE TALKING ABOUT?!
(￣▽￣))))
WHAT?! WHAT'S HE DOING AT THE CLUB?!
GYAAAH
DOES HE KNOW I WAS WORKING THERE?!
SCOUTER: KOJI
PLEEEASE! WE'RE SHORT ON GIRLS!
NOW I CAN'T GO BACK THERE EVEN IF THEY *BEG* ME.
NEVER AGAIN!
WOBBLE WOBBLE
NOPE, NOPE, NOPE!

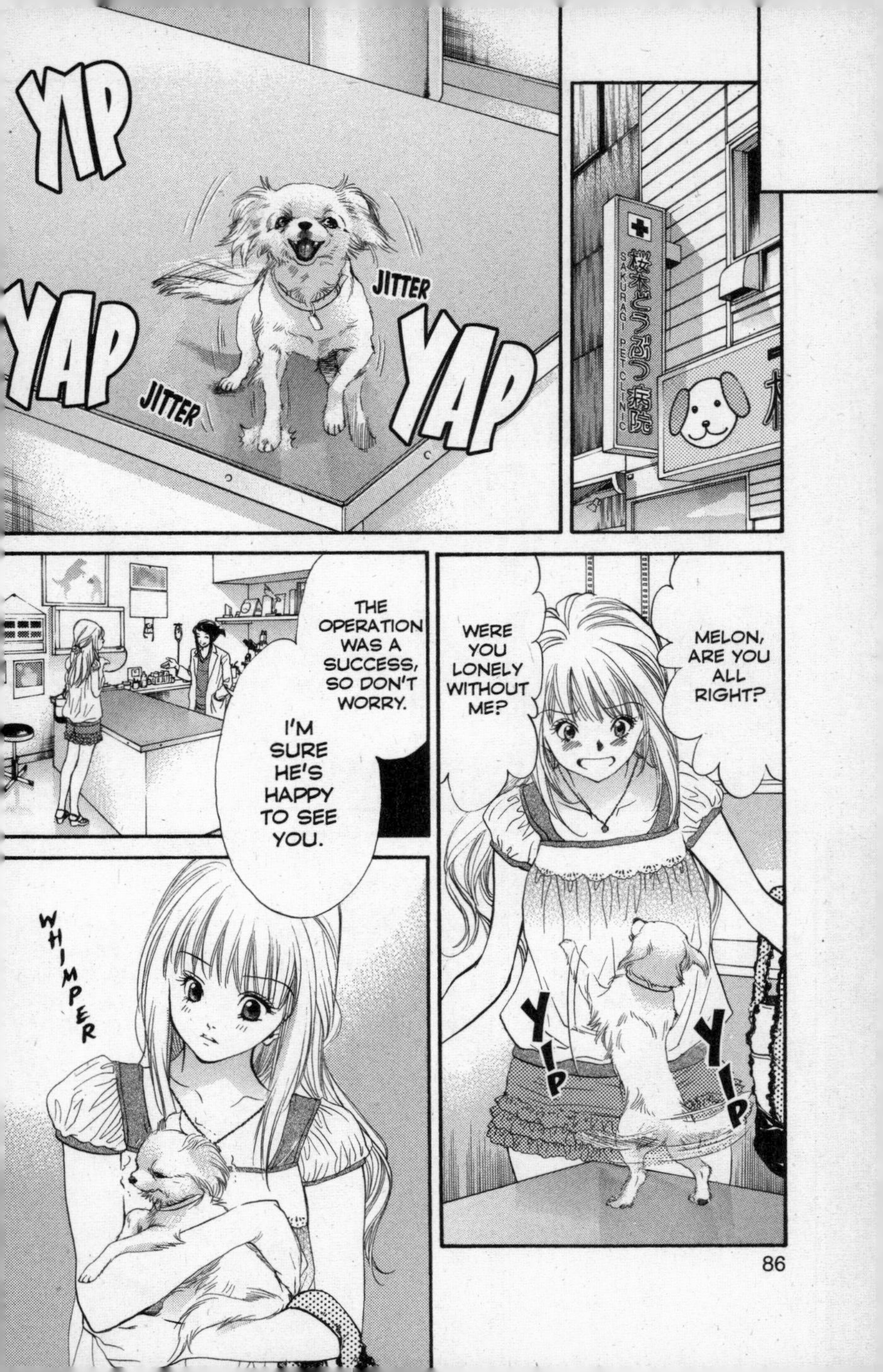
桜木どうぶつ病院
SAKURAGI PET CLINIC
YAP
JITTER
YIP
YAP
JITTER
MELON, ARE YOU ALL RIGHT?
WERE YOU LONELY WITHOUT ME?
YIP
YIP
THE OPERATION WAS A SUCCESS, SO DON'T WORRY.
I'M SURE HE'S HAPPY TO SEE YOU.
WHIMPER

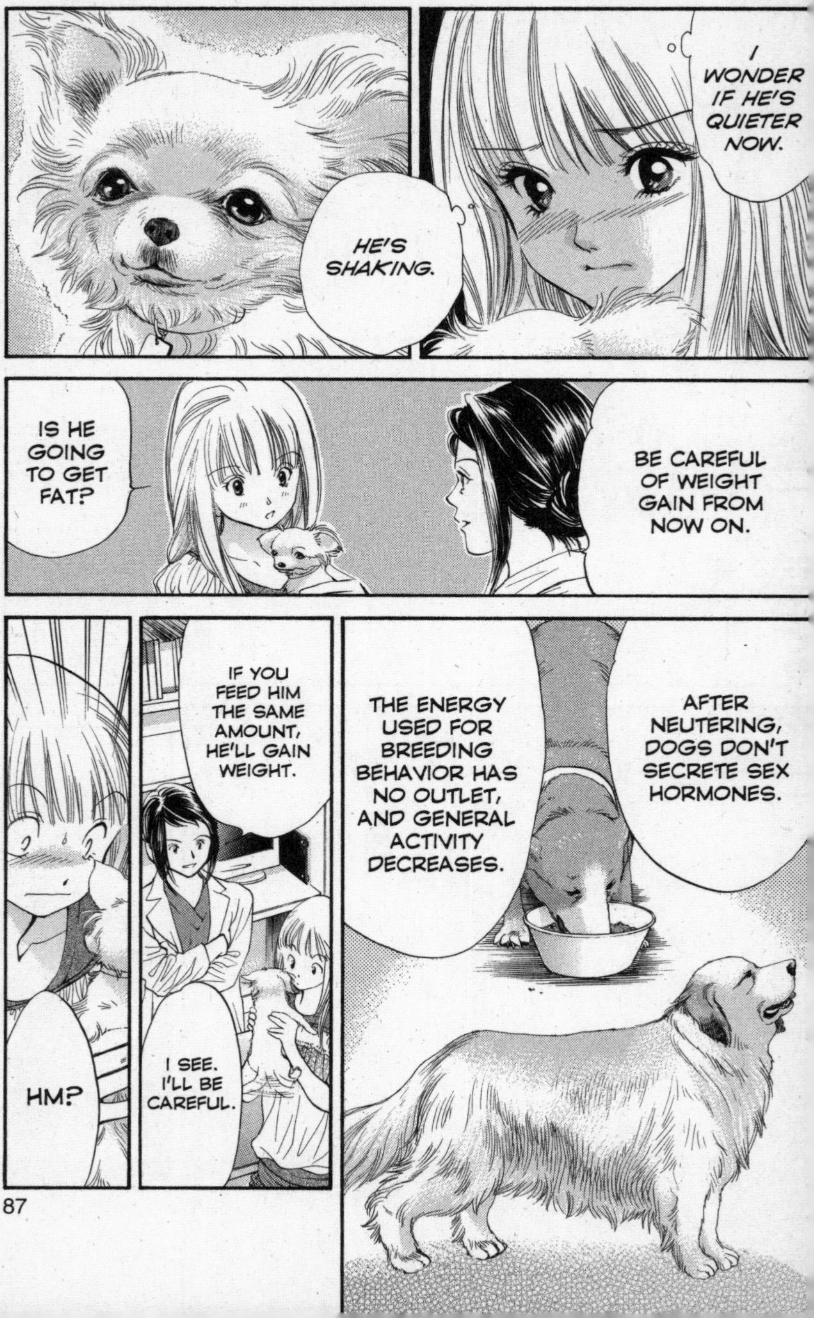
I WONDER IF HE'S QUIETER NOW.
HE'S SHAKING.
BE CAREFUL OF WEIGHT GAIN FROM NOW ON.
IS HE GOING TO GET FAT?
AFTER NEUTERING, DOGS DON'T SECRETE SEX HORMONES.
THE ENERGY USED FOR BREEDING BEHAVIOR HAS NO OUTLET, AND GENERAL ACTIVITY DECREASES.
IF YOU FEED HIM THE SAME AMOUNT, HE'LL GAIN WEIGHT.
I SEE. I'LL BE CAREFUL.
HM?

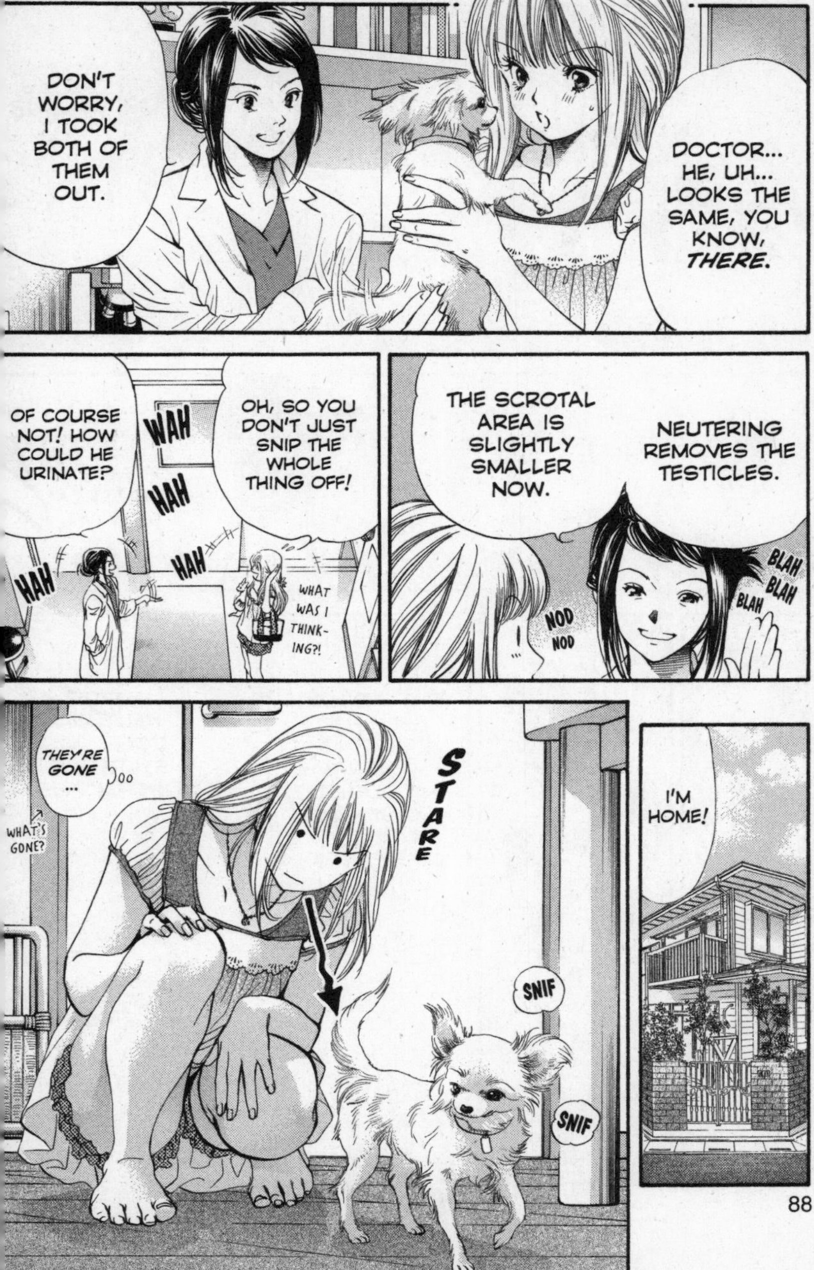
DOCTOR... HE, UH... LOOKS THE SAME, YOU KNOW, *THERE.*
DON'T WORRY, I TOOK BOTH OF THEM OUT.
NEUTERING REMOVES THE TESTICLES.
THE SCROTAL AREA IS SLIGHTLY SMALLER NOW.
BLAH BLAH BLAH
NOD NOD
OH, SO YOU DON'T JUST SNIP THE WHOLE THING OFF!
OF COURSE NOT! HOW COULD HE URINATE?
WAH
HAH
HAH
HAH
WHAT WAS I THINKING?!
I'M HOME!
STARE
SNIF
SNIF
THEY'RE GONE ...
WHAT'S GONE?

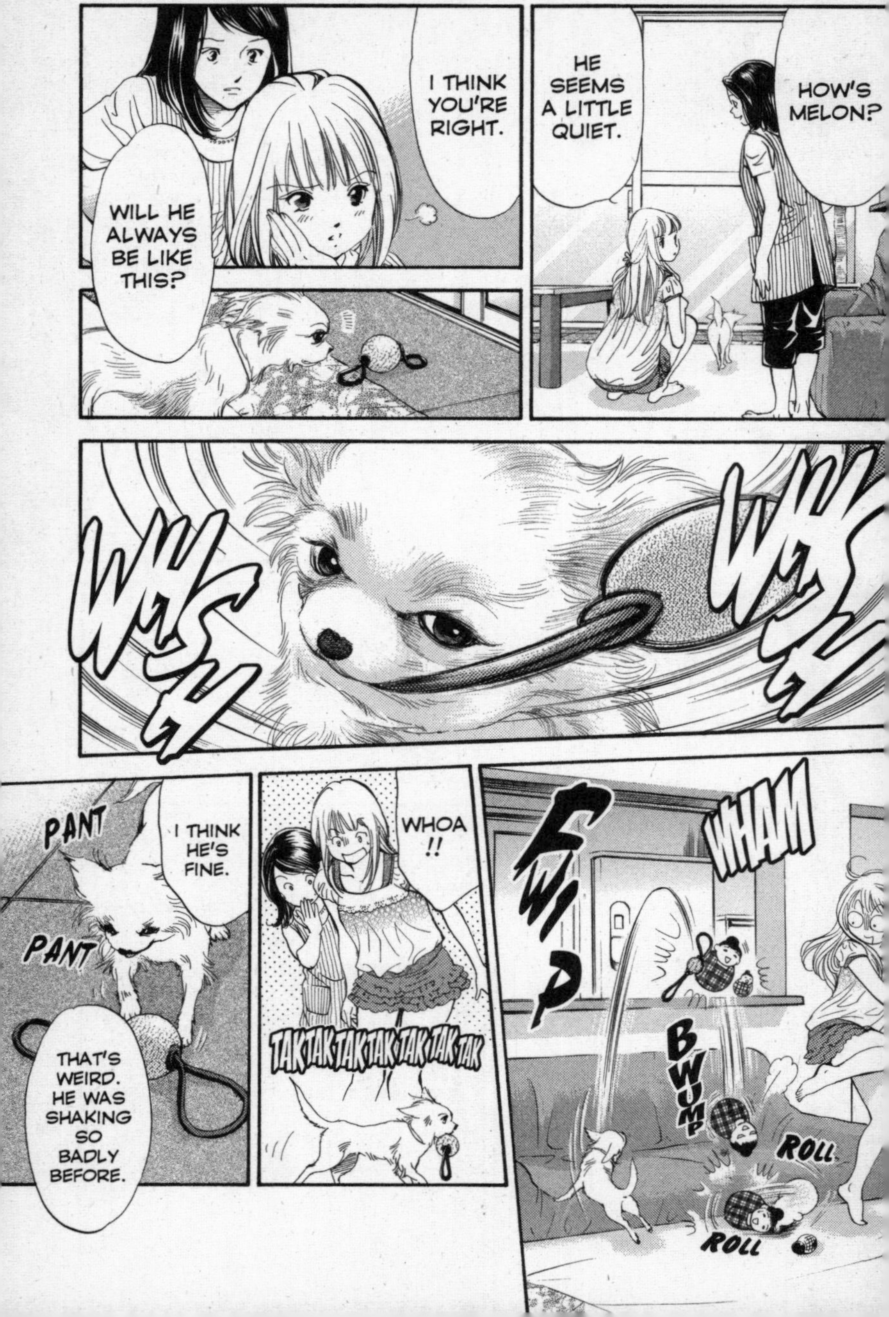
HOW'S MELON?
HE SEEMS A LITTLE QUIET.
I THINK YOU'RE RIGHT.
WILL HE ALWAYS BE LIKE THIS?
WHISH
WHISH
FWIP
WHAM
BWUMP
ROLL
ROLL
WHOA!!
TAK TAK TAK TAK TAK TAK TAK
I THINK HE'S FINE.
PANT
PANT
THAT'S WEIRD. HE WAS SHAKING SO BADLY BEFORE.

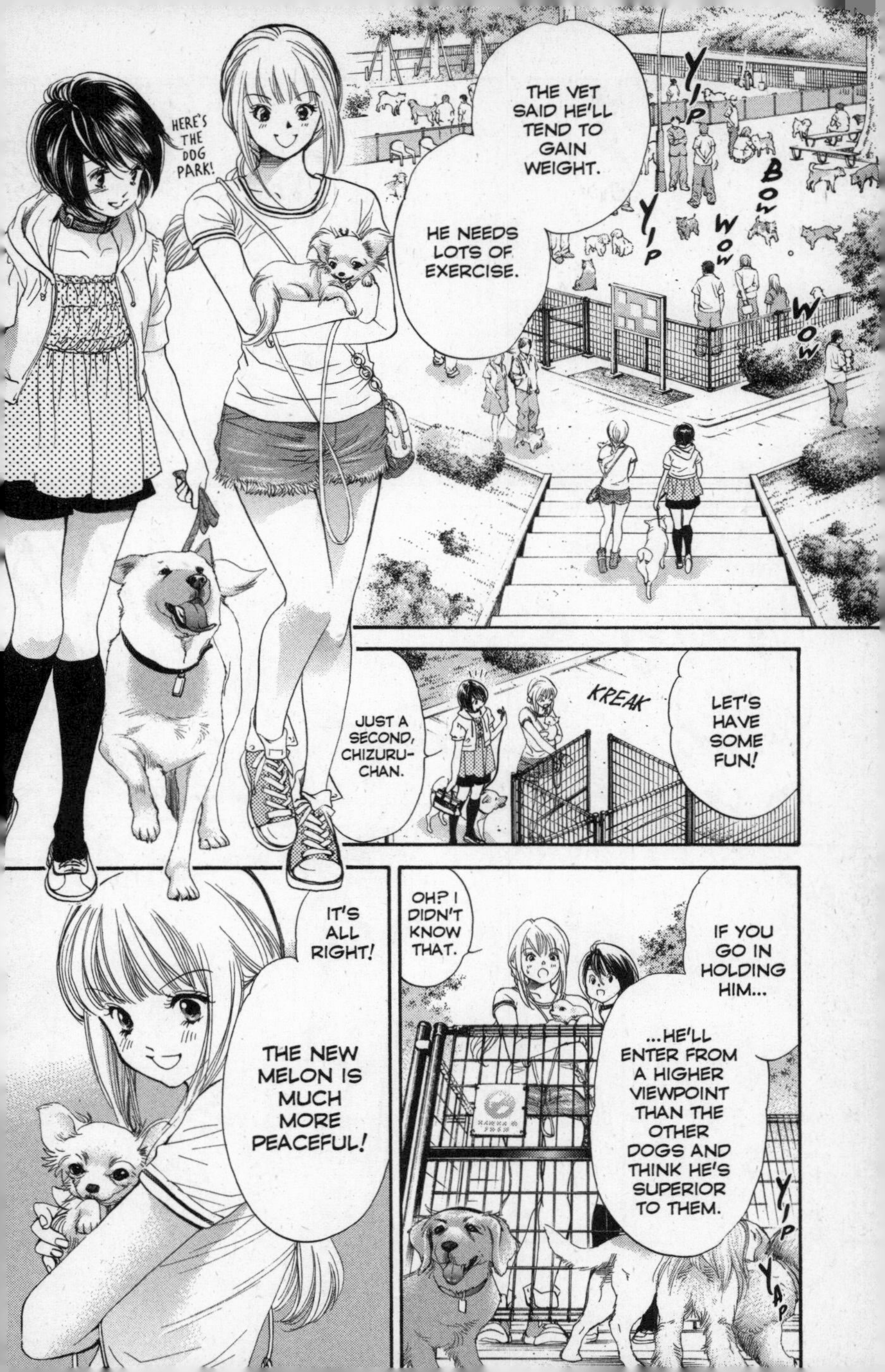
THE VET SAID HE'LL TEND TO GAIN WEIGHT.
HE NEEDS LOTS OF EXERCISE.
YIP
YIP
BOW
WOW
WOW
WOW
LET'S HAVE SOME FUN!
KREAK
JUST A SECOND, CHIZURU-CHAN.
HERE'S THE DOG PARK!
IF YOU GO IN HOLDING HIM...
...HE'LL ENTER FROM A HIGHER VIEWPOINT THAN THE OTHER DOGS AND THINK HE'S SUPERIOR TO THEM.
OH? I DIDN'T KNOW THAT.
YIP
YAP
IT'S ALL RIGHT!
THE NEW MELON IS MUCH MORE PEACEFUL!

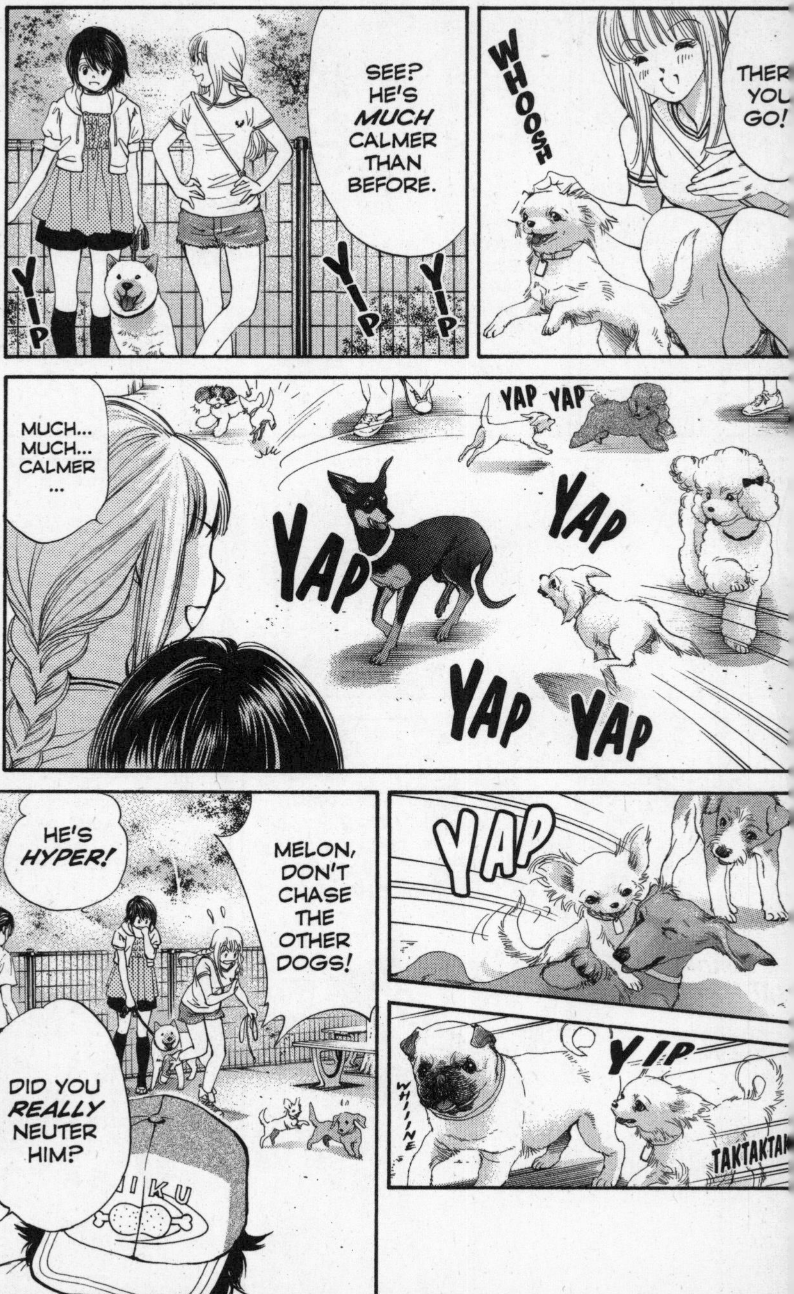
WHOOSH
THER YOU GO!
SEE? HE'S MUCH CALMER THAN BEFORE.
YIP
YIP
YIP
YAP YAP
YAP
YAP
MUCH... MUCH... CALMER ...
YAP
YAP
YAP
YIP
WHIIINE
TAKTAKTAK
MELON, DON'T CHASE THE OTHER DOGS!
HE'S HYPER!
DID YOU REALLY NEUTER HIM?
IKU

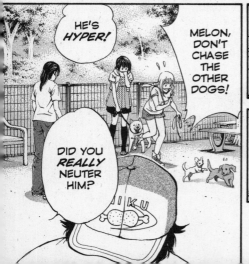

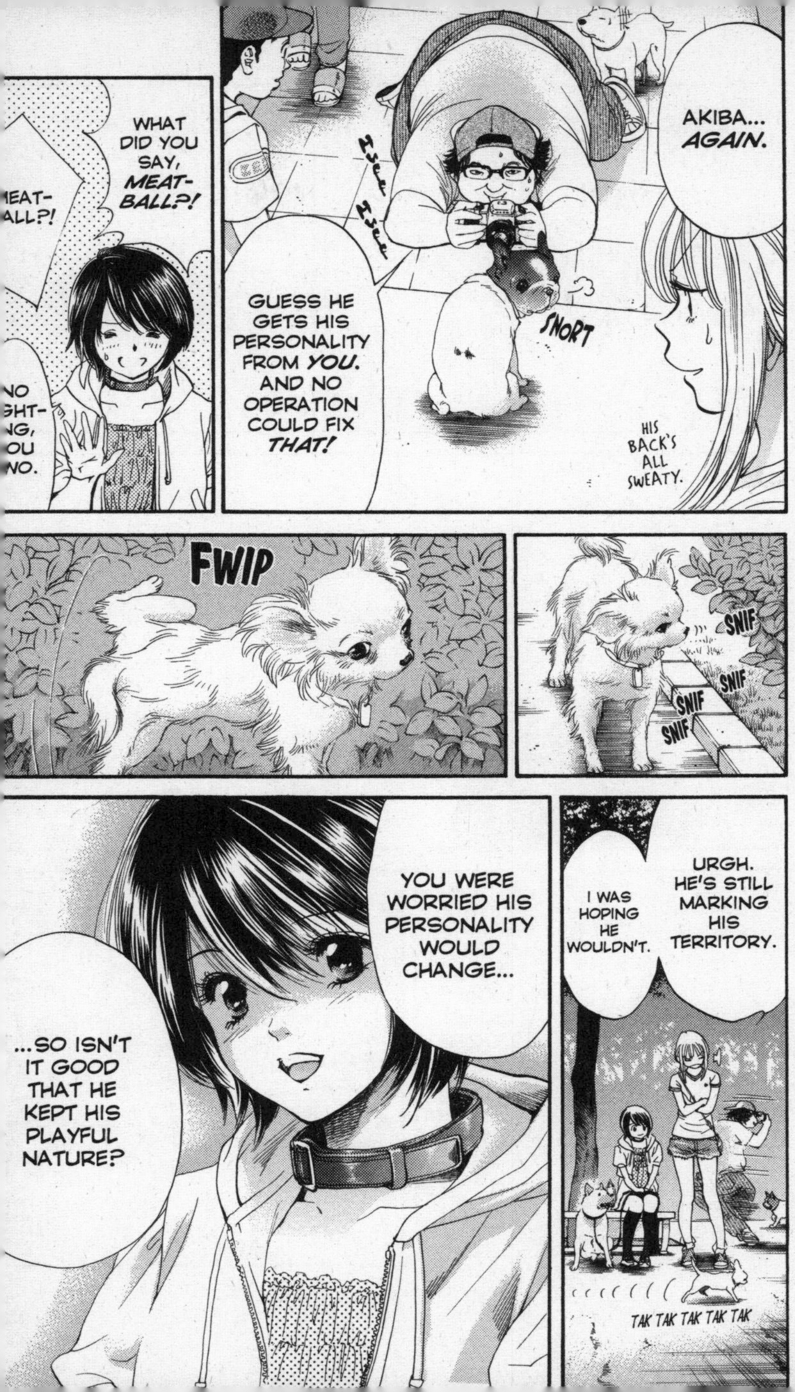
AKIBA... *AGAIN.*
GUESS HE GETS HIS PERSONALITY FROM *YOU.* AND NO OPERATION COULD FIX *THAT!*
SNORT
HIS BACK'S ALL SWEATY.
WHAT DID YOU SAY, *MEAT-BALL?!*
SNIF
SNIF
SNIF
SNIF
FWIP
URGH. HE'S STILL MARKING HIS TERRITORY.
I WAS HOPING HE WOULDN'T.
TAK TAK TAK TAK TAK
YOU WERE WORRIED HIS PERSONALITY WOULD CHANGE...
...SO ISN'T IT GOOD THAT HE KEPT HIS PLAYFUL NATURE?

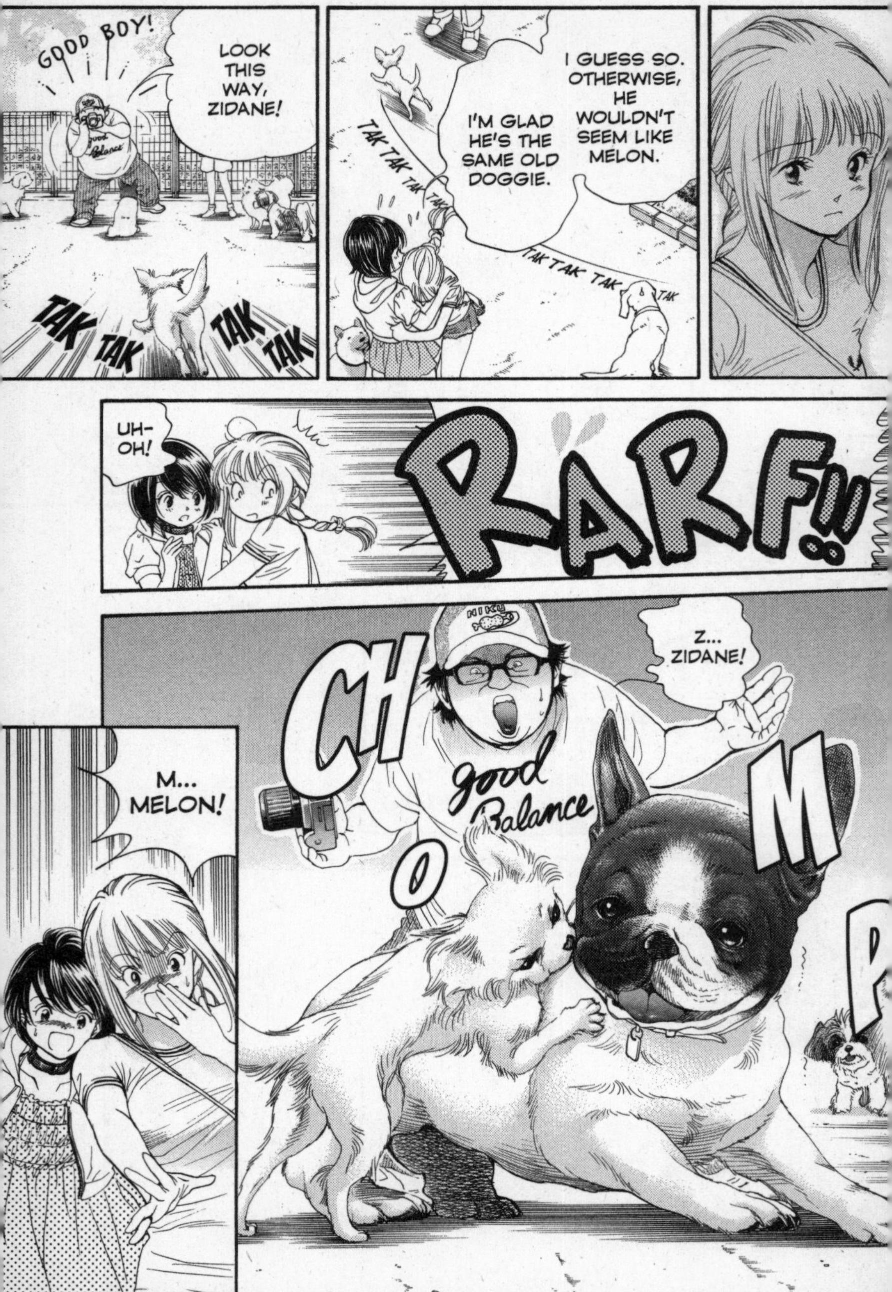

I'M GLAD HE'S THE SAME OLD DOGGIE.
I GUESS SO. OTHERWISE, HE WOULDN'T SEEM LIKE MELON.
TAK TAK TAK TAK
TAK TAK TAK TAK TAK
GOOD BOY!
LOOK THIS WAY, ZIDANE!
good Balance
TAK TAK TAK TAK
RARF!!
UH-OH!
Z... ZIDANE!
NIKU
CHOMP
good Balance
M... MELON!

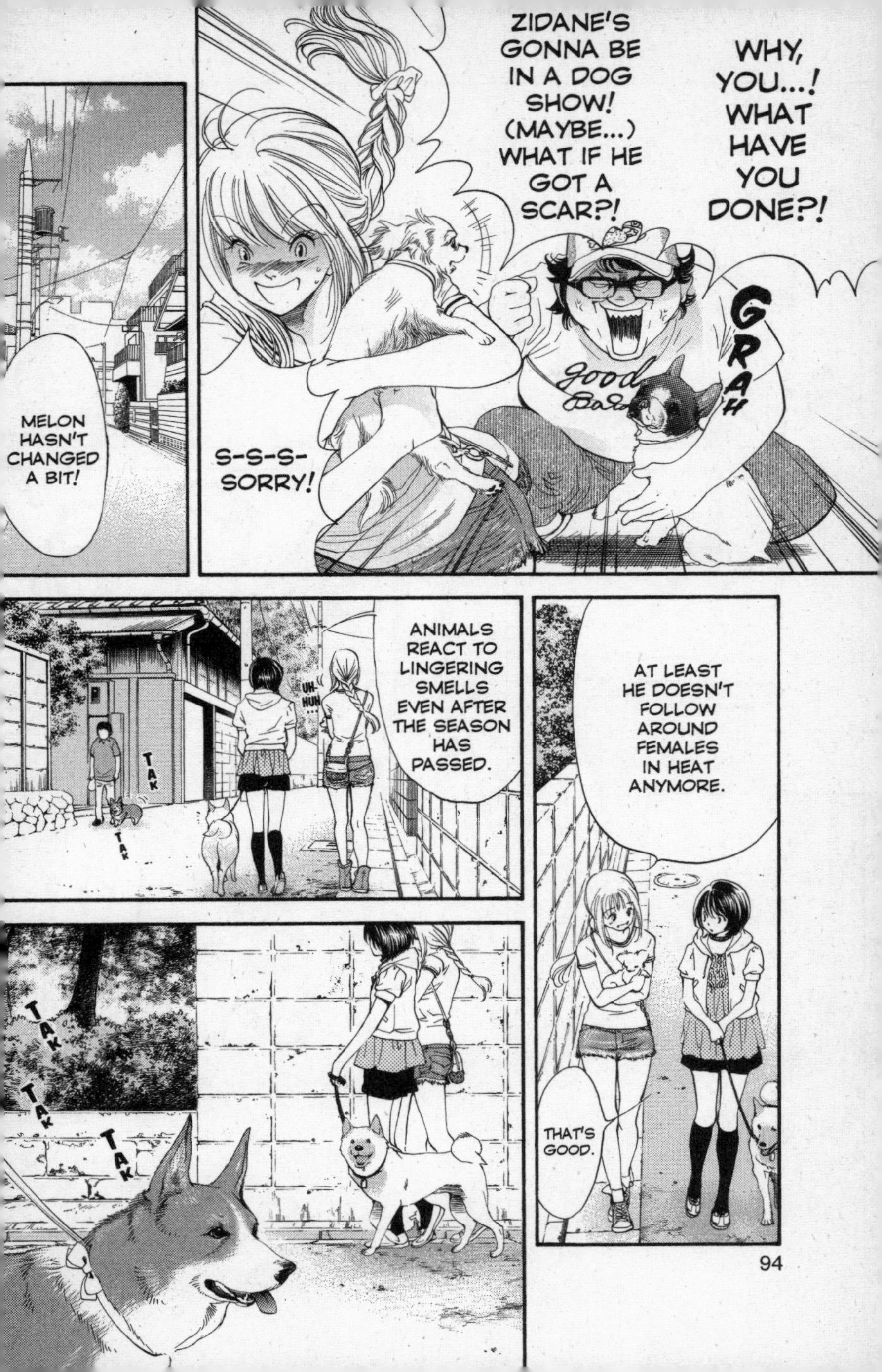
WHY, YOU...! WHAT HAVE YOU DONE?!
ZIDANE'S GONNA BE IN A DOG SHOW! (MAYBE...) WHAT IF HE GOT A SCAR?!
GRAH
S-S-S-SORRY!
MELON HASN'T CHANGED A BIT!
AT LEAST HE DOESN'T FOLLOW AROUND FEMALES IN HEAT ANYMORE.
THAT'S GOOD.
ANIMALS REACT TO LINGERING SMELLS EVEN AFTER THE SEASON HAS PASSED.
UH-HUH...
TAK
TAK
TAK
TAK
TAK
TAK

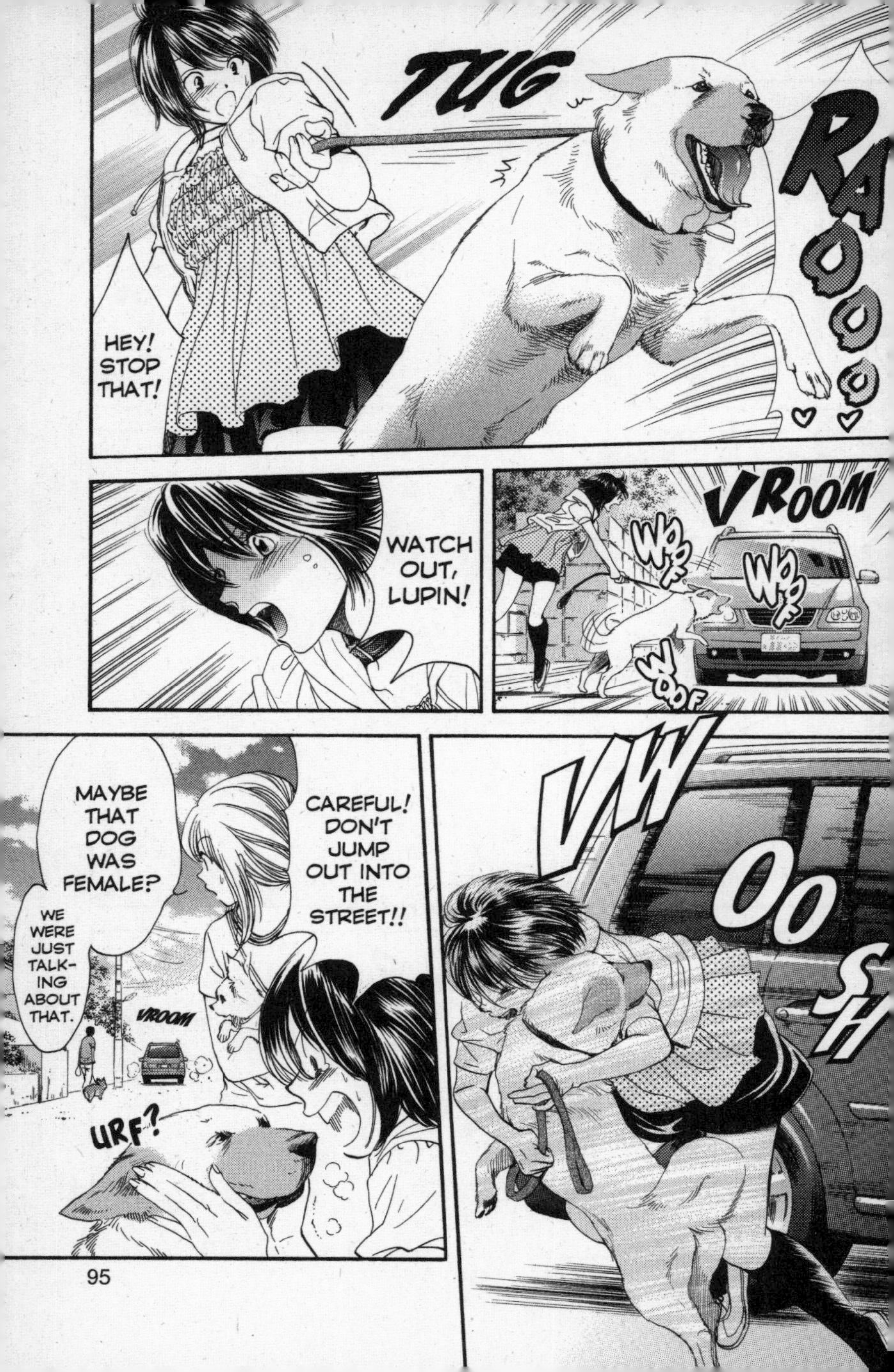
RAOOOOO
TUG
HEY! STOP THAT!
VROOM
WOOF
WOOF
WOOF
WATCH OUT, LUPIN!
VWOOSH
CAREFUL! DON'T JUMP OUT INTO THE STREET!!
MAYBE THAT DOG WAS FEMALE?
WE WERE JUST TALKING ABOUT THAT.
VROOM
URF?

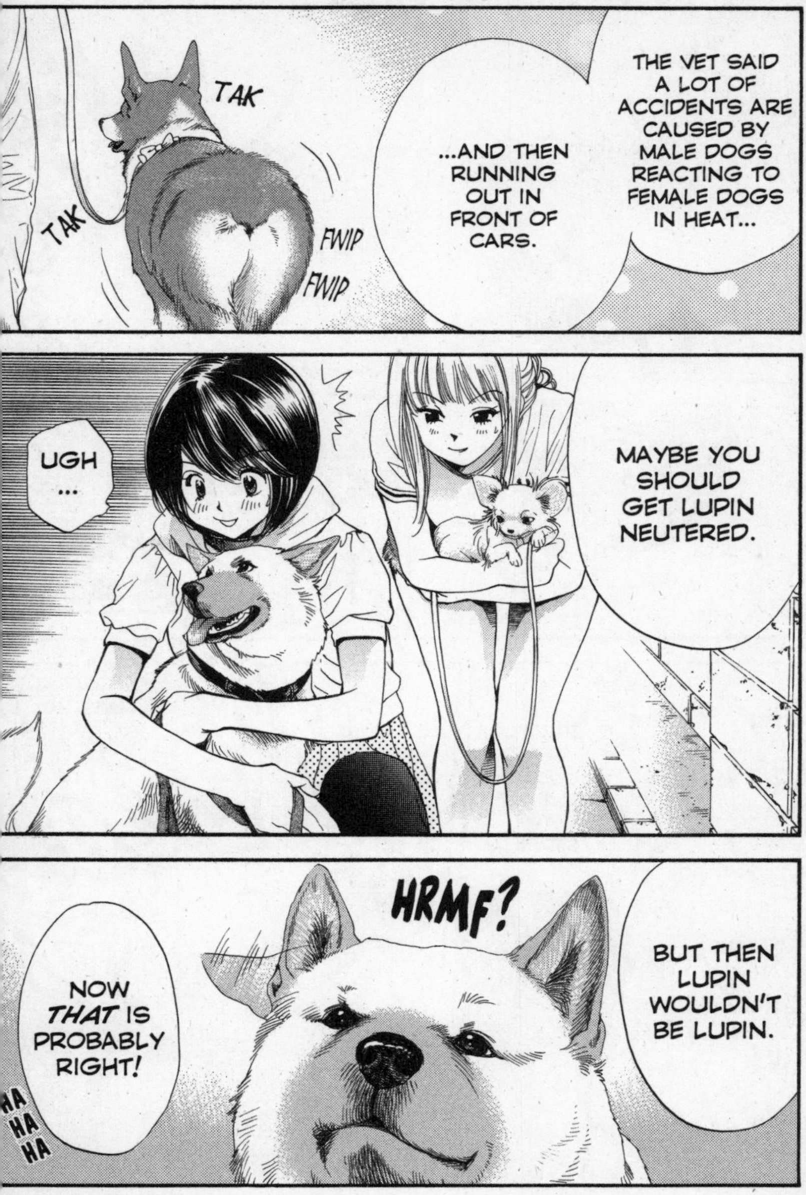
THE VET SAID A LOT OF ACCIDENTS ARE CAUSED BY MALE DOGS REACTING TO FEMALE DOGS IN HEAT...
...AND THEN RUNNING OUT IN FRONT OF CARS.
TAK
FWIP
FWIP
TAK
MAYBE YOU SHOULD GET LUPIN NEUTERED.
UGH ...
BUT THEN LUPIN WOULDN'T BE LUPIN.
HRMF?
NOW *THAT* IS PROBABLY RIGHT!
HA HA HA

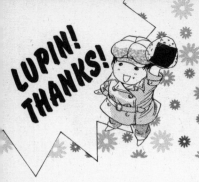

LUPIN! THANKS!

HERE I AM AGAIN, INVESTIGATOR RICE BALL, EVERYONE'S IDOL! (LOL) THIS TIME I HAVE A THANK-YOU LETTER FROM YUKIYAN SENSEI TO ALL OF YOU WHO SENT IN FOR THE LUPIN BAG.

HELLO, EVERYONE! IT'S ALREADY VOLUME 16. THANK YOU FOR SENDING IN SO MANY ENTRIES TO RECEIVE LUPIN'S BAG IN RESPONSE TO THE ADVERTISEMENT AT THE END O VOLUME 14 COMMEMORATING THE 150TH CHAPTER.* I WIS I COULD HAVE GIVEN ONE TO ALL OF YOU WHO APPLIED. SORRY IF YOU DIDN'T RECEIVE ONE DUE TO THE LIMITED NUMBERS. HOWEVER, IT WON'T BE LONG BEFORE WE CELEBRATE CHAPTER 200! MAYBE WE'LL HAVE ANOTHER PRESENT FOR YOU THEN! THE MAGAZINE SERIAL IS PUBLISHED AHEAD OF THE GRAPHIC NOVEL, BUT MAYBE WE CAN COME UP WITH SOME SORT OF GIFT JUST FOR THE GRAPHIC NOVELS AS WELL. LOOK FORWARD TO IT!! ALTHOUGH...I STILL DON'T HAVE ANY IDEA WHAT IT WILL BE...
KEEP READING!
YUKIYA SAKURAGI

*CONTEST IN JAPAN ONLY

...KEEP READING! ♡

WHETHER YOU WON OR DIDN'T...

RUFF

I'M USING THE BAG TOO! ☆

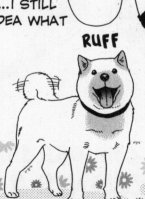

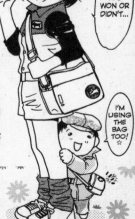

SEND ME YOUR ILLUSTRATIONS AND THOUGHTS ON THE MANGA! ♡

SEND TO YUKIYA SAKURAGI, C/O VIZ MEDIA, LLC; INUBAKA EDITOR; P.O. BOX 77010; SAN FRANCISCO, CA 94107.

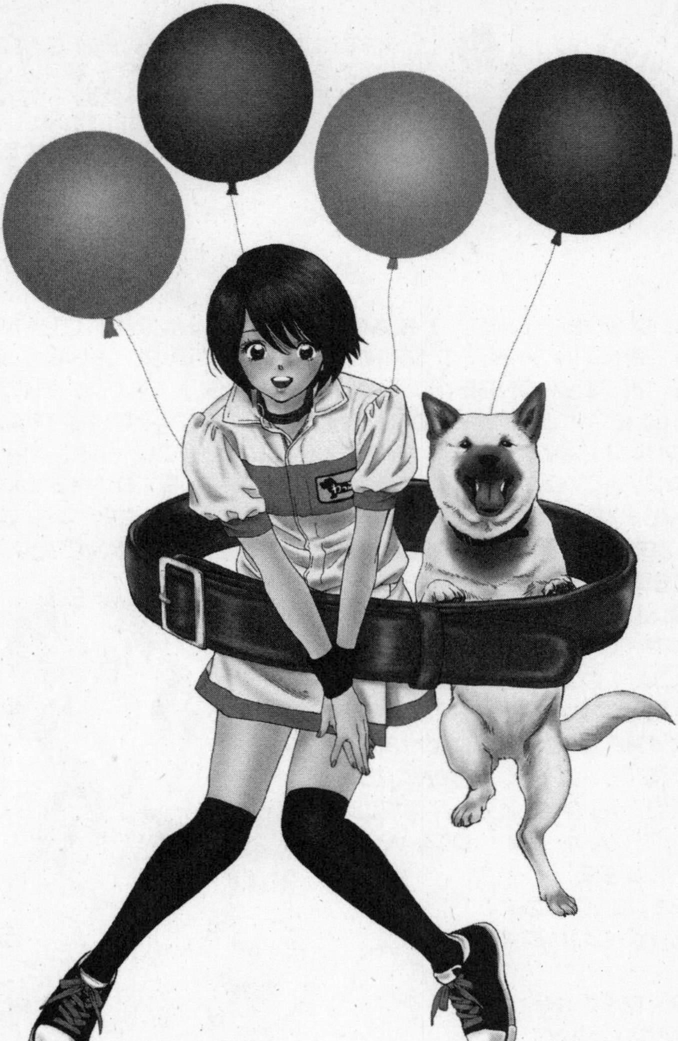

CHAPTER 168:
SERINA WANTS A DOGGIE!

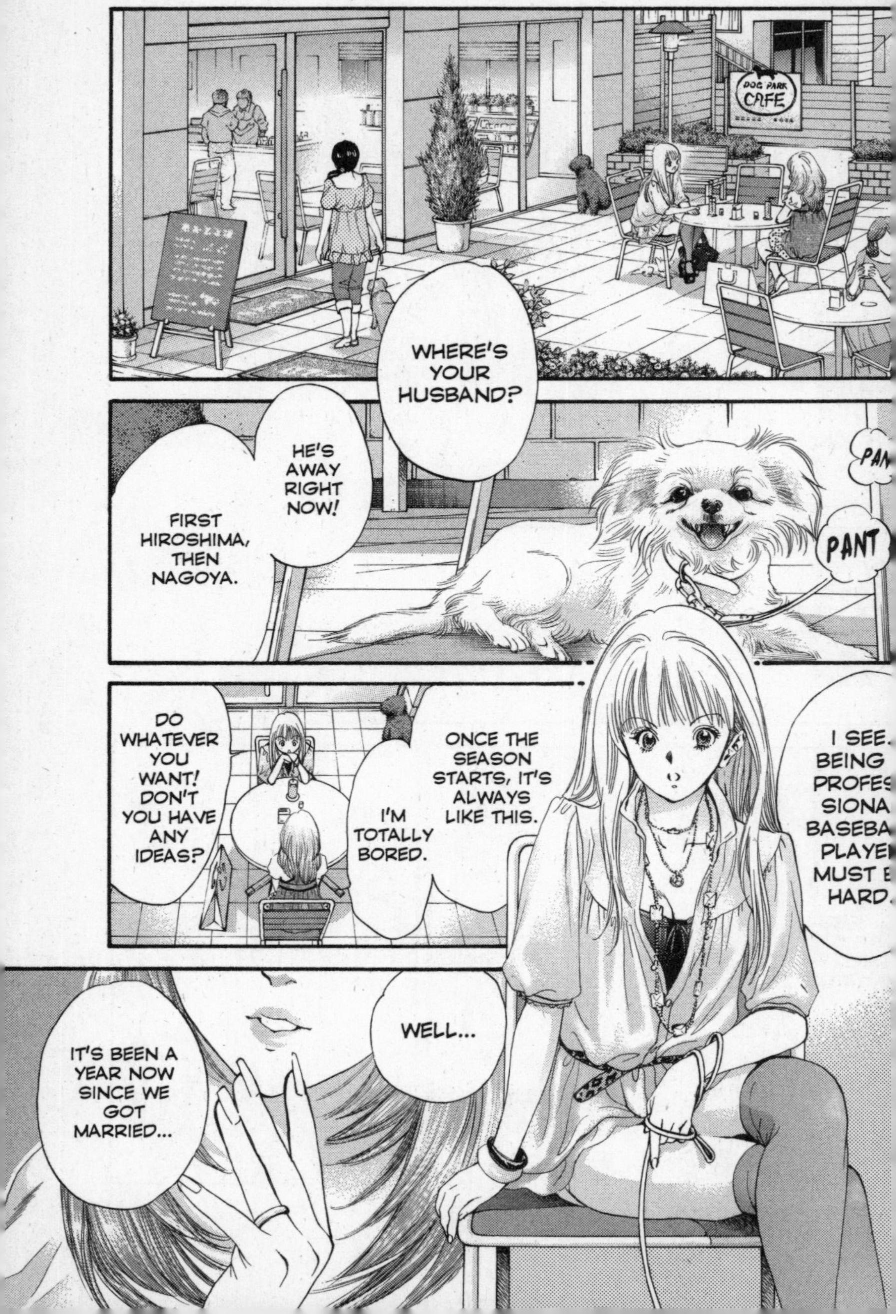

DOG PARK CAFE
WHERE'S YOUR HUSBAND?
PAN
PANT
HE'S AWAY RIGHT NOW!
FIRST HIROSHIMA, THEN NAGOYA.
I SEE. BEING PROFES SIONA BASEBA PLAYE MUST B HARD.
ONCE THE SEASON STARTS, IT'S ALWAYS LIKE THIS.
I'M TOTALLY BORED.
DO WHATEVER YOU WANT! DON'T YOU HAVE ANY IDEAS?
WELL...
IT'S BEEN A YEAR NOW SINCE WE GOT MARRIED...

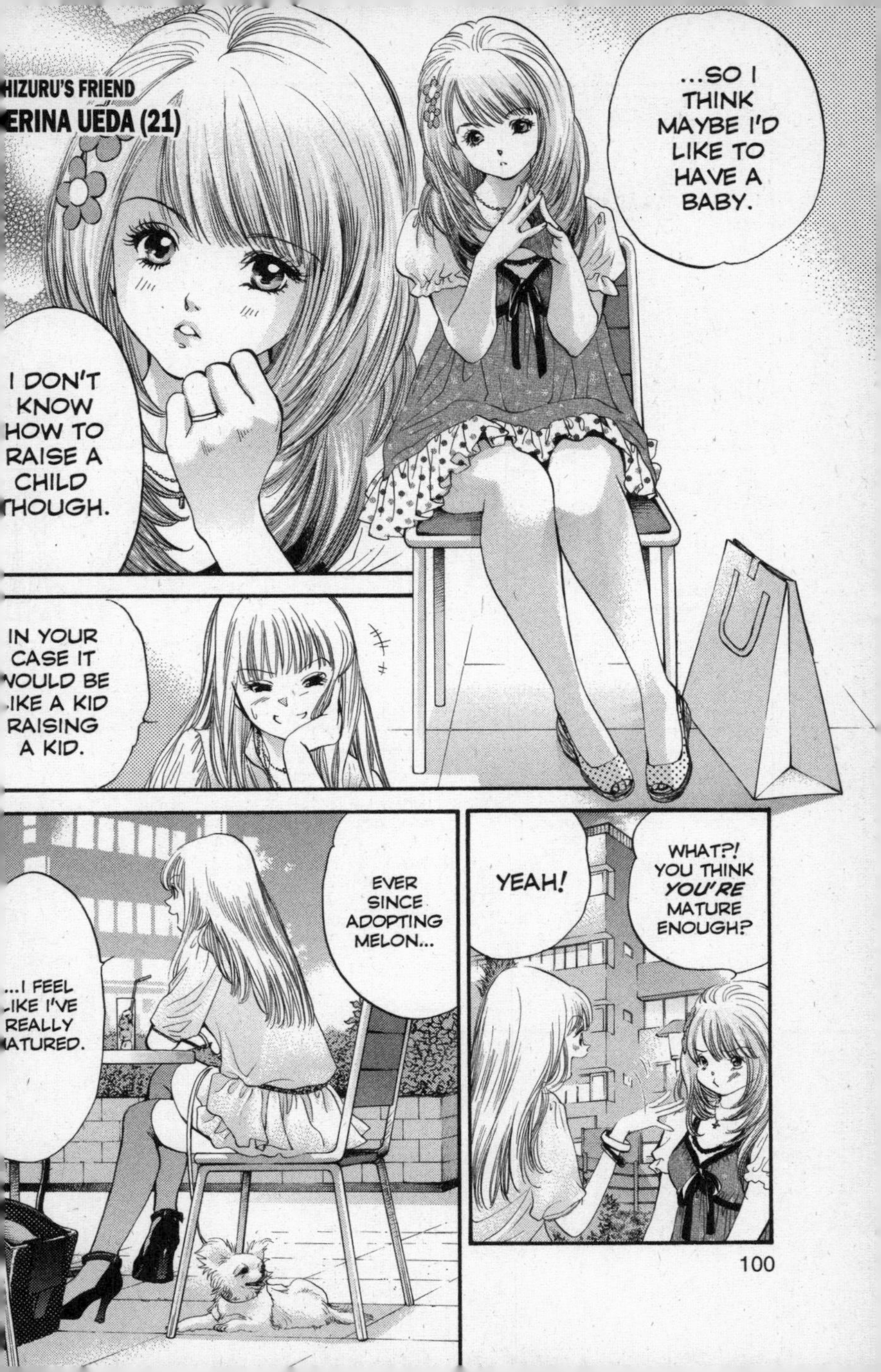
...SO I THINK MAYBE I'D LIKE TO HAVE A BABY.
HIZURU'S FRIEND ERINA UEDA (21)
I DON'T KNOW HOW TO RAISE A CHILD THOUGH.
IN YOUR CASE IT WOULD BE LIKE A KID RAISING A KID.
WHAT?! YOU THINK *YOU'RE* MATURE ENOUGH?
YEAH!
EVER SINCE ADOPTING MELON...
...I FEEL LIKE I'VE REALLY MATURED.

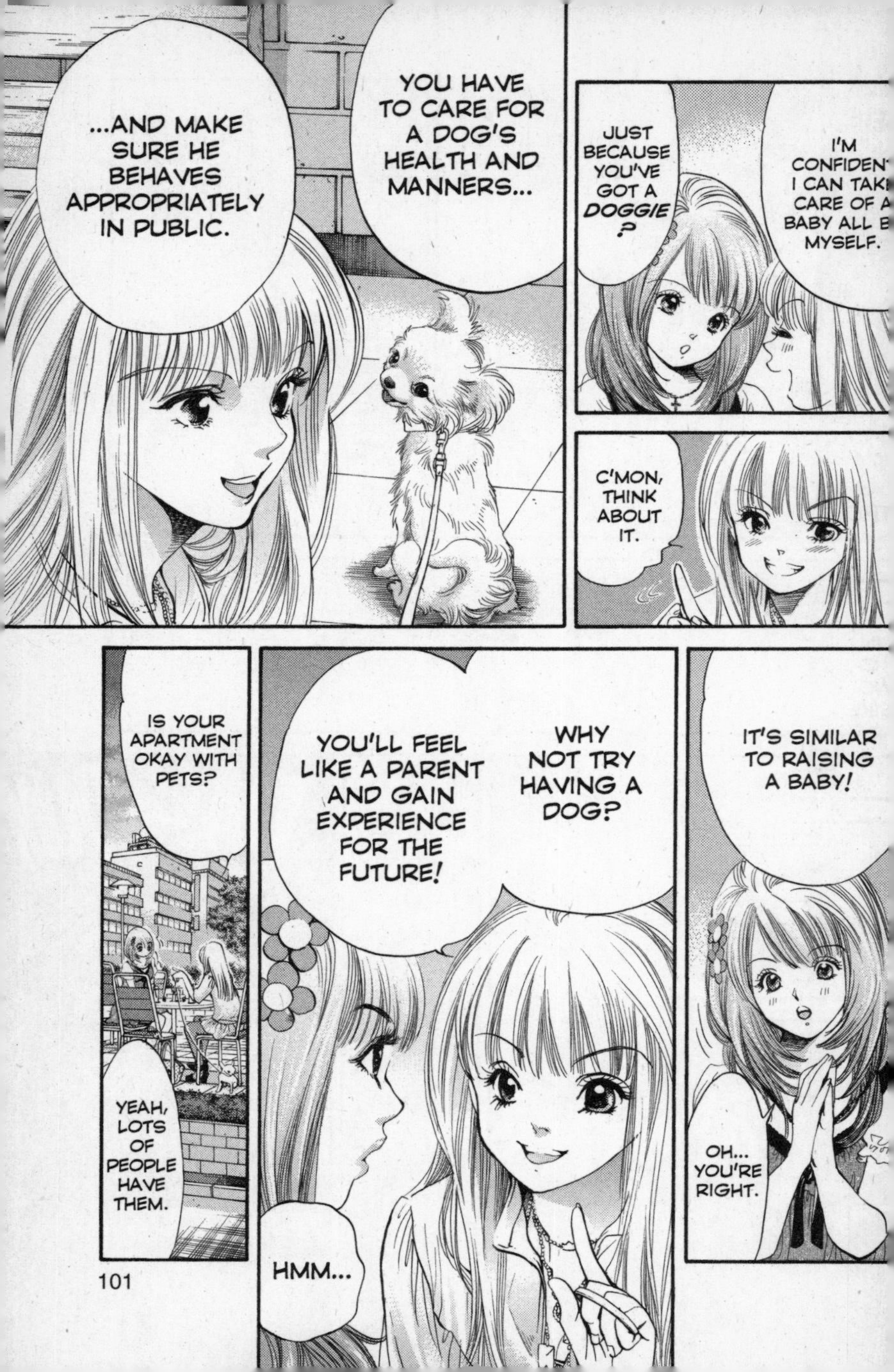
I'M CONFIDEN I CAN TAK CARE OF A BABY ALL B MYSELF.
JUST BECAUSE YOU'VE GOT A *DOGGIE*?
C'MON, THINK ABOUT IT.
YOU HAVE TO CARE FOR A DOG'S HEALTH AND MANNERS...
...AND MAKE SURE HE BEHAVES APPROPRIATELY IN PUBLIC.
IT'S SIMILAR TO RAISING A BABY!
OH... YOU'RE RIGHT.
WHY NOT TRY HAVING A DOG?
YOU'LL FEEL LIKE A PARENT AND GAIN EXPERIENCE FOR THE FUTURE!
HMM...
IS YOUR APARTMENT OKAY WITH PETS?
YEAH, LOTS OF PEOPLE HAVE THEM.

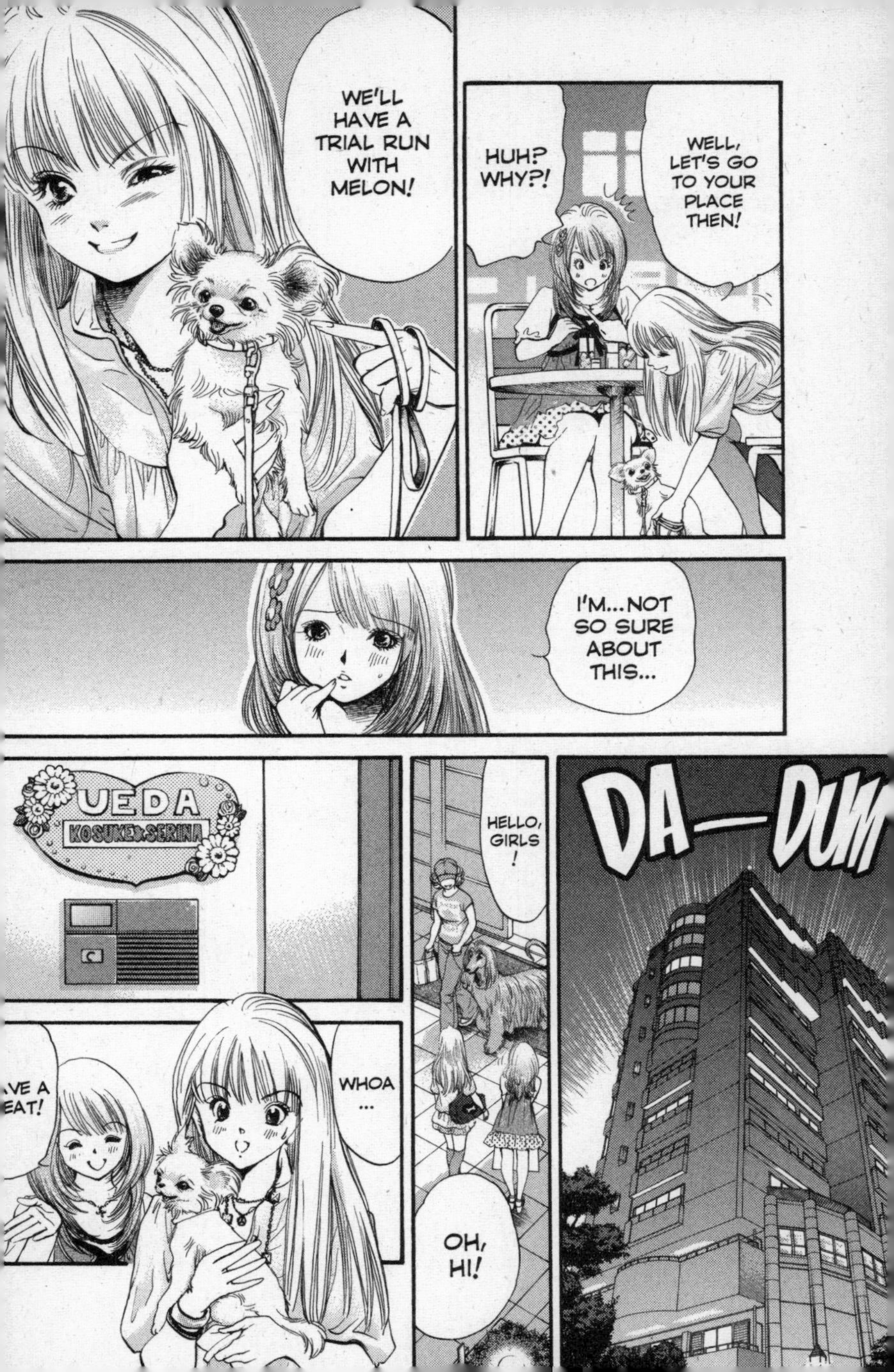
WELL, LET'S GO TO YOUR PLACE THEN!
HUH? WHY?!
WE'LL HAVE A TRIAL RUN WITH MELON!
I'M...NOT SO SURE ABOUT THIS...
DA—DUM
HELLO, GIRLS!
OH, HI!
UEDA
KOSUKE&SERINA
WHOA...
AVE A EAT!

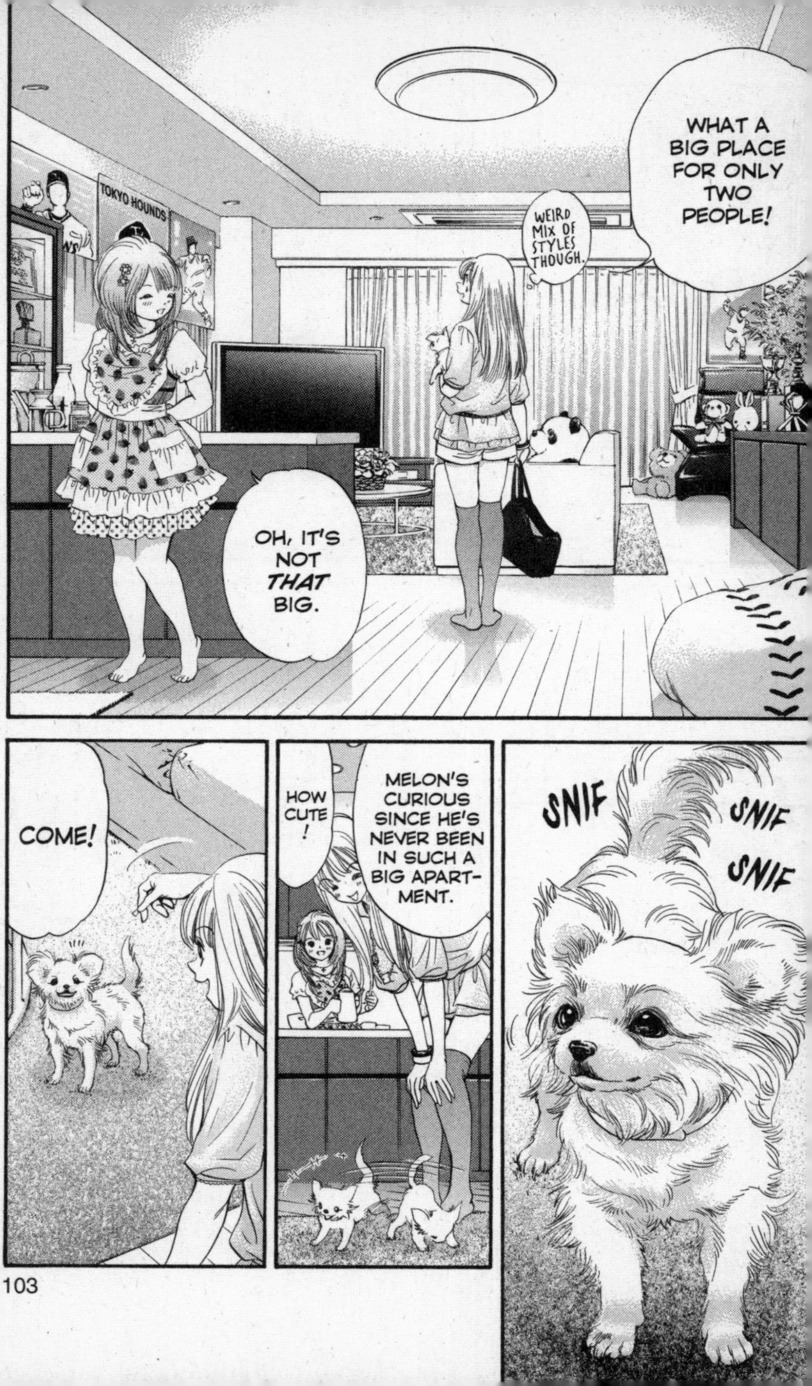
WHAT A BIG PLACE FOR ONLY TWO PEOPLE!
WEIRD MIX OF STYLES THOUGH.
TOKYO HOUNDS
OH, IT'S NOT *THAT* BIG.
SNIF
SNIF
SNIF
MELON'S CURIOUS SINCE HE'S NEVER BEEN IN SUCH A BIG APARTMENT.
HOW CUTE!
COME!

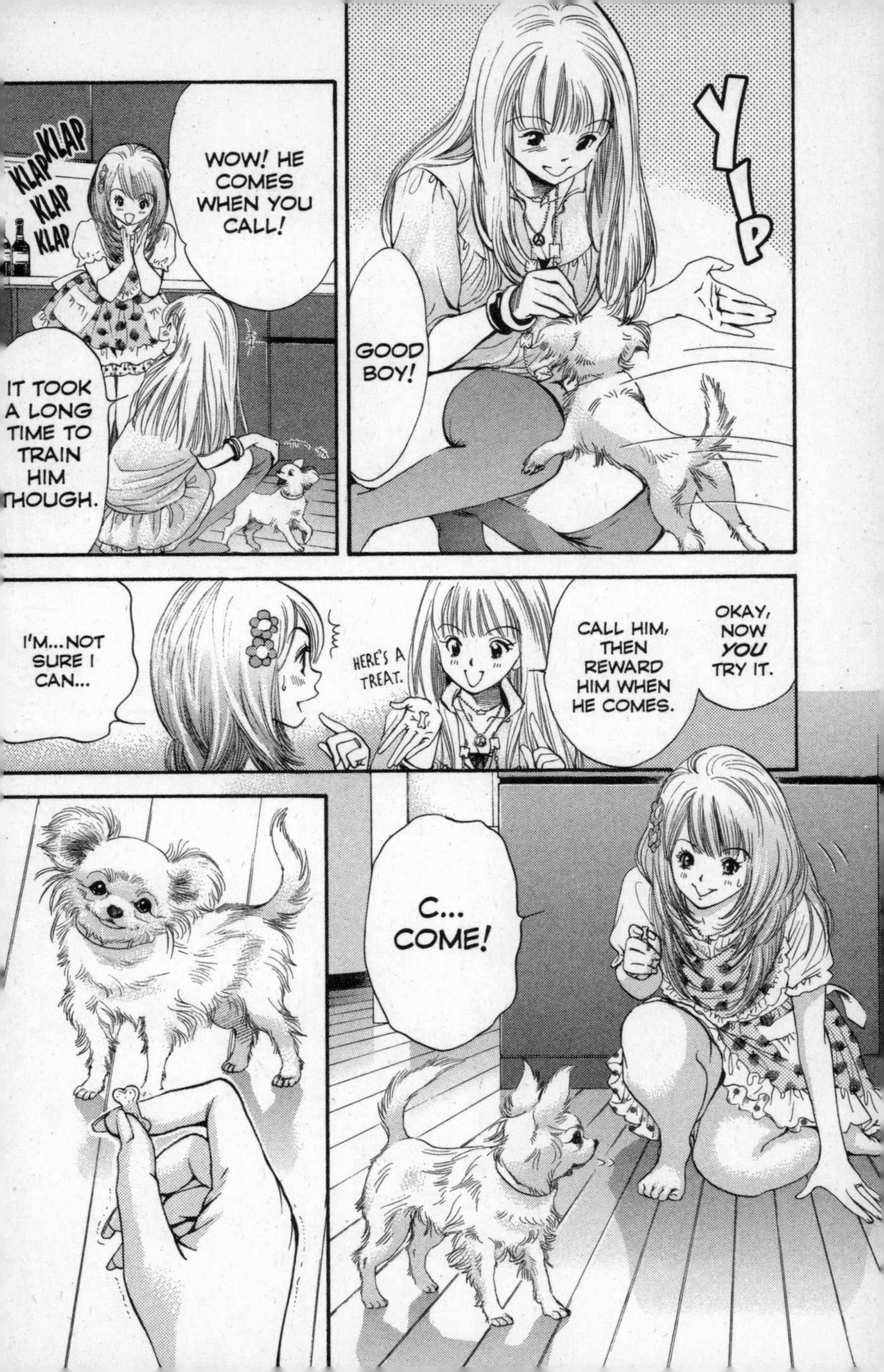
YIP
GOOD BOY!
KLAP KLAP KLAP KLAP KLAP
WOW! HE COMES WHEN YOU CALL!
IT TOOK A LONG TIME TO TRAIN HIM THOUGH.
OKAY, NOW *YOU* TRY IT.
CALL HIM, THEN REWARD HIM WHEN HE COMES.
HERE'S A TREAT.
I'M...NOT SURE I CAN...
C... COME!

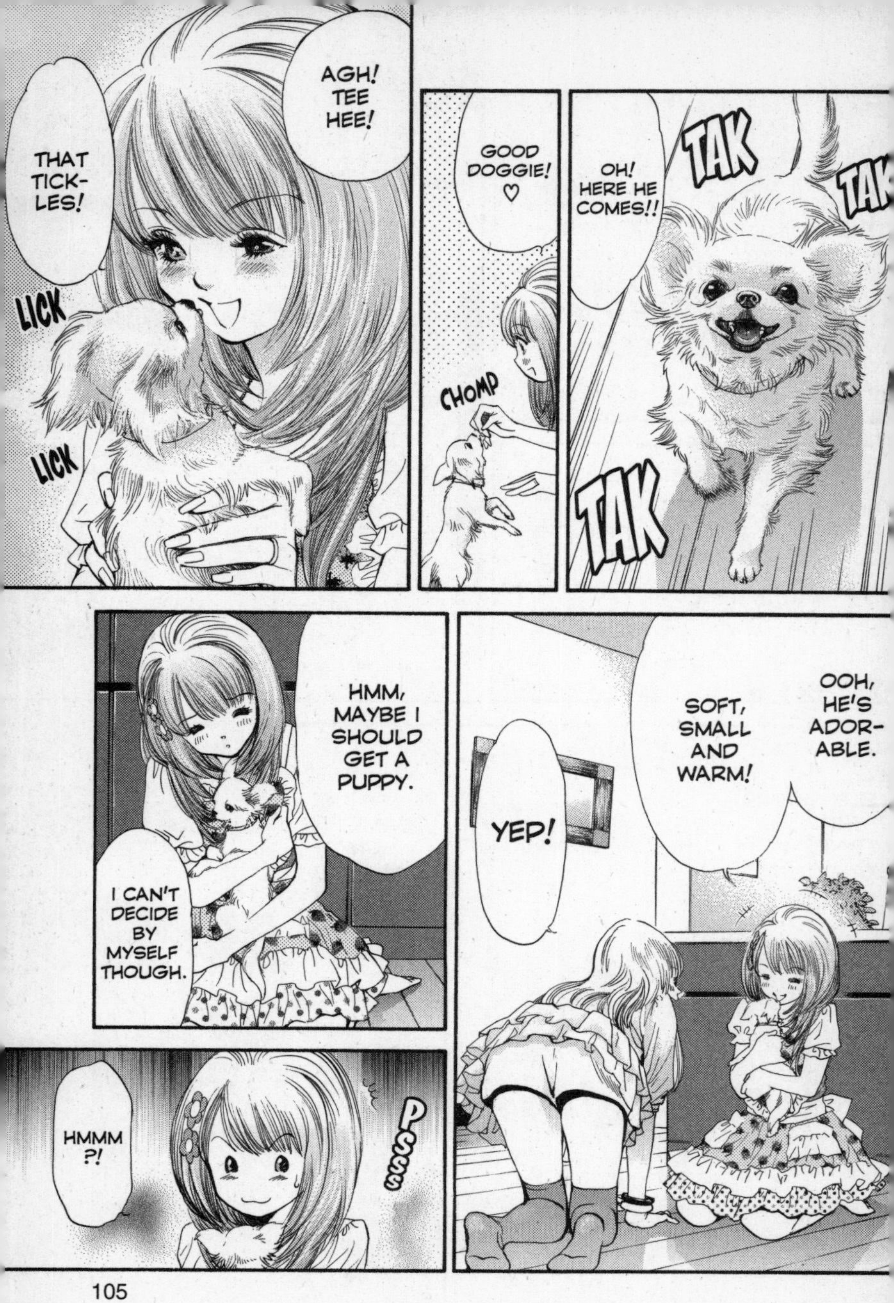
TAK
TAK
OH! HERE HE COMES!!
TAK
GOOD DOGGIE! ♡
CHOMP
AGH! TEE HEE!
THAT TICK-LES!
LICK
LICK
OOH, HE'S ADOR-ABLE.
SOFT, SMALL AND WARM!
YEP!
HMM, MAYBE I SHOULD GET A PUPPY.
I CAN'T DECIDE BY MYSELF THOUGH.
PSSS
HMMM ?!

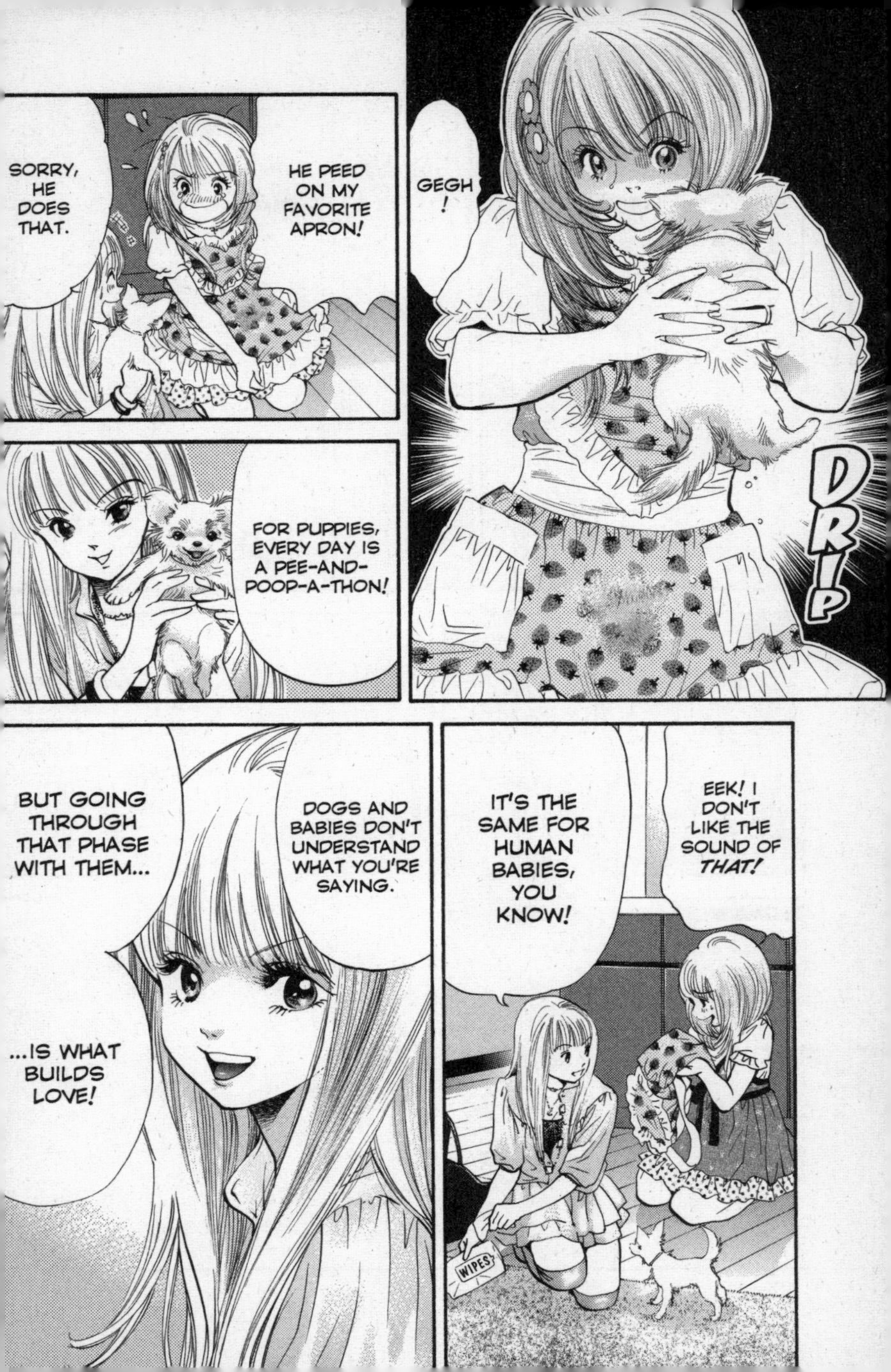
GEGH!
DRIP
HE PEED ON MY FAVORITE APRON!
SORRY, HE DOES THAT.
FOR PUPPIES, EVERY DAY IS A PEE-AND-POOP-A-THON!
EEK! I DON'T LIKE THE SOUND OF *THAT!*
IT'S THE SAME FOR HUMAN BABIES, YOU KNOW!
WIPES
DOGS AND BABIES DON'T UNDERSTAND WHAT YOU'RE SAYING.
BUT GOING THROUGH THAT PHASE WITH THEM...
...IS WHAT BUILDS LOVE!

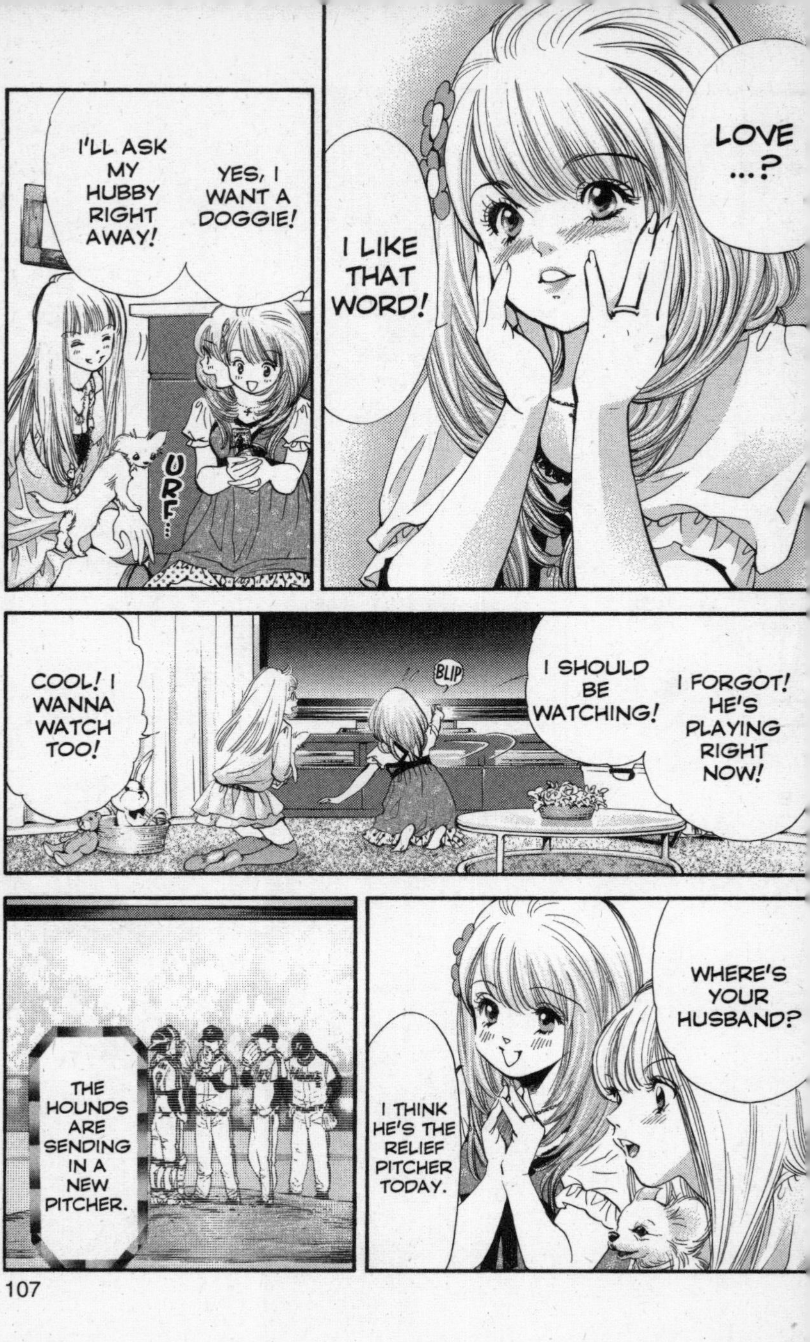
LOVE ...?
I LIKE THAT WORD!
YES, I WANT A DOGGIE!
I'LL ASK MY HUBBY RIGHT AWAY!
URF...
I FORGOT! HE'S PLAYING RIGHT NOW!
I SHOULD BE WATCHING!
BLIP
COOL! I WANNA WATCH TOO!
WHERE'S YOUR HUSBAND?
I THINK HE'S THE RELIEF PITCHER TODAY.
THE HOUNDS ARE SENDING IN A NEW PITCHER.

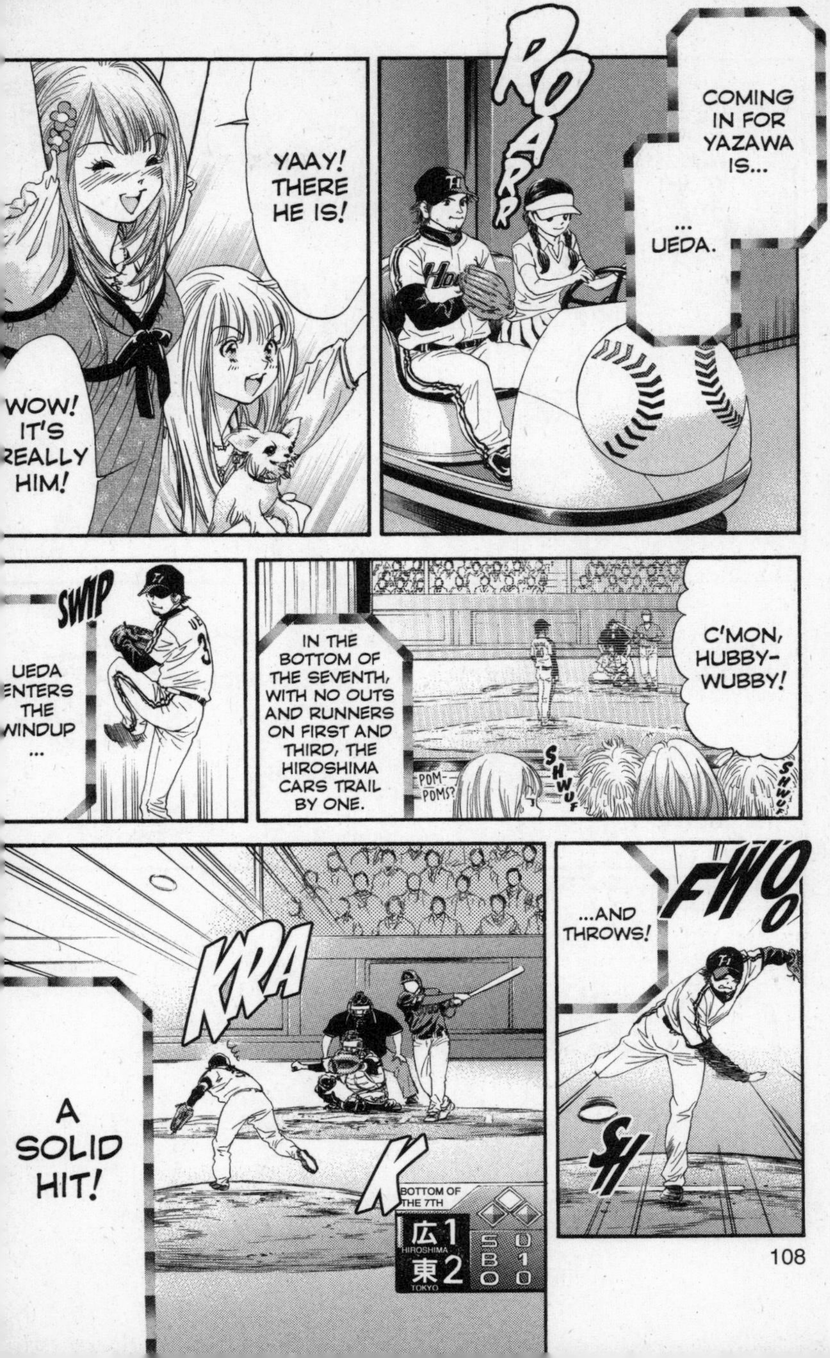
ROARR
COMING IN FOR YAZAWA IS...
... UEDA.
YAAY! THERE HE IS!
WOW! IT'S REALLY HIM!
C'MON, HUBBY-WUBBY!
SHWUF
SHWUF
IN THE BOTTOM OF THE SEVENTH, WITH NO OUTS AND RUNNERS ON FIRST AND THIRD, THE HIROSHIMA CARS TRAIL BY ONE.
POM-POMS?
SWIP
UEDA ENTERS THE WINDUP ...
FWOO
...AND THROWS!
SH
KRA
K
A SOLID HIT!
BOTTOM OF THE 7TH
広1 HIROSHIMA
東2 TOKYO
S 0
B 1
O 0

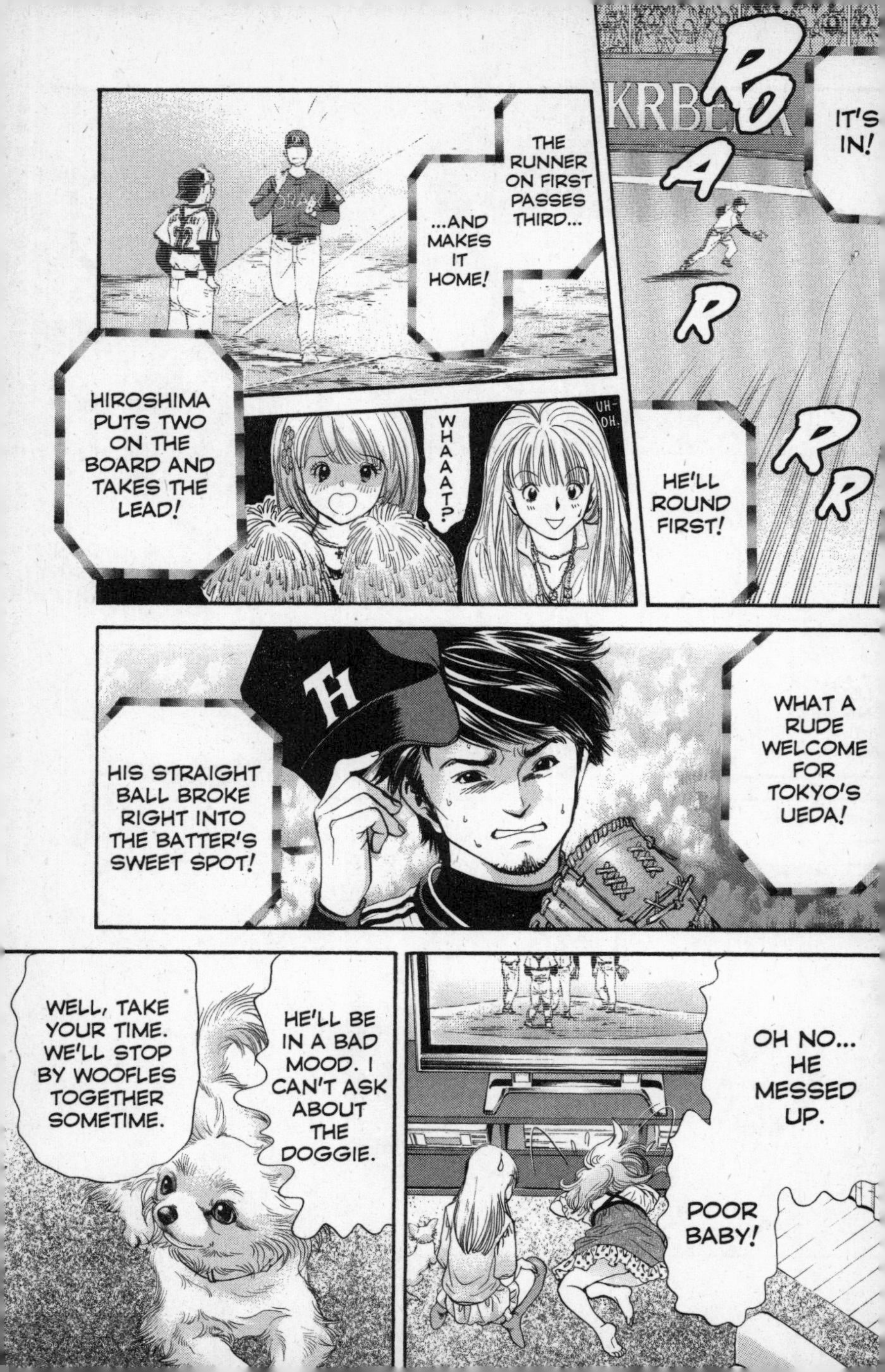
ROARRR
IT'S IN!
HE'LL ROUND FIRST!
THE RUNNER ON FIRST PASSES THIRD...
...AND MAKES IT HOME!
UH-OH.
WHAAAT?
HIROSHIMA PUTS TWO ON THE BOARD AND TAKES THE LEAD!
WHAT A RUDE WELCOME FOR TOKYO'S UEDA!
HIS STRAIGHT BALL BROKE RIGHT INTO THE BATTER'S SWEET SPOT!
OH NO... HE MESSED UP.
POOR BABY!
HE'LL BE IN A BAD MOOD. I CAN'T ASK ABOUT THE DOGGIE.
WELL, TAKE YOUR TIME. WE'LL STOP BY WOOFLES TOGETHER SOMETIME.

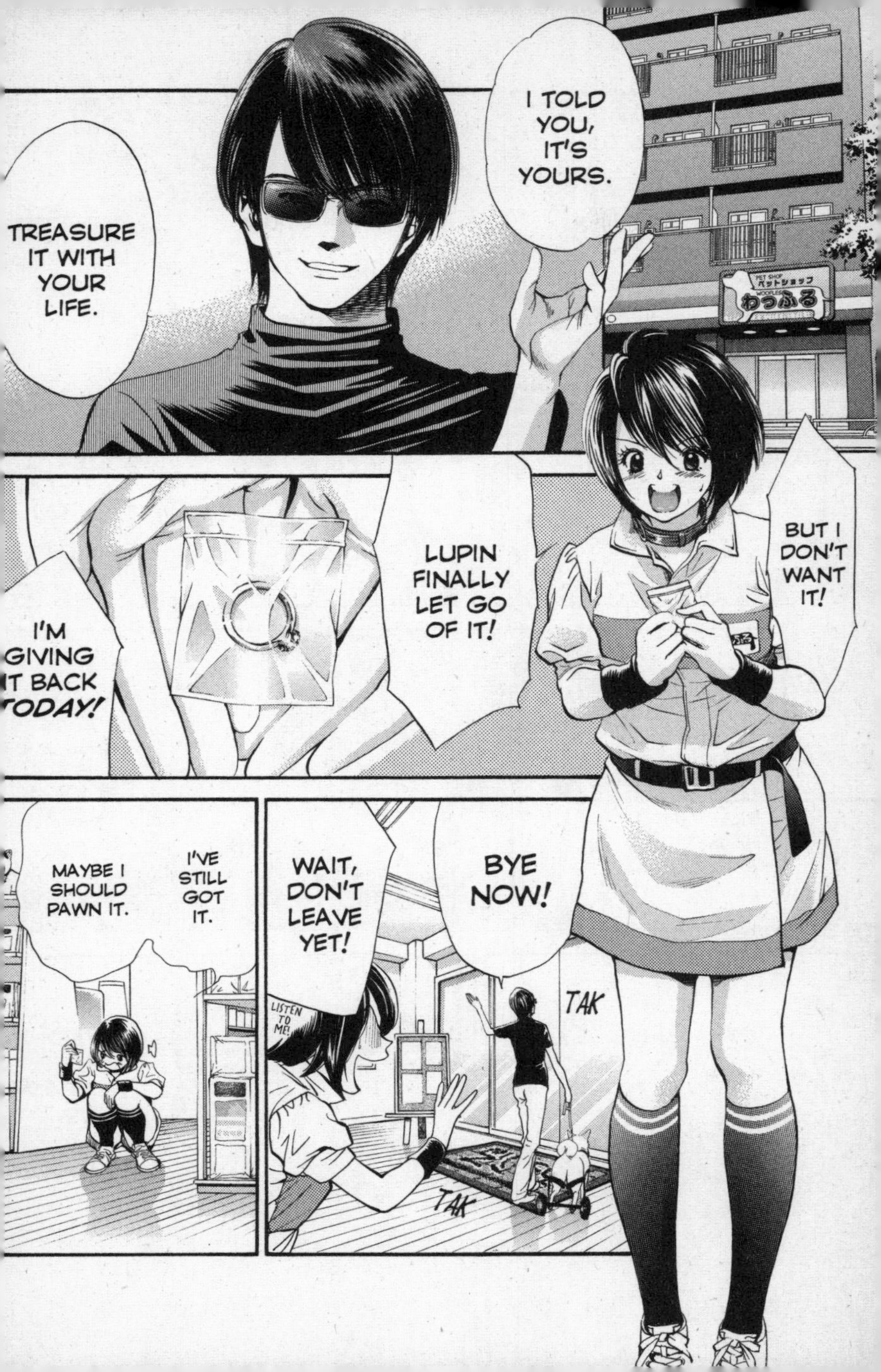
I TOLD YOU, IT'S YOURS.
PET SHOP
ペットショップ
WOOFLES
わっふる
TREASURE IT WITH YOUR LIFE.
BUT I DON'T WANT IT!
LUPIN FINALLY LET GO OF IT!
I'M GIVING IT BACK TODAY!
BYE NOW!
TAK
WAIT, DON'T LEAVE YET!
LISTEN TO ME!
TAK
I'VE STILL GOT IT.
MAYBE I SHOULD PAWN IT.

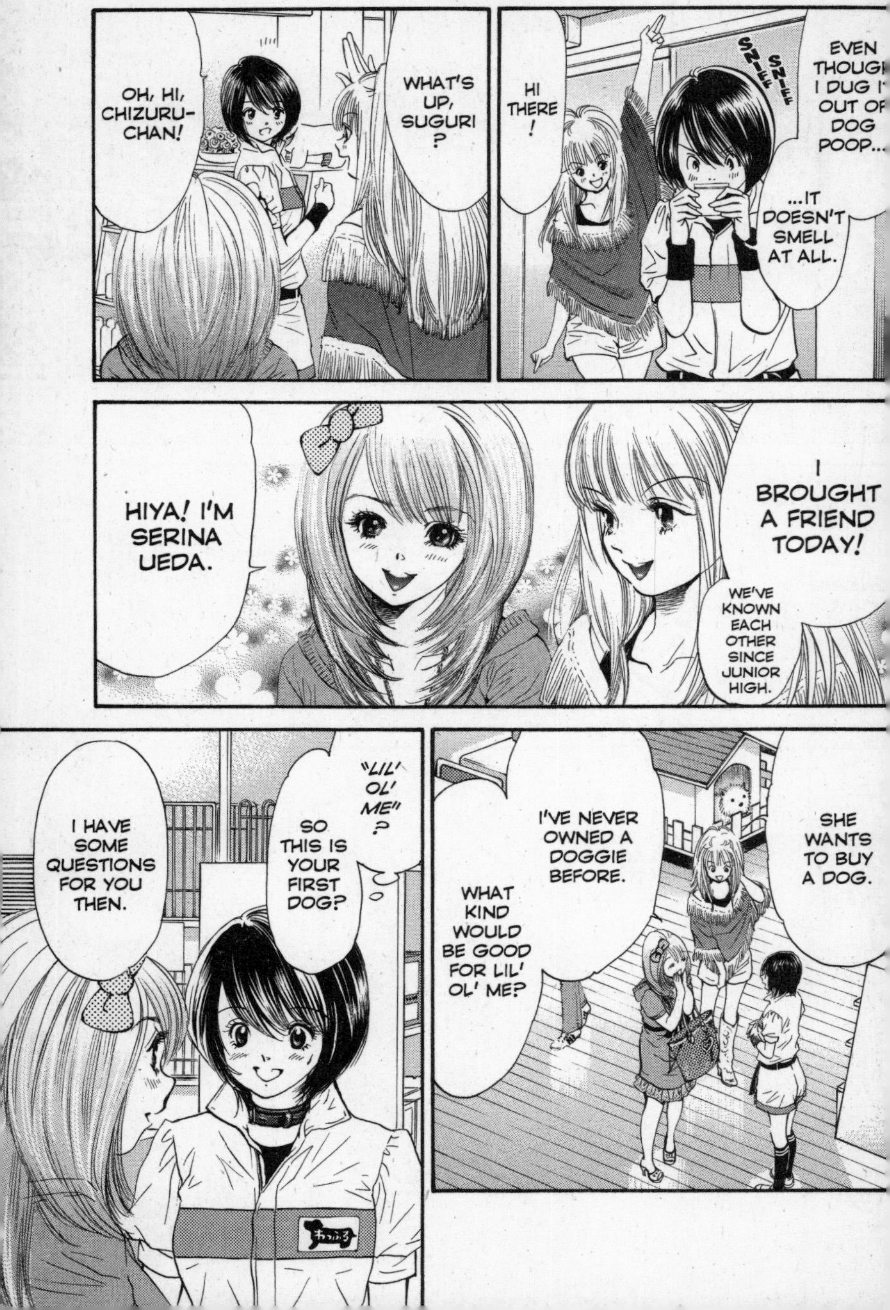
EVEN THOUG I DUG I OUT OF DOG POOP...
SNIFF SNIFF
...IT DOESN'T SMELL AT ALL.
HI THERE!
WHAT'S UP, SUGURI?
OH, HI, CHIZURU-CHAN!
I BROUGHT A FRIEND TODAY!
WE'VE KNOWN EACH OTHER SINCE JUNIOR HIGH.
HIYA! I'M SERINA UEDA.
SHE WANTS TO BUY A DOG.
I'VE NEVER OWNED A DOGGIE BEFORE.
WHAT KIND WOULD BE GOOD FOR LIL' OL' ME?
"LIL' OL' ME"?
SO THIS IS YOUR FIRST DOG?
I HAVE SOME QUESTIONS FOR YOU THEN.

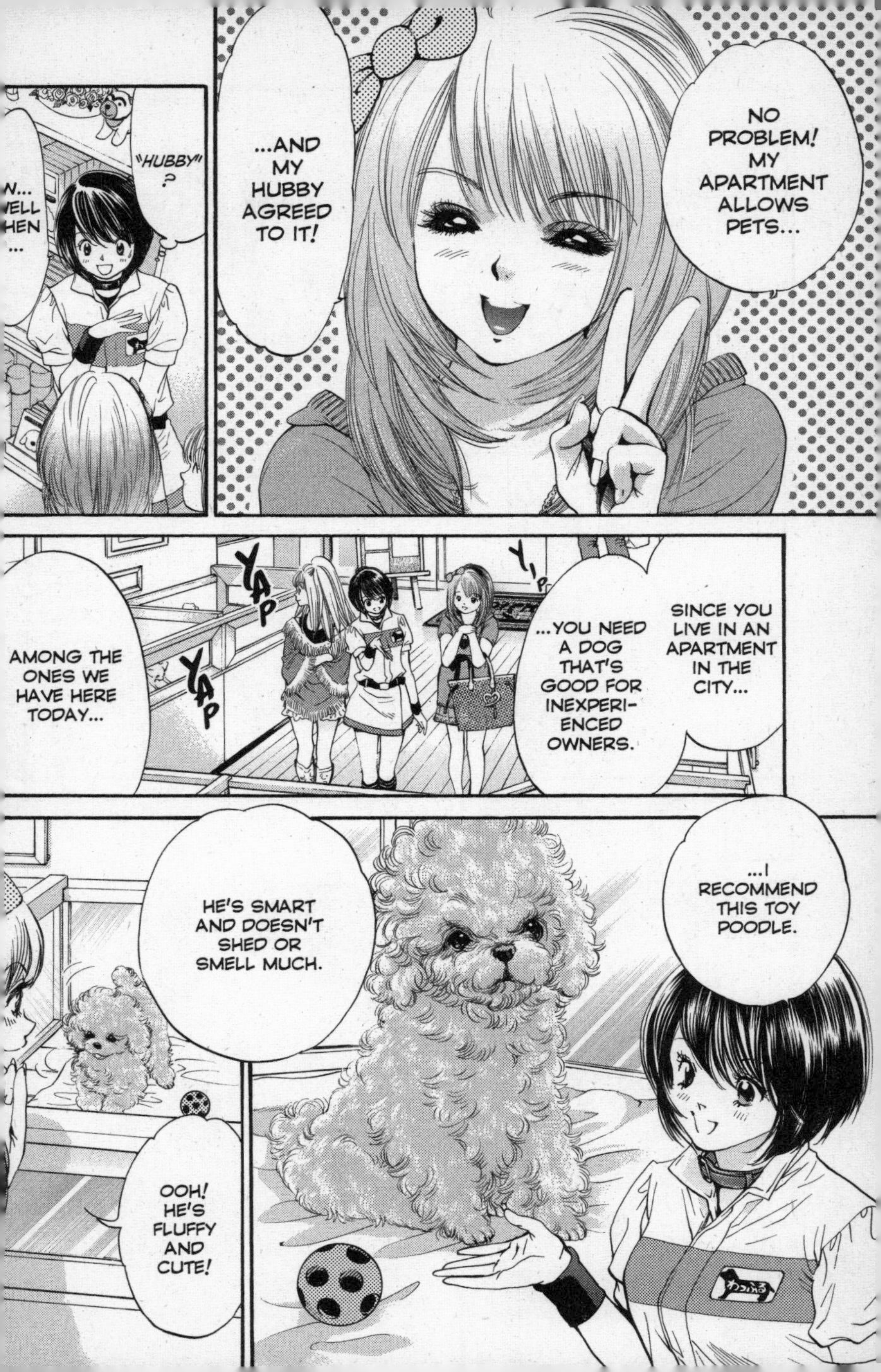
NO PROBLEM! MY APARTMENT ALLOWS PETS...
...AND MY HUBBY AGREED TO IT!
"HUBBY"?
SINCE YOU LIVE IN AN APARTMENT IN THE CITY...
...YOU NEED A DOG THAT'S GOOD FOR INEXPERI-ENCED OWNERS.
YIP
YAP
YAP
AMONG THE ONES WE HAVE HERE TODAY...
...I RECOMMEND THIS TOY POODLE.
HE'S SMART AND DOESN'T SHED OR SMELL MUCH.
OOH! HE'S FLUFFY AND CUTE!

YORKSHIRE TERRIERS DON'T SHED MUCH EITHER.
YIP
YIP
THEIR COATS ARE SO BEAUTIFUL THAT PEOPLE CALL THEM LIVING JEWELS.
THEY'RE TINY BUT ACTIVE!
I ALSO RECOM-MEND A MALTESE.
WHIMPER
WHIMPER
THEY'RE BRIGHT AND LIVELY AND GOOD LEARNERS.
THEY DON'T SHED MUCH EITHER.
IF YOU WANT SOMETHING UNIQUE, YOU MIGHT LIKE A PUG.
HE DOESN'T LIKE HEAT, BUT HIS CALM PERSONALITY MAKES HIM PERFECT AS AN INSIDE PET.

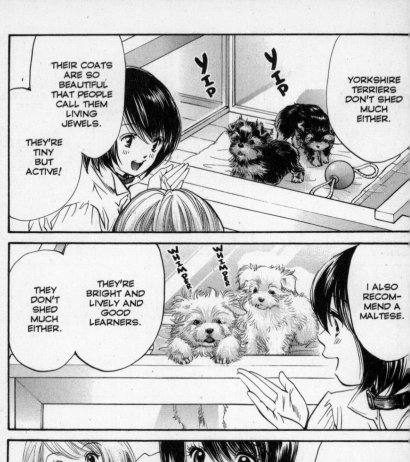

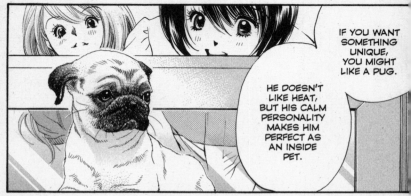

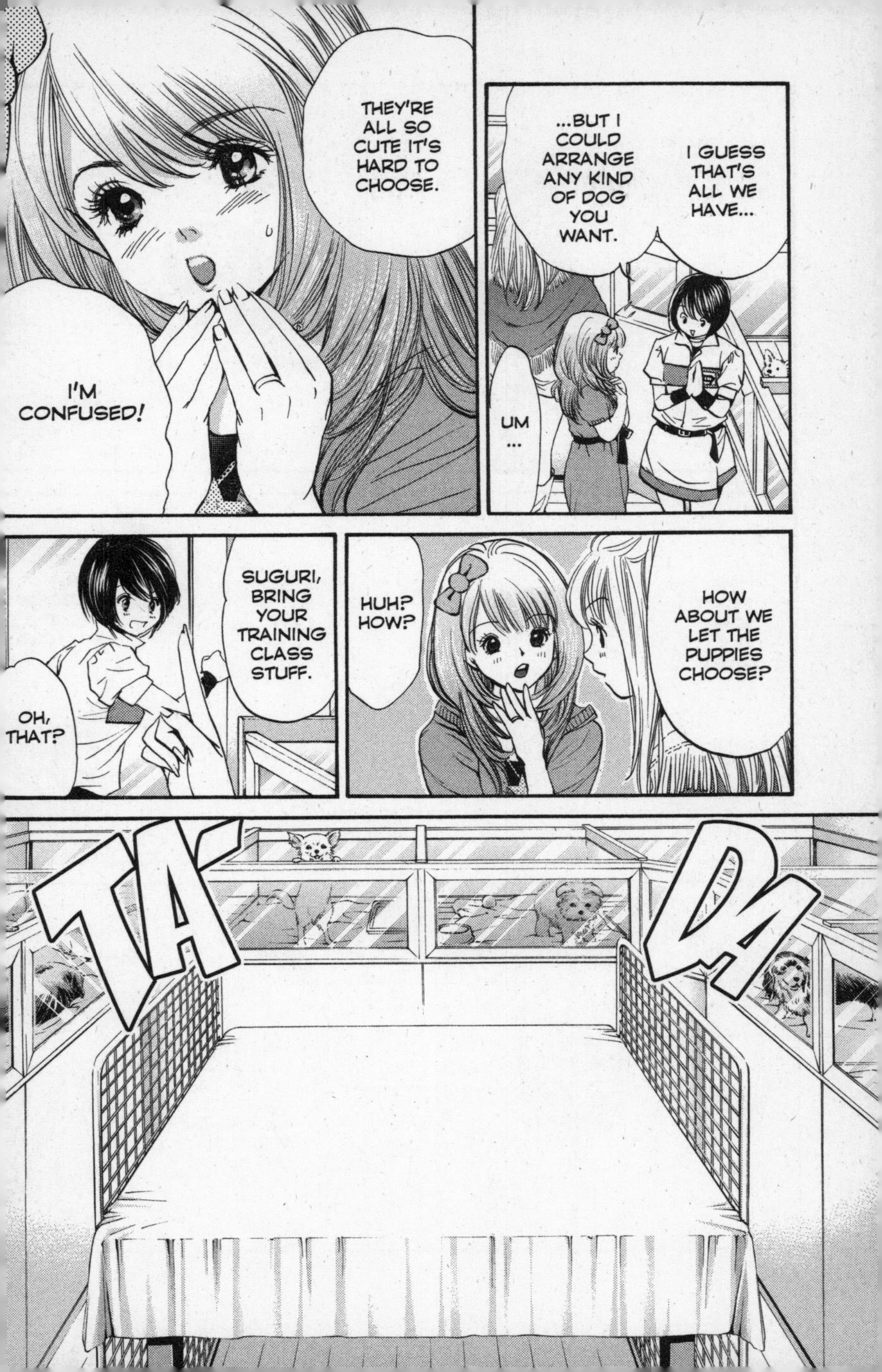
I GUESS THAT'S ALL WE HAVE...
...BUT I COULD ARRANGE ANY KIND OF DOG YOU WANT.
UM ...
THEY'RE ALL SO CUTE IT'S HARD TO CHOOSE.
I'M CONFUSED!
HOW ABOUT WE LET THE PUPPIES CHOOSE?
HUH? HOW?
SUGURI, BRING YOUR TRAINING CLASS STUFF.
OH, THAT?
TA DA

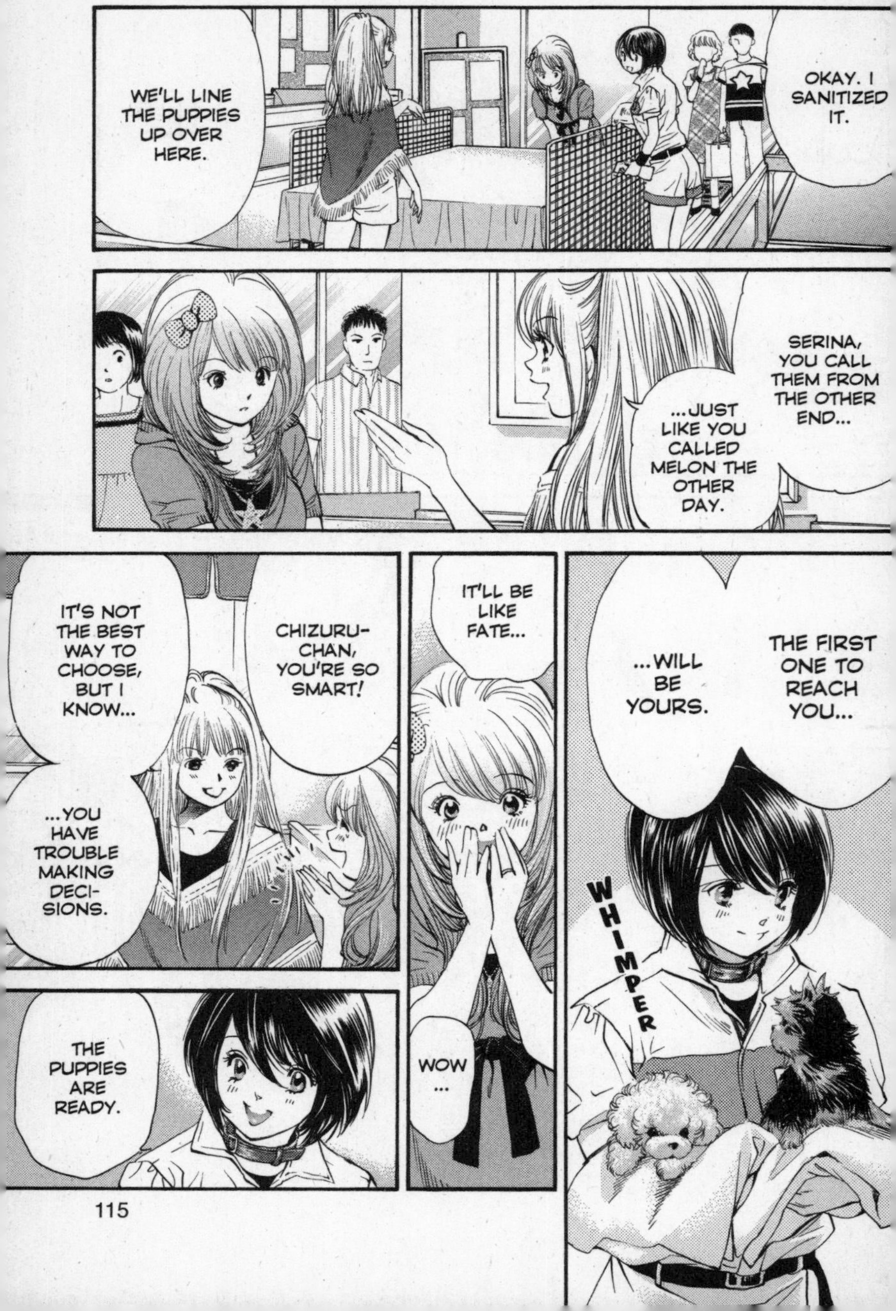
OKAY. I SANITIZED IT.
WE'LL LINE THE PUPPIES UP OVER HERE.
SERINA, YOU CALL THEM FROM THE OTHER END...
...JUST LIKE YOU CALLED MELON THE OTHER DAY.
THE FIRST ONE TO REACH YOU...
...WILL BE YOURS.
WHIMPER
IT'LL BE LIKE FATE...
WOW...
CHIZURU-CHAN, YOU'RE SO SMART!
IT'S NOT THE BEST WAY TO CHOOSE, BUT I KNOW...
...YOU HAVE TROUBLE MAKING DECISIONS.
THE PUPPIES ARE READY.

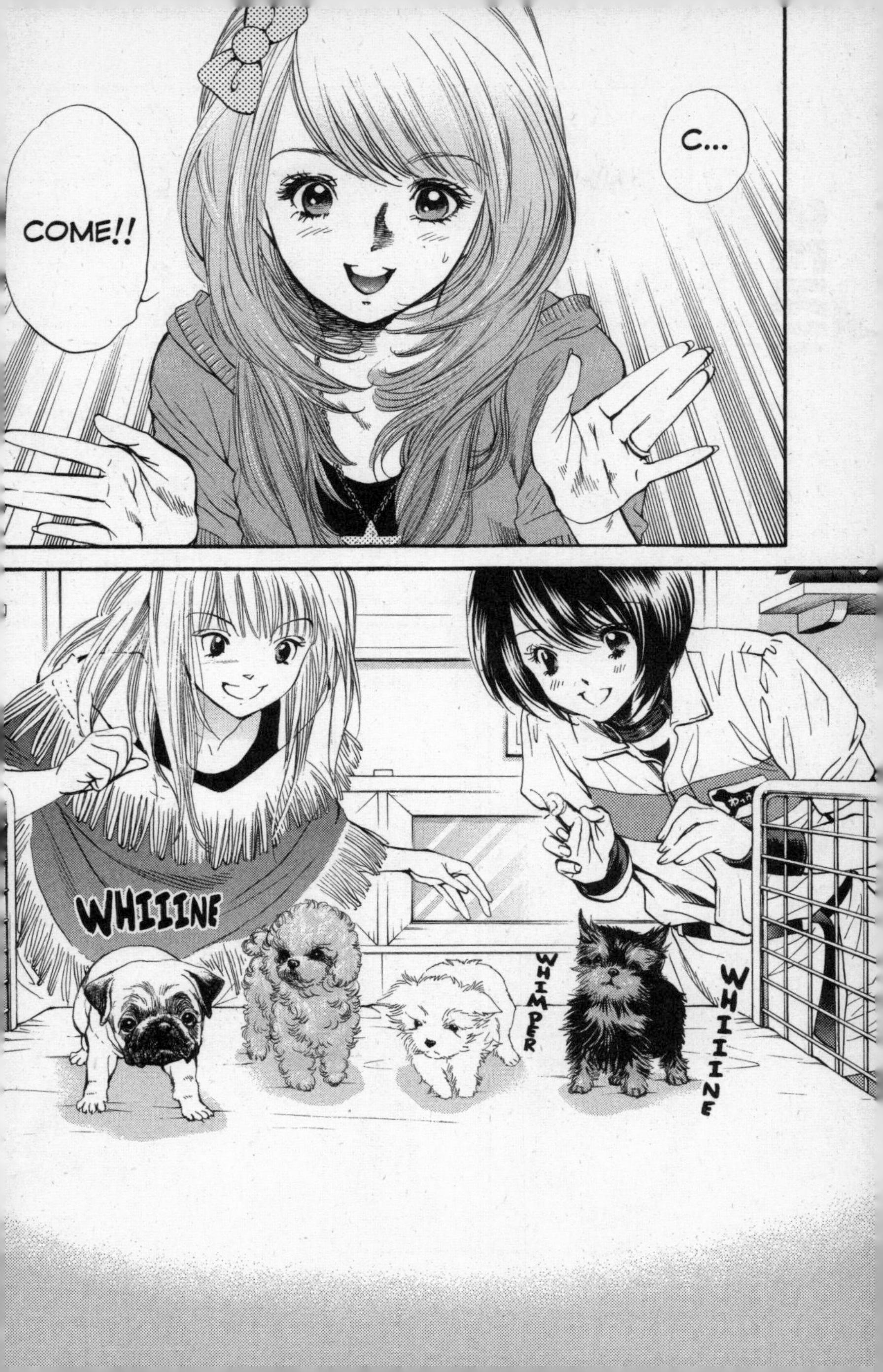
C...
COME!!
WHIIINE
WHIMPER
WHIIINE

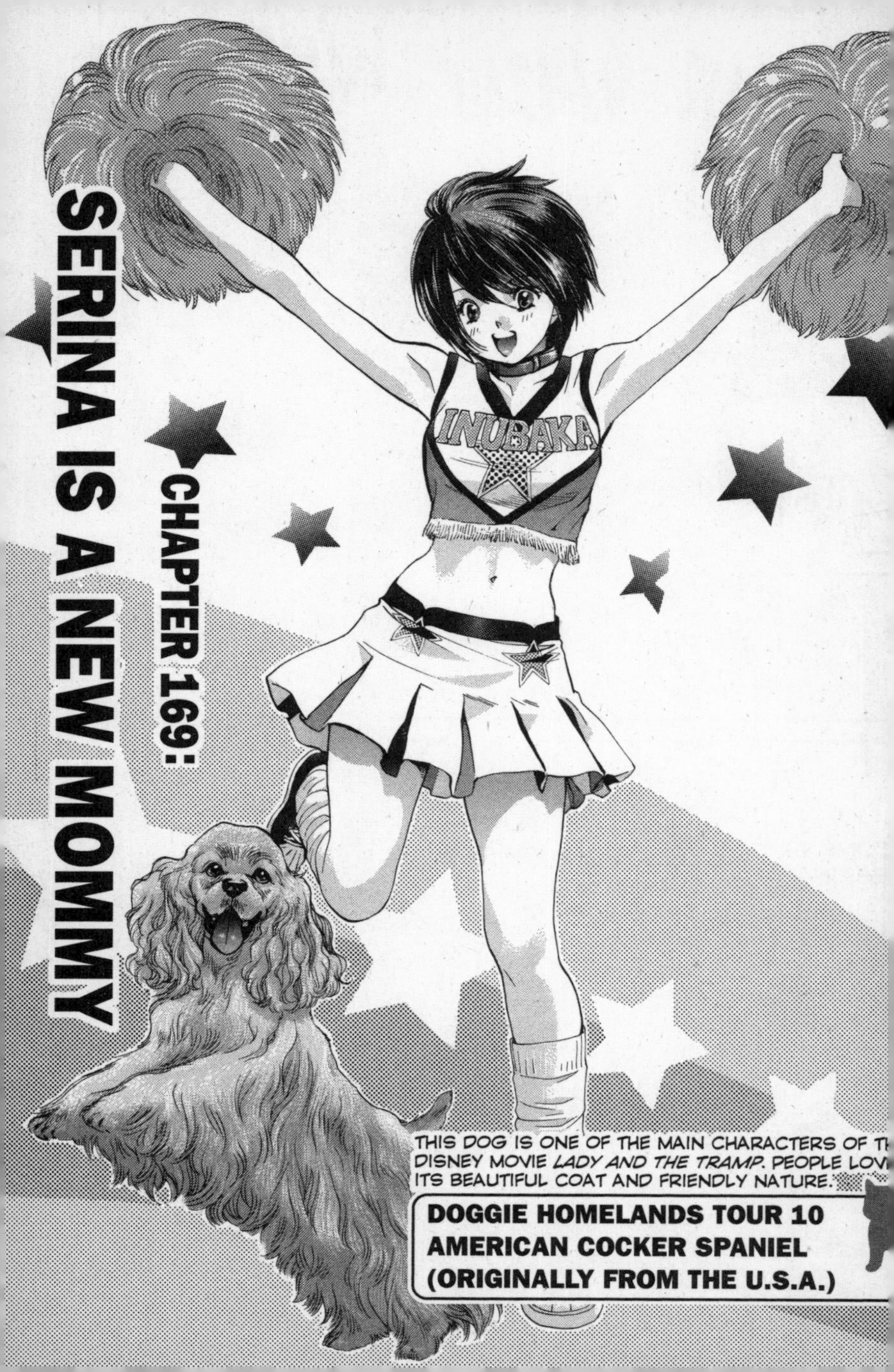
CHAPTER 169:
SERINA IS A NEW MOMMY
INUBAKA
THIS DOG IS ONE OF THE MAIN CHARACTERS OF T
DISNEY MOVIE *LADY AND THE TRAMP*. PEOPLE LOV
ITS BEAUTIFUL COAT AND FRIENDLY NATURE.
DOGGIE HOMELANDS TOUR 10
AMERICAN COCKER SPANIEL
(ORIGINALLY FROM THE U.S.A.)

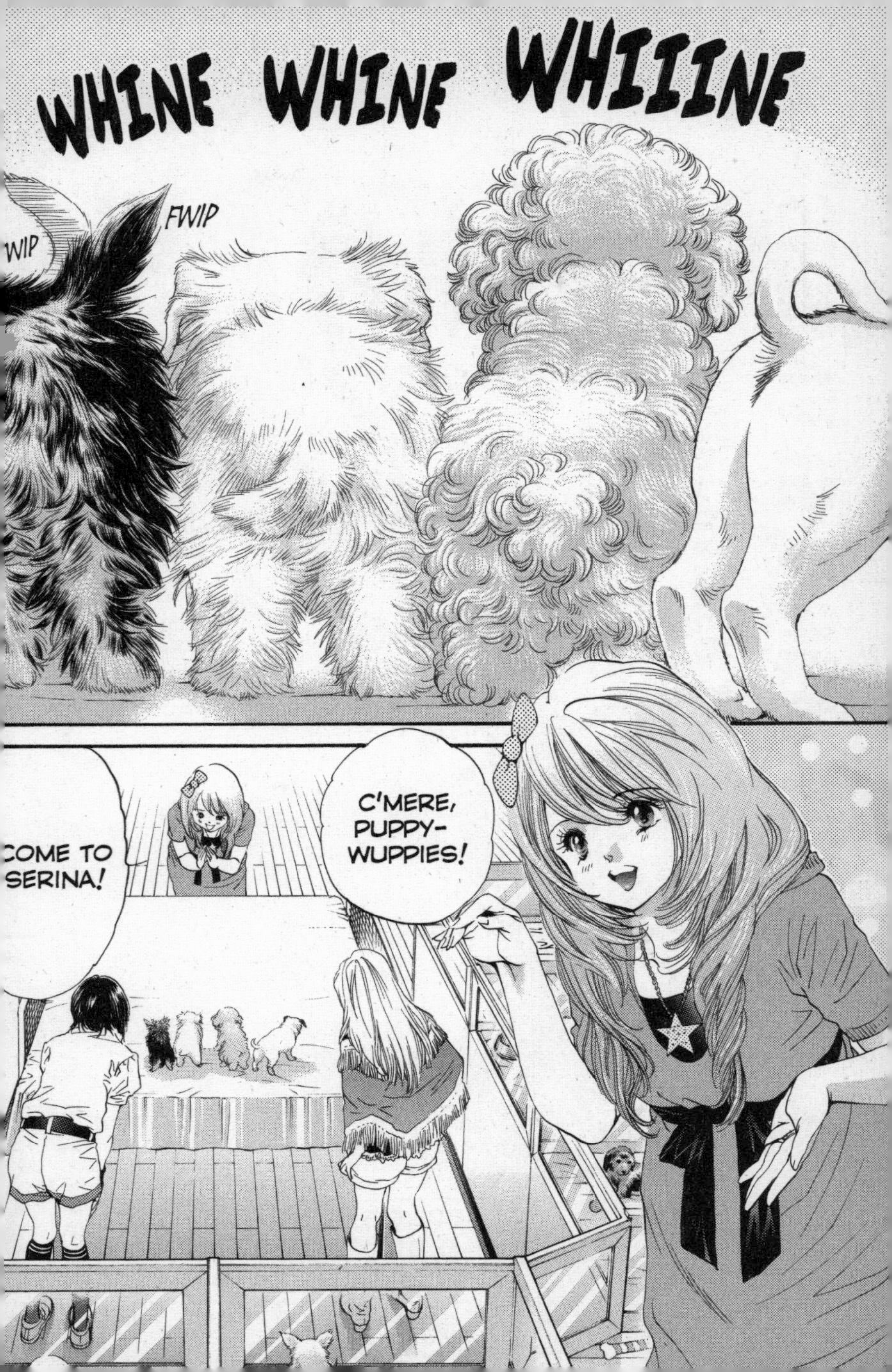
WHINE WHINE WHIIINE
FWIP
WIP
C'MERE, PUPPY-WUPPIES!
COME TO SERINA!

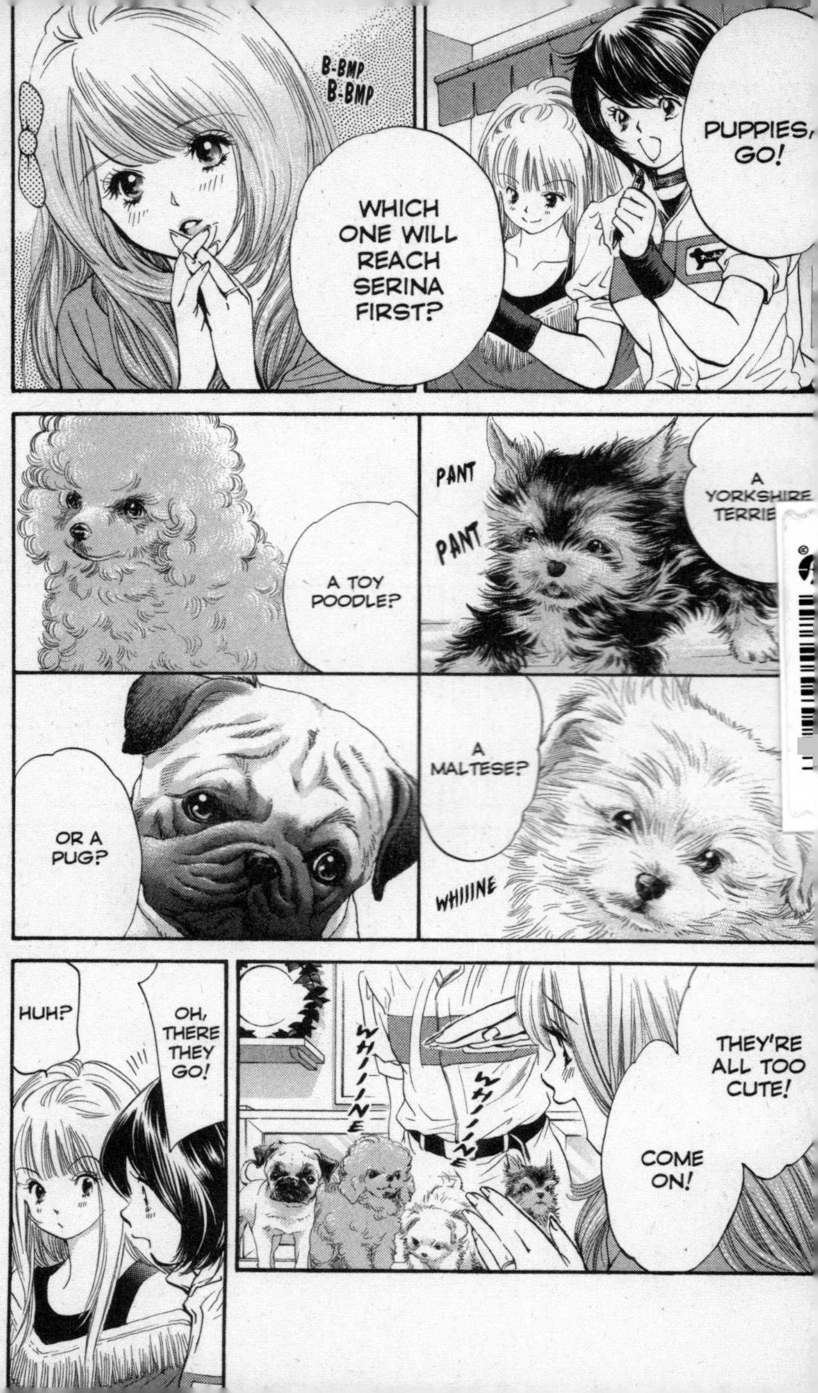
PUPPIES, GO!
B-BMP B-BMP
WHICH ONE WILL REACH SERINA FIRST?
A YORKSHIRE TERRIE
PANT
PANT
A TOY POODLE?
A MALTESE?
WHIIINE
OR A PUG?
THEY'RE ALL TOO CUTE!
COME ON!
WHIIIINE
WHIIIINE
OH, THERE THEY GO!
HUH?

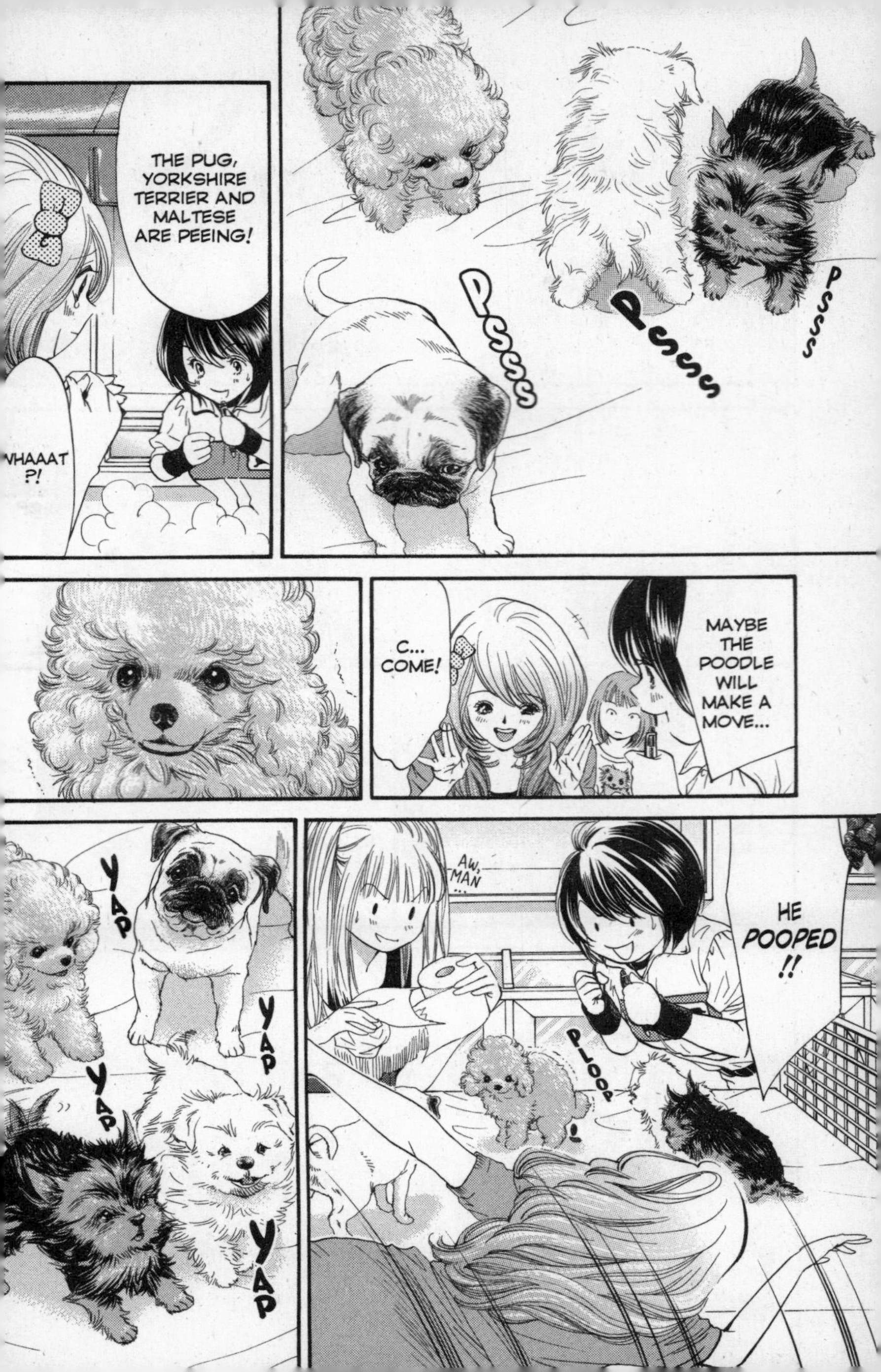
PSSS
PSSSS
PSSS
THE PUG, YORKSHIRE TERRIER AND MALTESE ARE PEEING!
WHAAAT?!
MAYBE THE POODLE WILL MAKE A MOVE...
C... COME!
HE POOPED!!
AW, MAN...
PLOOP
YAP
YAP
YAP
YAP

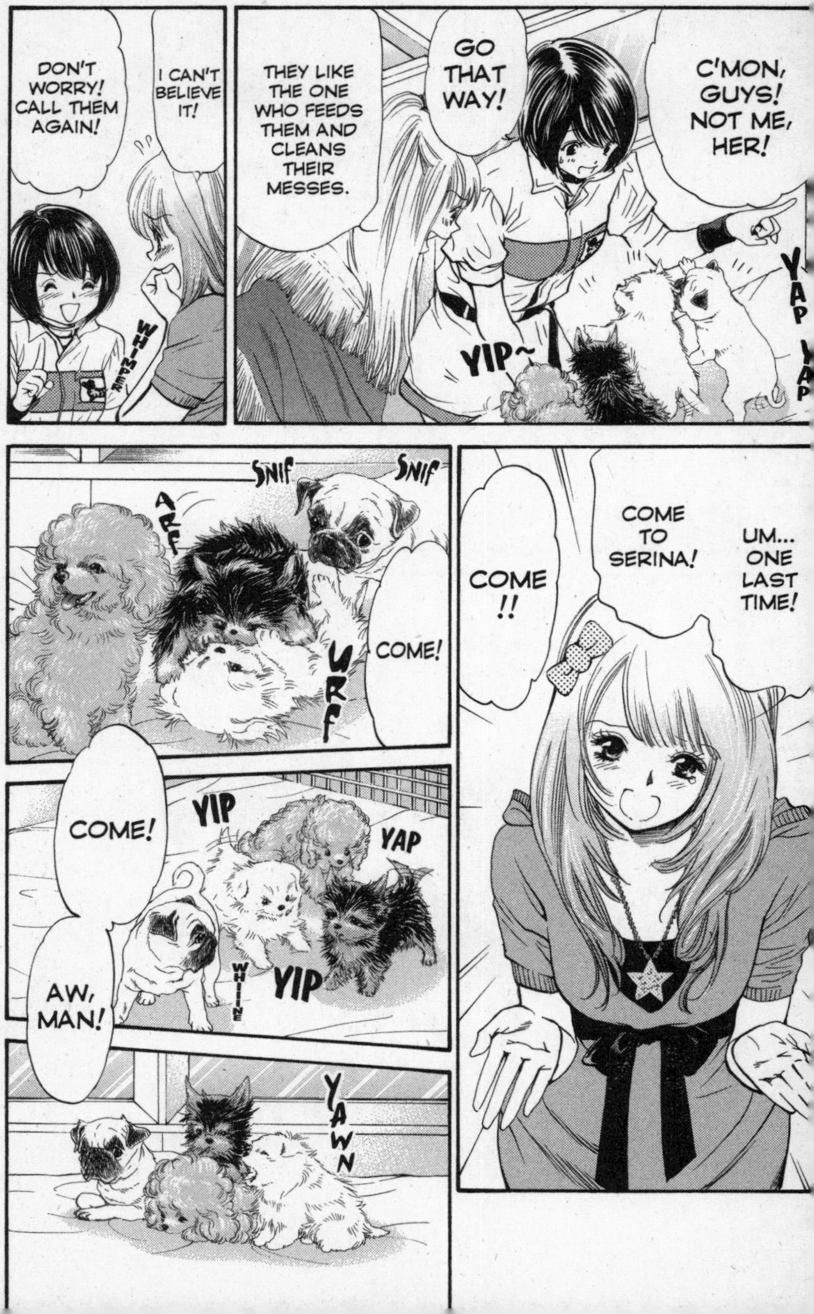
C'MON, GUYS! NOT ME, HER!
GO THAT WAY!
THEY LIKE THE ONE WHO FEEDS THEM AND CLEANS THEIR MESSES.
YAP YAP
YIP~
I CAN'T BELIEVE IT!
DON'T WORRY! CALL THEM AGAIN!
WHIMPER
UM... ONE LAST TIME!
COME TO SERINA!
COME !!
SNIF
SNIF
ARF
COME!
URF
COME!
YIP
YAP
WHINE
YIP
AW, MAN!
YAWN

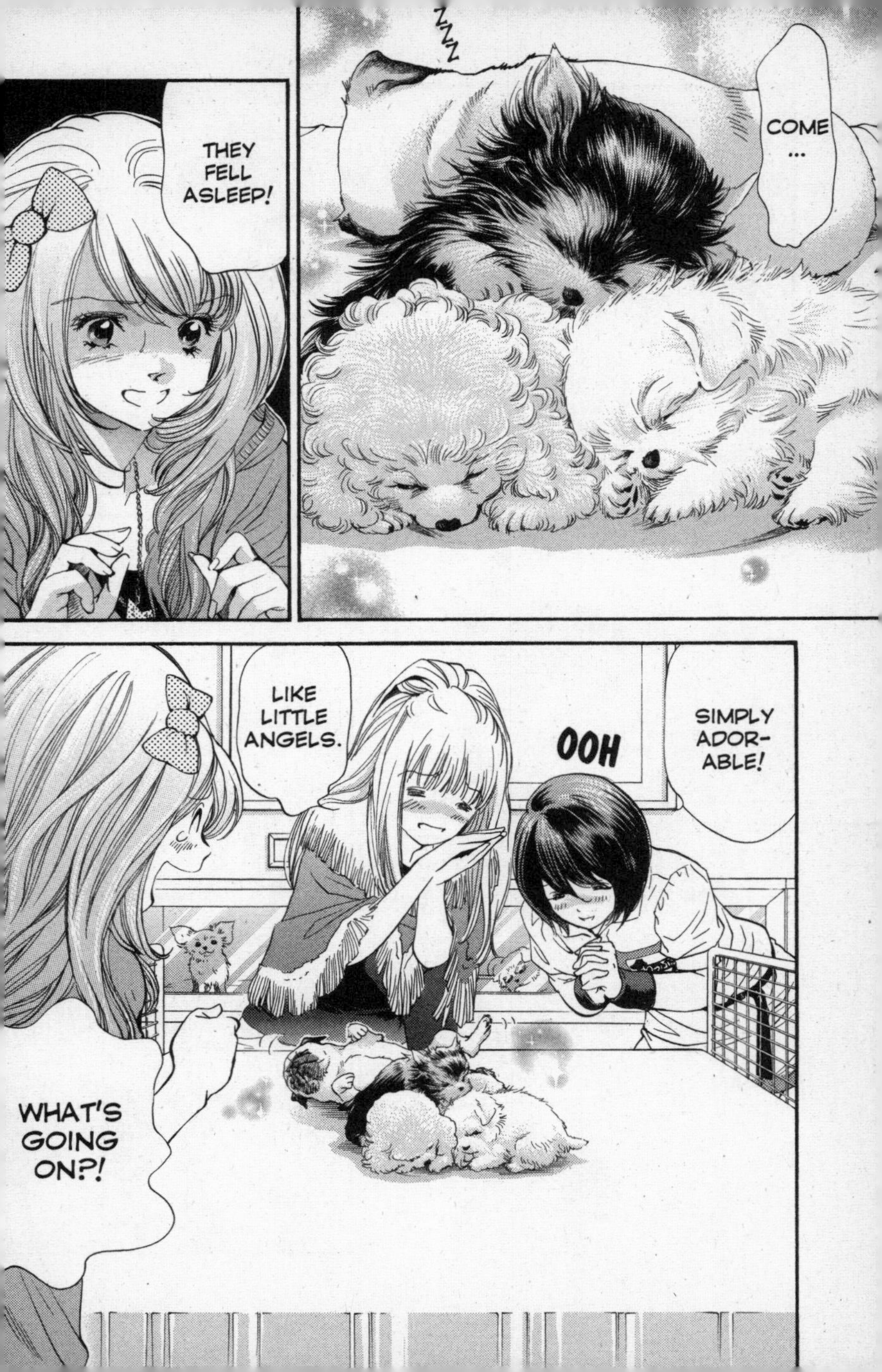
ZZZ
COME ...
THEY FELL ASLEEP!
SIMPLY ADORABLE!
OOH
LIKE LITTLE ANGELS.
WHAT'S GOING ON?!

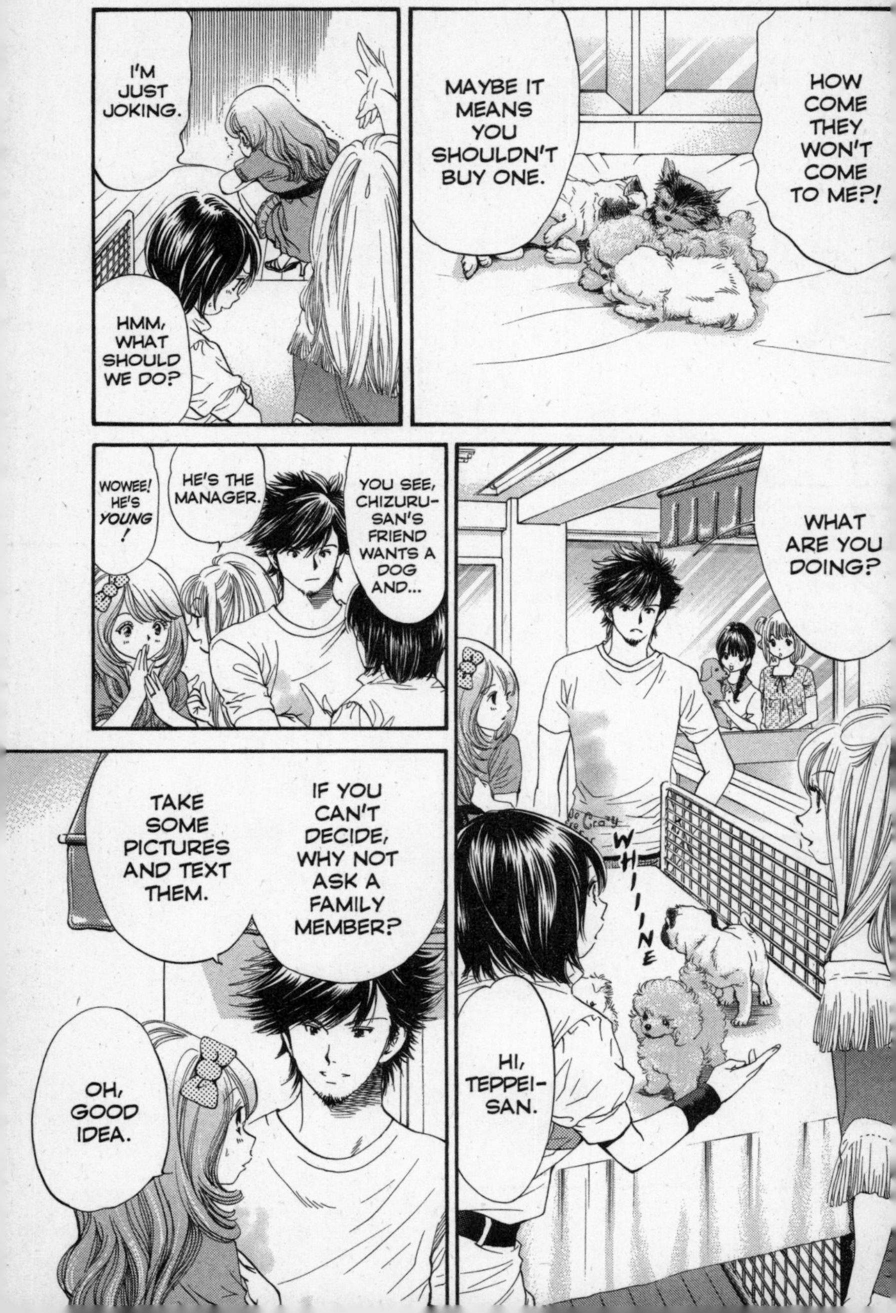
HOW COME THEY WON'T COME TO ME?!
MAYBE IT MEANS YOU SHOULDN'T BUY ONE.
I'M JUST JOKING.
HMM, WHAT SHOULD WE DO?
WHAT ARE YOU DOING?
WHIIINE
HI, TEPPEI-SAN.
YOU SEE, CHIZURU-SAN'S FRIEND WANTS A DOG AND...
HE'S THE MANAGER.
WOWEE! HE'S *YOUNG*!
IF YOU CAN'T DECIDE, WHY NOT ASK A FAMILY MEMBER?
TAKE SOME PICTURES AND TEXT THEM.
OH, GOOD IDEA.

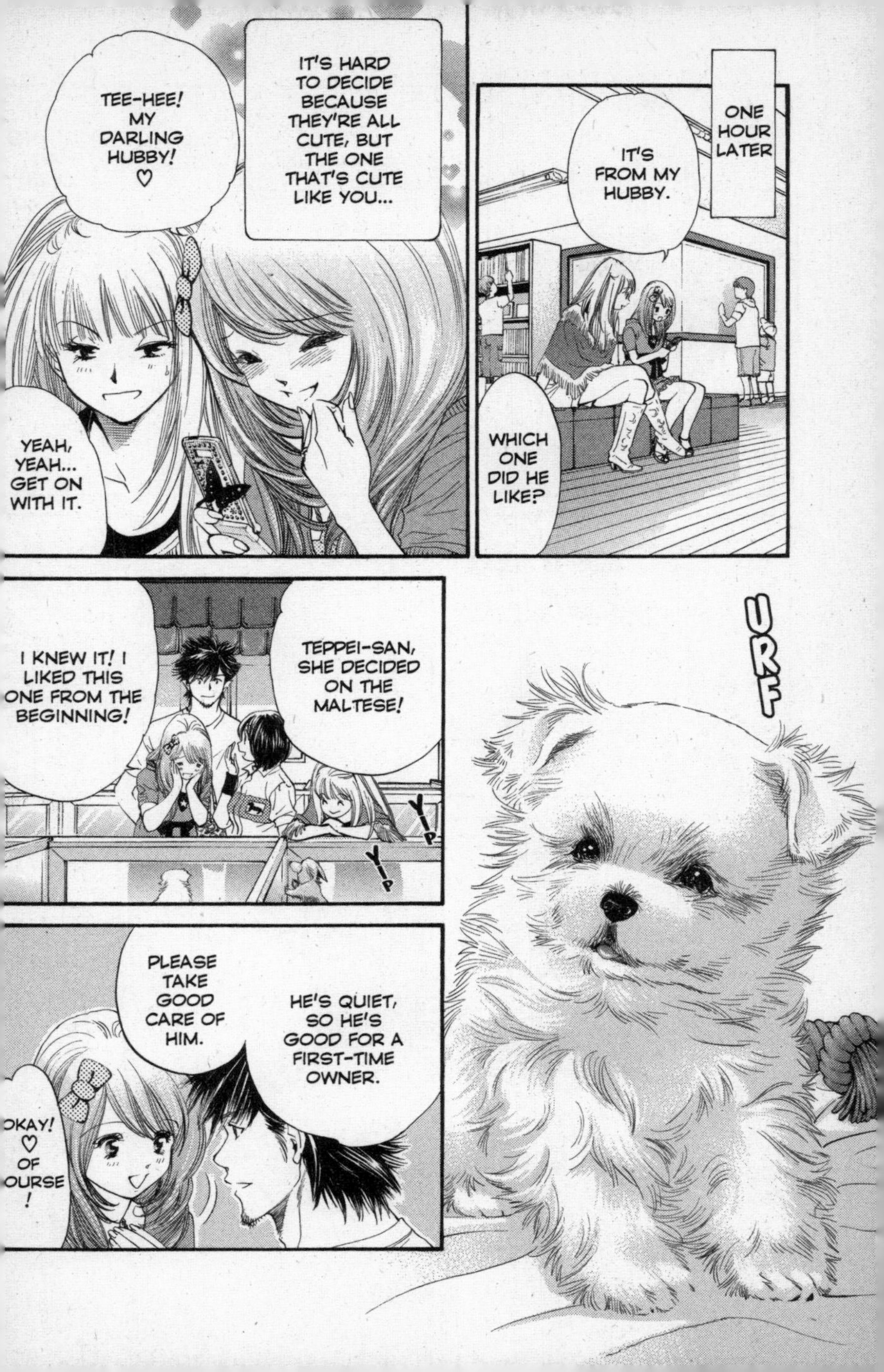
ONE HOUR LATER
IT'S FROM MY HUBBY.
WHICH ONE DID HE LIKE?
IT'S HARD TO DECIDE BECAUSE THEY'RE ALL CUTE, BUT THE ONE THAT'S CUTE LIKE YOU...
TEE-HEE! MY DARLING HUBBY! ♡
YEAH, YEAH... GET ON WITH IT.
URF
TEPPEI-SAN, SHE DECIDED ON THE MALTESE!
I KNEW IT! I LIKED THIS ONE FROM THE BEGINNING!
YIP
YIP
HE'S QUIET, SO HE'S GOOD FOR A FIRST-TIME OWNER.
PLEASE TAKE GOOD CARE OF HIM.
OKAY! ♡ OF OURSE!

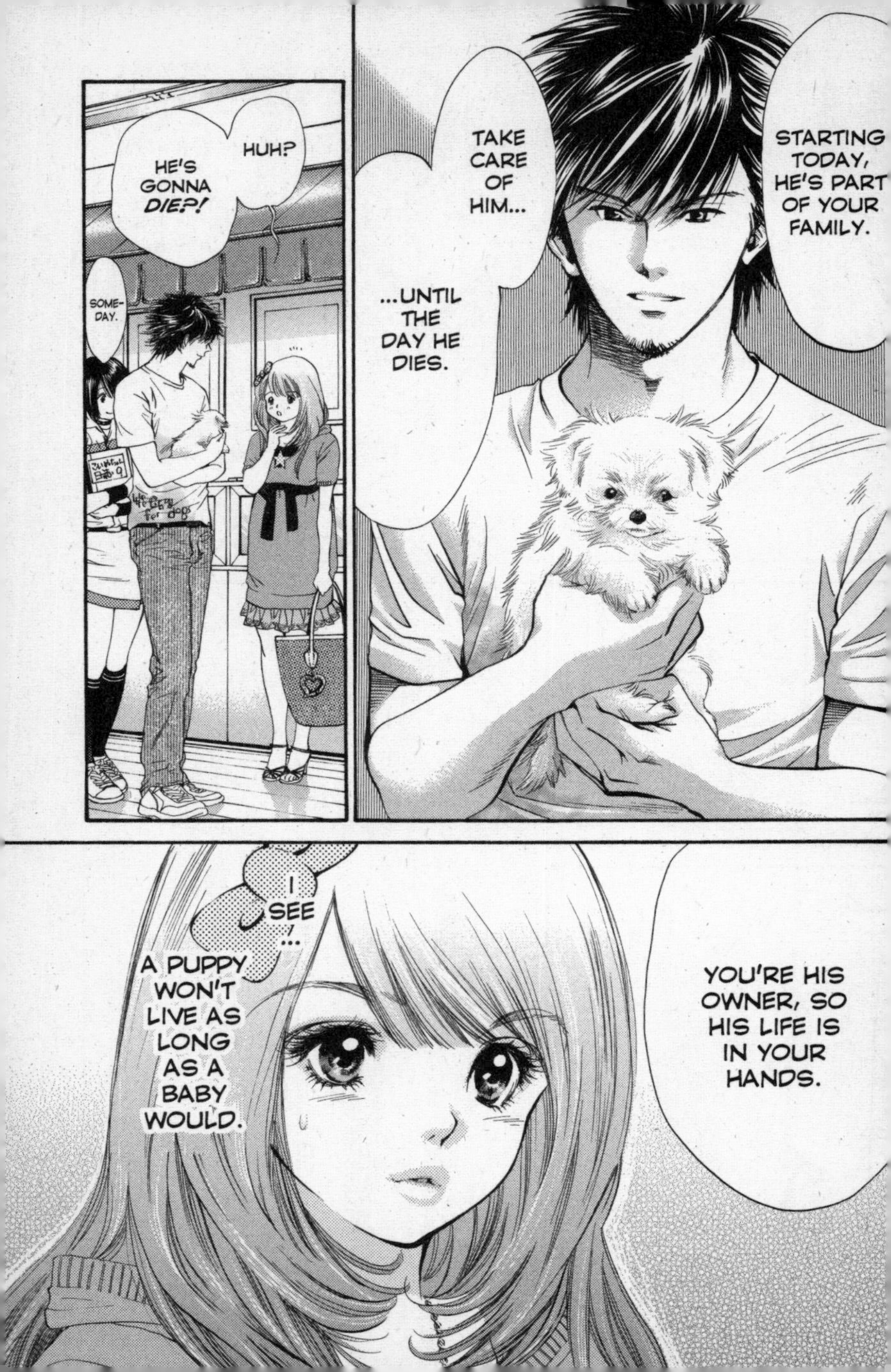
STARTING TODAY, HE'S PART OF YOUR FAMILY.
TAKE CARE OF HIM...
...UNTIL THE DAY HE DIES.
HUH?
HE'S GONNA *DIE?!*
SOME-DAY.
YOU'RE HIS OWNER, SO HIS LIFE IS IN YOUR HANDS.
I SEE...
A PUPPY WON'T LIVE AS LONG AS A BABY WOULD.

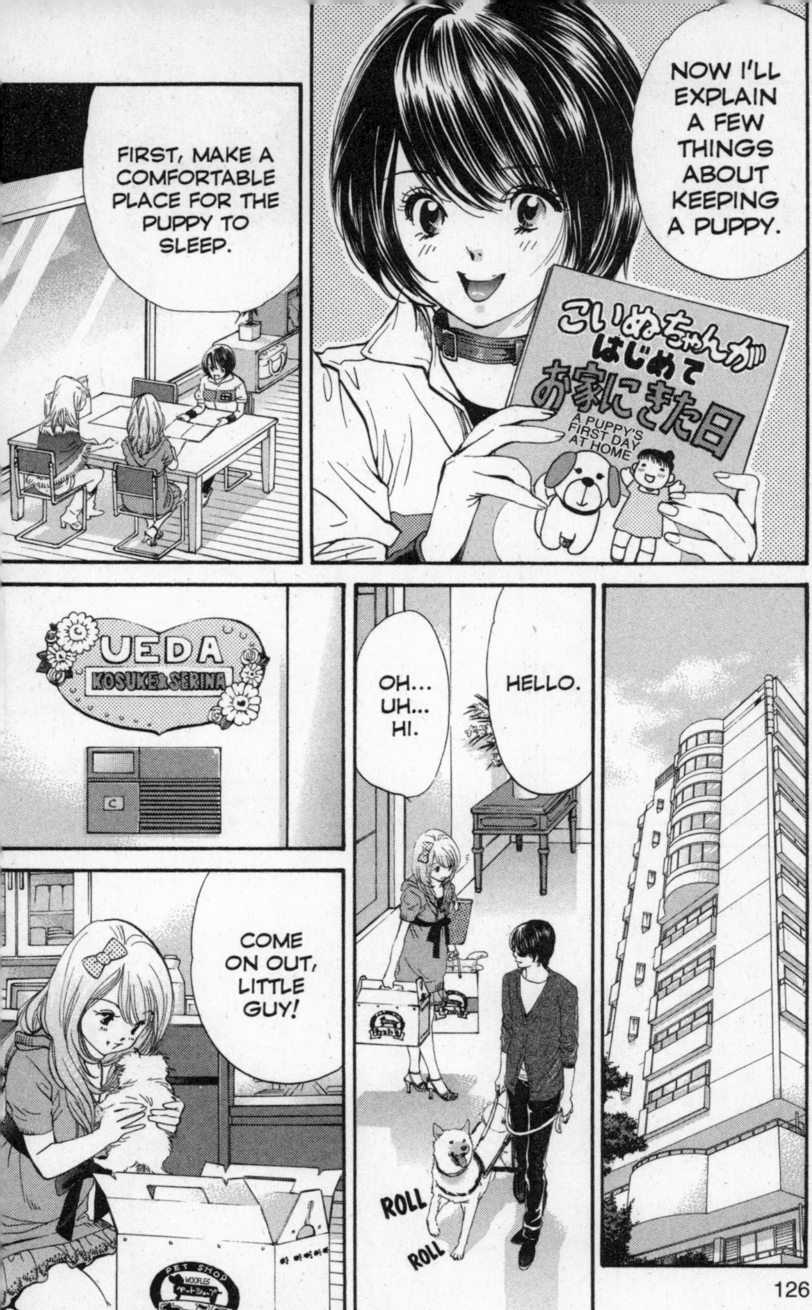

NOW I'LL EXPLAIN A FEW THINGS ABOUT KEEPING A PUPPY.
こいぬちゃんが はじめて お家にきた日
A PUPPY'S FIRST DAY AT HOME
FIRST, MAKE A COMFORTABLE PLACE FOR THE PUPPY TO SLEEP.
HELLO.
OH... UH... HI.
ROLL
ROLL
UEDA
KOSUKE & SERINA
COME ON OUT, LITTLE GUY!
PET SHOP
WOOFLES
わっふる

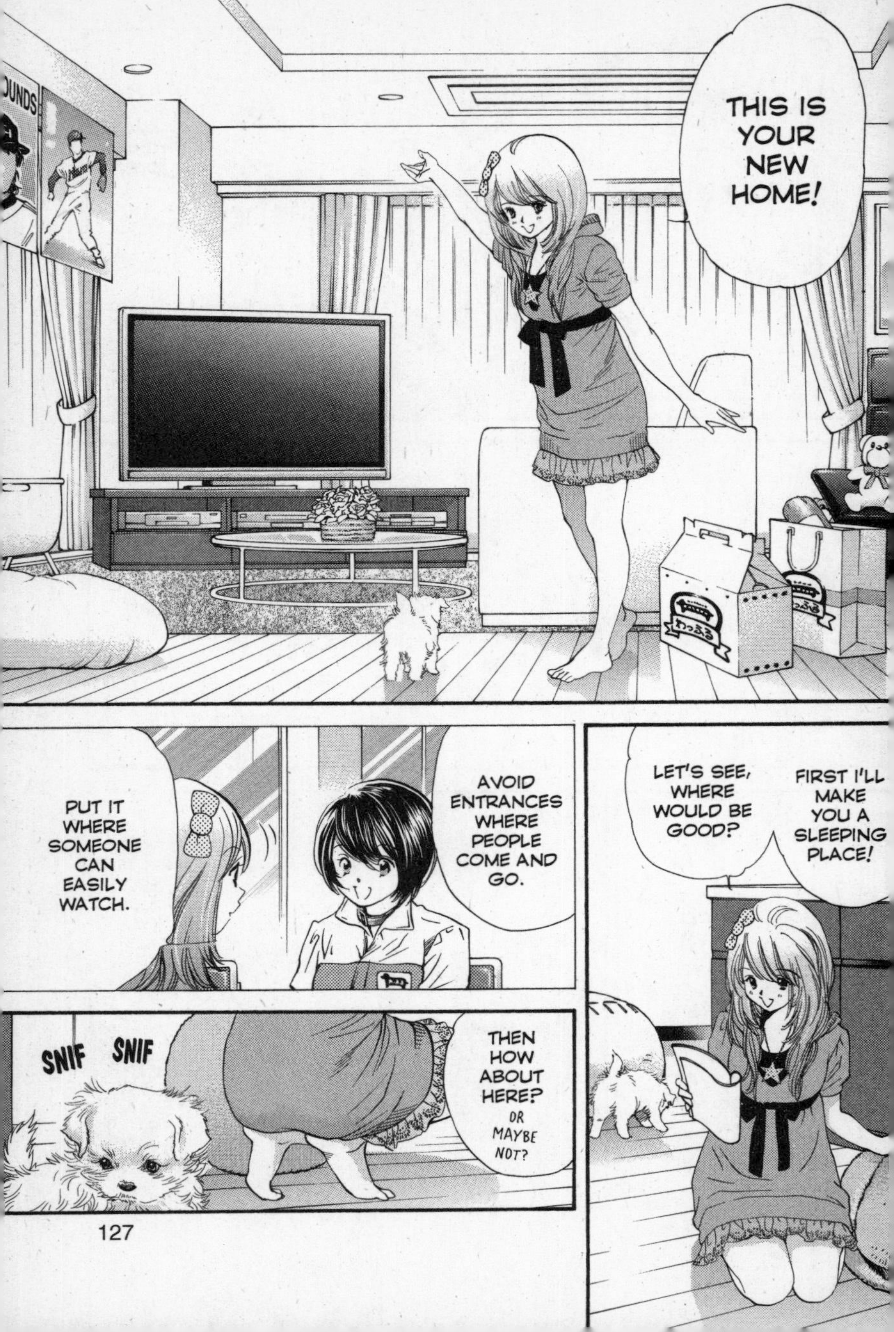
THIS IS YOUR NEW HOME!
FIRST I'LL MAKE YOU A SLEEPING PLACE!
LET'S SEE, WHERE WOULD BE GOOD?
AVOID ENTRANCES WHERE PEOPLE COME AND GO.
PUT IT WHERE SOMEONE CAN EASILY WATCH.
THEN HOW ABOUT HERE?
OR MAYBE NOT?
SNIF SNIF

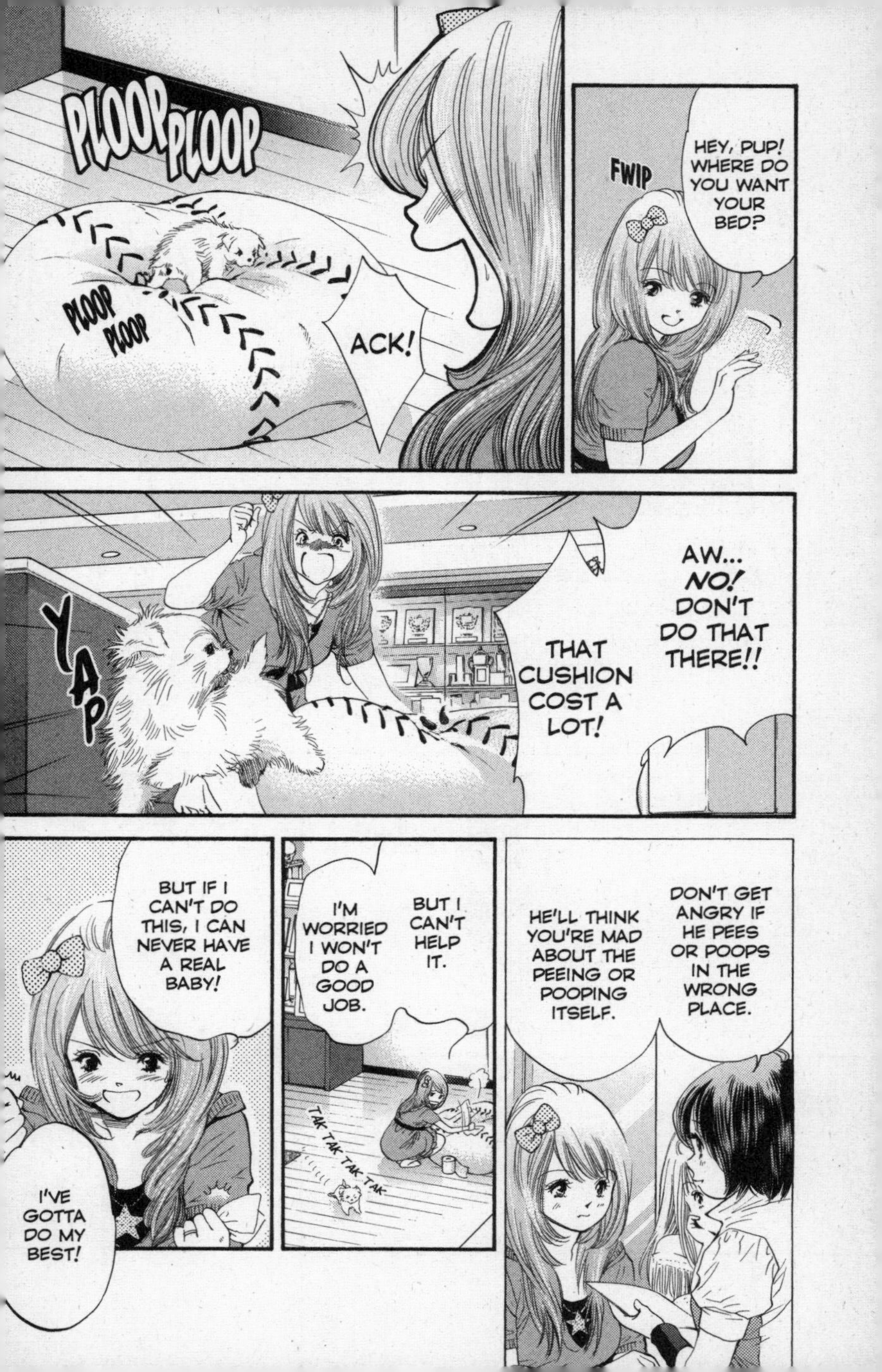
FWIP
HEY, PUP! WHERE DO YOU WANT YOUR BED?
ACK!
PLOOP PLOOP
PLOOP PLOOP
AW... *NO!* DON'T DO THAT THERE!!
THAT CUSHION COST A LOT!
YAP
DON'T GET ANGRY IF HE PEES OR POOPS IN THE WRONG PLACE.
HE'LL THINK YOU'RE MAD ABOUT THE PEEING OR POOPING ITSELF.
BUT I CAN'T HELP IT.
I'M WORRIED I WON'T DO A GOOD JOB.
TAK TAK TAK TAK
BUT IF I CAN'T DO THIS, I CAN NEVER HAVE A REAL BABY!
I'VE GOTTA DO MY BEST!

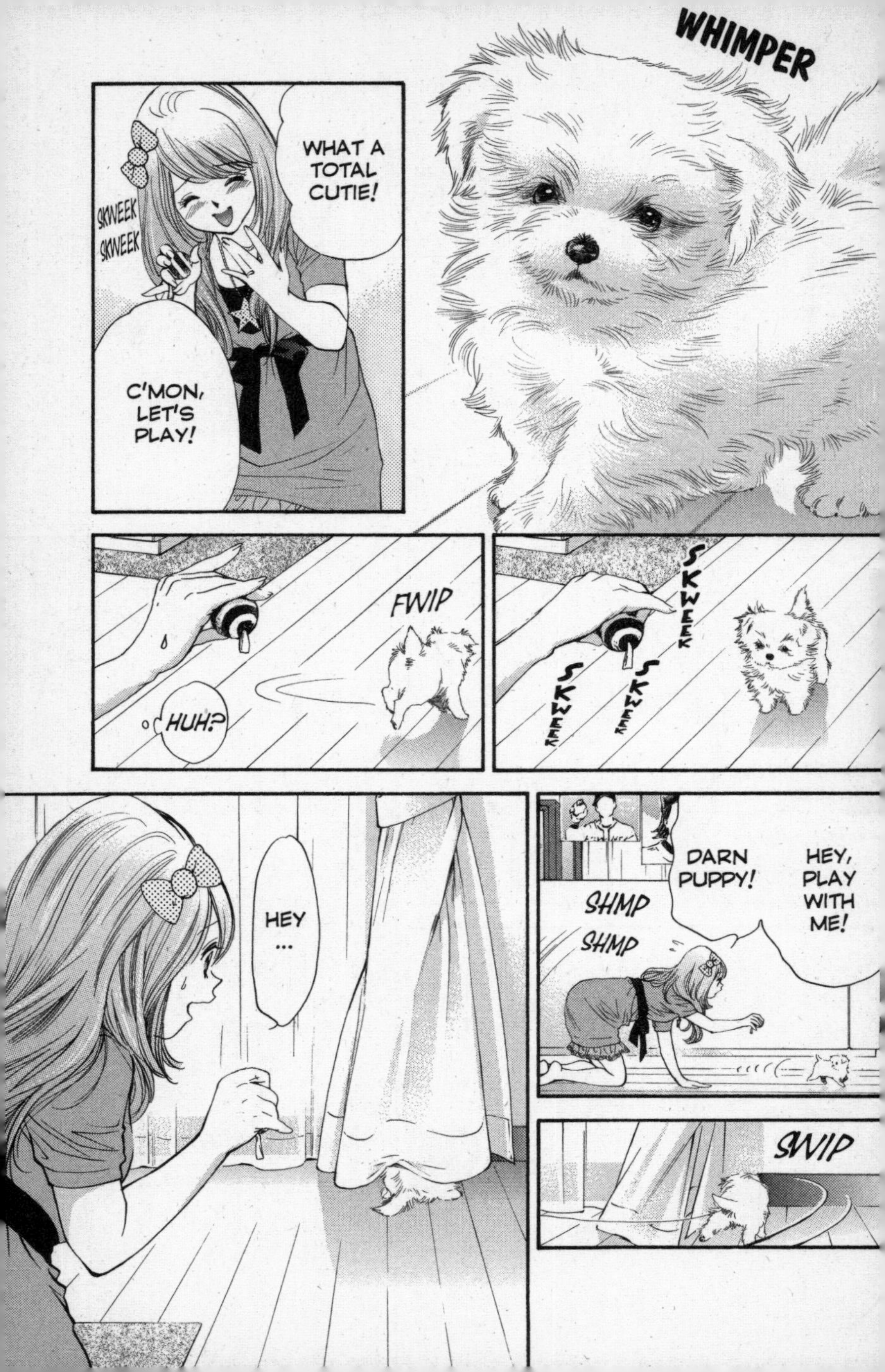
WHIMPER
WHAT A TOTAL CUTIE!
SKWEEK SKWEEK
C'MON, LET'S PLAY!
SKWEEK
SKWEEK
SKWEEK
FWIP
HUH?
HEY, PLAY WITH ME!
DARN PUPPY!
SHMP SHMP
SWIP
HEY ...

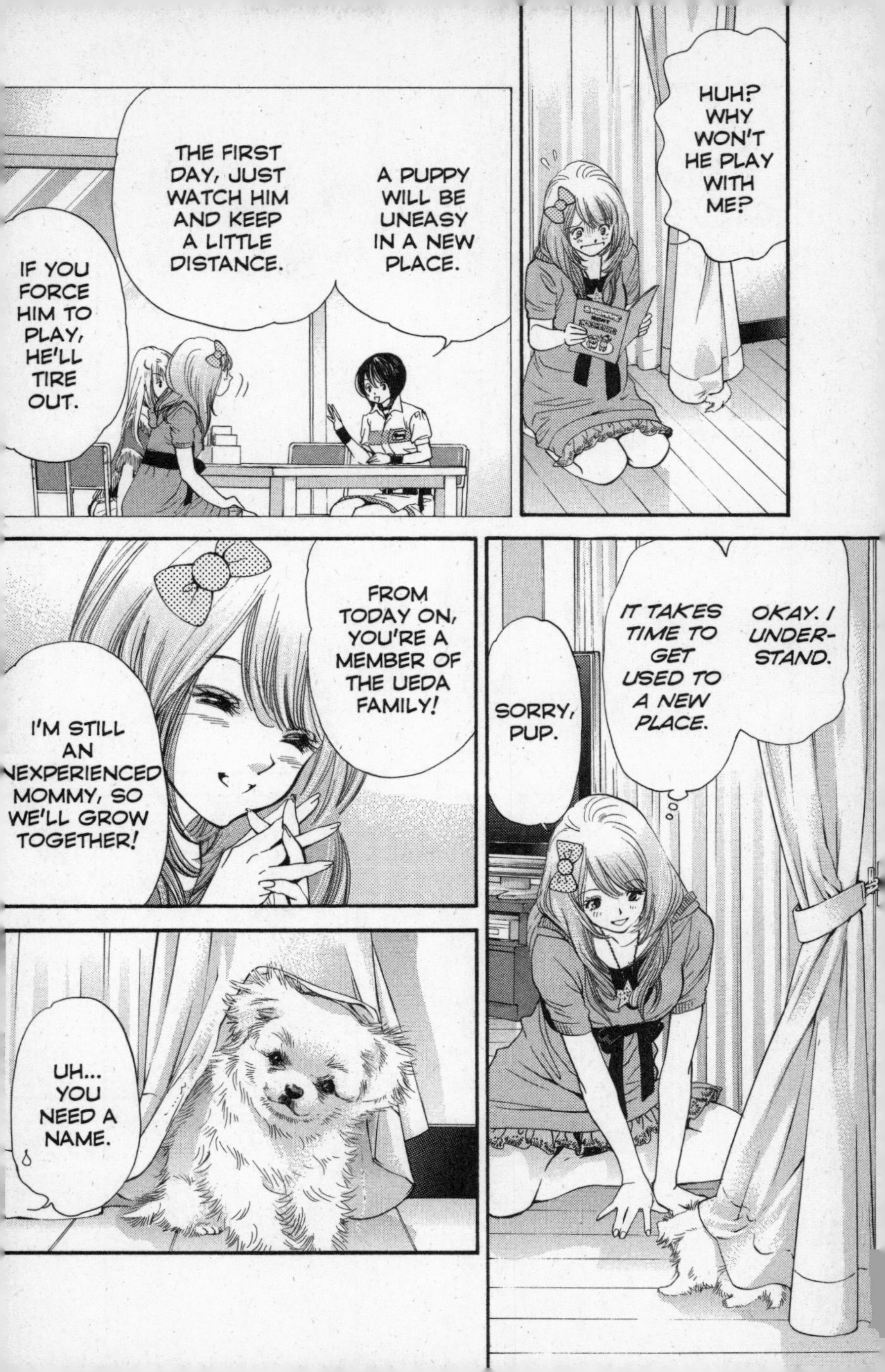

HUH? WHY WON'T HE PLAY WITH ME?
A PUPPY WILL BE UNEASY IN A NEW PLACE.
THE FIRST DAY, JUST WATCH HIM AND KEEP A LITTLE DISTANCE.
IF YOU FORCE HIM TO PLAY, HE'LL TIRE OUT.
OKAY. I UNDERSTAND.
IT TAKES TIME TO GET USED TO A NEW PLACE.
SORRY, PUP.
FROM TODAY ON, YOU'RE A MEMBER OF THE UEDA FAMILY!
I'M STILL AN INEXPERIENCED MOMMY, SO WE'LL GROW TOGETHER!
UH... YOU NEED A NAME.

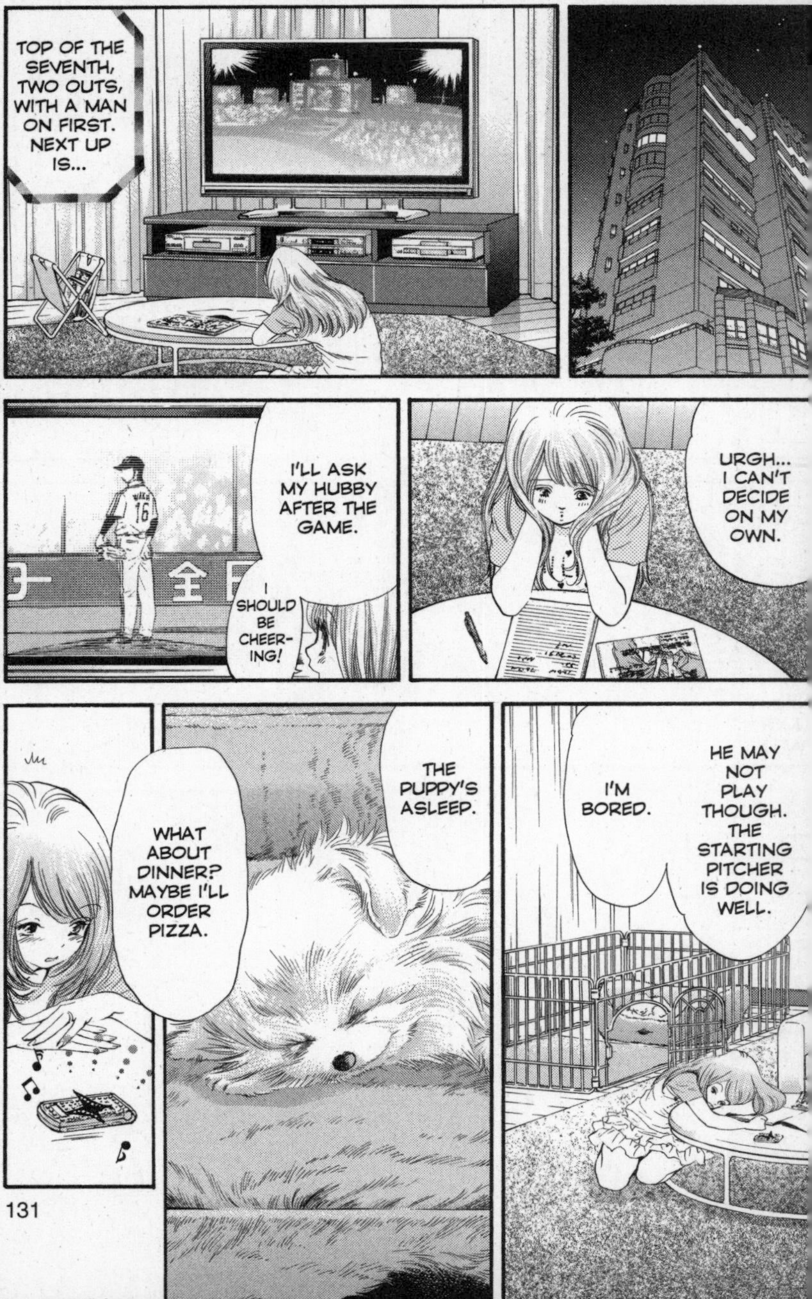
TOP OF THE SEVENTH, TWO OUTS, WITH A MAN ON FIRST. NEXT UP IS...
URGH... I CAN'T DECIDE ON MY OWN.
I'LL ASK MY HUBBY AFTER THE GAME.
I SHOULD BE CHEERING!
HE MAY NOT PLAY THOUGH. THE STARTING PITCHER IS DOING WELL.
I'M BORED.
THE PUPPY'S ASLEEP.
WHAT ABOUT DINNER? MAYBE I'LL ORDER PIZZA.

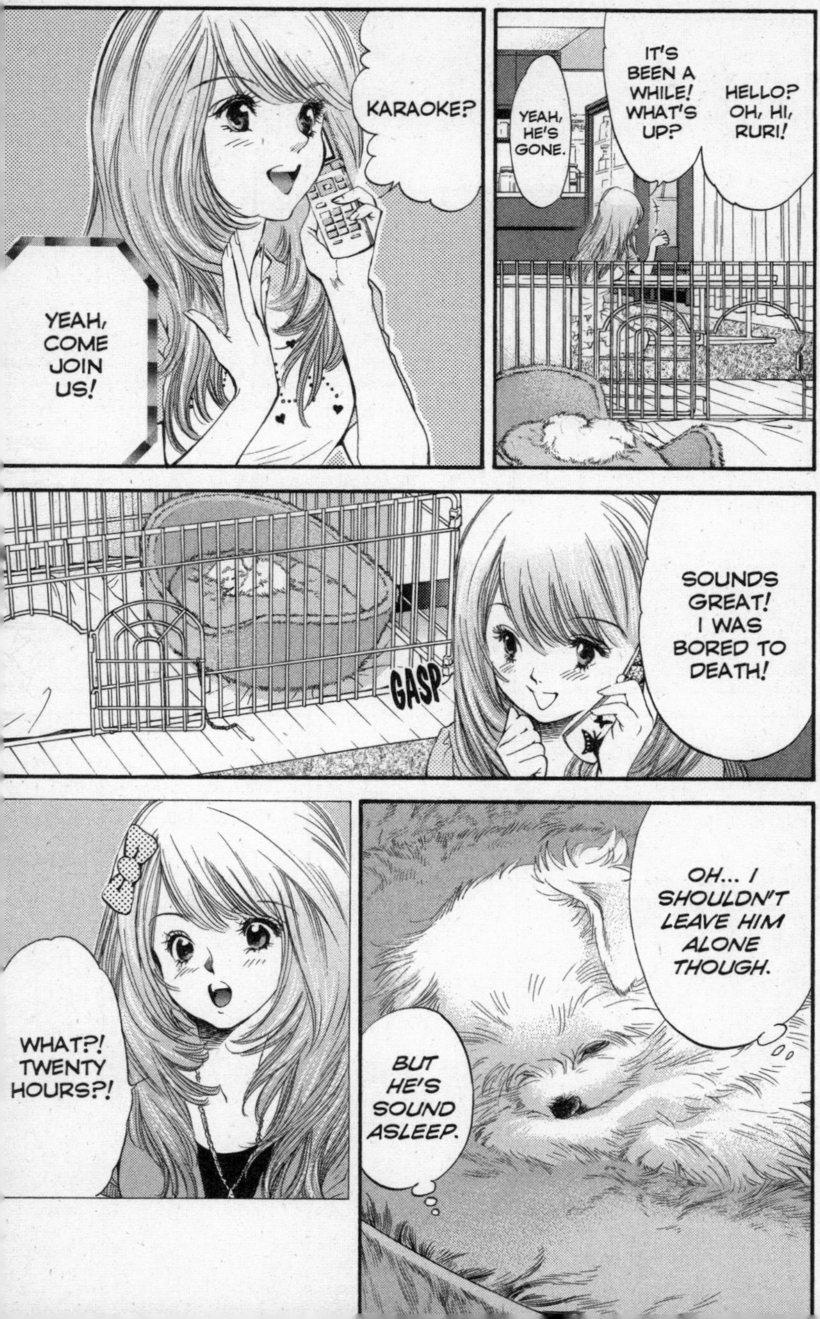
HELLO? OH, HI, RURI!
IT'S BEEN A WHILE! WHAT'S UP?
YEAH, HE'S GONE.
KARAOKE?
YEAH, COME JOIN US!
SOUNDS GREAT! I WAS BORED TO DEATH!
GASP
OH... I SHOULDN'T LEAVE HIM ALONE THOUGH.
BUT HE'S SOUND ASLEEP.
WHAT?! TWENTY HOURS?!

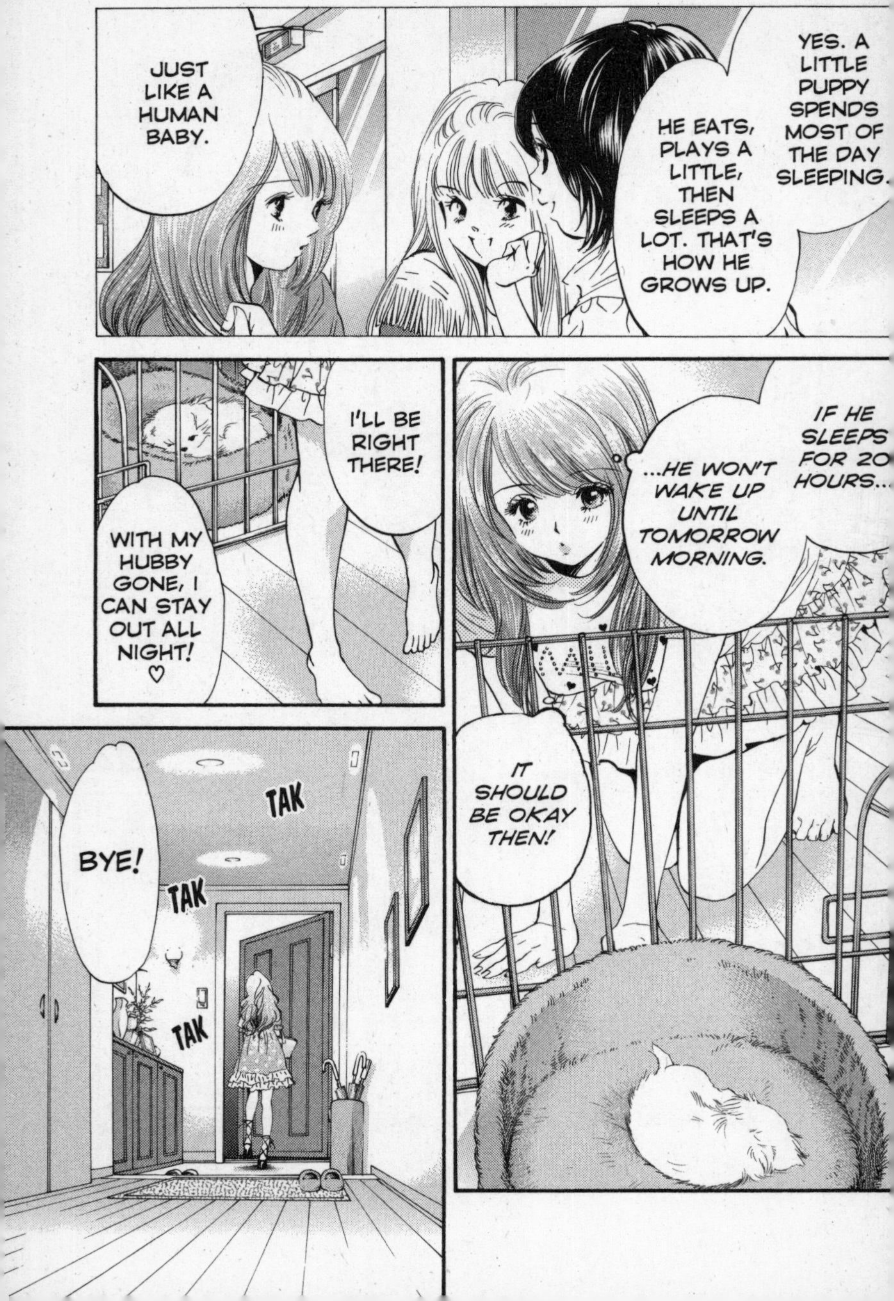
YES. A LITTLE PUPPY SPENDS MOST OF THE DAY SLEEPING.
HE EATS, PLAYS A LITTLE, THEN SLEEPS A LOT. THAT'S HOW HE GROWS UP.
JUST LIKE A HUMAN BABY.
IF HE SLEEPS FOR 20 HOURS...
...HE WON'T WAKE UP UNTIL TOMORROW MORNING.
IT SHOULD BE OKAY THEN!
I'LL BE RIGHT THERE!
WITH MY HUBBY GONE, I CAN STAY OUT ALL NIGHT! ♡
TAK
TAK
TAK
BYE!

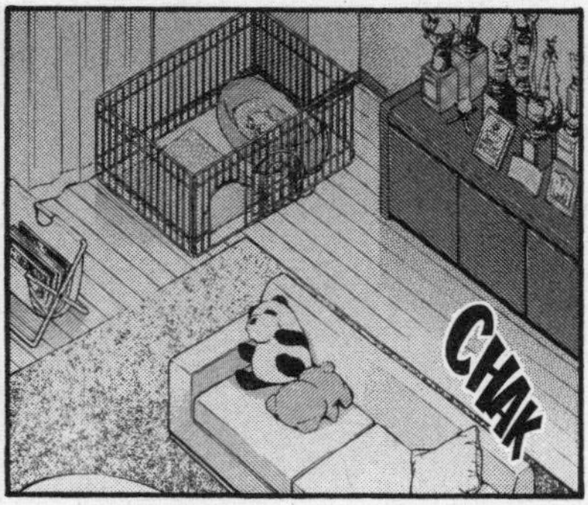
CHAK
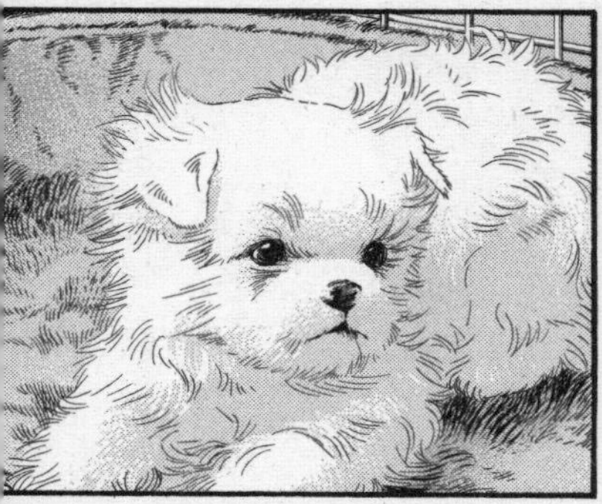
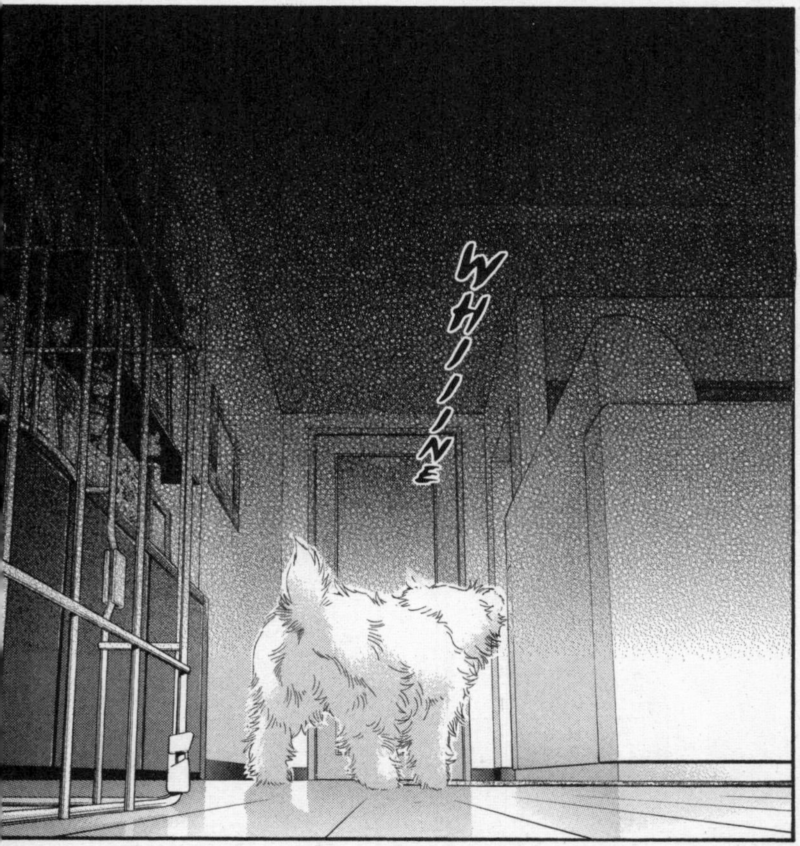
WHIIIINE

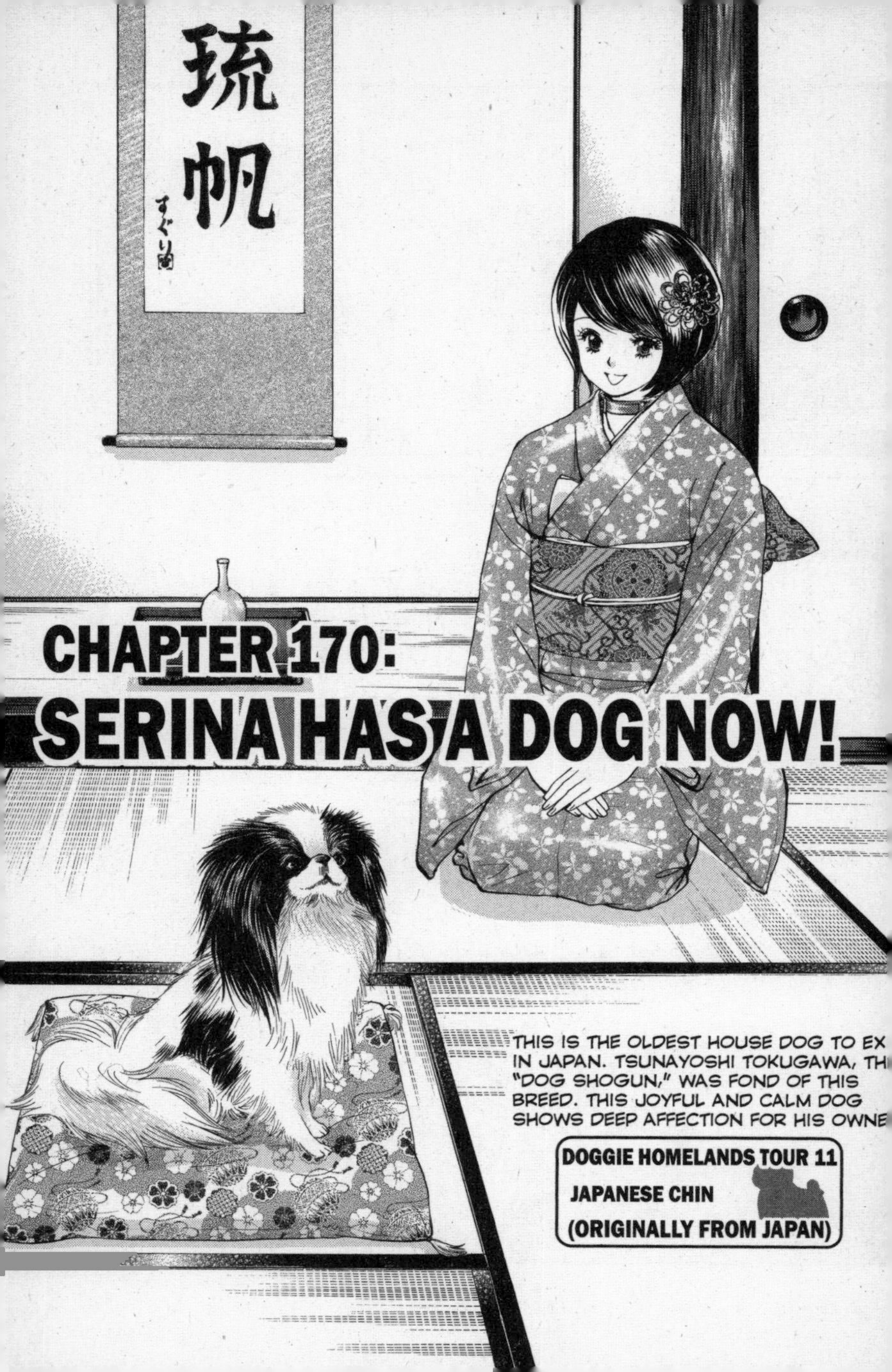
琉帆
すぐり
CHAPTER 170:
SERINA HAS A DOG NOW!
THIS IS THE OLDEST HOUSE DOG TO EX IN JAPAN. TSUNAYOSHI TOKUGAWA, TH "DOG SHOGUN," WAS FOND OF THIS BREED. THIS JOYFUL AND CALM DOG SHOWS DEEP AFFECTION FOR HIS OWNE
DOGGIE HOMELANDS TOUR 11
JAPANESE CHIN
(ORIGINALLY FROM JAPAN)

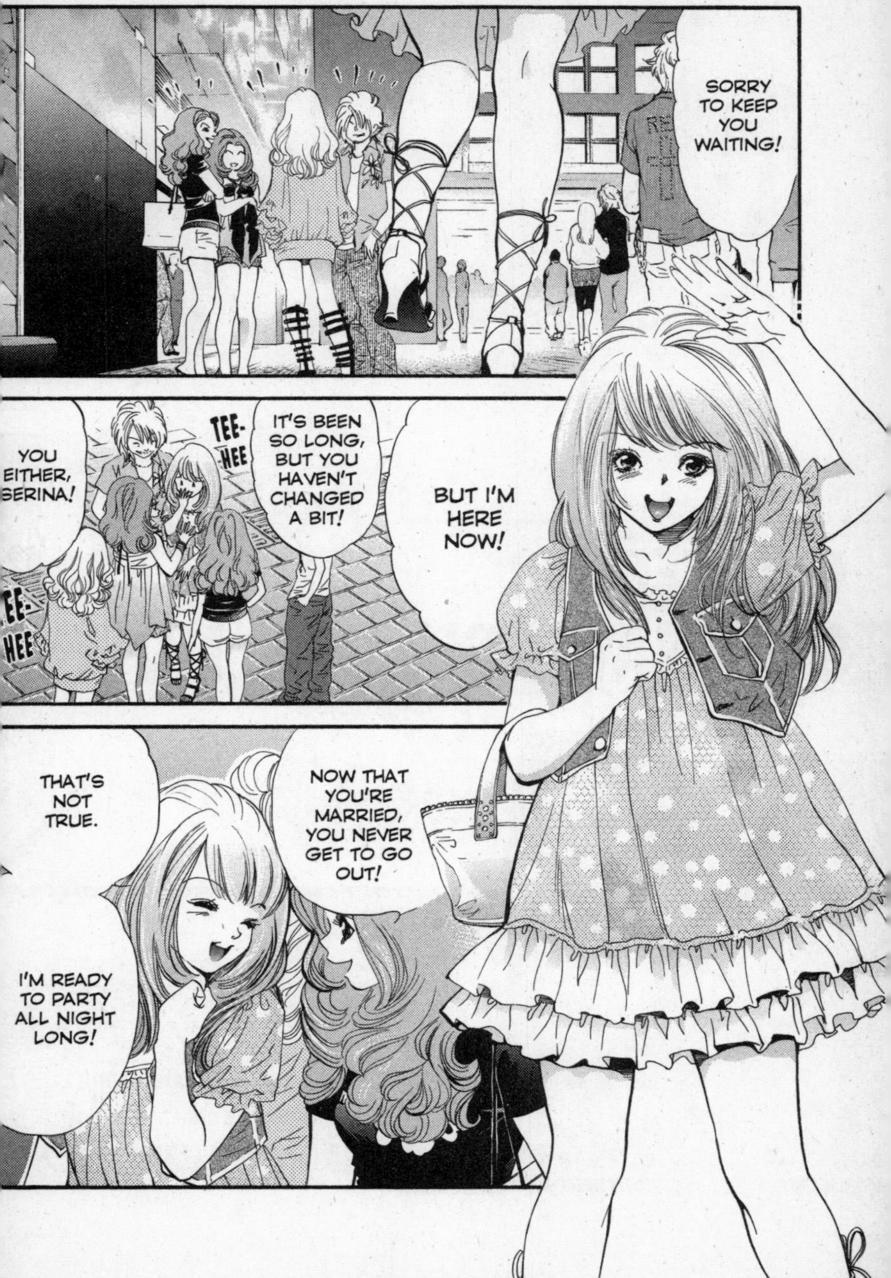
SORRY TO KEEP YOU WAITING!
BUT I'M HERE NOW!
IT'S BEEN SO LONG, BUT YOU HAVEN'T CHANGED A BIT!
TEE-HEE
YOU EITHER, SERINA!
EE-HEE
NOW THAT YOU'RE MARRIED, YOU NEVER GET TO GO OUT!
THAT'S NOT TRUE.
I'M READY TO PARTY ALL NIGHT LONG!

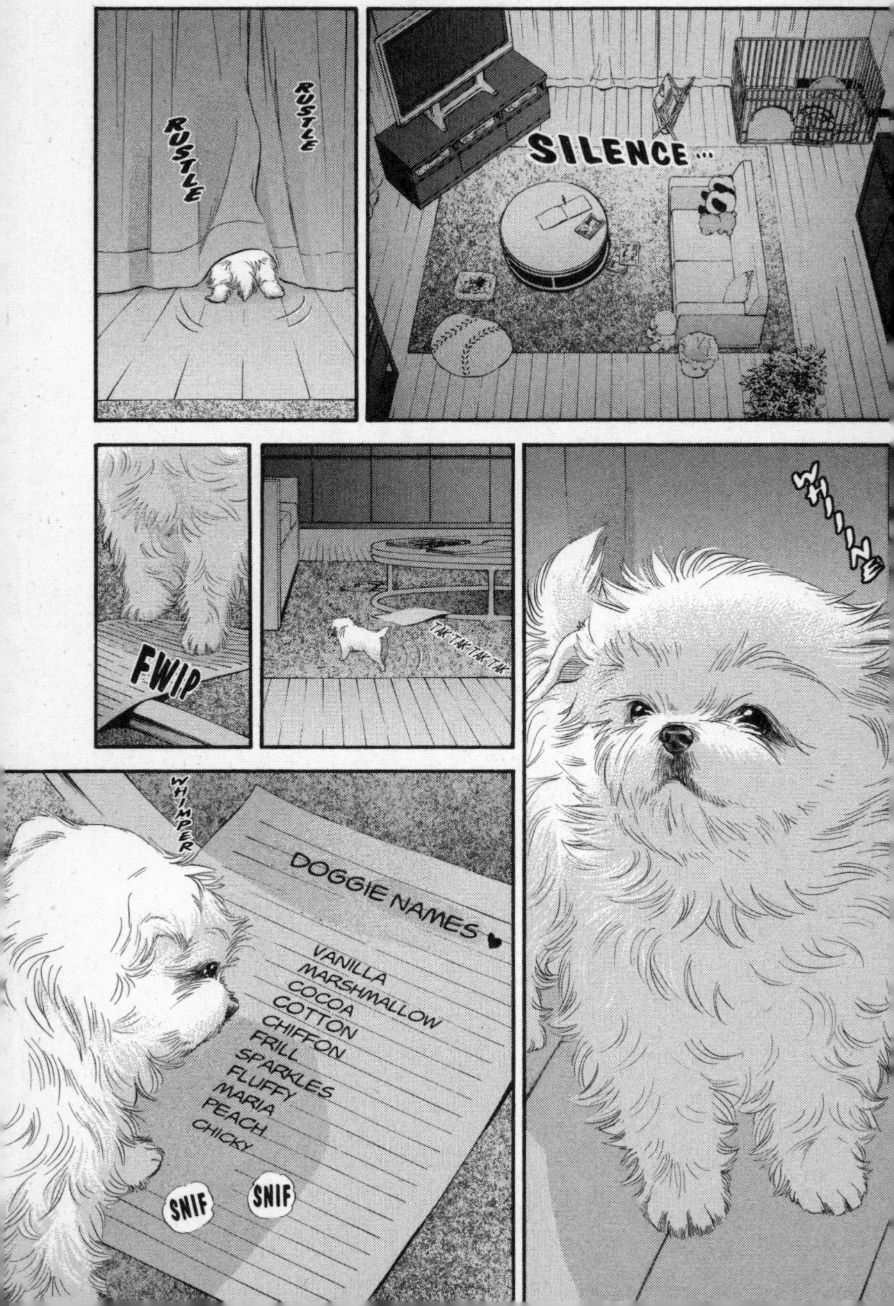
SILENCE...
RUSTLE
RUSTLE
WHIIINE
TAK TAK TAK TAK
FWIP
WHIMPER
DOGGIE NAMES ♥
VANILLA
MARSHMALLOW
COCOA
COTTON
CHIFFON
FRILL
SPARKLES
FLUFFY
MARIA
PEACH
CHICKY
SNIF
SNIF

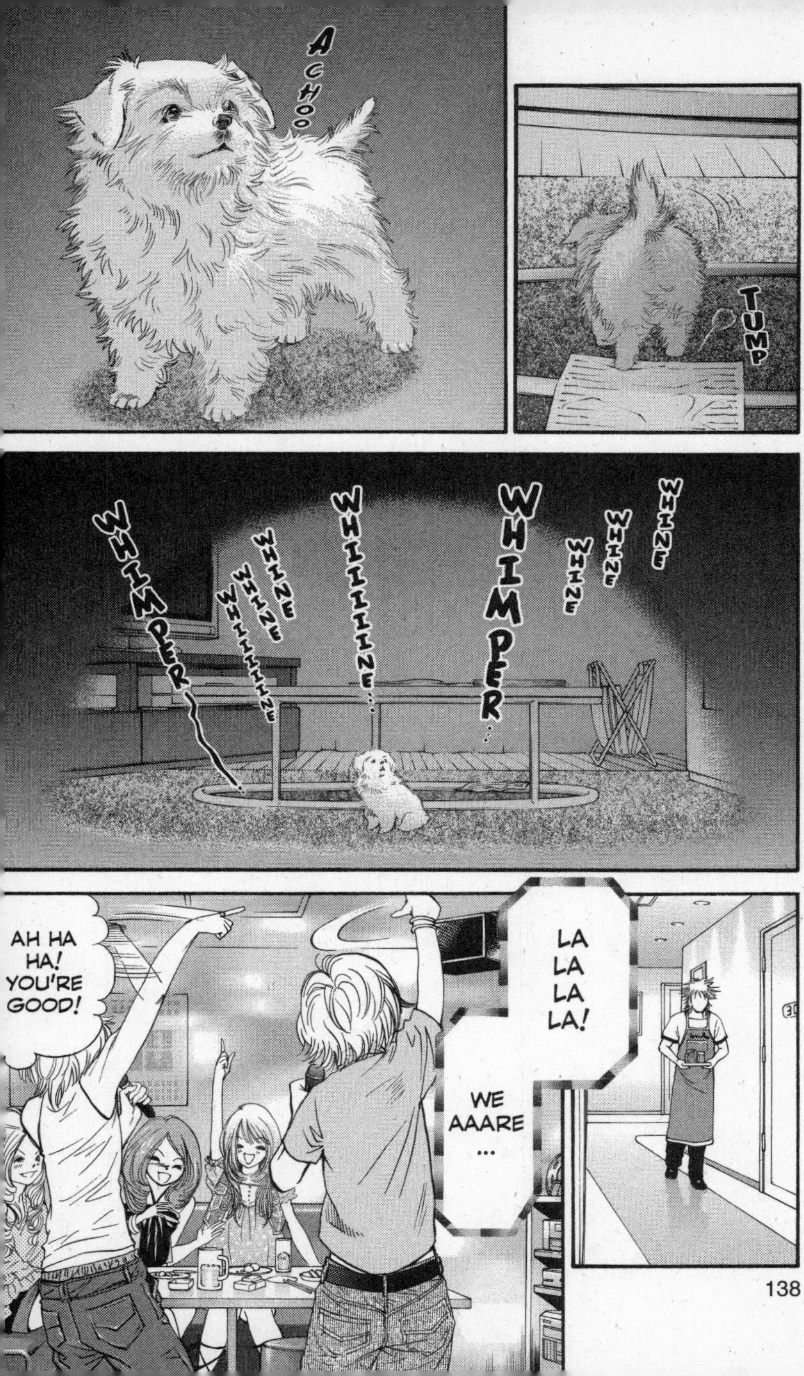
TUMP
ACHOO
WHINE
WHINE
WHINE
WHIMPER...
WHIIIIINE...
WHINE
WHINE
WHIIIIIINE
WHIMPER~
LA LA LA LA!
WE AAARE...
AH HA HA! YOU'RE GOOD!

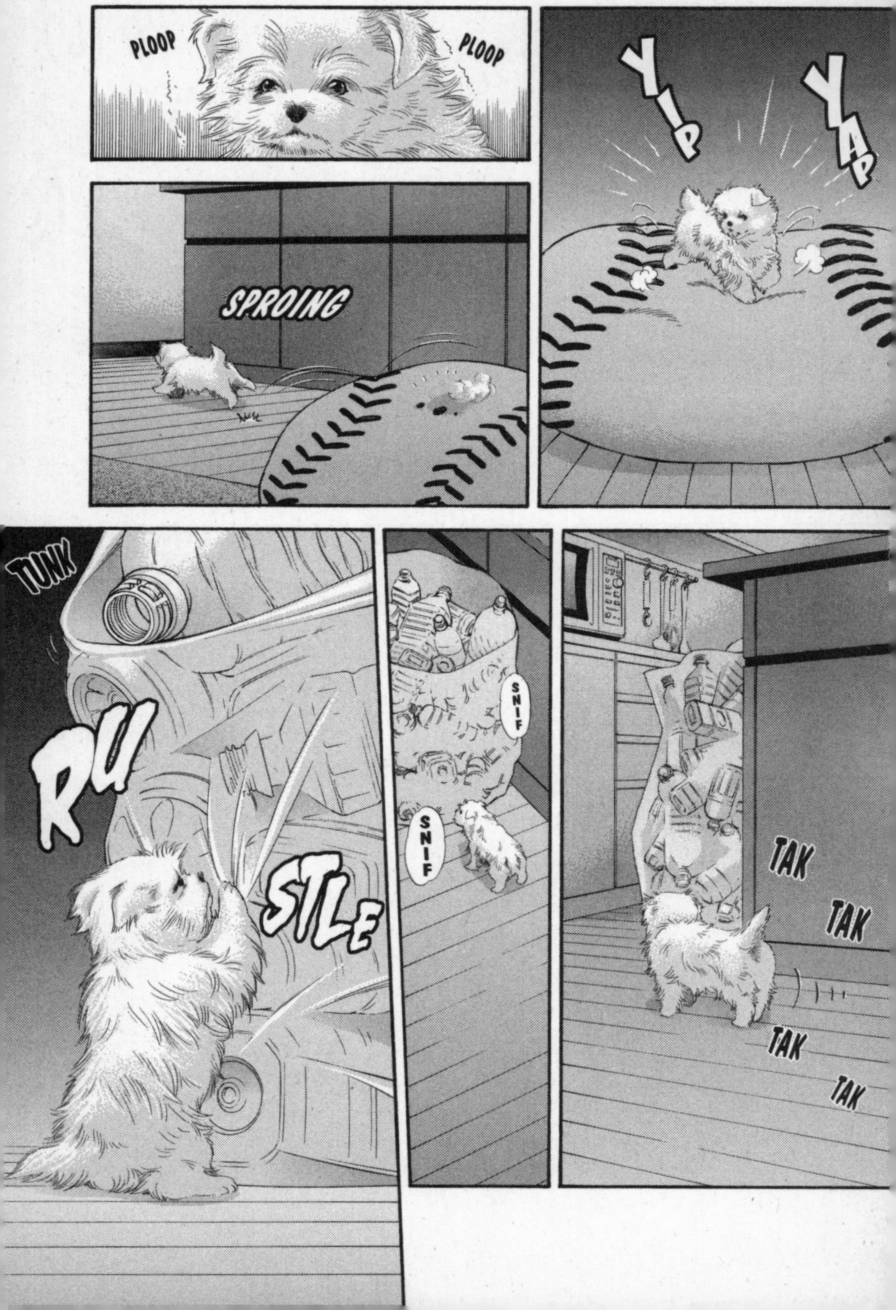
YIP
YAP
PLOOP
PLOOP
SPROING
TAK
TAK
TAK
TAK
SNIF
SNIF
TUNK
RUSTLE

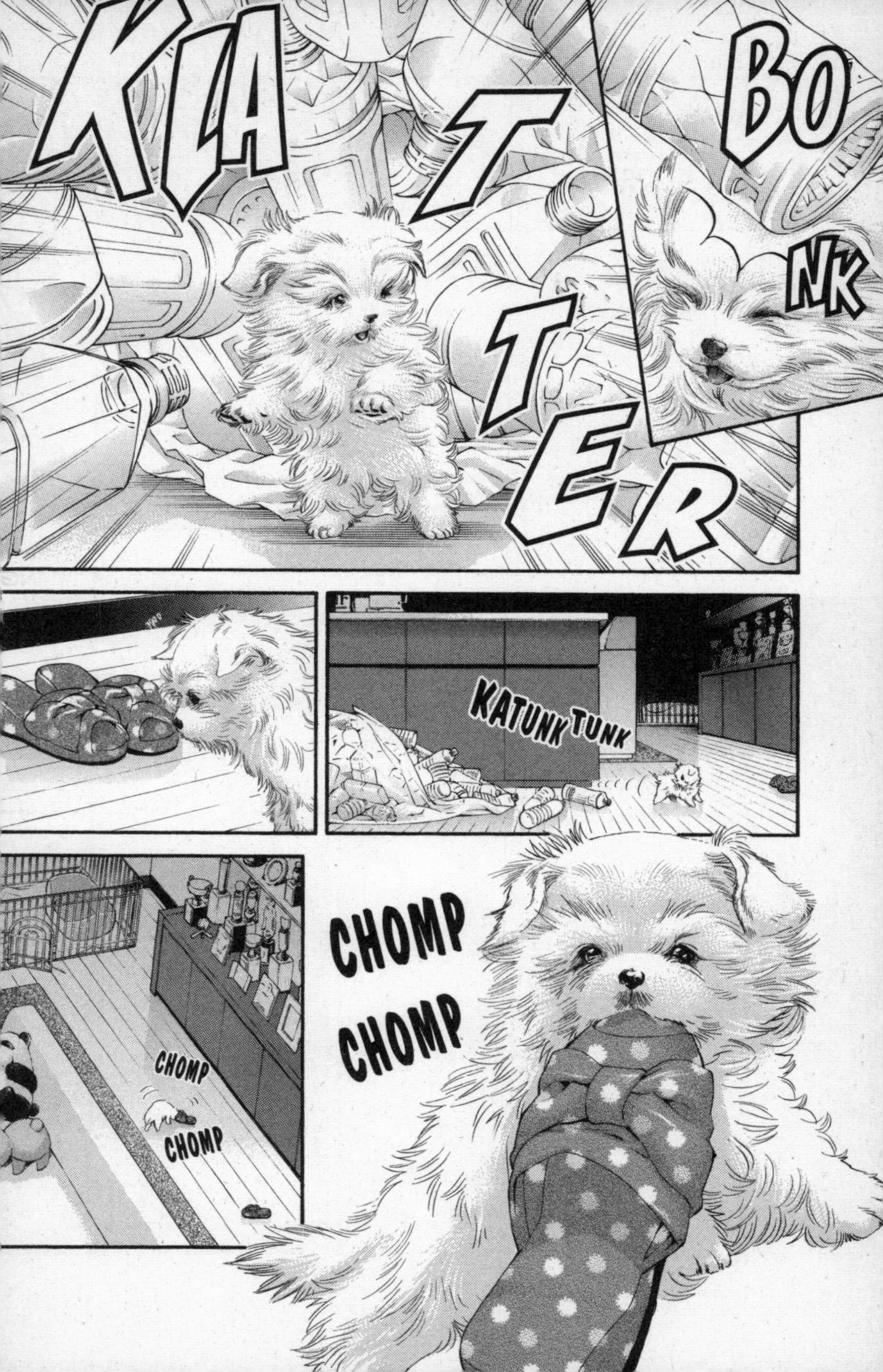
BONK
KLATTER
KATUNK TUNK
CHOMP CHOMP
CHOMP CHOMP

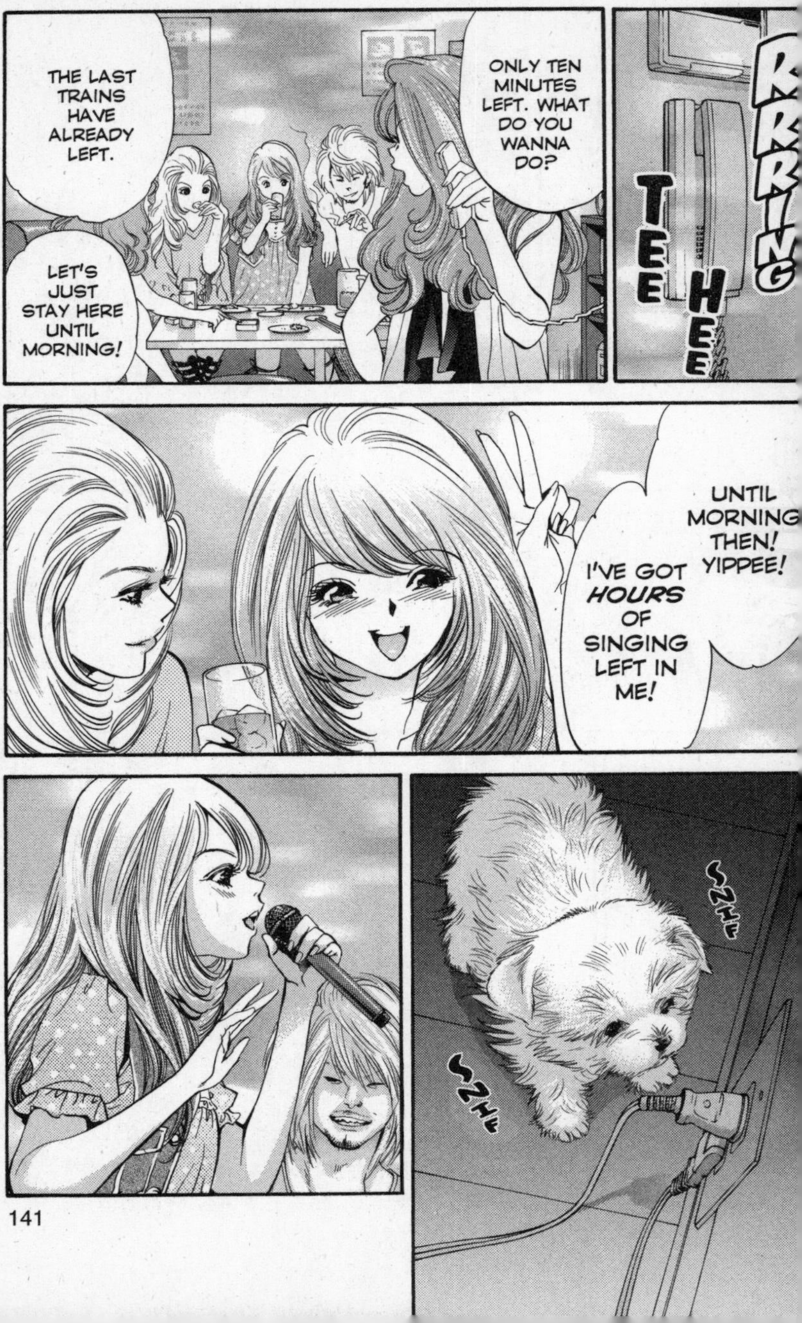
RRRING
TEE HEE
ONLY TEN MINUTES LEFT. WHAT DO YOU WANNA DO?
THE LAST TRAINS HAVE ALREADY LEFT.
LET'S JUST STAY HERE UNTIL MORNING!
UNTIL MORNING THEN! YIPPEE!
I'VE GOT *HOURS* OF SINGING LEFT IN ME!
SNIF
SNIF

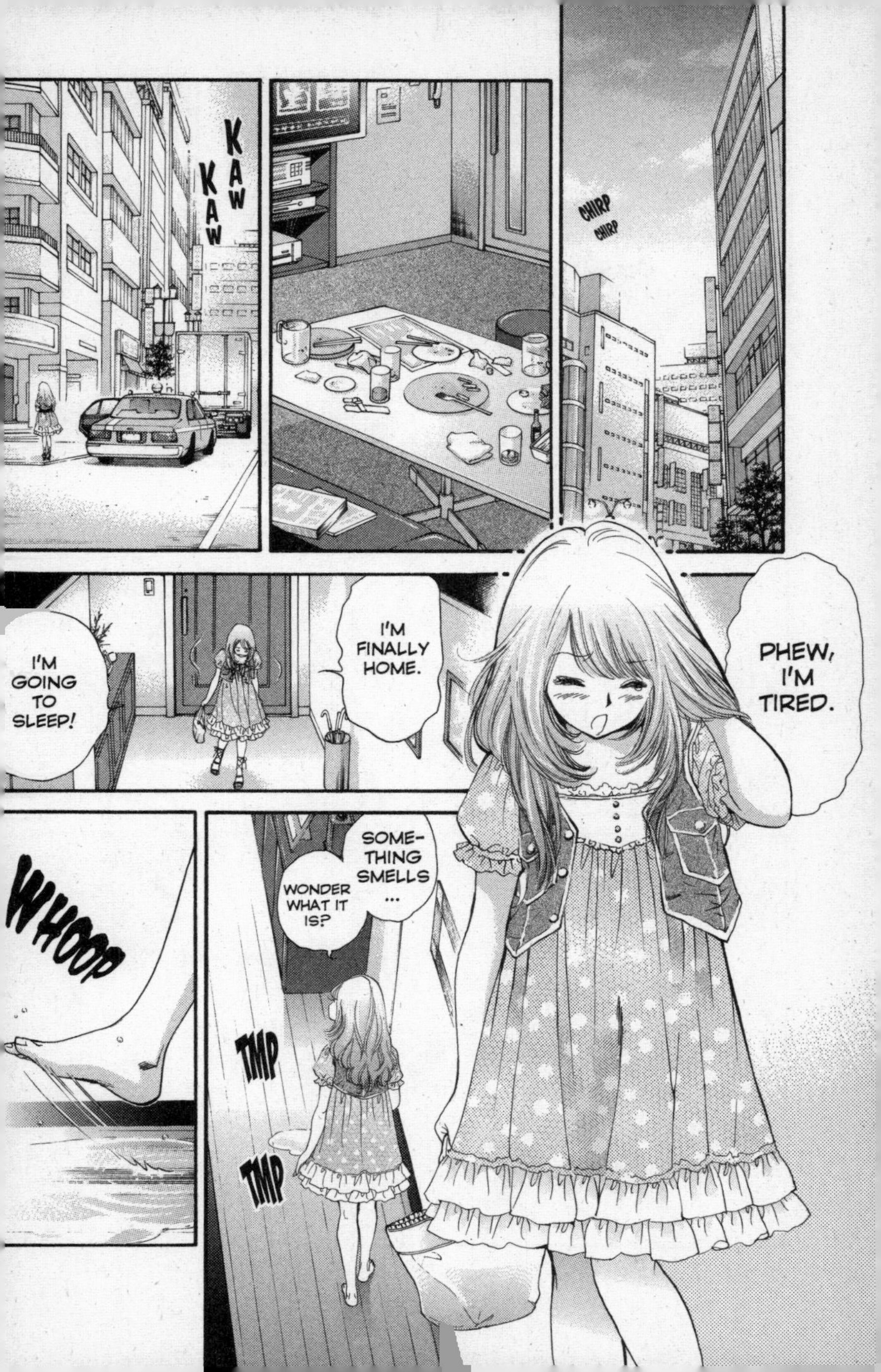
CHIRP CHIRP
KAW KAW
PHEW, I'M TIRED.
I'M FINALLY HOME.
I'M GOING TO SLEEP!
SOME-THING SMELLS...
WONDER WHAT IT IS?
TMP
TMP
WHOOP

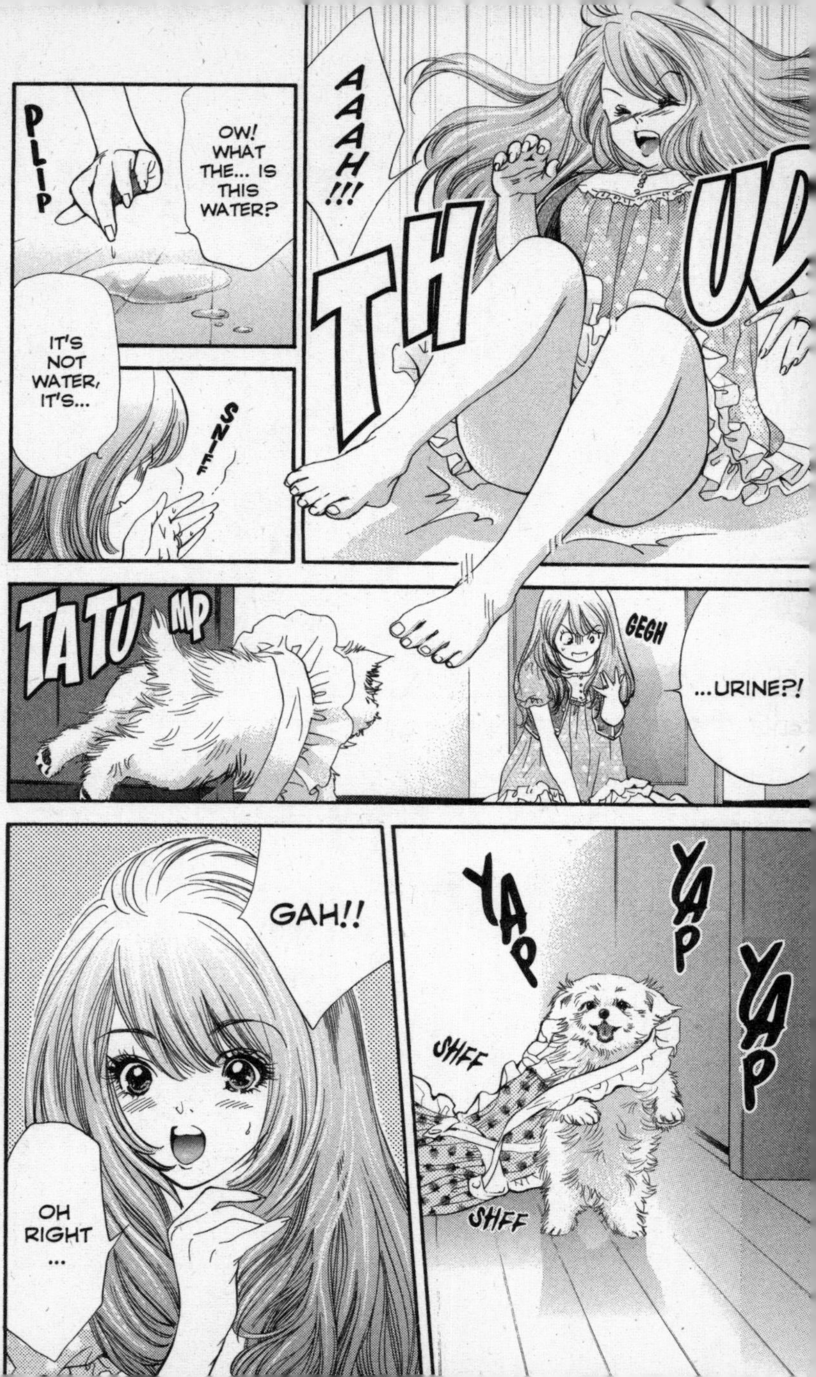
AAAAH!!!
THUD
PLIP
OW! WHAT THE... IS THIS WATER?
IT'S NOT WATER, IT'S...
SNIFF
GEGH
...URINE?!
TATUMP
YAP
YAP
YAP
YAP
SHFF
SHFF
GAH!!
OH RIGHT ...

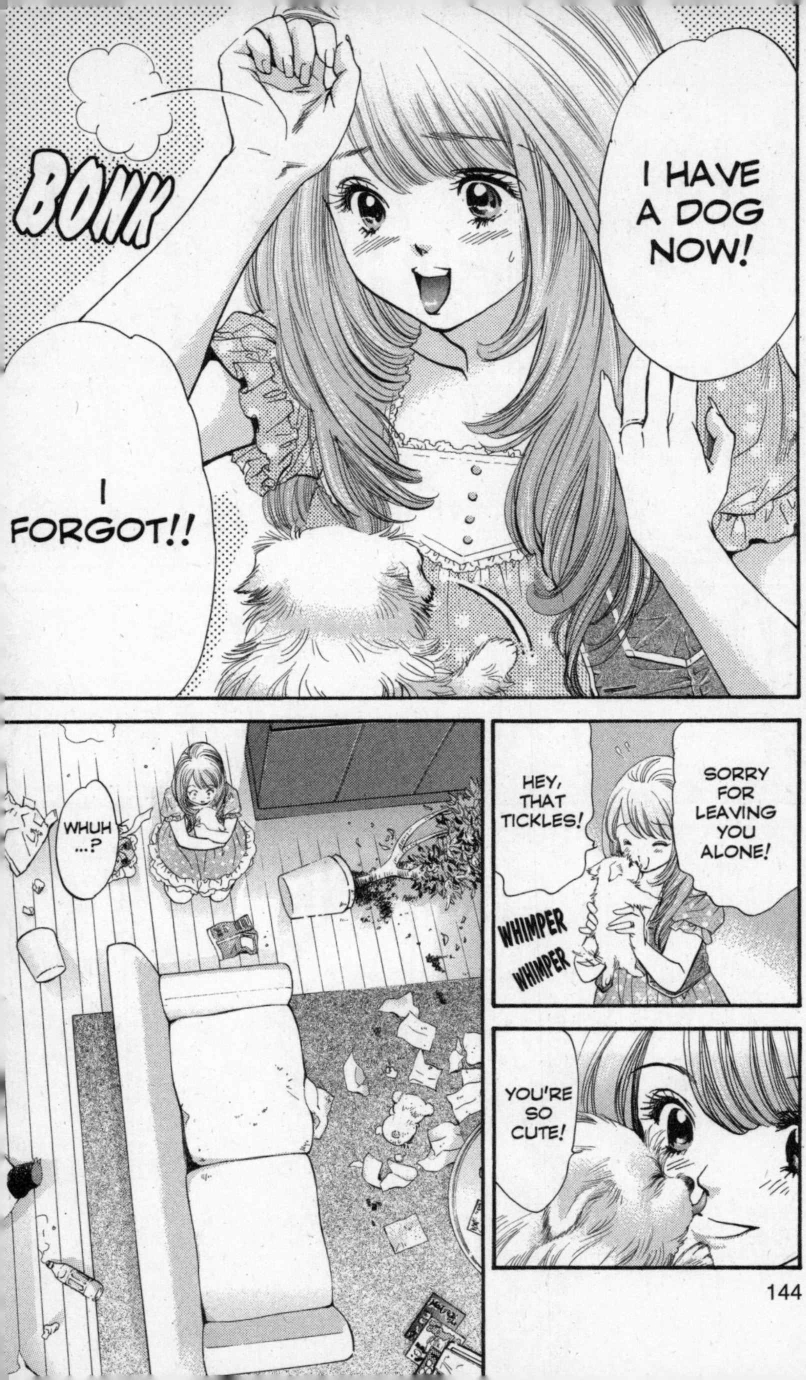
I HAVE A DOG NOW!
BONK
I FORGOT!!
SORRY FOR LEAVING YOU ALONE!
HEY, THAT TICKLES!
WHIMPER
WHIMPER
YOU'RE SO CUTE!
WHUH …?

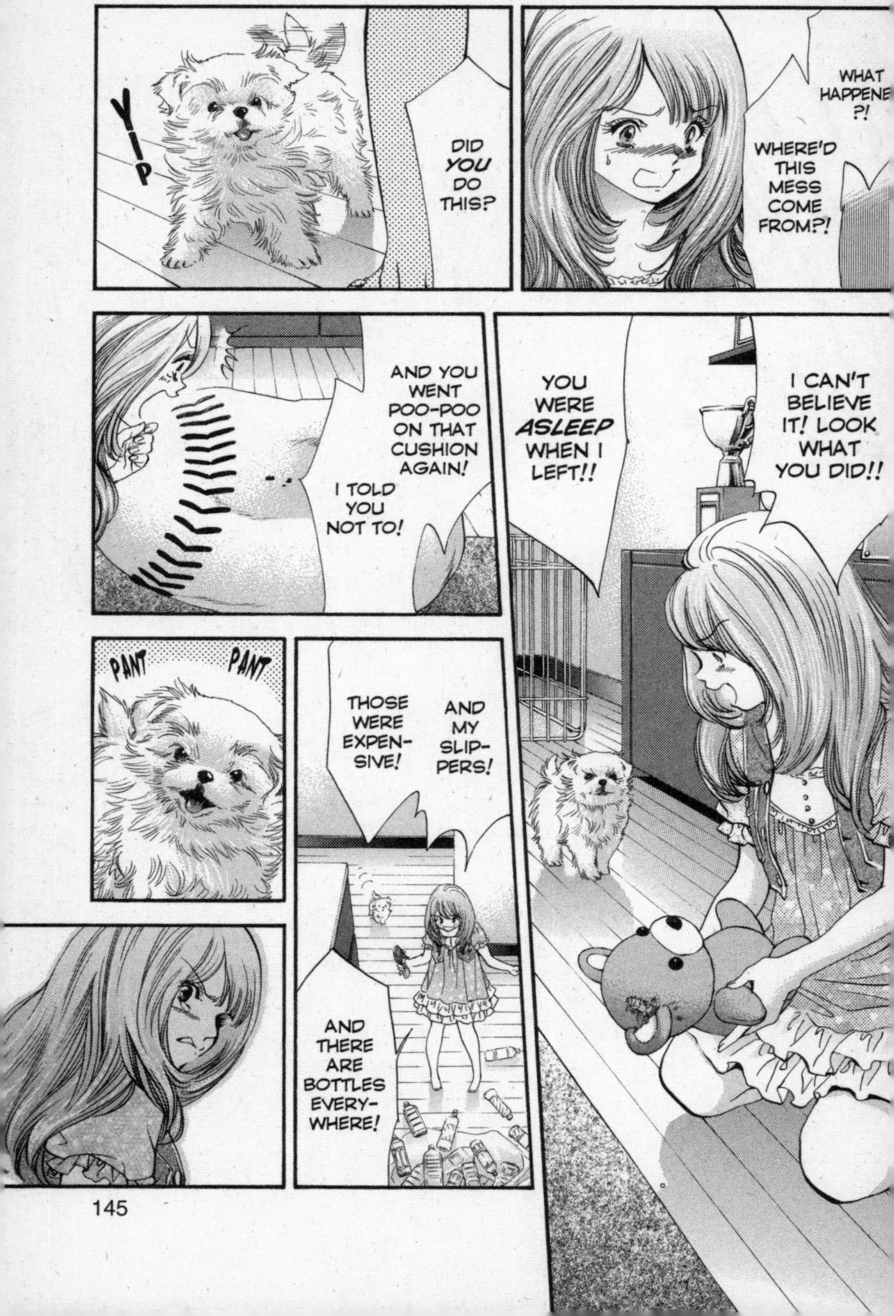
WHAT HAPPENE ?!
WHERE'D THIS MESS COME FROM?!
DID *YOU* DO THIS?
YIP
I CAN'T BELIEVE IT! LOOK WHAT YOU DID!!
YOU WERE *ASLEEP* WHEN I LEFT!!
AND YOU WENT POO-POO ON THAT CUSHION AGAIN!
I TOLD YOU NOT TO!
AND MY SLIP-PERS!
THOSE WERE EXPEN-SIVE!
AND THERE ARE BOTTLES EVERY-WHERE!
PANT
PANT

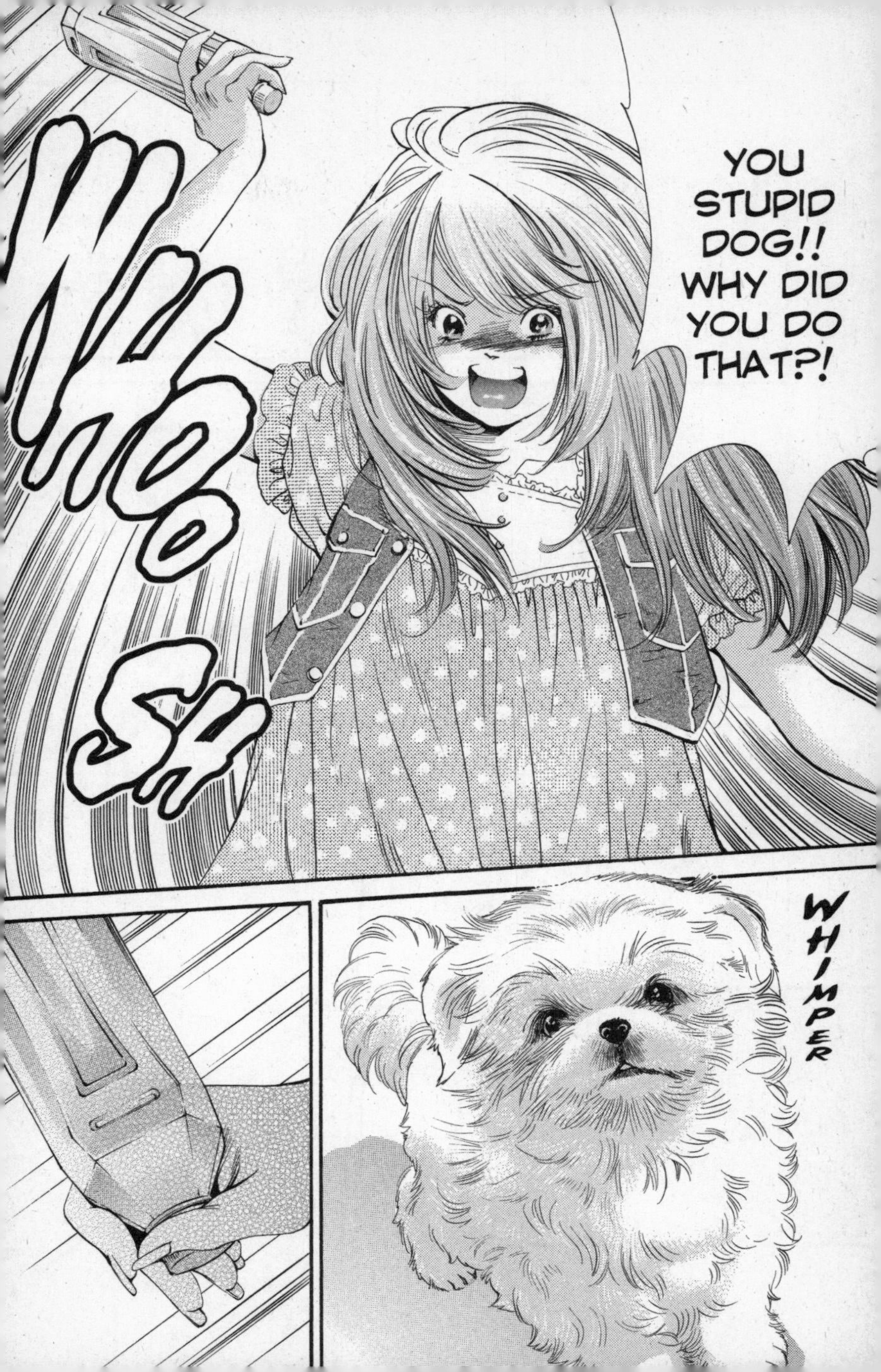
YOU STUPID DOG!! WHY DID YOU DO THAT?!
WHOOSH
WHIMPER

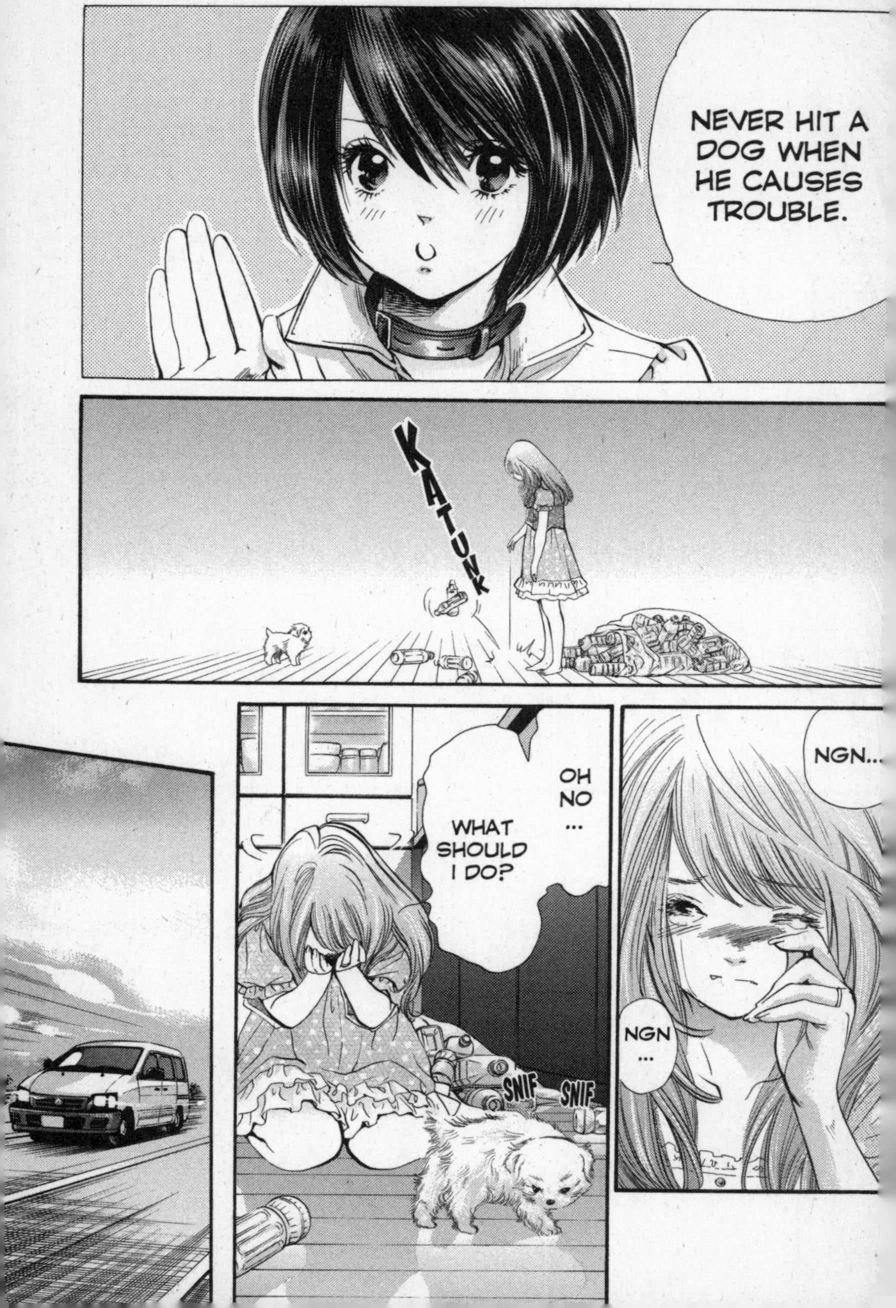
NEVER HIT A DOG WHEN HE CAUSES TROUBLE.
KATUNK
NGN...
NGN ...
OH NO ...
WHAT SHOULD I DO?
SNIF
SNIF

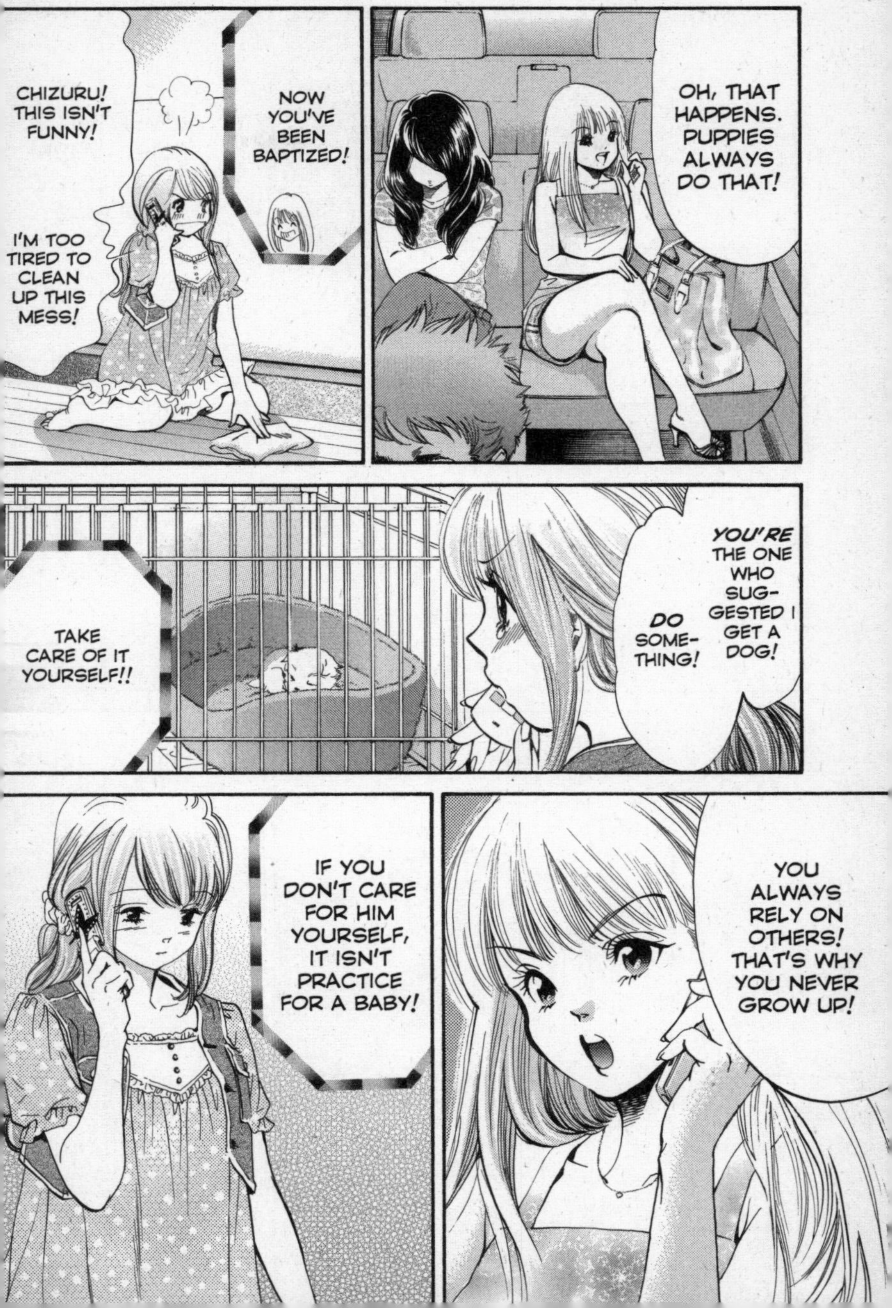
OH, THAT HAPPENS. PUPPIES ALWAYS DO THAT!
NOW YOU'VE BEEN BAPTIZED!
CHIZURU! THIS ISN'T FUNNY!
I'M TOO TIRED TO CLEAN UP THIS MESS!
YOU'RE THE ONE WHO SUG-GESTED I GET A DOG!
DO SOME-THING!
TAKE CARE OF IT YOURSELF!!
YOU ALWAYS RELY ON OTHERS! THAT'S WHY YOU NEVER GROW UP!
IF YOU DON'T CARE FOR HIM YOURSELF, IT ISN'T PRACTICE FOR A BABY!

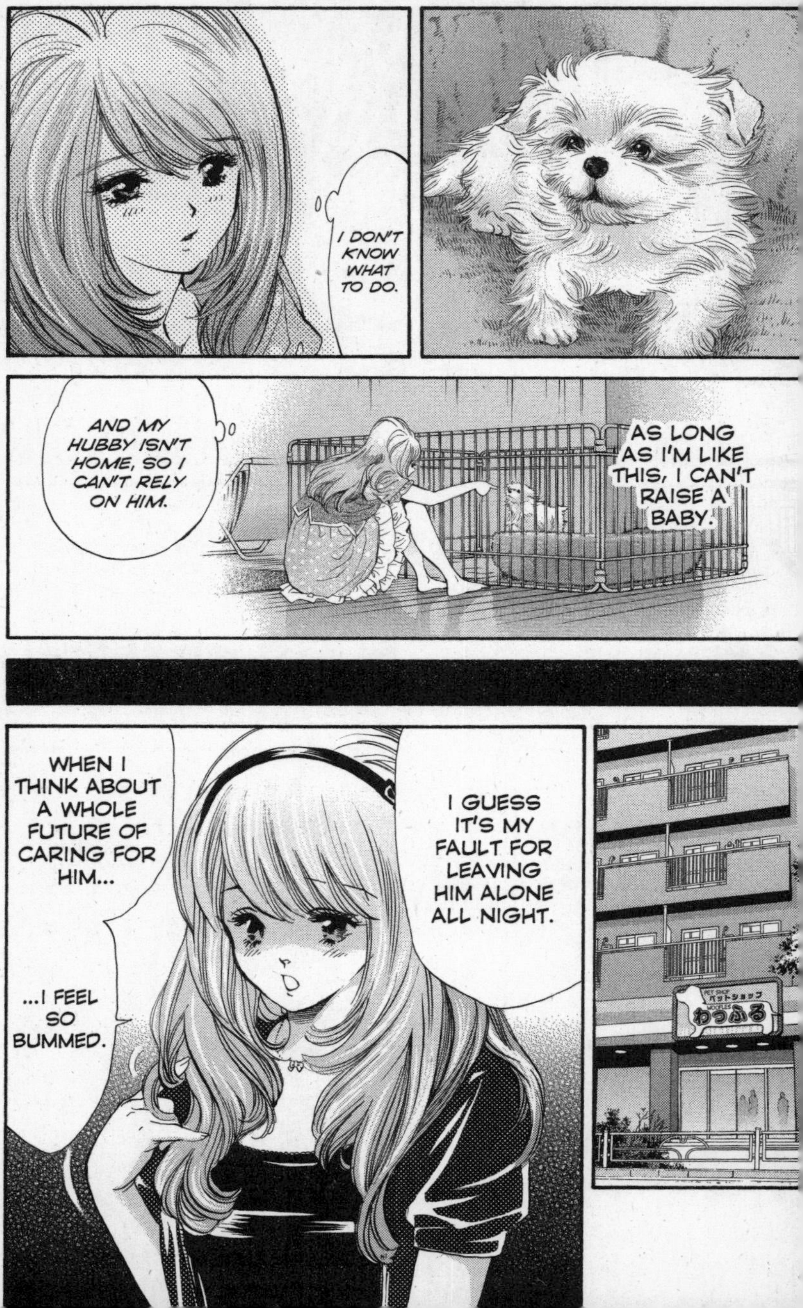
I DON'T KNOW WHAT TO DO.
AS LONG AS I'M LIKE THIS, I CAN'T RAISE A BABY.
AND MY HUBBY ISN'T HOME, SO I CAN'T RELY ON HIM.
PET SHOP
ペットショップ
WOOFLES
わっふる
I GUESS IT'S MY FAULT FOR LEAVING HIM ALONE ALL NIGHT.
WHEN I THINK ABOUT A WHOLE FUTURE OF CARING FOR HIM...
...I FEEL SO BUMMED.

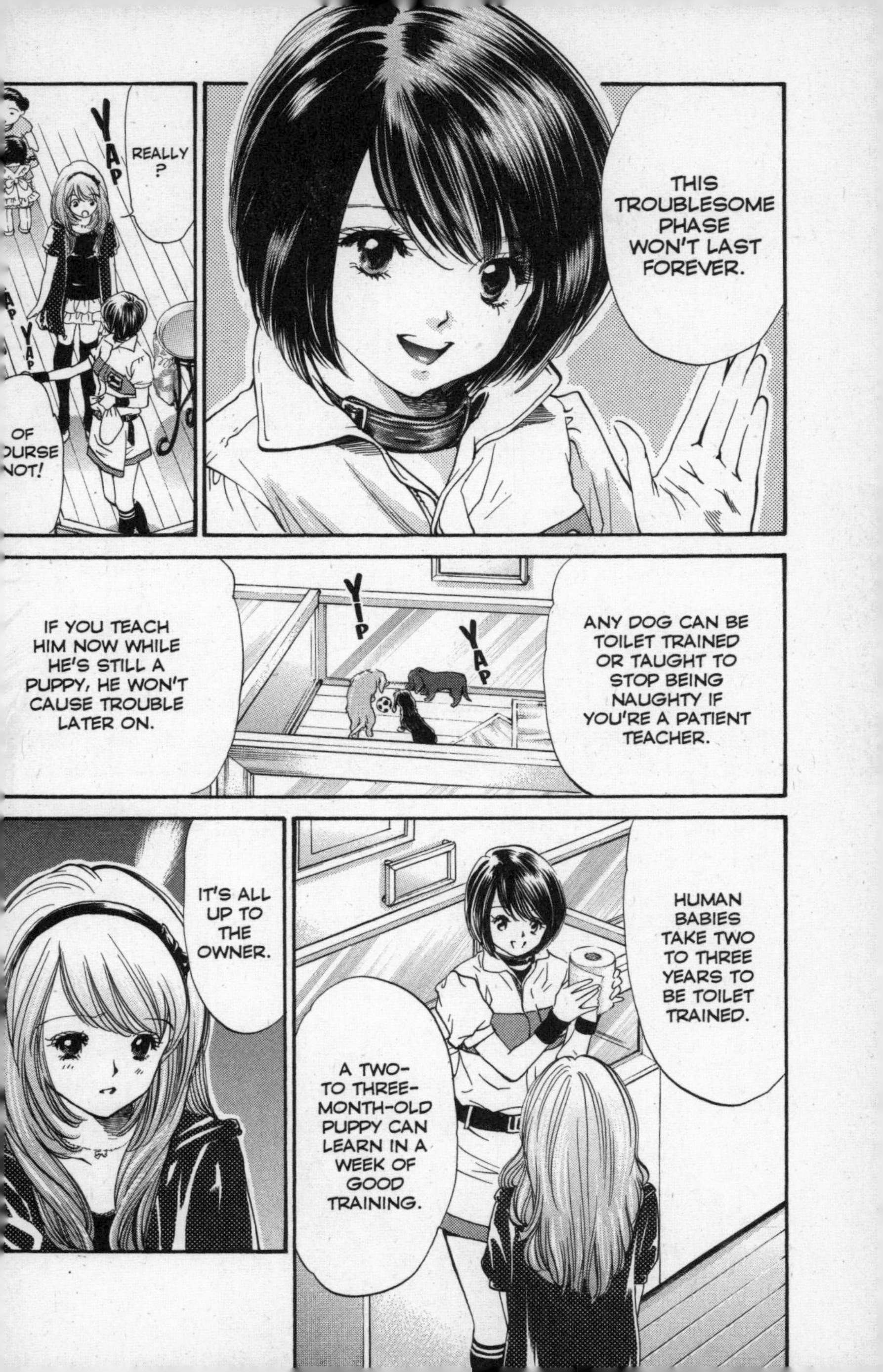
THIS TROUBLESOME PHASE WON'T LAST FOREVER.
YAP
REALLY?
YAP
YAP
OF
OURSE
NOT!
ANY DOG CAN BE TOILET TRAINED OR TAUGHT TO STOP BEING NAUGHTY IF YOU'RE A PATIENT TEACHER.
YAP
YIP
IF YOU TEACH HIM NOW WHILE HE'S STILL A PUPPY, HE WON'T CAUSE TROUBLE LATER ON.
HUMAN BABIES TAKE TWO TO THREE YEARS TO BE TOILET TRAINED.
A TWO- TO THREE-MONTH-OLD PUPPY CAN LEARN IN A WEEK OF GOOD TRAINING.
IT'S ALL UP TO THE OWNER.

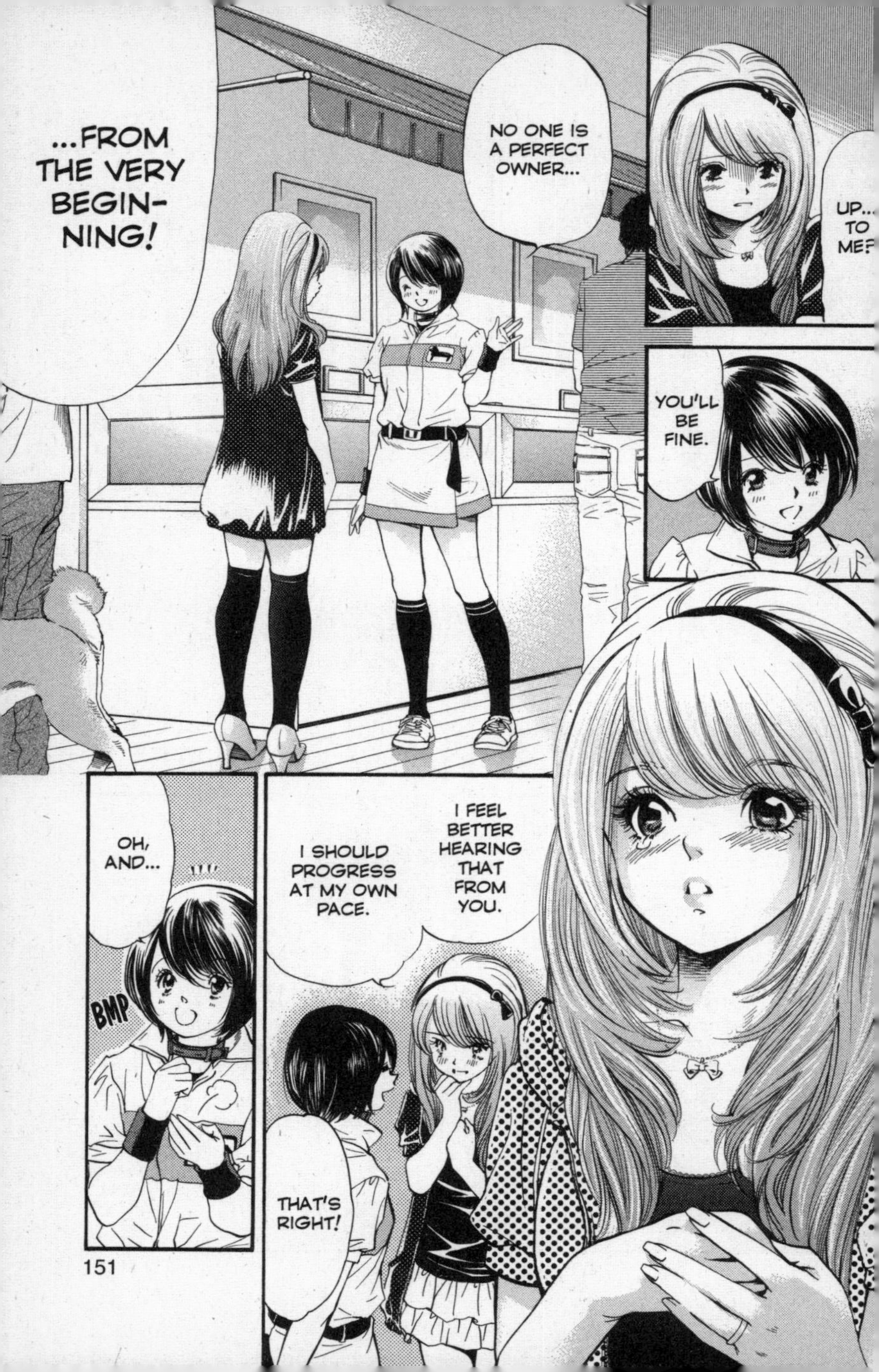
UP... TO ME?
YOU'LL BE FINE.
NO ONE IS A PERFECT OWNER...
...FROM THE VERY BEGIN-NING!
I FEEL BETTER HEARING THAT FROM YOU.
I SHOULD PROGRESS AT MY OWN PACE.
THAT'S RIGHT!
OH, AND...
!!!
BMP

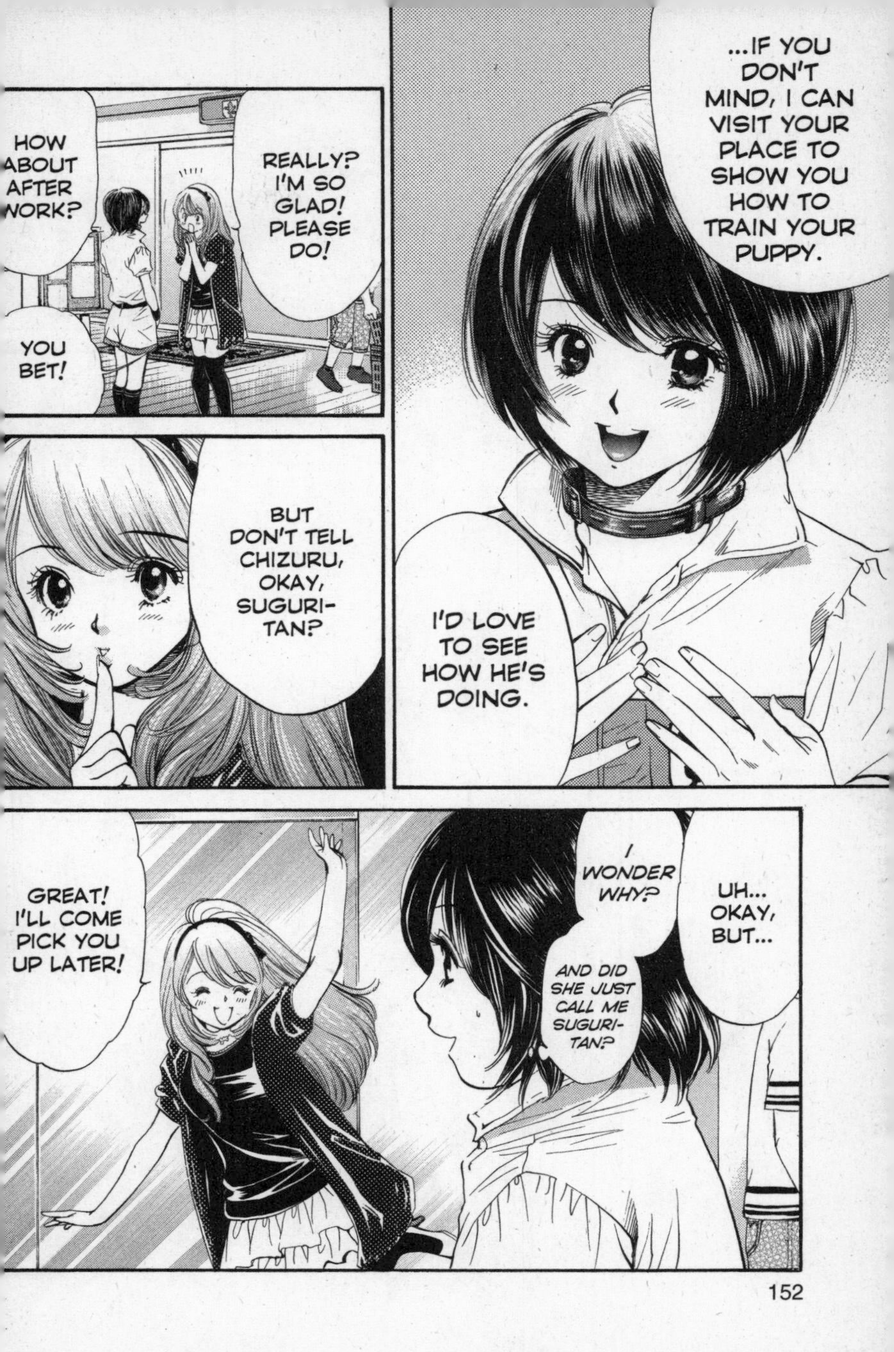
...IF YOU DON'T MIND, I CAN VISIT YOUR PLACE TO SHOW YOU HOW TO TRAIN YOUR PUPPY.
I'D LOVE TO SEE HOW HE'S DOING.
REALLY? I'M SO GLAD! PLEASE DO!
HOW ABOUT AFTER WORK?
YOU BET!
BUT DON'T TELL CHIZURU, OKAY, SUGURI-TAN?
UH... OKAY, BUT...
I WONDER WHY?
AND DID SHE JUST CALL ME SUGURI-TAN?
GREAT! I'LL COME PICK YOU UP LATER!

CHAPTER 171: SERINA LOSES HEART...

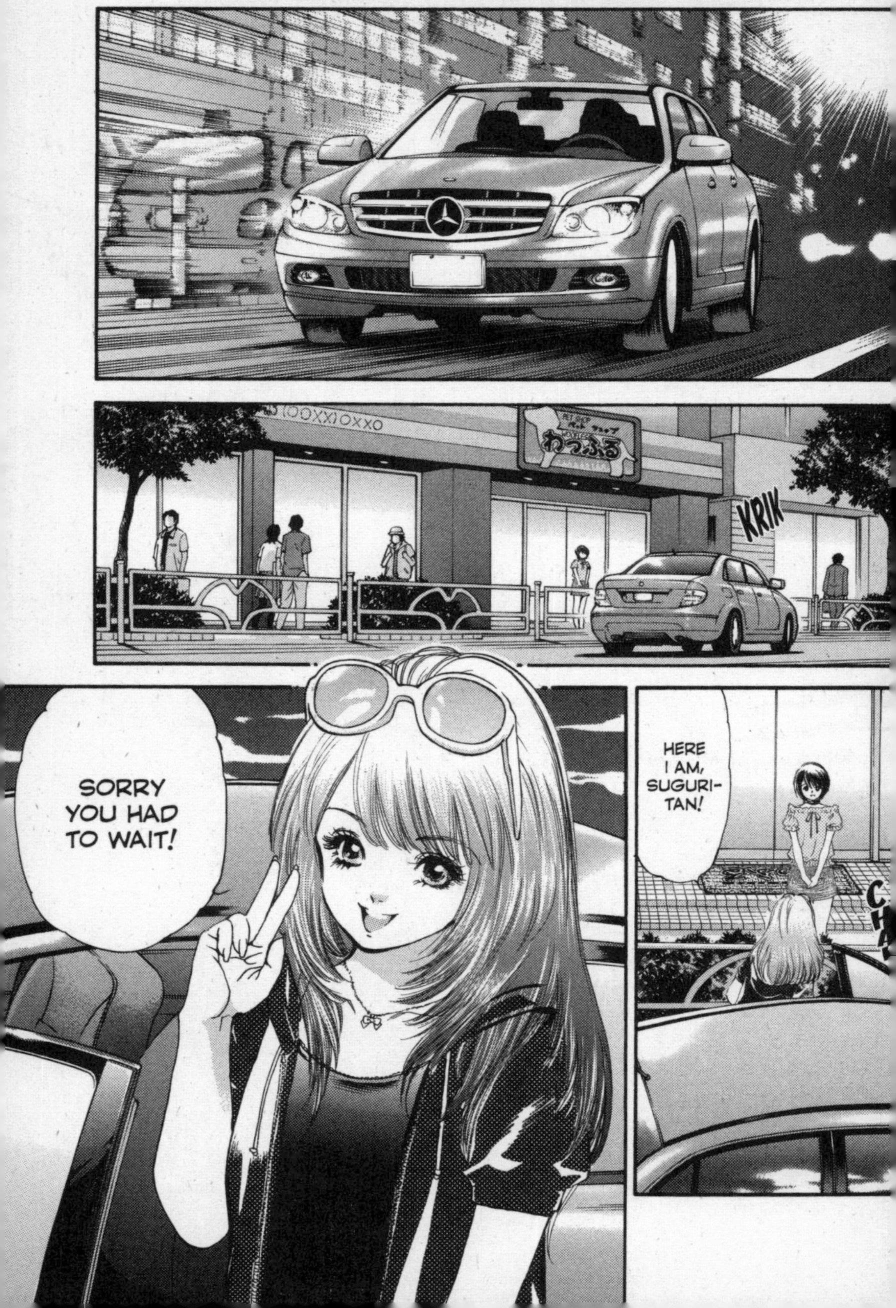
わっふる
KRIK
HERE I AM, SUGURI-TAN!
SORRY YOU HAD TO WAIT!

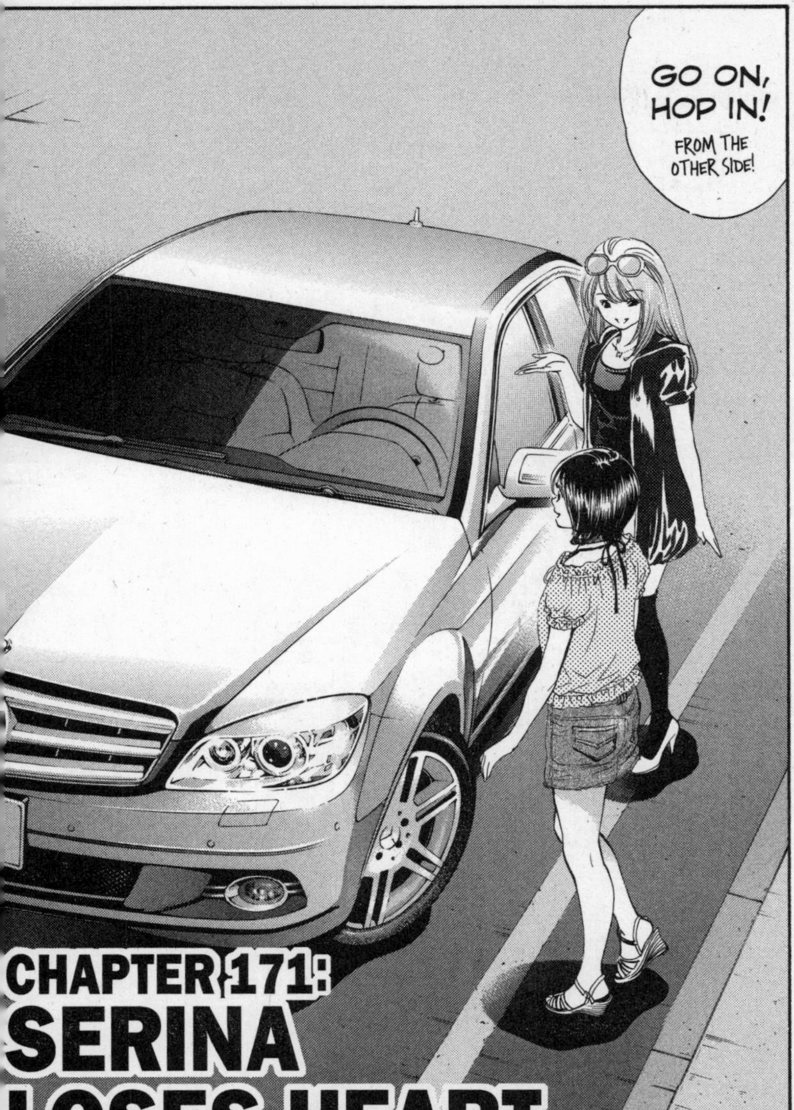
GO ON, HOP IN!
FROM THE OTHER SIDE!
CHAPTER 171: SERINA LOSES HEART...

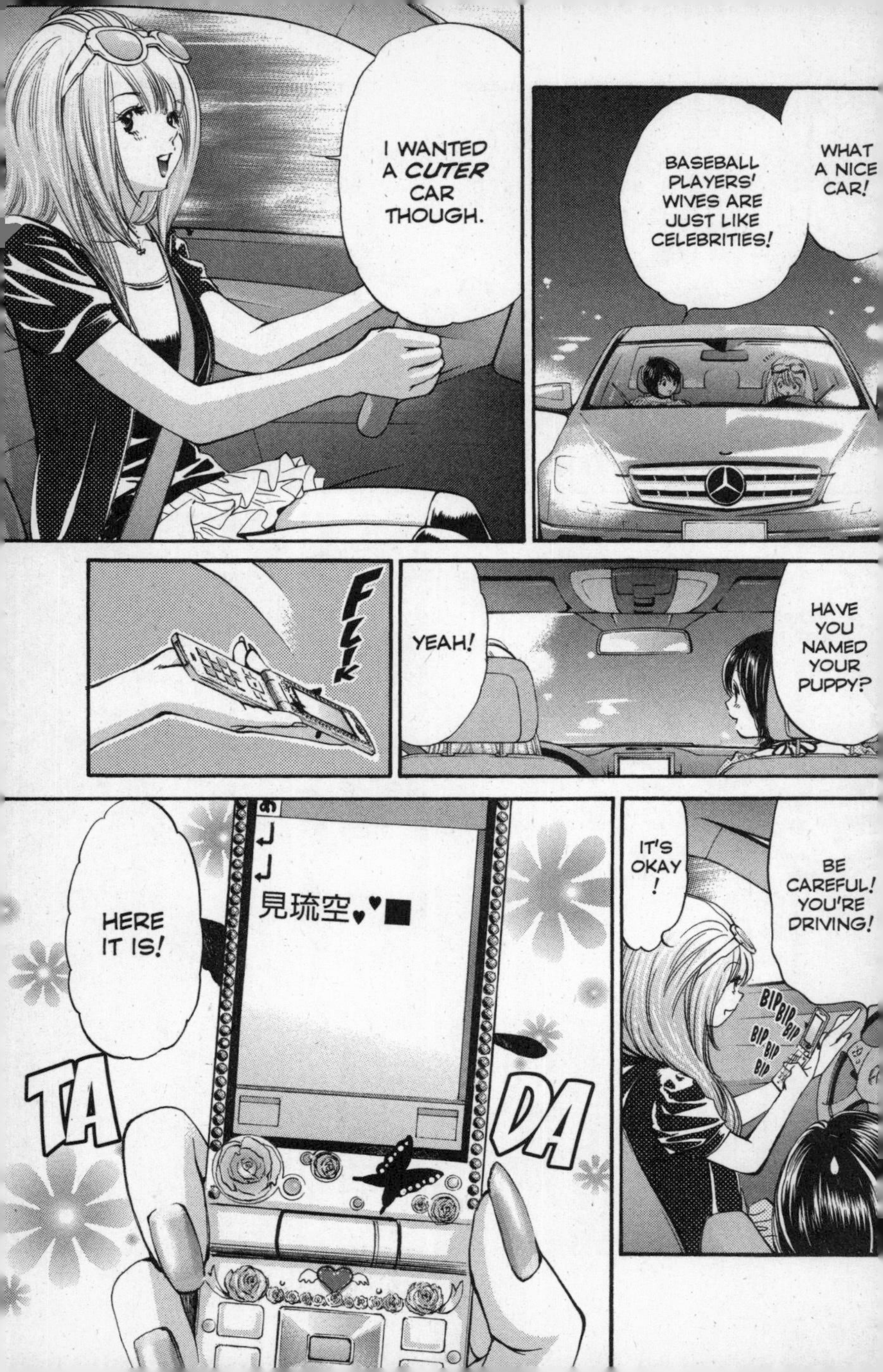
WHAT A NICE CAR!
BASEBALL PLAYERS' WIVES ARE JUST LIKE CELEBRITIES!
I WANTED A *CUTER* CAR THOUGH.
HAVE YOU NAMED YOUR PUPPY?
YEAH!
FLIK
BE CAREFUL! YOU'RE DRIVING!
IT'S OKAY!
BIP BIP BIP
BIP BIP BIP
HERE IT IS!
見琉空
TA DA

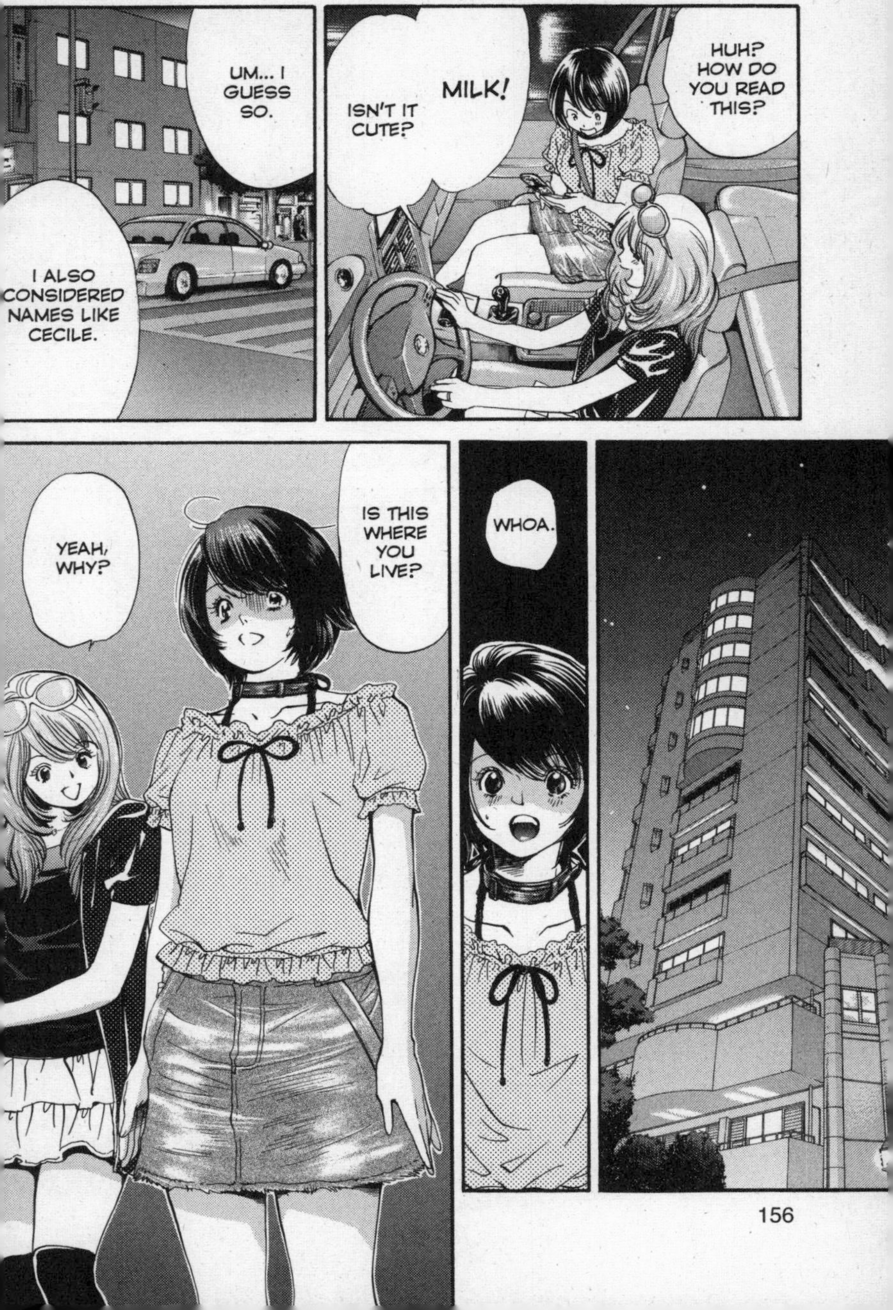
HUH? HOW DO YOU READ THIS?
MILK!
ISN'T IT CUTE?
UM... I GUESS SO.
I ALSO CONSIDERED NAMES LIKE CECILE.
WHOA.
IS THIS WHERE YOU LIVE?
YEAH, WHY?

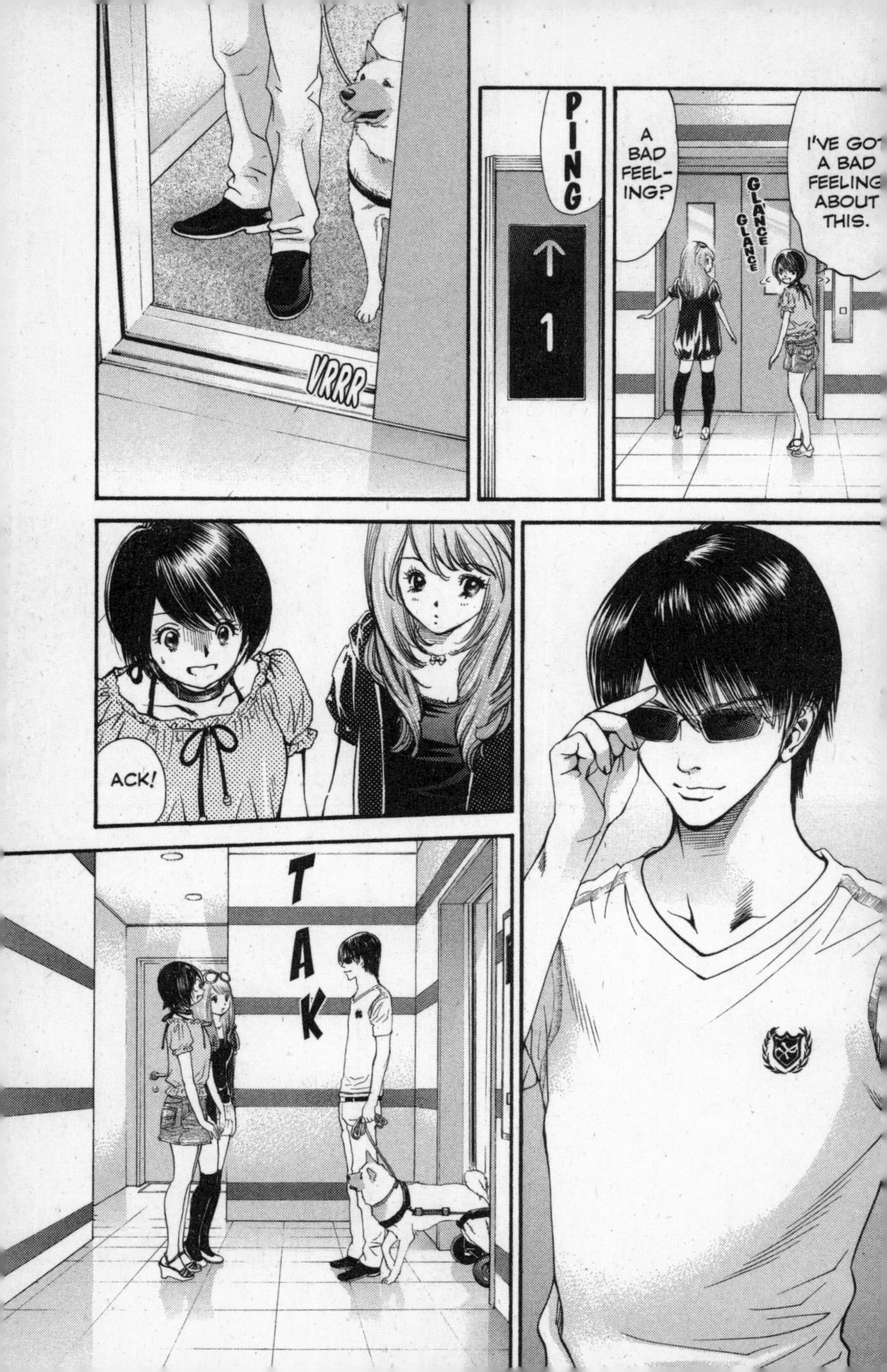
I'VE GOT A BAD FEELING ABOUT THIS.
A BAD FEEL-ING?
GLANCE
GLANCE
PING
VRRR
ACK!
TAK

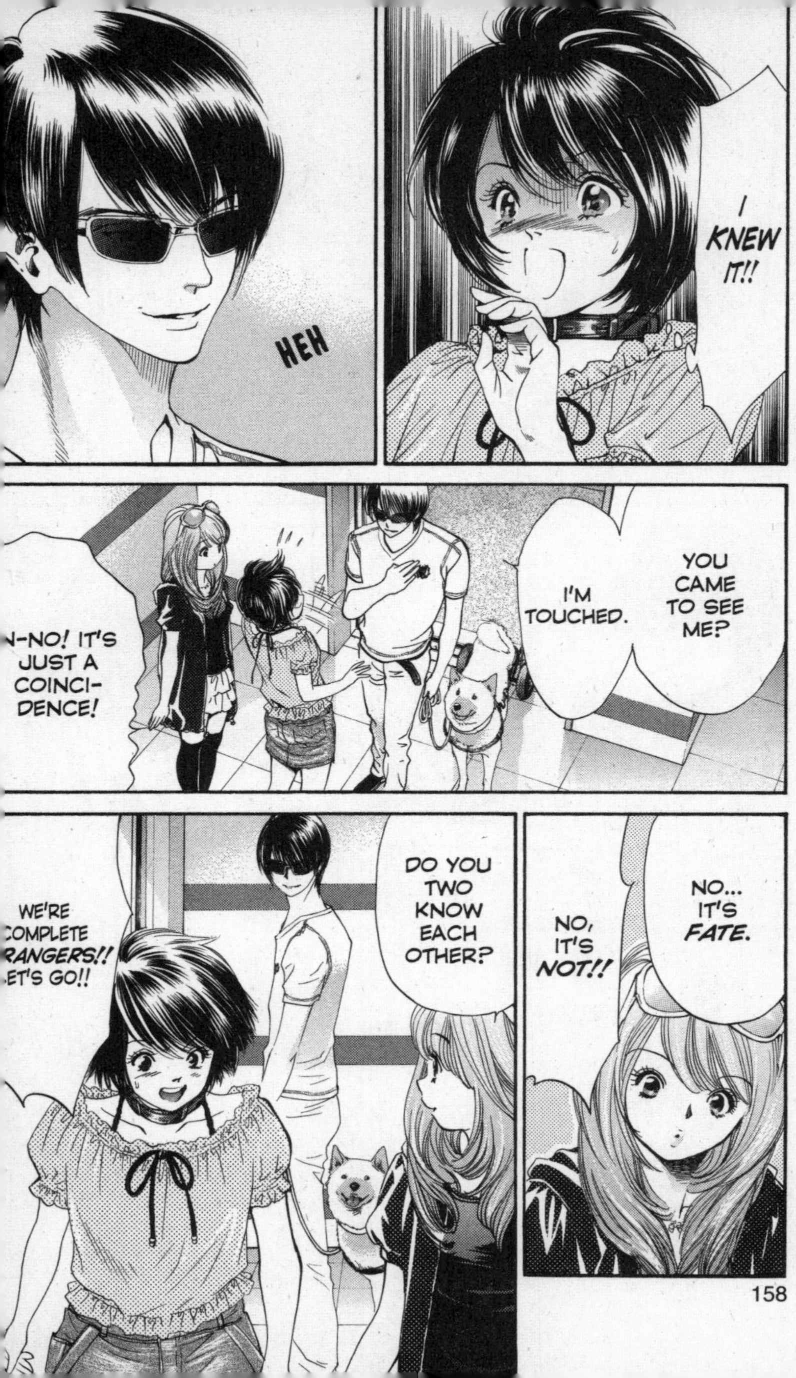
I KNEW IT!!
HEH
YOU CAME TO SEE ME?
I'M TOUCHED.
N-NO! IT'S JUST A COINCI-DENCE!
NO... IT'S FATE.
NO, IT'S NOT!!
DO YOU TWO KNOW EACH OTHER?
WE'RE COMPLETE RANGERS!! ET'S GO!!

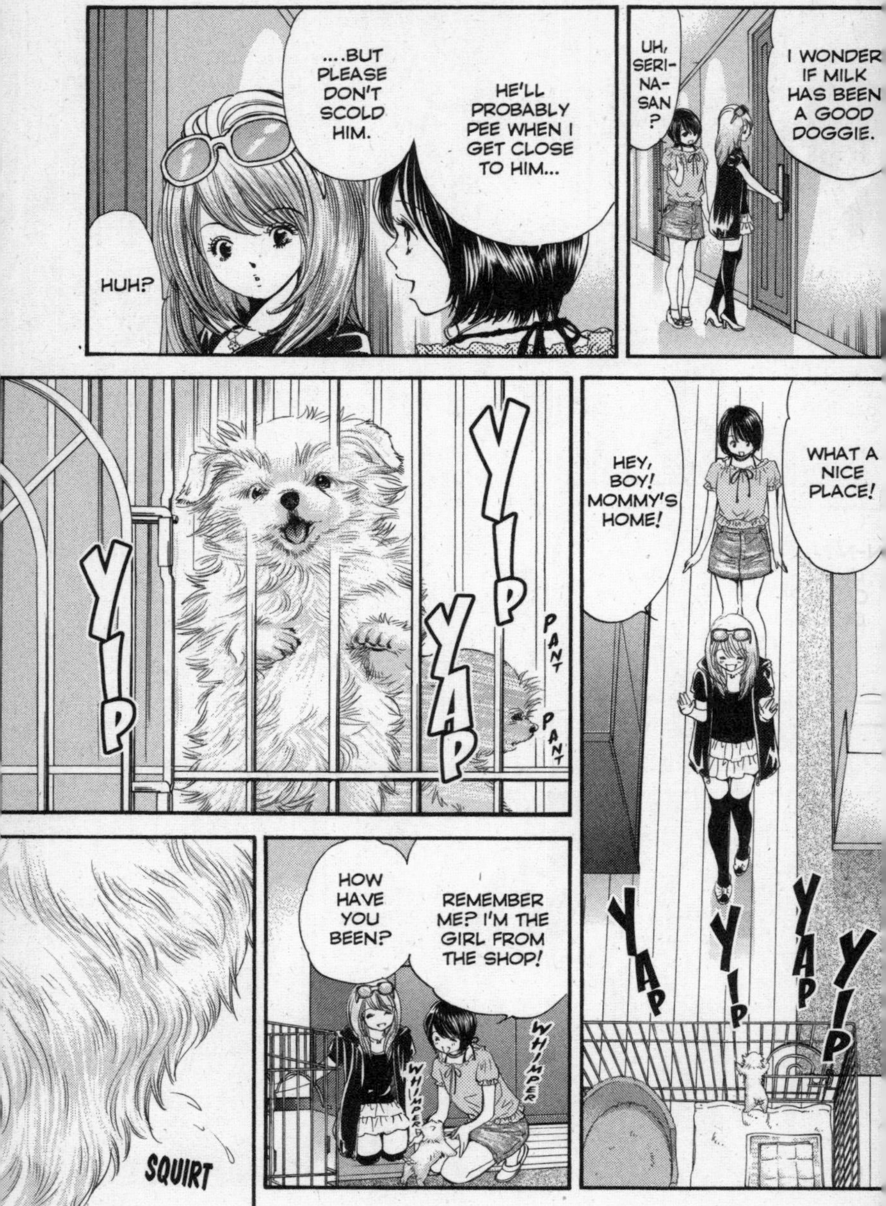
I WONDER IF MILK HAS BEEN A GOOD DOGGIE.
UH, SERI-NA-SAN?
HE'LL PROBABLY PEE WHEN I GET CLOSE TO HIM...
....BUT PLEASE DON'T SCOLD HIM.
HUH?
WHAT A NICE PLACE!
HEY, BOY! MOMMY'S HOME!
YIP
YAP
YIP
YAP
PANT PANT
YAP
YIP
YIP
REMEMBER ME? I'M THE GIRL FROM THE SHOP!
HOW HAVE YOU BEEN?
WHIMPER
WHIMPER
SQUIRT

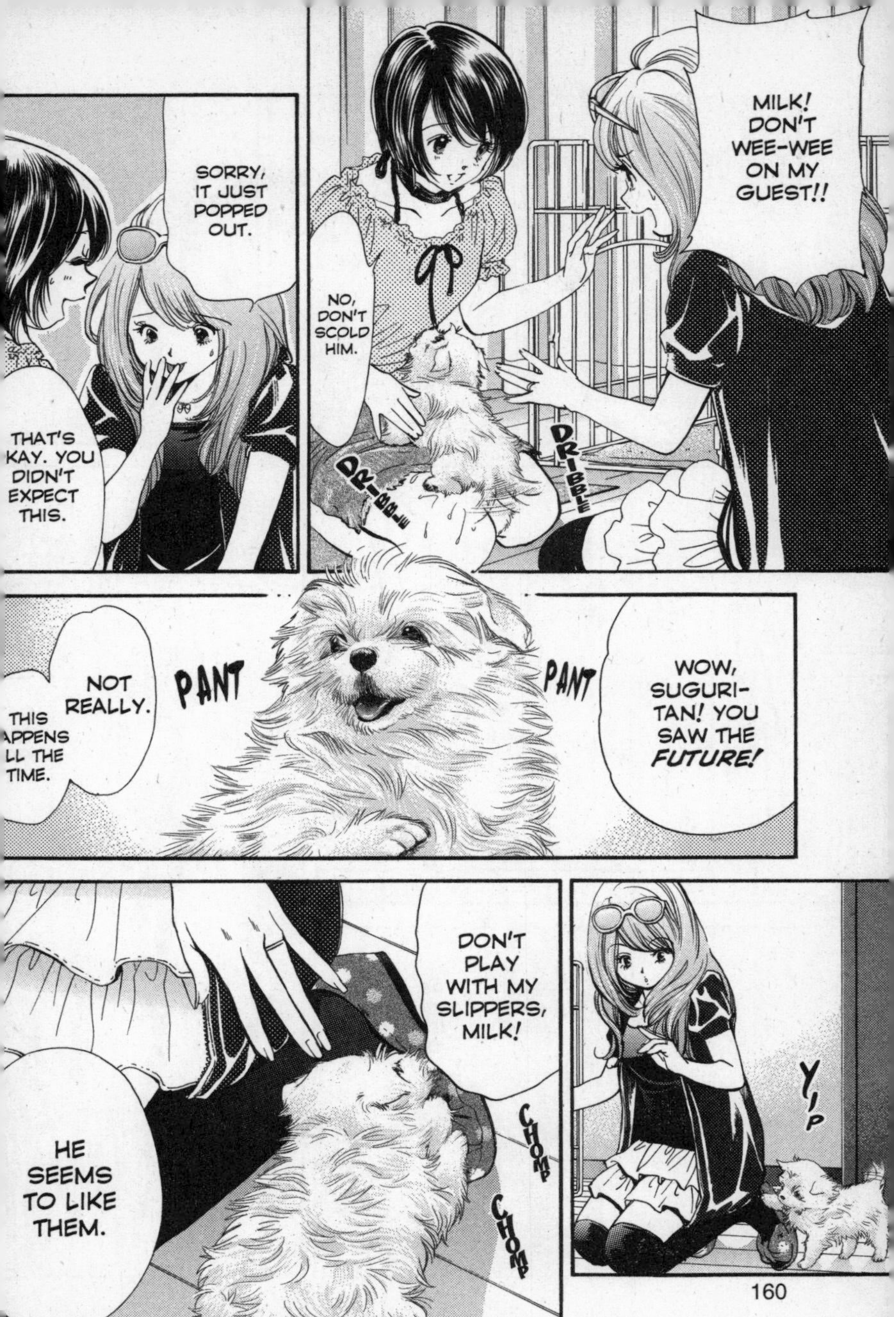
MILK! DON'T WEE-WEE ON MY GUEST!!
NO, DON'T SCOLD HIM.
DRIBBLE
DRI-BBLE
SORRY, IT JUST POPPED OUT.
THAT'S KAY. YOU DIDN'T EXPECT THIS.
WOW, SUGURI-TAN! YOU SAW THE *FUTURE!*
PANT
PANT
NOT REALLY.
THIS APPENS LL THE TIME.
YIP
DON'T PLAY WITH MY SLIPPERS, MILK!
CHOMP
CHOMP
HE SEEMS TO LIKE THEM.

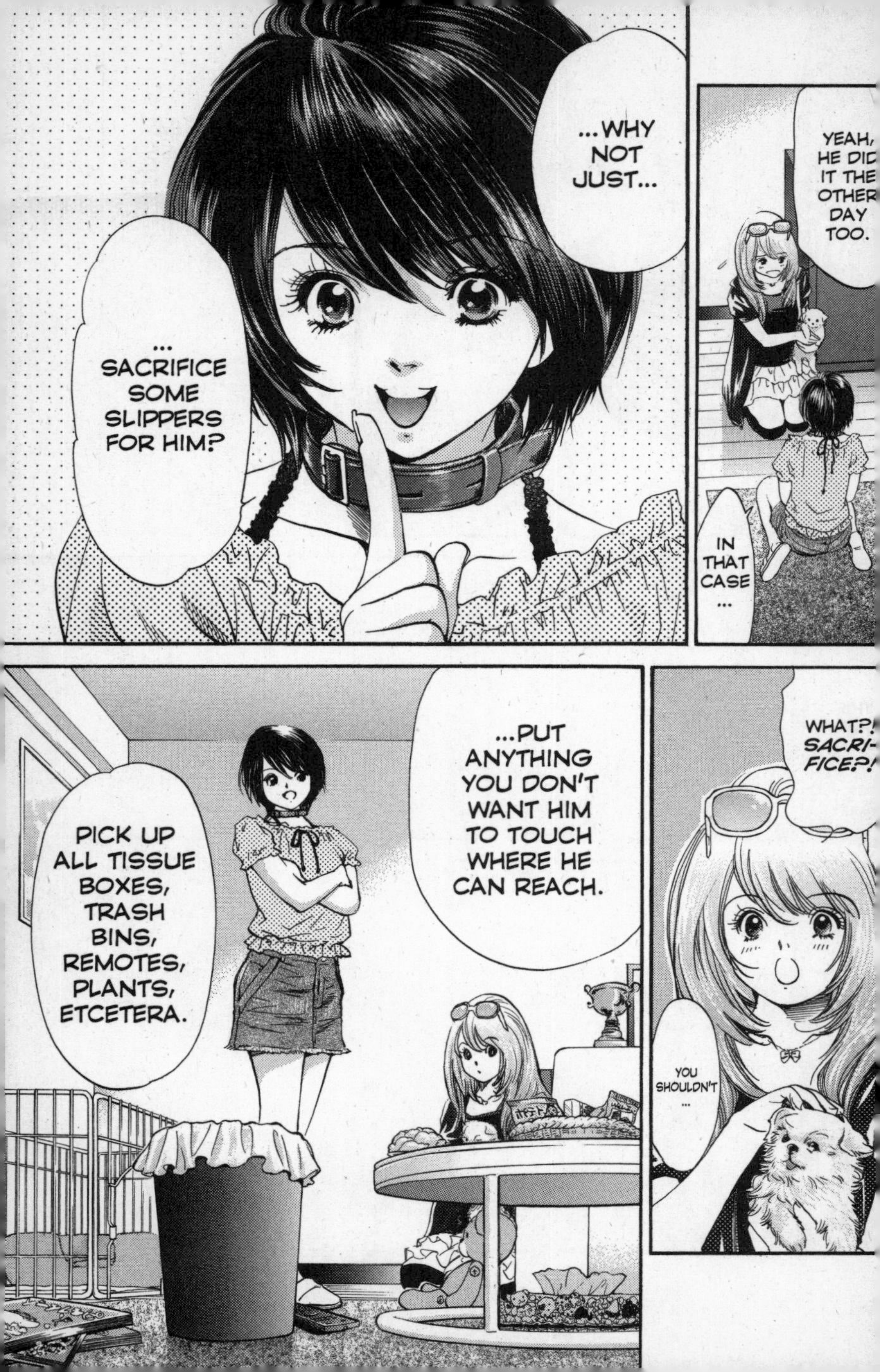
YEAH, HE DID IT THE OTHER DAY TOO.
IN THAT CASE...
...WHY NOT JUST...
...SACRIFICE SOME SLIPPERS FOR HIM?
WHAT?! SACRIFICE?!
YOU SHOULDN'T...
...PUT ANYTHING YOU DON'T WANT HIM TO TOUCH WHERE HE CAN REACH.
PICK UP ALL TISSUE BOXES, TRASH BINS, REMOTES, PLANTS, ETCETERA.

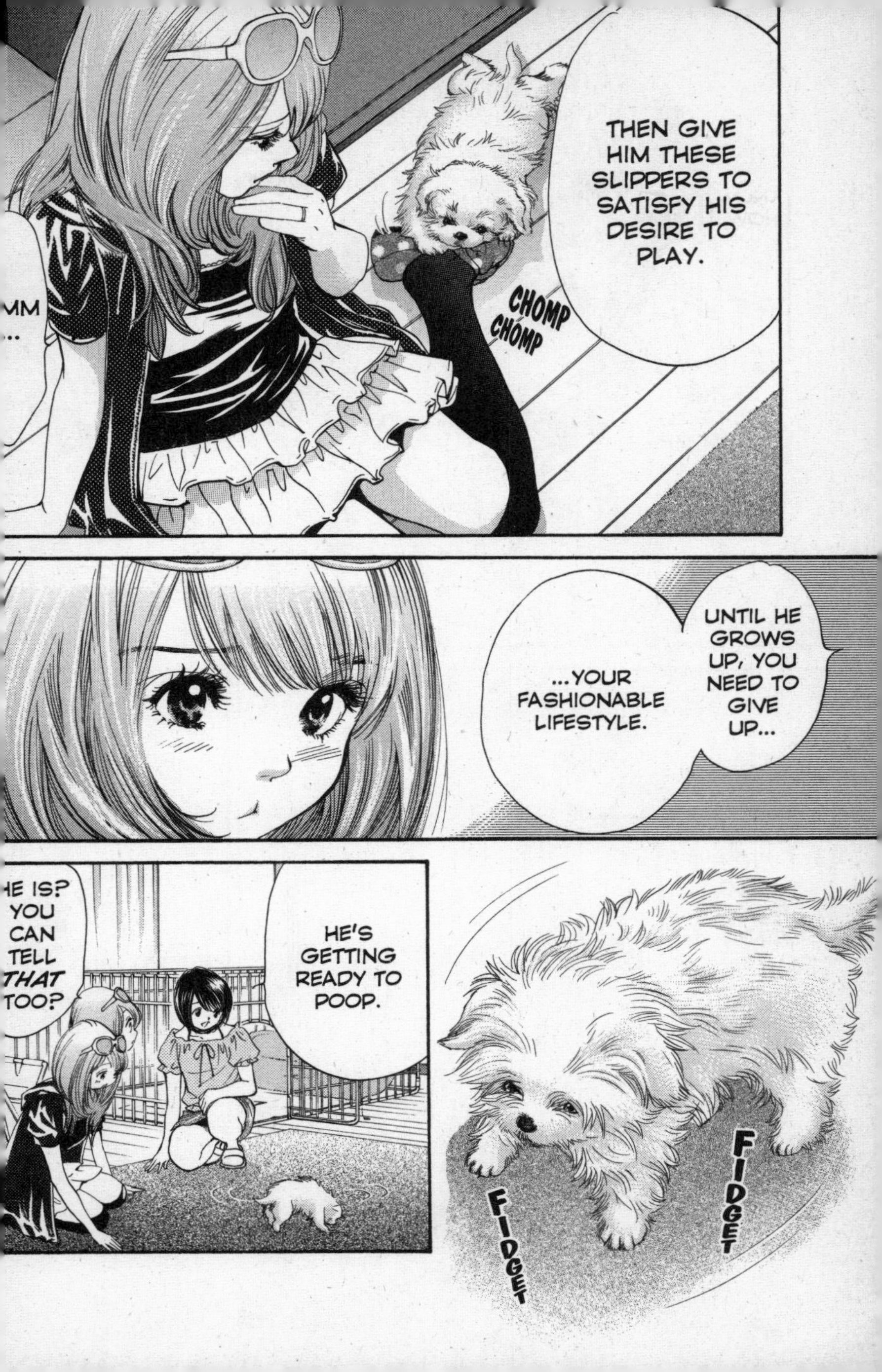
THEN GIVE HIM THESE SLIPPERS TO SATISFY HIS DESIRE TO PLAY.
CHOMP CHOMP
MM...
UNTIL HE GROWS UP, YOU NEED TO GIVE UP...
...YOUR FASHIONABLE LIFESTYLE.
FIDGET FIDGET
HE'S GETTING READY TO POOP.
HE IS? YOU CAN TELL *THAT* TOO?

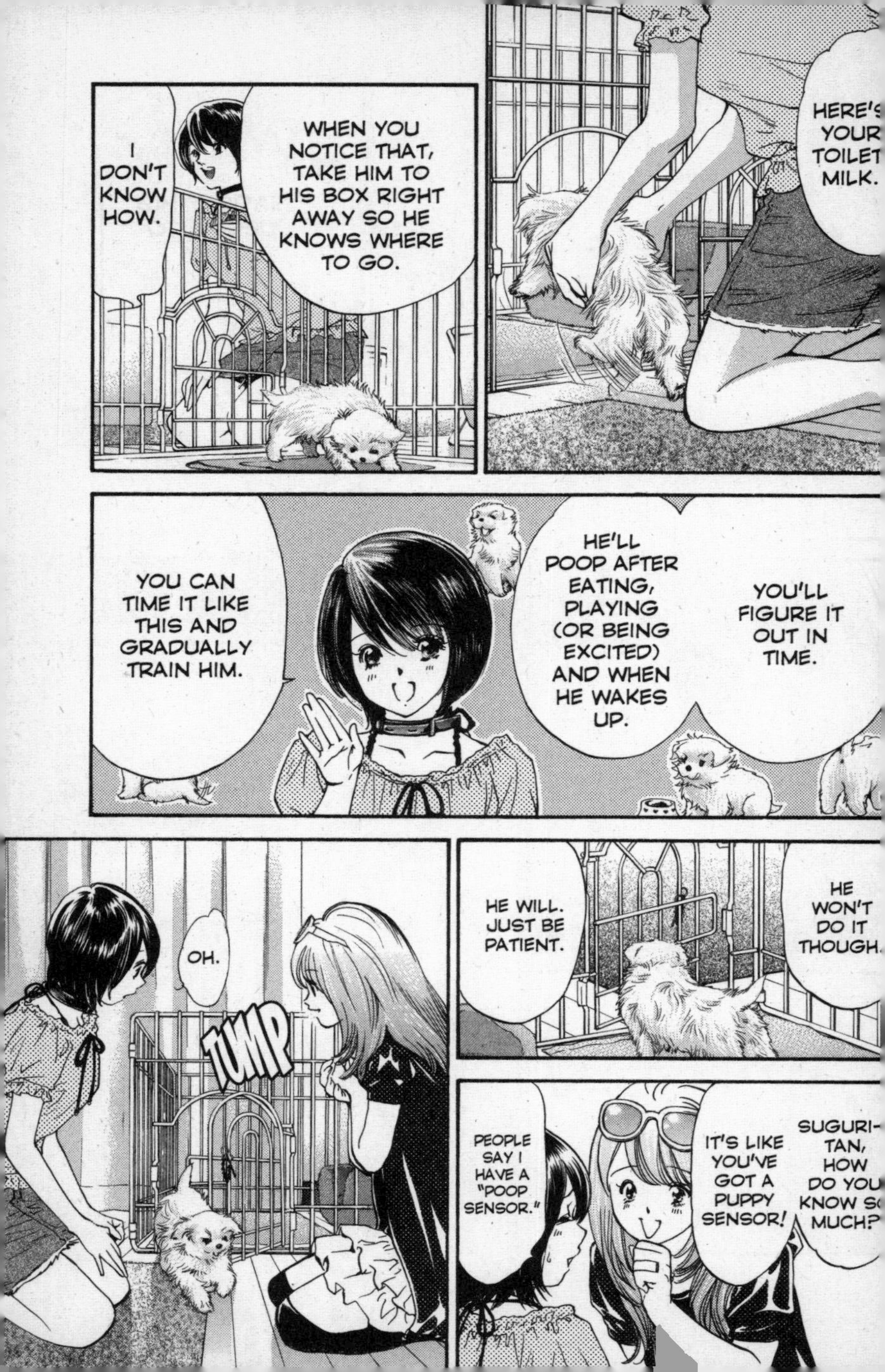
HERE'S YOUR TOILET MILK.
WHEN YOU NOTICE THAT, TAKE HIM TO HIS BOX RIGHT AWAY SO HE KNOWS WHERE TO GO.
I DON'T KNOW HOW.
YOU'LL FIGURE IT OUT IN TIME.
HE'LL POOP AFTER EATING, PLAYING (OR BEING EXCITED) AND WHEN HE WAKES UP.
YOU CAN TIME IT LIKE THIS AND GRADUALLY TRAIN HIM.
HE WON'T DO IT THOUGH.
HE WILL. JUST BE PATIENT.
SUGURI-TAN, HOW DO YOU KNOW S MUCH?
IT'S LIKE YOU'VE GOT A PUPPY SENSOR!
PEOPLE SAY I HAVE A "POOP SENSOR."
OH.
TUMP

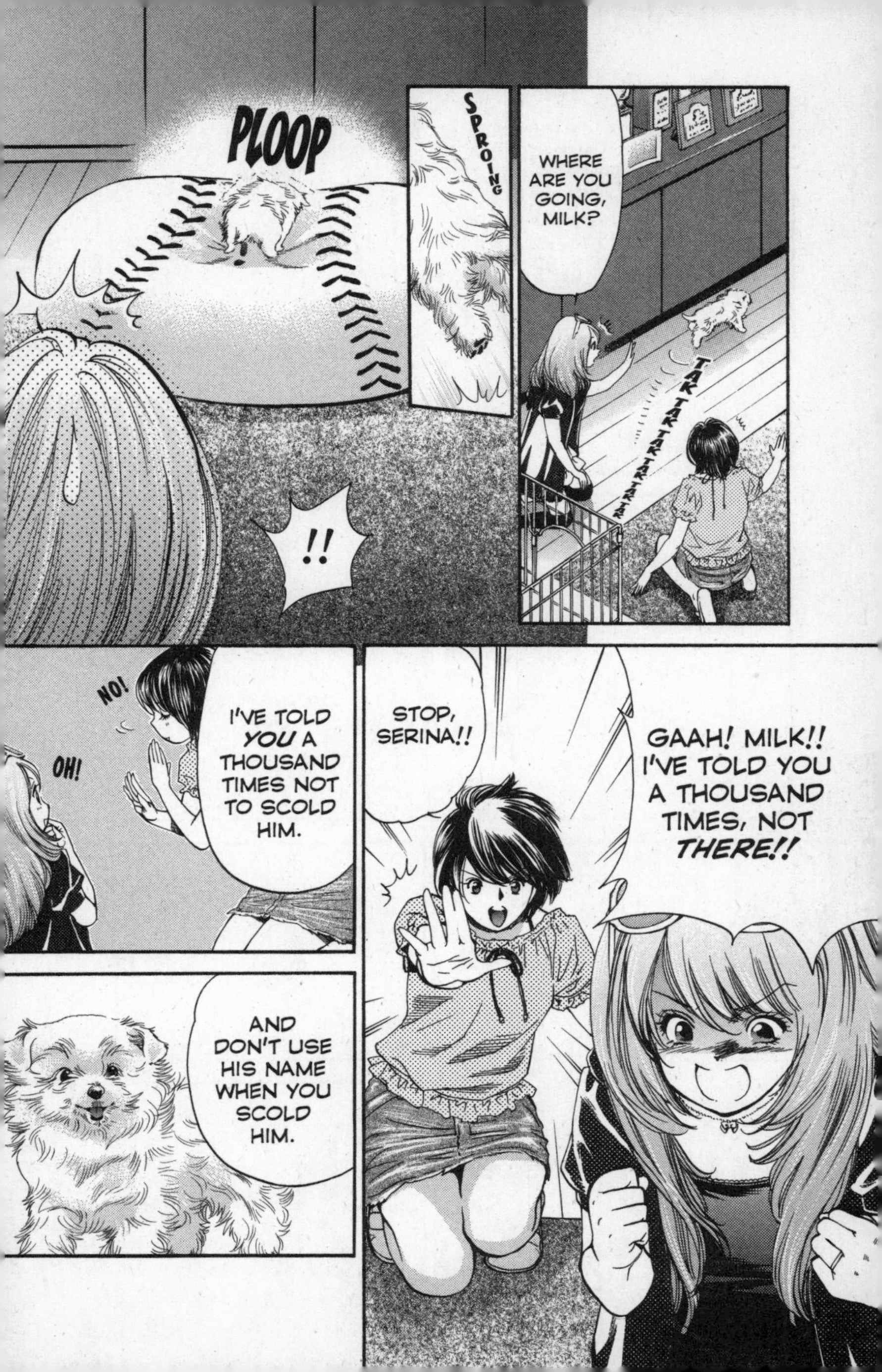
WHERE ARE YOU GOING, MILK?
TAK TAK TAK TAK TAK TAK
SPROING
PLOOP
!!
GAAH! MILK!! I'VE TOLD YOU A THOUSAND TIMES, NOT *THERE!!*
STOP, SERINA!!
NO!
OH!
I'VE TOLD *YOU* A THOUSAND TIMES NOT TO SCOLD HIM.
AND DON'T USE HIS NAME WHEN YOU SCOLD HIM.

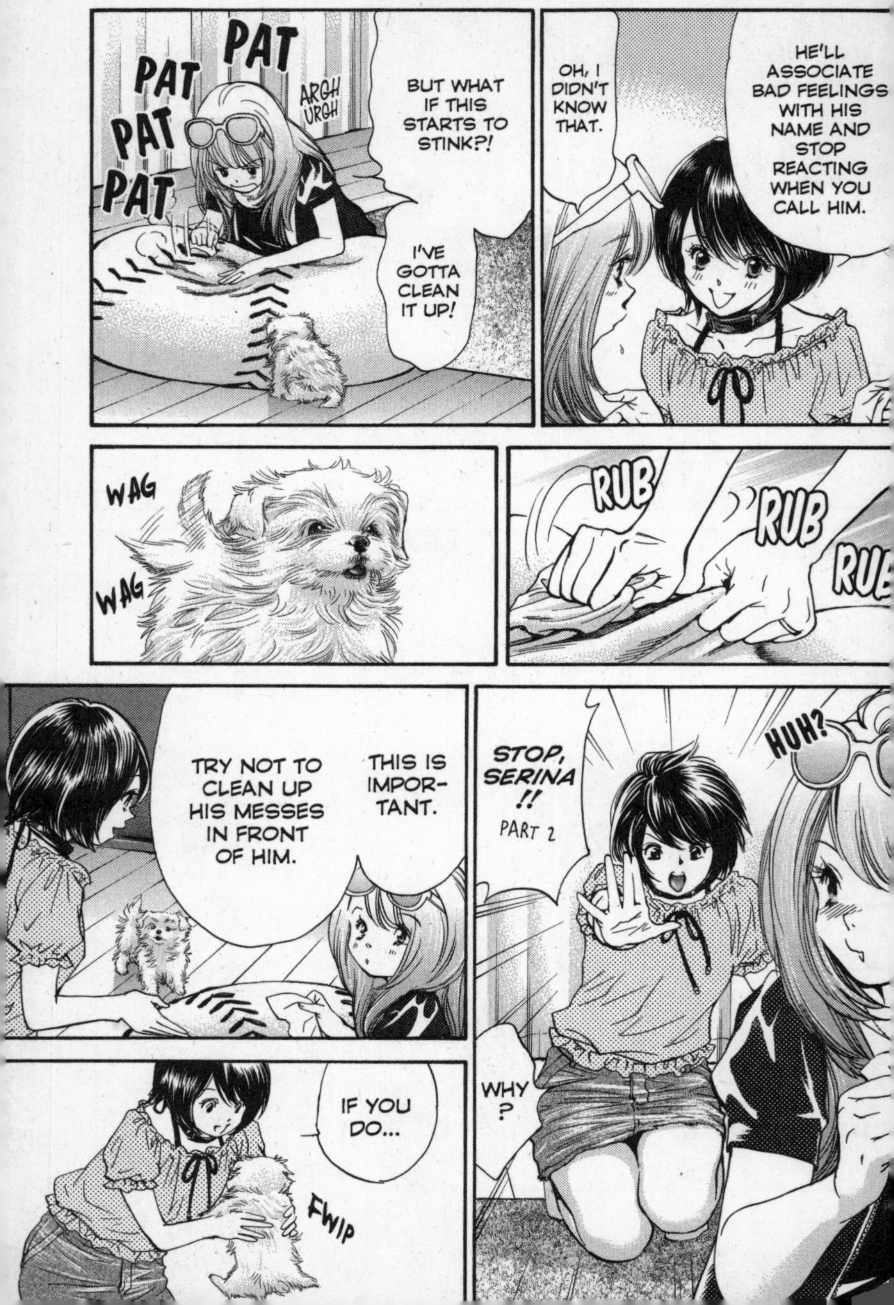

HE'LL ASSOCIATE BAD FEELINGS WITH HIS NAME AND STOP REACTING WHEN YOU CALL HIM.
OH, I DIDN'T KNOW THAT.
BUT WHAT IF THIS STARTS TO STINK?!
I'VE GOTTA CLEAN IT UP!
ARGH URGH
PAT
PAT
PAT
PAT
RUB
RUB
WAG
WAG
HUH?
STOP, SERINA!!
PART 2
WHY?
THIS IS IMPOR-TANT.
TRY NOT TO CLEAN UP HIS MESSES IN FRONT OF HIM.
IF YOU DO...
FWIP

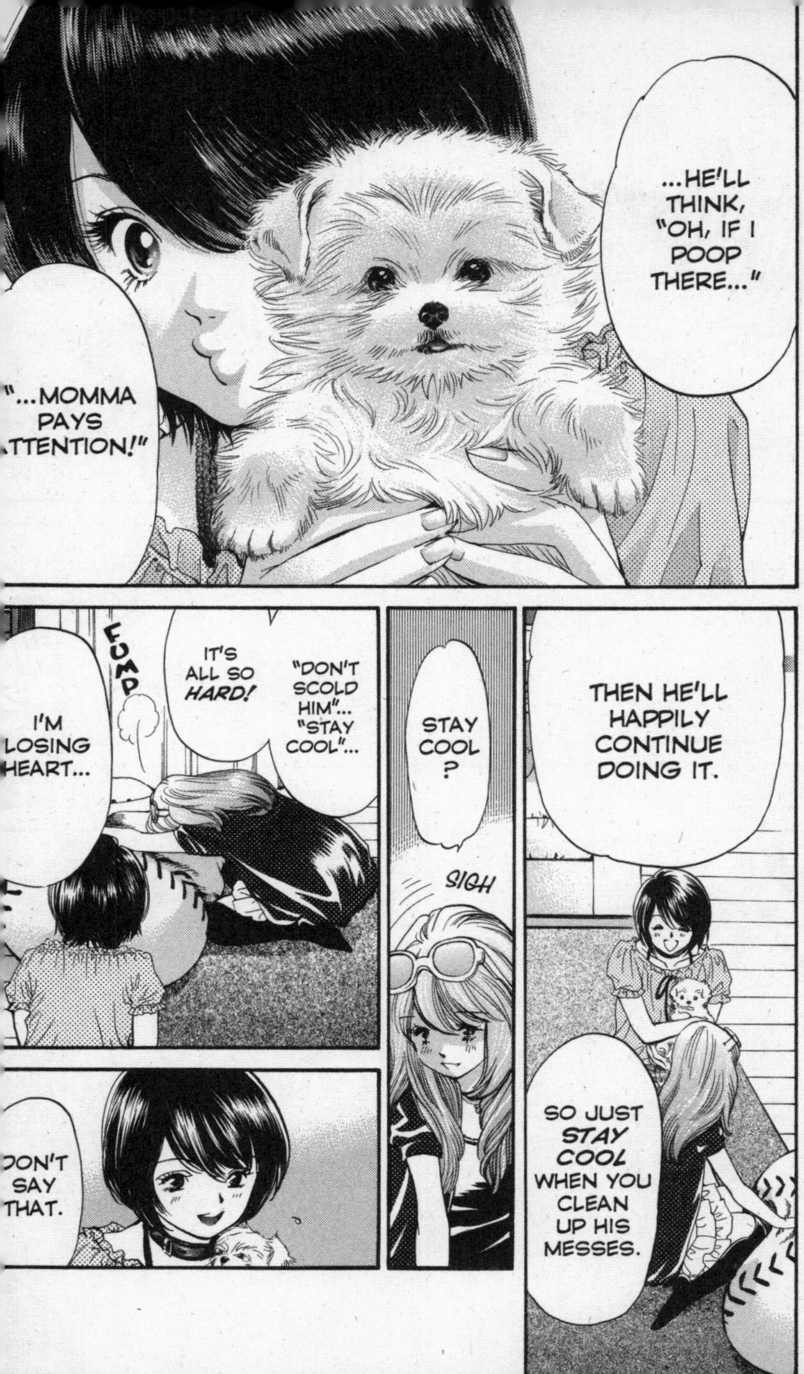
...HE'LL THINK, "OH, IF I POOP THERE..."
"...MOMMA PAYS TTENTION!"
THEN HE'LL HAPPILY CONTINUE DOING IT.
SO JUST *STAY COOL* WHEN YOU CLEAN UP HIS MESSES.
STAY COOL ?
SIGH
"DON'T SCOLD HIM"... "STAY COOL"...
IT'S ALL SO *HARD!*
FUMP
I'M LOSING HEART...
ON'T SAY THAT.

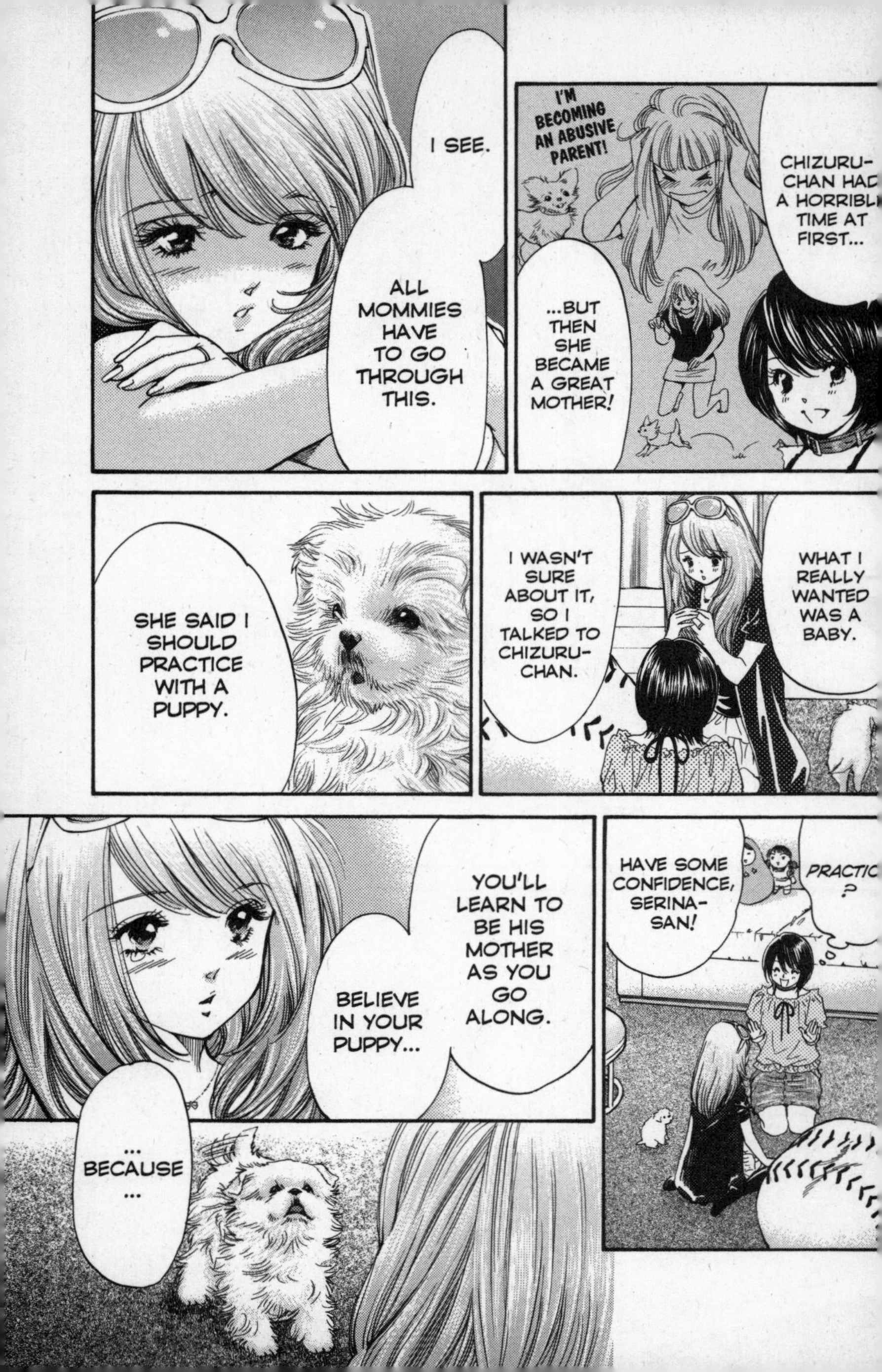
CHIZURU-CHAN HAD A HORRIBL TIME AT FIRST...
I'M BECOMING AN ABUSIVE PARENT!
...BUT THEN SHE BECAME A GREAT MOTHER!
I SEE.
ALL MOMMIES HAVE TO GO THROUGH THIS.
WHAT I REALLY WANTED WAS A BABY.
I WASN'T SURE ABOUT IT, SO I TALKED TO CHIZURU-CHAN.
SHE SAID I SHOULD PRACTICE WITH A PUPPY.
PRACTIC ?
HAVE SOME CONFIDENCE, SERINA-SAN!
YOU'LL LEARN TO BE HIS MOTHER AS YOU GO ALONG.
BELIEVE IN YOUR PUPPY...
...BECAUSE...

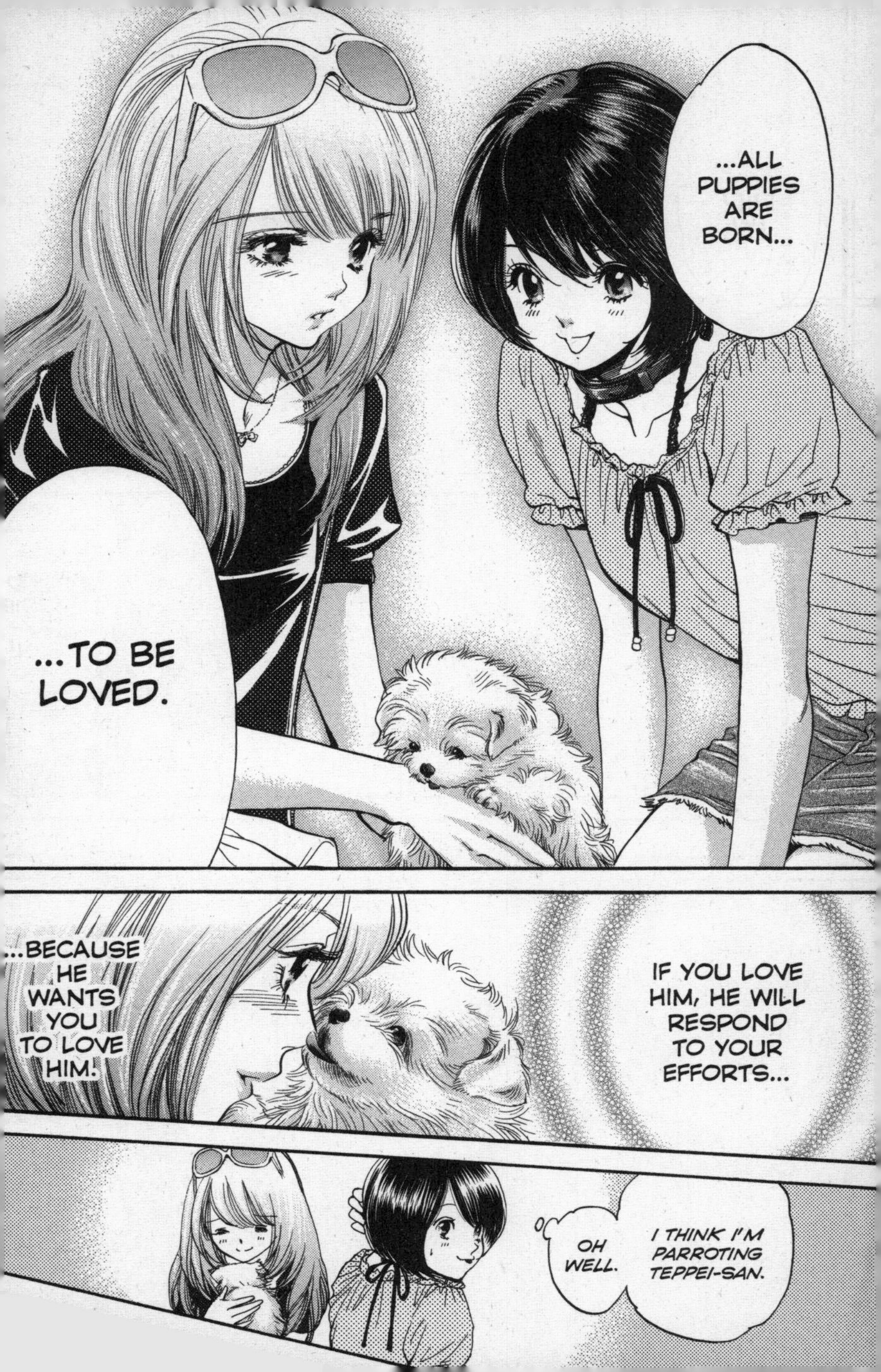
...ALL PUPPIES ARE BORN...
...TO BE LOVED.
IF YOU LOVE HIM, HE WILL RESPOND TO YOUR EFFORTS...
...BECAUSE HE WANTS YOU TO LOVE HIM.
I THINK I'M PARROTING TEPPEI-SAN.
OH WELL.

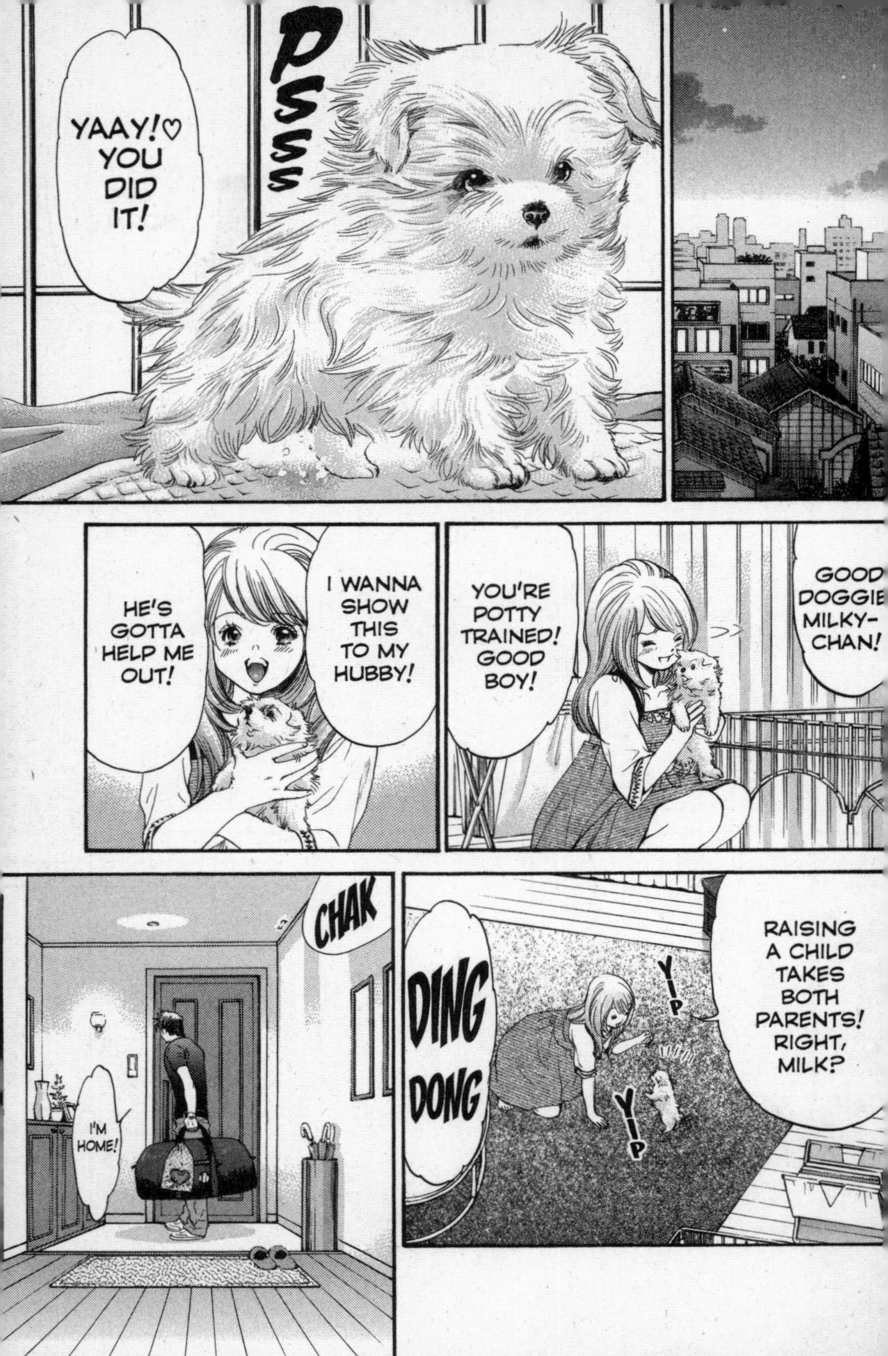
PSSS
YAAY!♡ YOU DID IT!
GOOD DOGGIE MILKY-CHAN!
YOU'RE POTTY TRAINED! GOOD BOY!
I WANNA SHOW THIS TO MY HUBBY!
HE'S GOTTA HELP ME OUT!
RAISING A CHILD TAKES BOTH PARENTS! RIGHT, MILK?
YIP
YIP
DING DONG
CHAK
I'M HOME!

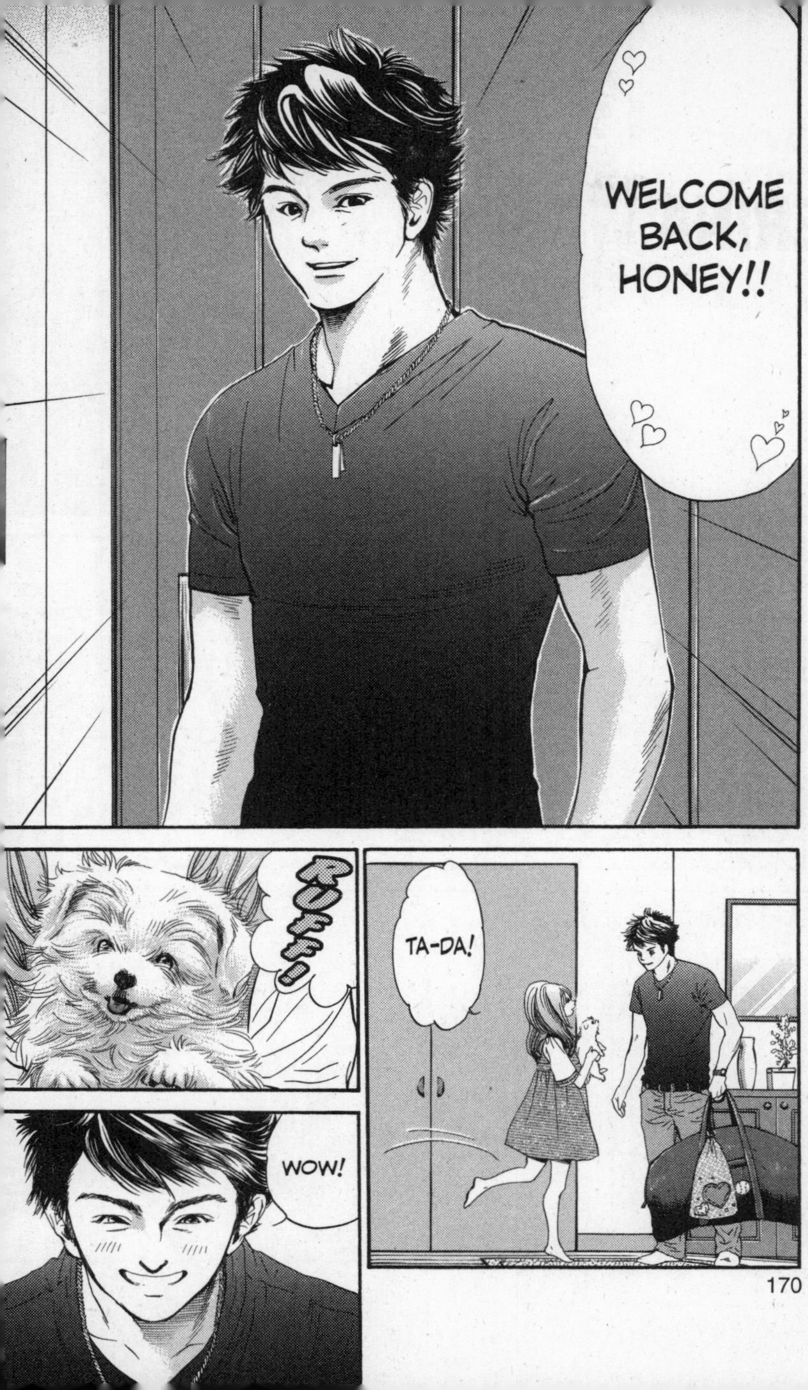
WELCOME BACK, HONEY!!
TA-DA!
POFF!
WOW!

CHAPTER 172: SERINA WANTS A BABY SOON

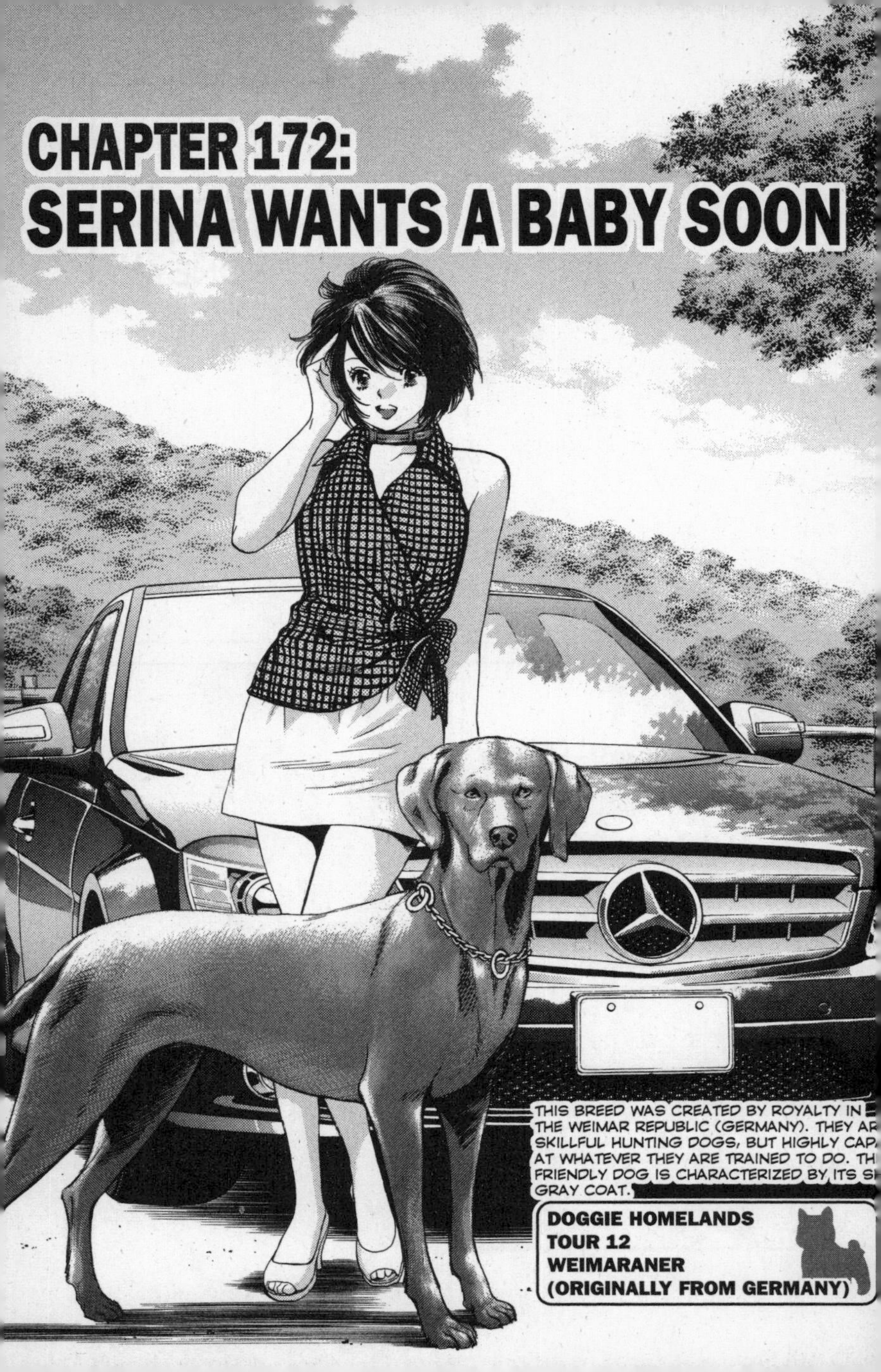
THIS BREED WAS CREATED BY ROYALTY IN
THE WEIMAR REPUBLIC (GERMANY). THEY AR
SKILLFUL HUNTING DOGS, BUT HIGHLY CAP
AT WHATEVER THEY ARE TRAINED TO DO. TH
FRIENDLY DOG IS CHARACTERIZED BY ITS S
GRAY COAT.
DOGGIE HOMELANDS
TOUR 12
WEIMARANER
(ORIGINALLY FROM GERMANY)

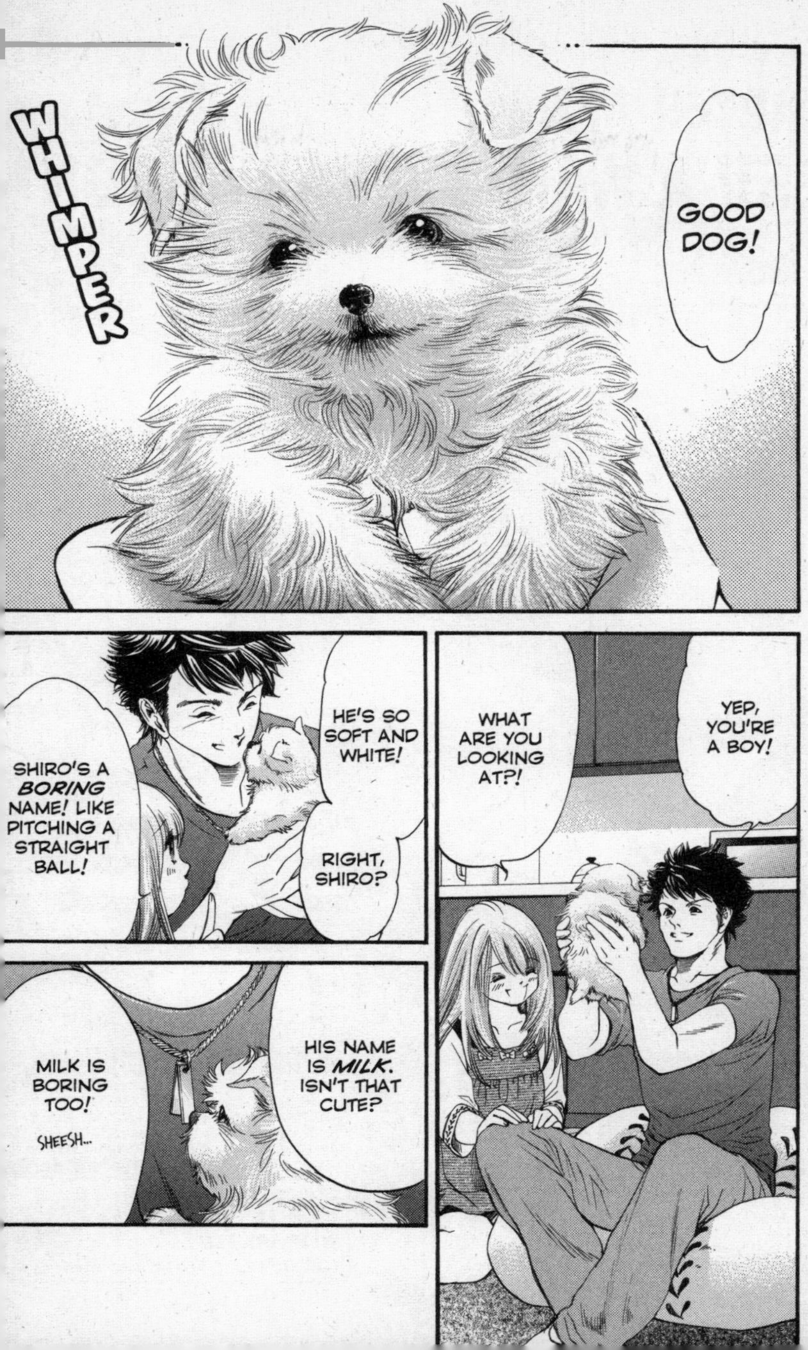
GOOD DOG!
WHIMPER
YEP, YOU'RE A BOY!
WHAT ARE YOU LOOKING AT?!
HE'S SO SOFT AND WHITE!
RIGHT, SHIRO?
SHIRO'S A *BORING* NAME! LIKE PITCHING A STRAIGHT BALL!
HIS NAME IS *MILK*. ISN'T THAT CUTE?
MILK IS BORING TOO!
SHEESH...

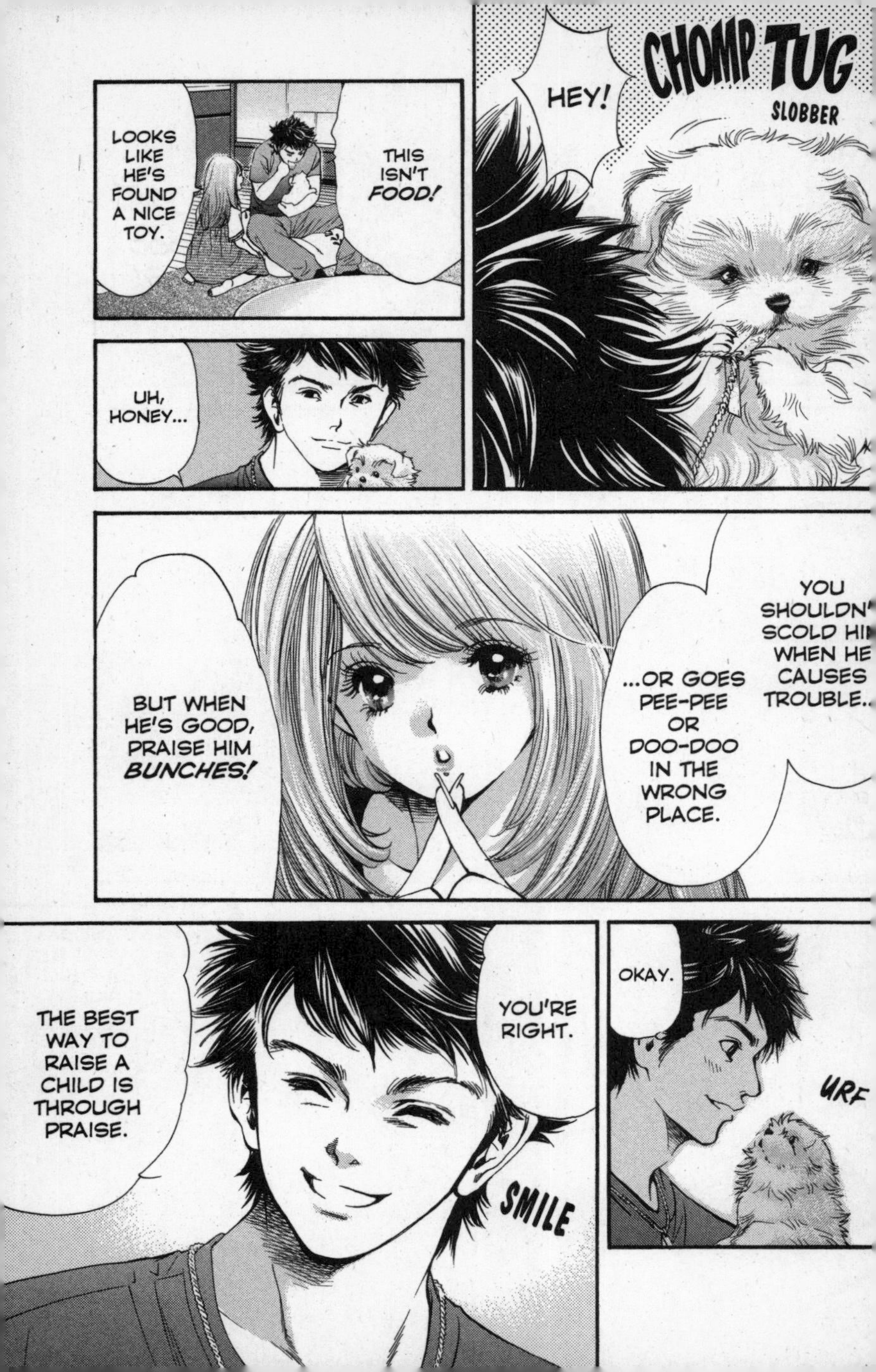
HEY!
CHOMP TUG
SLOBBER
THIS ISN'T *FOOD!*
LOOKS LIKE HE'S FOUND A NICE TOY.
UH, HONEY...
YOU SHOULDN' SCOLD HI WHEN HE CAUSES TROUBLE..
...OR GOES PEE-PEE OR DOO-DOO IN THE WRONG PLACE.
BUT WHEN HE'S GOOD, PRAISE HIM *BUNCHES!*
OKAY.
URF
YOU'RE RIGHT.
THE BEST WAY TO RAISE A CHILD IS THROUGH PRAISE.
SMILE

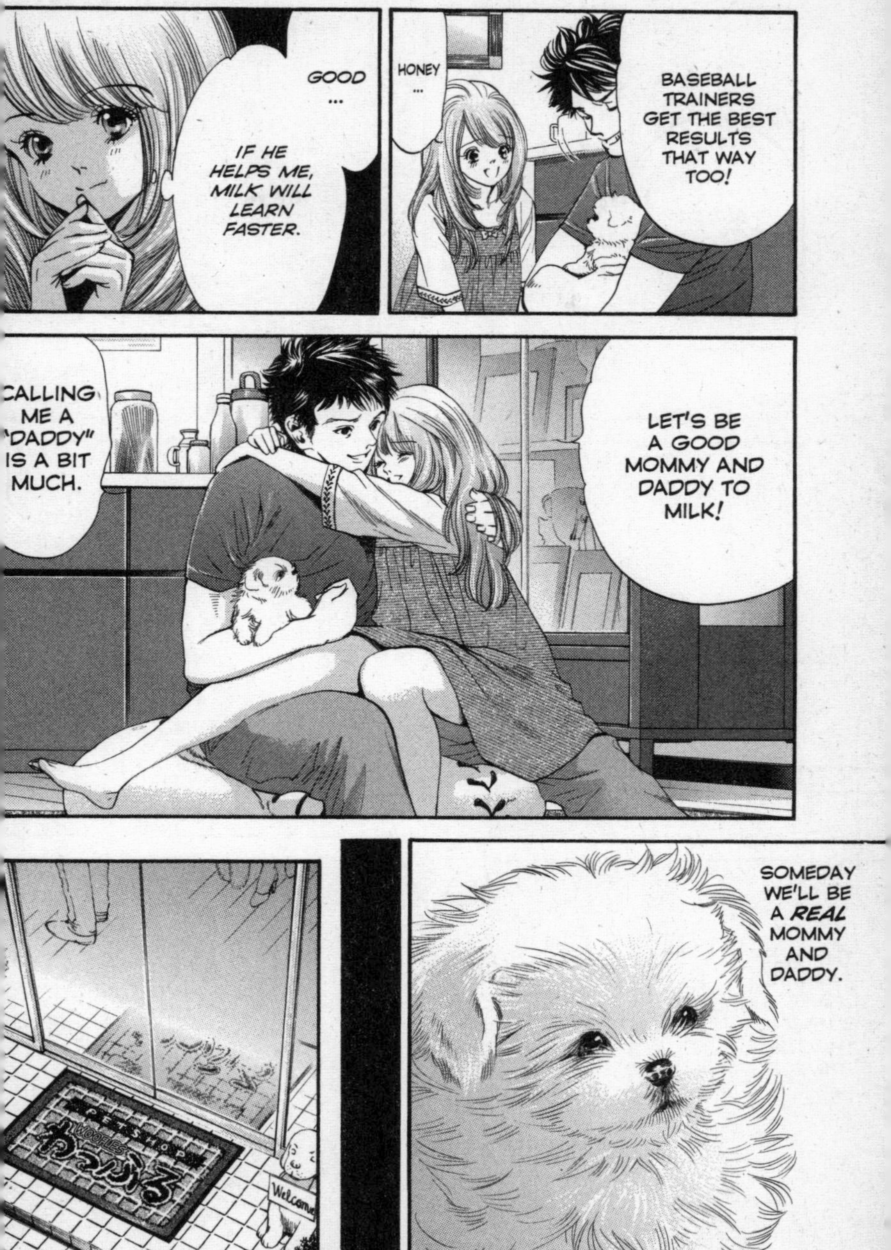
BASEBALL TRAINERS GET THE BEST RESULTS THAT WAY TOO!
HONEY ...
GOOD ...
IF HE HELPS ME, MILK WILL LEARN FASTER.
LET'S BE A GOOD MOMMY AND DADDY TO MILK!
CALLING ME A "DADDY" IS A BIT MUCH.
SOMEDAY WE'LL BE A *REAL* MOMMY AND DADDY.
PET SHOP
WOOFIES
Welcome

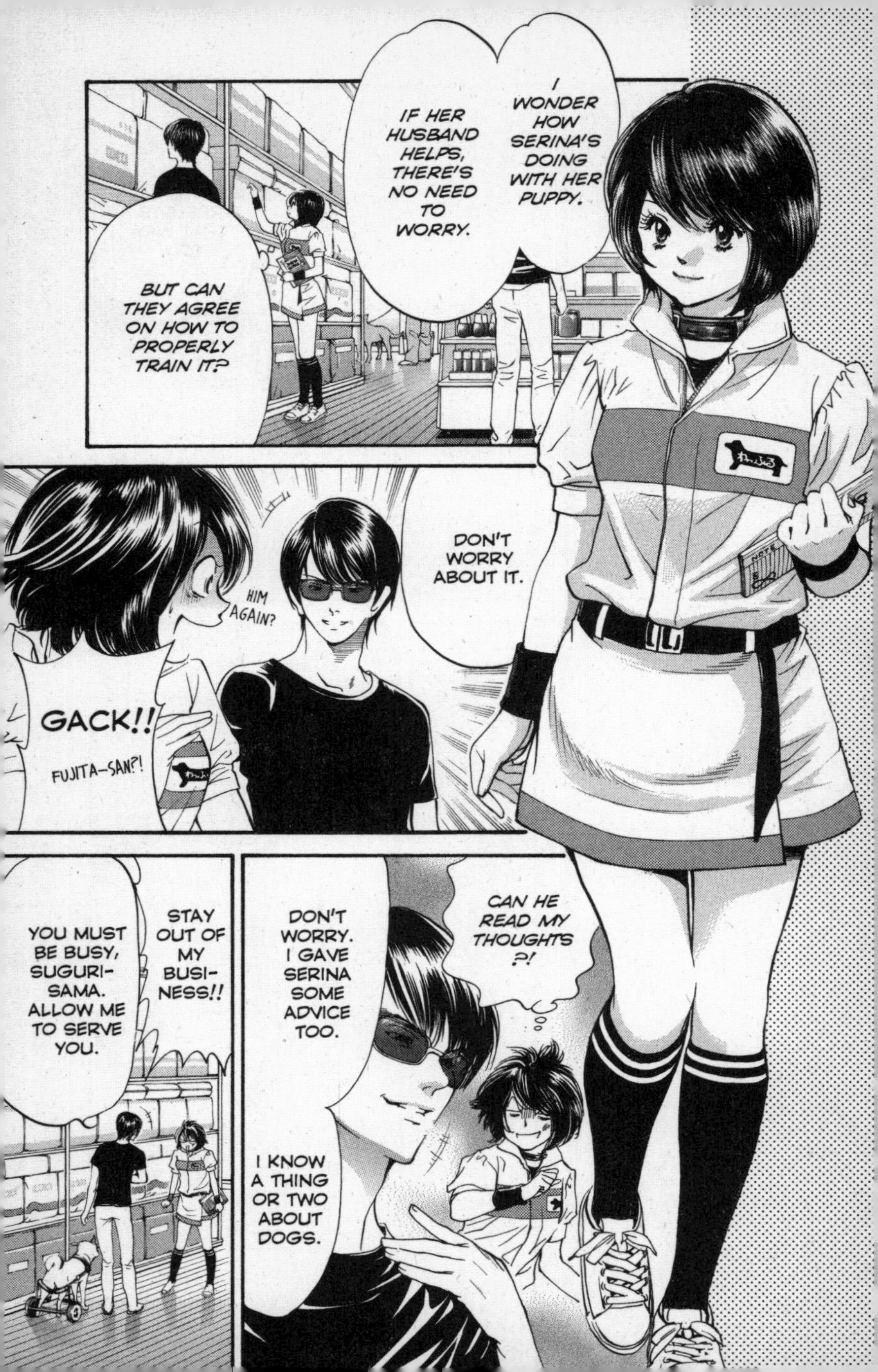
I WONDER HOW SERINA'S DOING WITH HER PUPPY.
IF HER HUSBAND HELPS, THERE'S NO NEED TO WORRY.
BUT CAN THEY AGREE ON HOW TO PROPERLY TRAIN IT?
DON'T WORRY ABOUT IT.
HIM AGAIN?
GACK!!
FUJITA-SAN?!
CAN HE READ MY THOUGHTS?!
DON'T WORRY. I GAVE SERINA SOME ADVICE TOO.
I KNOW A THING OR TWO ABOUT DOGS.
STAY OUT OF MY BUSINESS!!
YOU MUST BE BUSY, SUGURI-SAMA. ALLOW ME TO SERVE YOU.

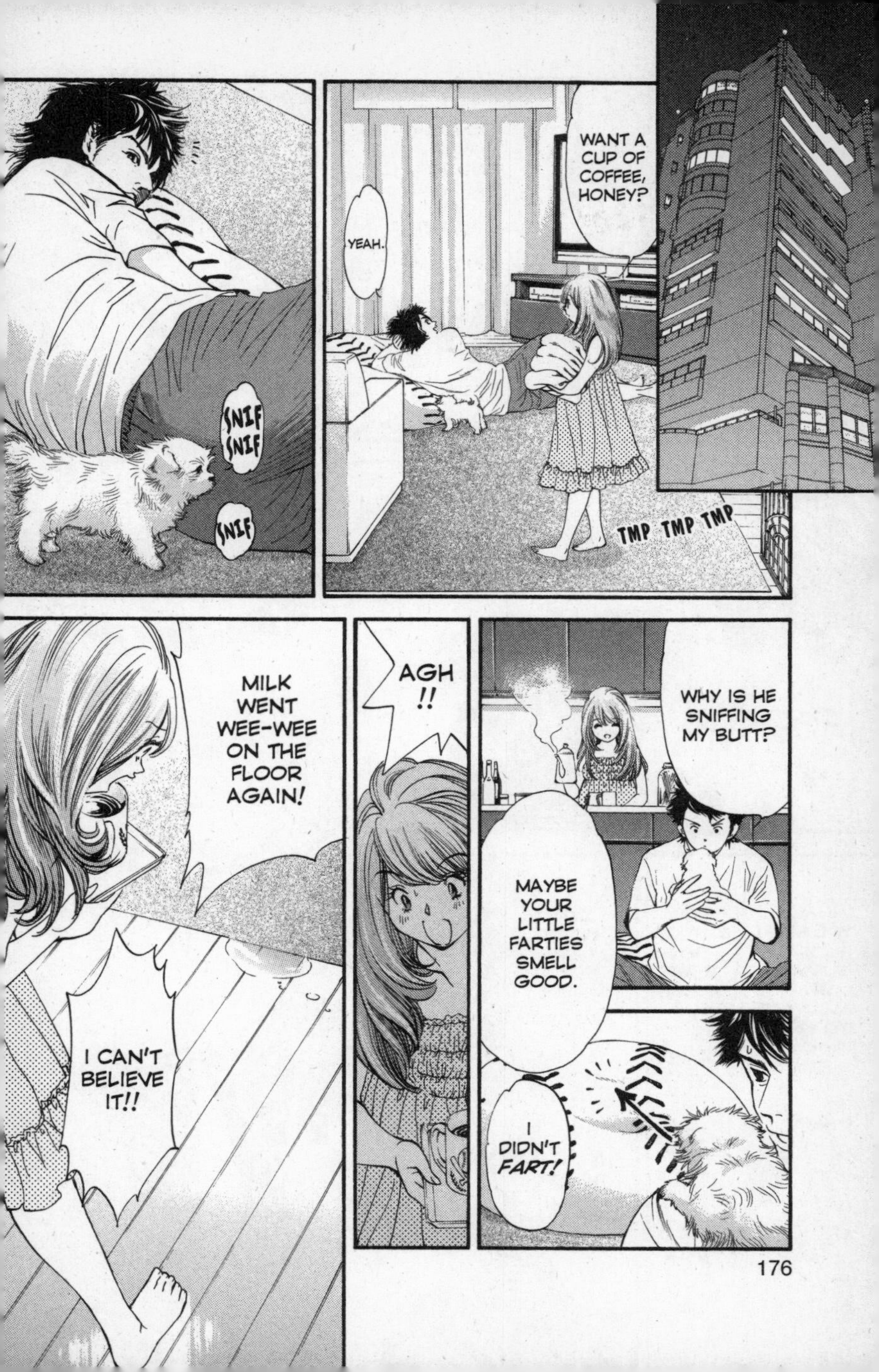
WANT A CUP OF COFFEE, HONEY?
YEAH.
TMP TMP TMP
SNIF SNIF
SNIF
WHY IS HE SNIFFING MY BUTT?
MAYBE YOUR LITTLE FARTIES SMELL GOOD.
I DIDN'T *FART!*
AGH!!
MILK WENT WEE-WEE ON THE FLOOR AGAIN!
I CAN'T BELIEVE IT!!

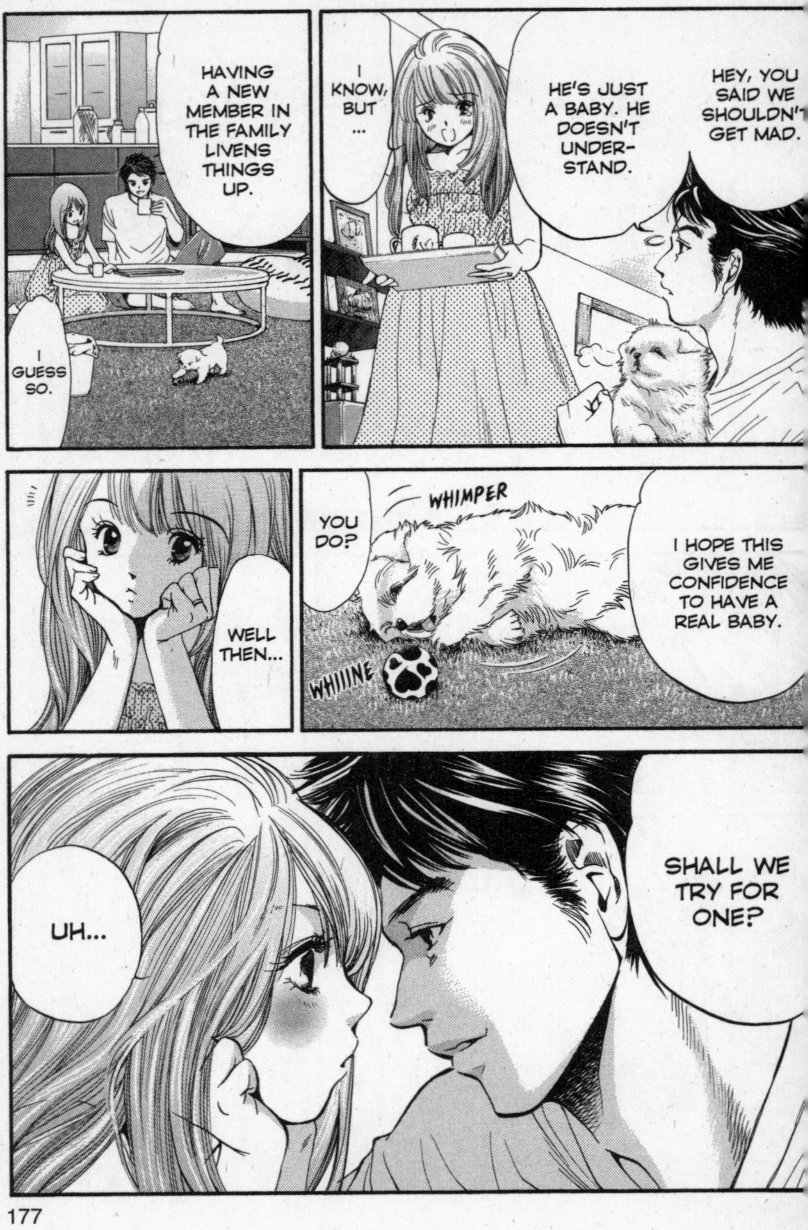
HEY, YOU SAID WE SHOULDN'T GET MAD.
HE'S JUST A BABY. HE DOESN'T UNDER-STAND.
I KNOW, BUT ...
HAVING A NEW MEMBER IN THE FAMILY LIVENS THINGS UP.
I GUESS SO.
I HOPE THIS GIVES ME CONFIDENCE TO HAVE A REAL BABY.
WHIMPER
YOU DO?
WHIIINE
WELL THEN...
SHALL WE TRY FOR ONE?
UH...

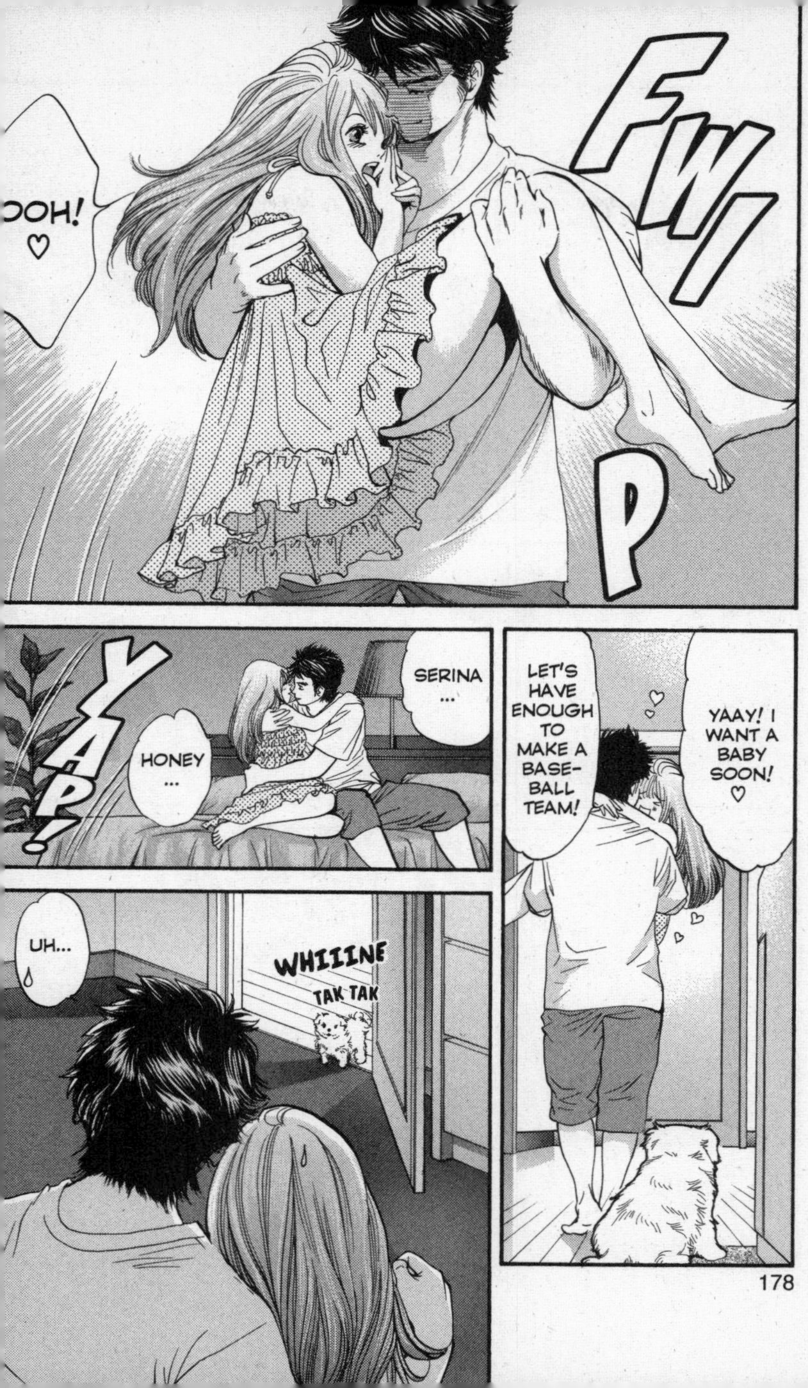
FWIP
OOH! ♡
YAAY! I WANT A BABY SOON! ♡
LET'S HAVE ENOUGH TO MAKE A BASE-BALL TEAM!
SERINA ...
HONEY ...
YAP!
WHIIINE
TAK TAK
UH...

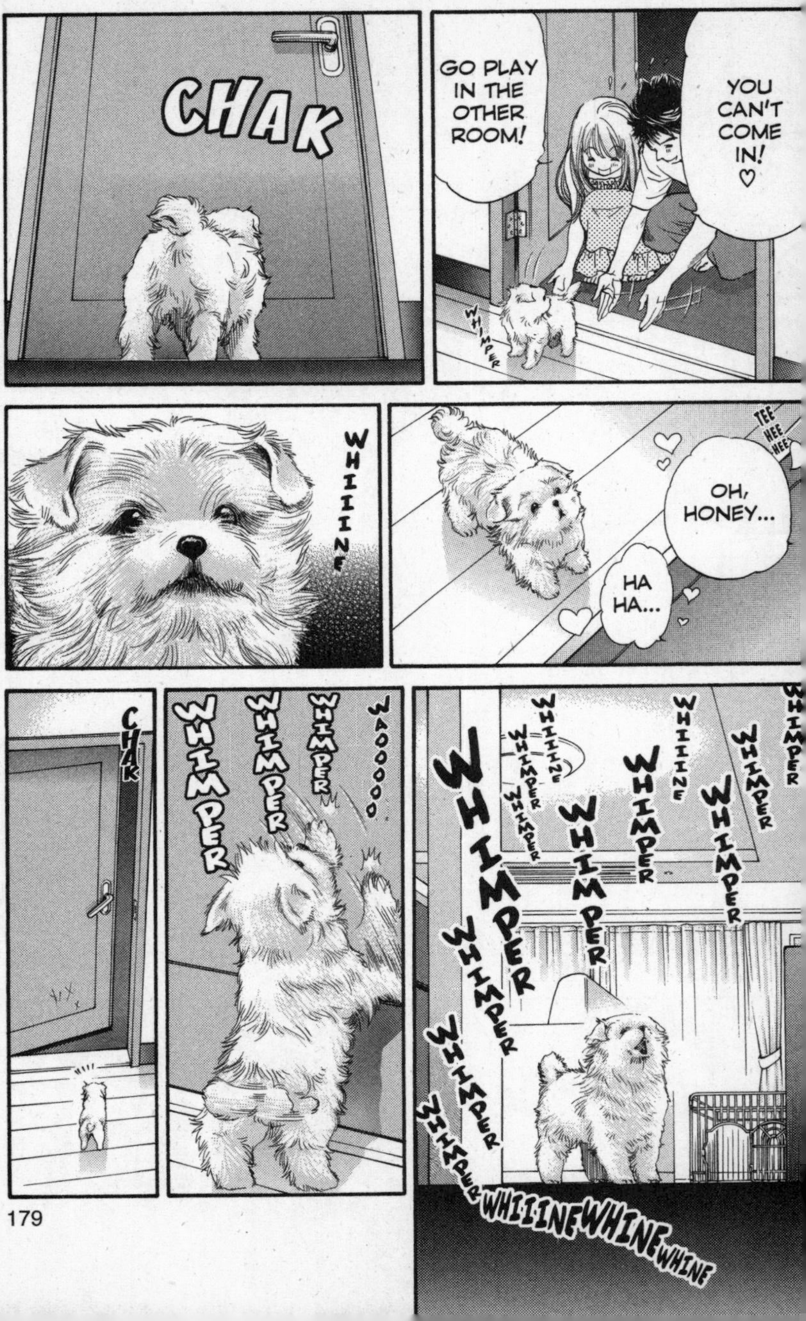
YOU CAN'T COME IN! ♡
GO PLAY IN THE OTHER ROOM!
WHIMPER
CHAK
TEE HEE HEE
OH, HONEY...
HA HA...
WHIIIINE
WHIMPER
WHIMPER
WHIMPER
WHIIIINE
WHIMPER
WHIMPER
WHIIIINE
WHIMPER
WHIMPER
WHIMPER
WHIMPER
WHIMPER
WHIMPER
WHIMPER
WHIIINE WHINE WHINE
WAOOOOO
WHIMPER
WHIMPER
WHIMPER
CHAK

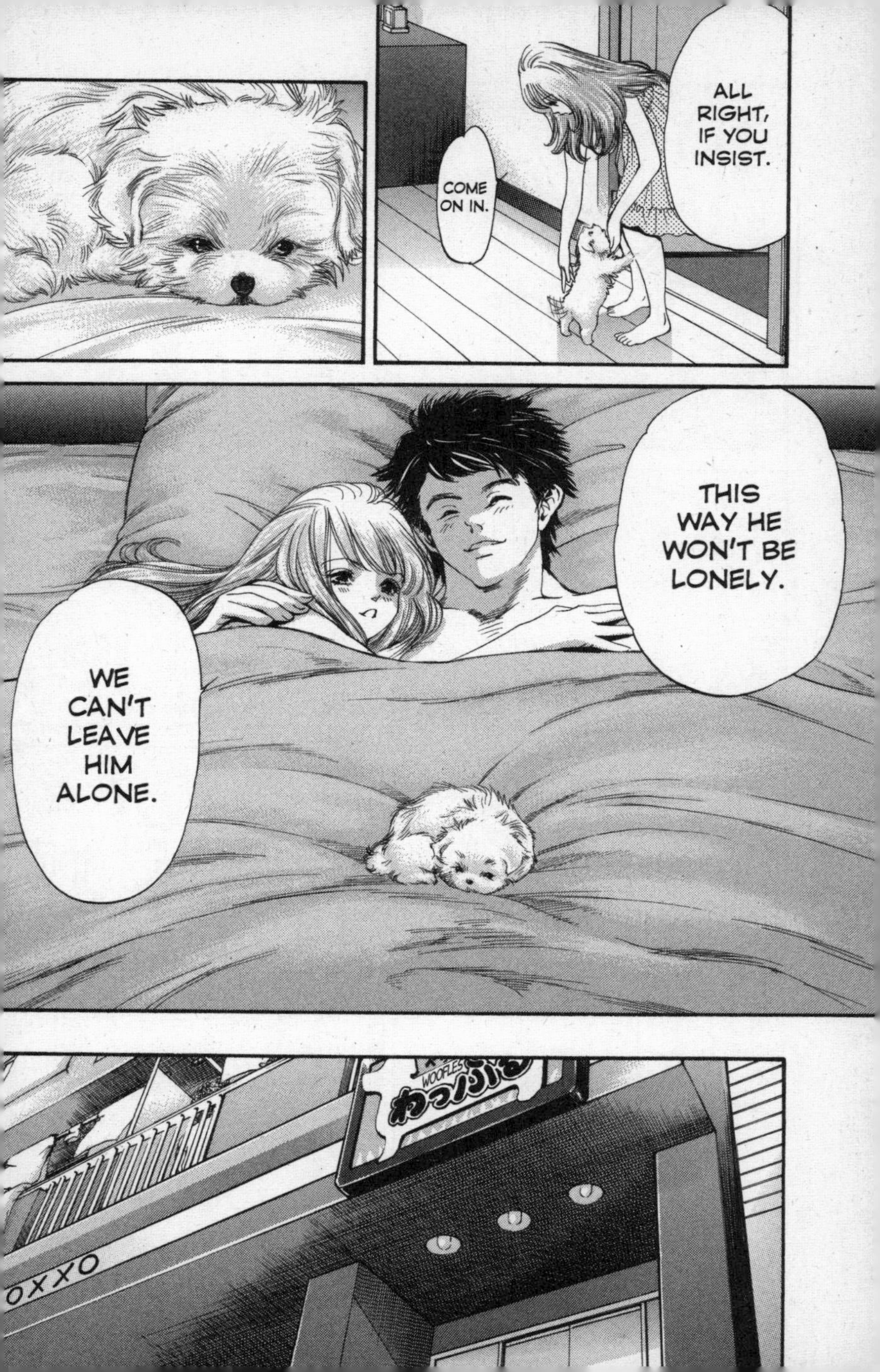
ALL RIGHT, IF YOU INSIST.
COME ON IN.
THIS WAY HE WON'T BE LONELY.
WE CAN'T LEAVE HIM ALONE.
WOOFLES

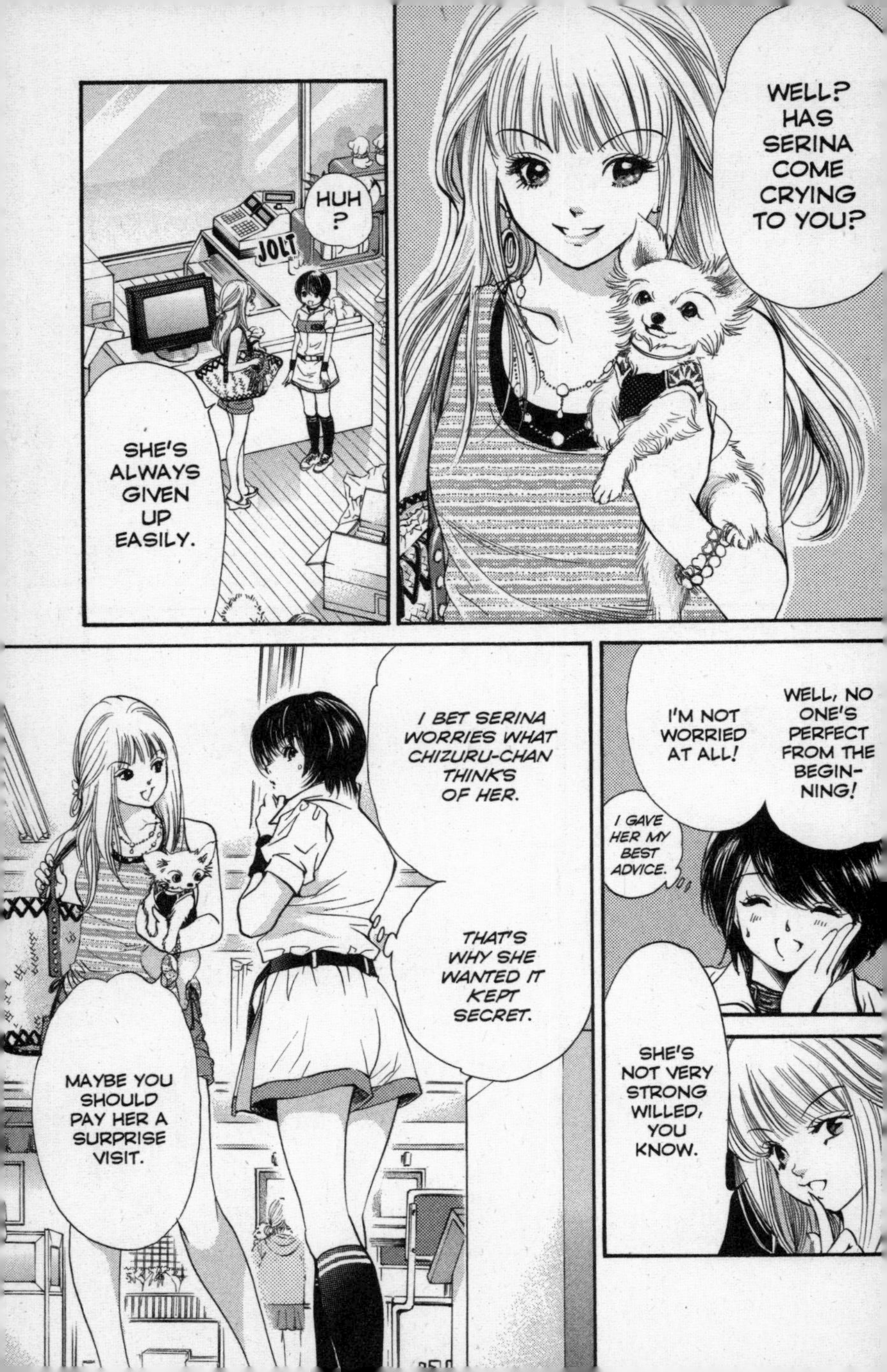
WELL? HAS SERINA COME CRYING TO YOU?
HUH?
JOLT
SHE'S ALWAYS GIVEN UP EASILY.
WELL, NO ONE'S PERFECT FROM THE BEGINNING!
I'M NOT WORRIED AT ALL!
I GAVE HER MY BEST ADVICE.
SHE'S NOT VERY STRONG WILLED, YOU KNOW.
I BET SERINA WORRIES WHAT CHIZURU-CHAN THINKS OF HER.
THAT'S WHY SHE WANTED IT KEPT SECRET.
MAYBE YOU SHOULD PAY HER A SURPRISE VISIT.

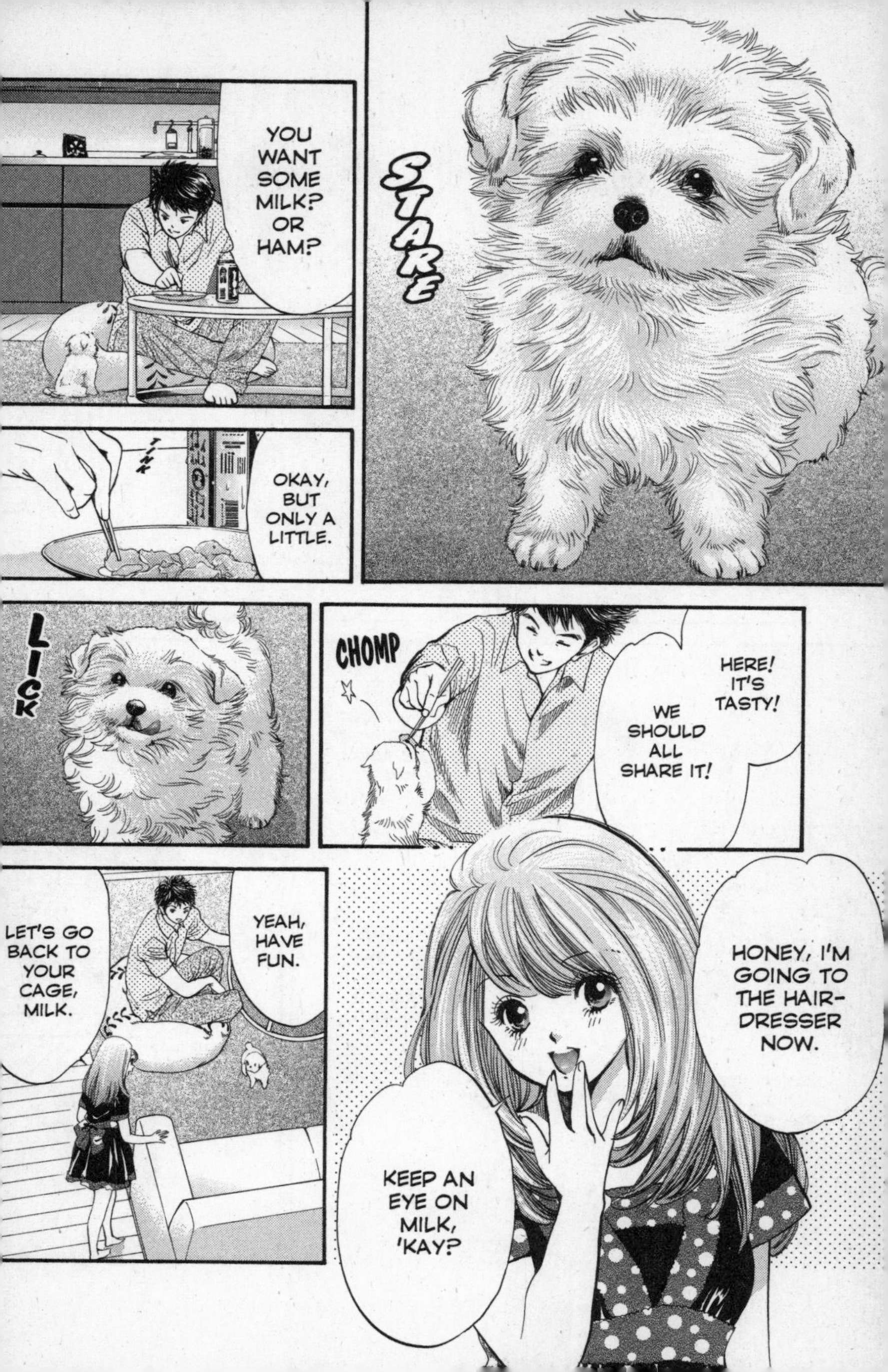
STARE
YOU WANT SOME MILK? OR HAM?
TINK
OKAY, BUT ONLY A LITTLE.
CHOMP
HERE! IT'S TASTY!
WE SHOULD ALL SHARE IT!
LICK
HONEY, I'M GOING TO THE HAIR-DRESSER NOW.
KEEP AN EYE ON MILK, 'KAY?
YEAH, HAVE FUN.
LET'S GO BACK TO YOUR CAGE, MILK.

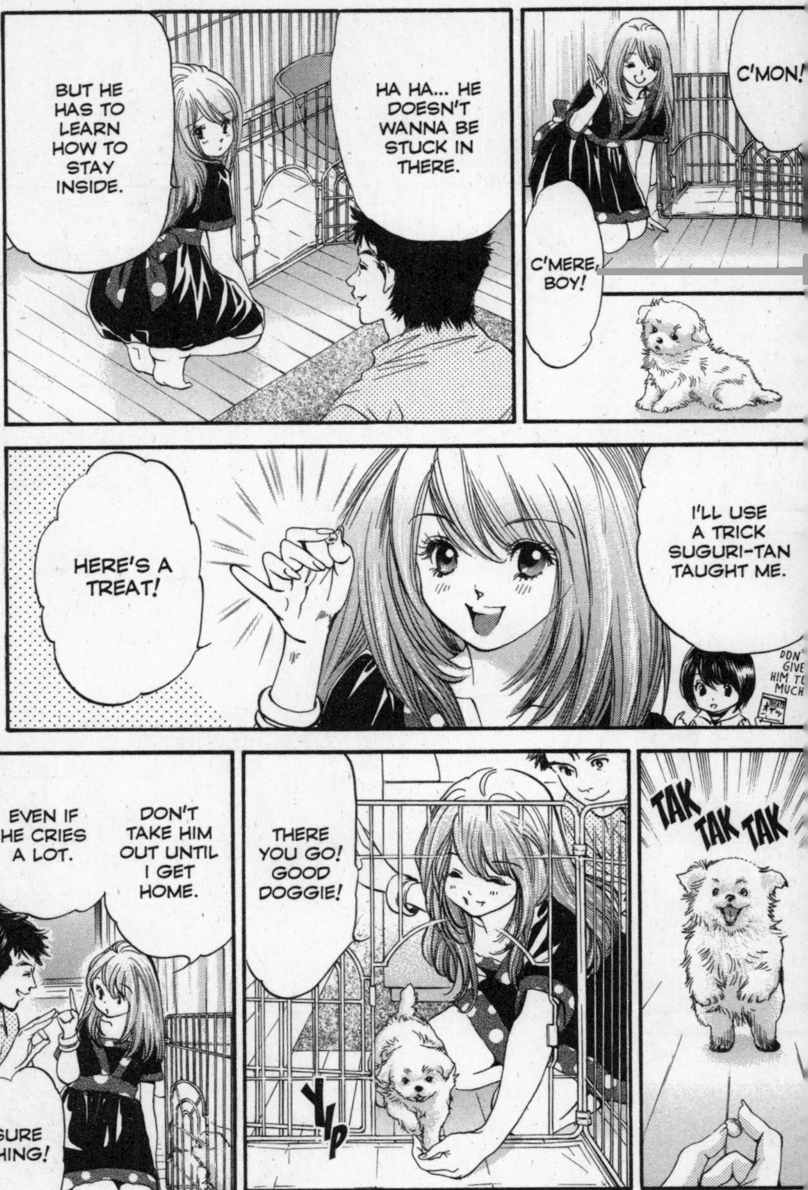
C'MON!
C'MERE, BOY!
HA HA... HE DOESN'T WANNA BE STUCK IN THERE.
BUT HE HAS TO LEARN HOW TO STAY INSIDE.
I'LL USE A TRICK SUGURI-TAN TAUGHT ME.
HERE'S A TREAT!
TAK TAK TAK
THERE YOU GO! GOOD DOGGIE!
YIP
DON'T TAKE HIM OUT UNTIL I GET HOME.
EVEN IF HE CRIES A LOT.
SURE THING!

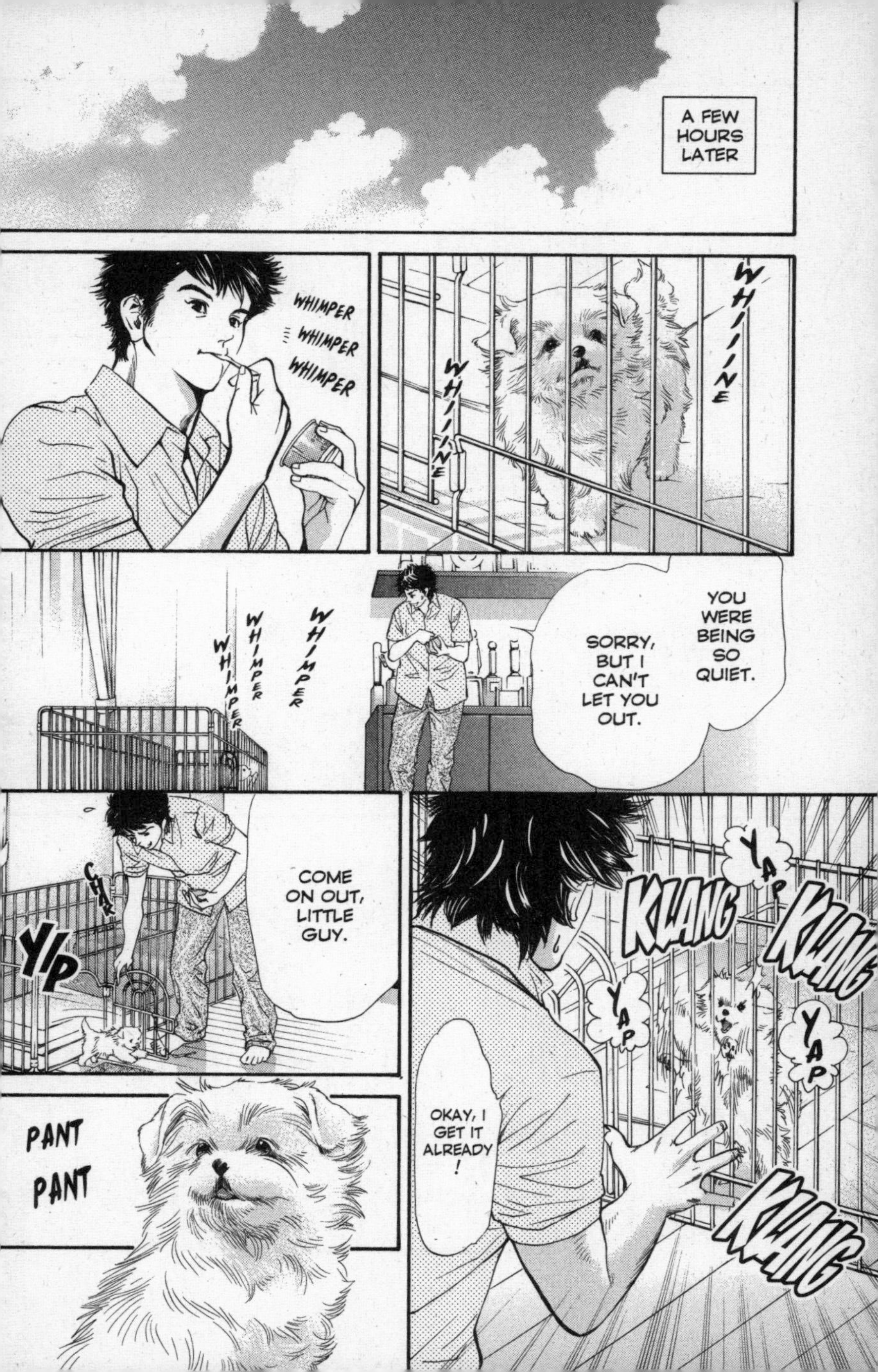
A FEW HOURS LATER
WHIIIINE
WHIIIINE
WHIMPER
WHIMPER
WHIMPER
YOU WERE BEING SO QUIET.
SORRY, BUT I CAN'T LET YOU OUT.
WHIMPER
WHIMPER
WHIMPER
YAP
KLANG
KLANG
YAP
YAP
OKAY, I GET IT ALREADY!
KLANG
COME ON OUT, LITTLE GUY.
CHAK
YIP
PANT
PANT

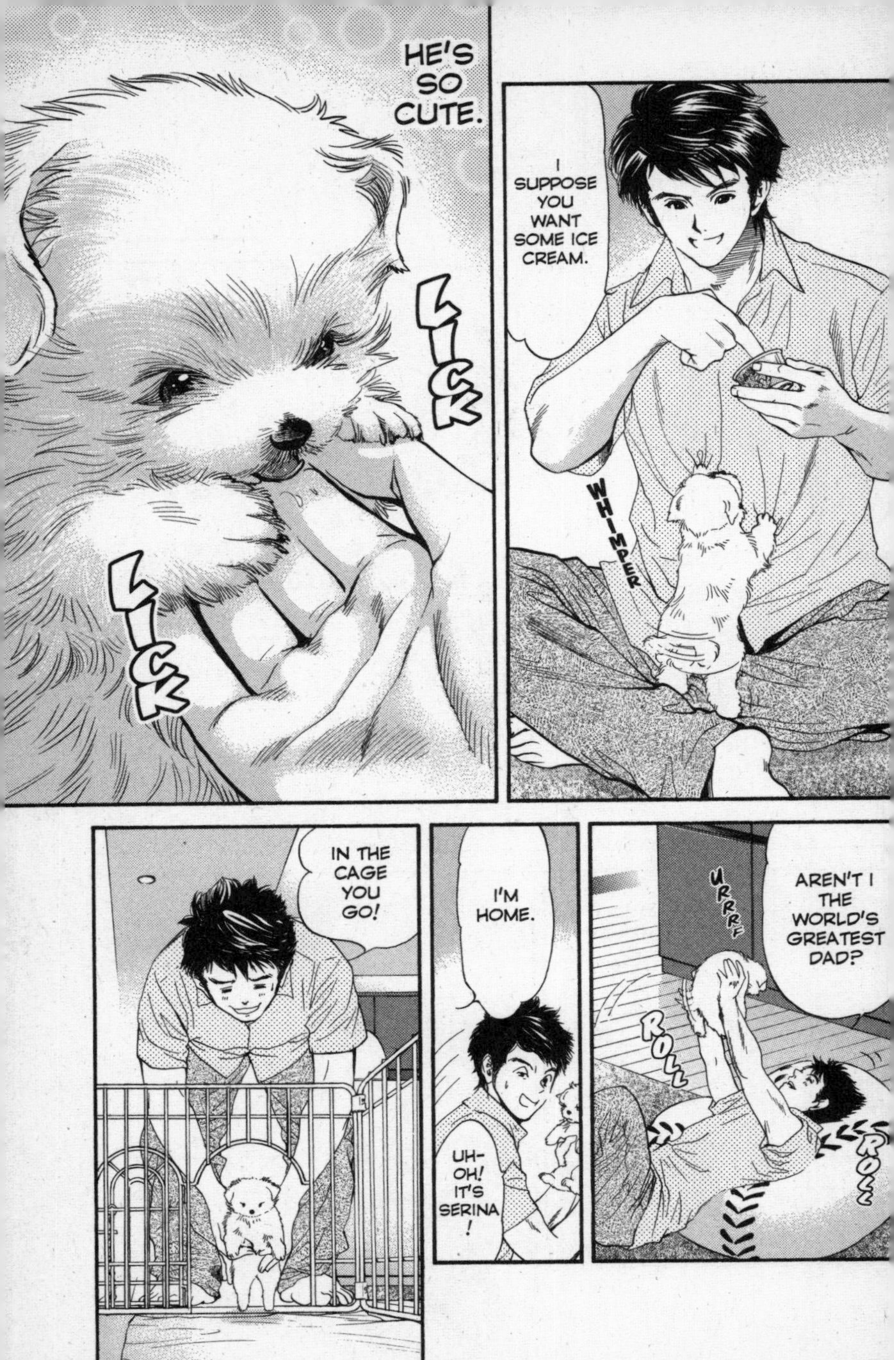
I SUPPOSE YOU WANT SOME ICE CREAM.
WHIMPER
HE'S SO CUTE.
LICK
LICK
AREN'T I THE WORLD'S GREATEST DAD?
URRRF
ROLL
ROLL
I'M HOME.
UH-OH! IT'S SERINA!
IN THE CAGE YOU GO!

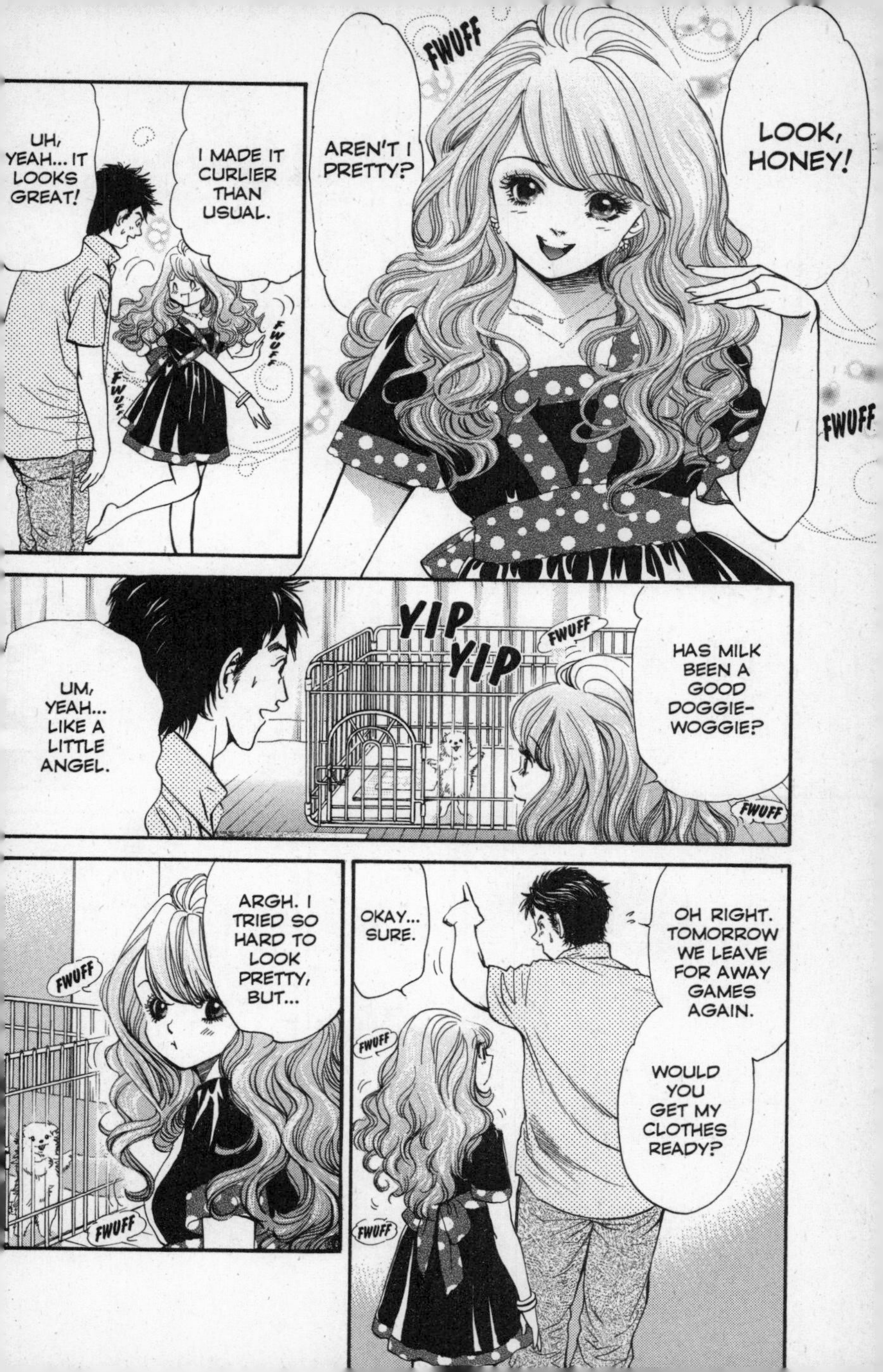
LOOK, HONEY!
FWUFF
FWUFF
AREN'T I PRETTY?
I MADE IT CURLIER THAN USUAL.
FWUFF
FWUFF
UH, YEAH... IT LOOKS GREAT!
HAS MILK BEEN A GOOD DOGGIE-WOGGIE?
FWUFF
FWUFF
YIP YIP
UM, YEAH... LIKE A LITTLE ANGEL.
OH RIGHT. TOMORROW WE LEAVE FOR AWAY GAMES AGAIN.
WOULD YOU GET MY CLOTHES READY?
OKAY... SURE.
FWUFF
FWUFF
ARGH. I TRIED SO HARD TO LOOK PRETTY, BUT...
FWUFF
FWUFF

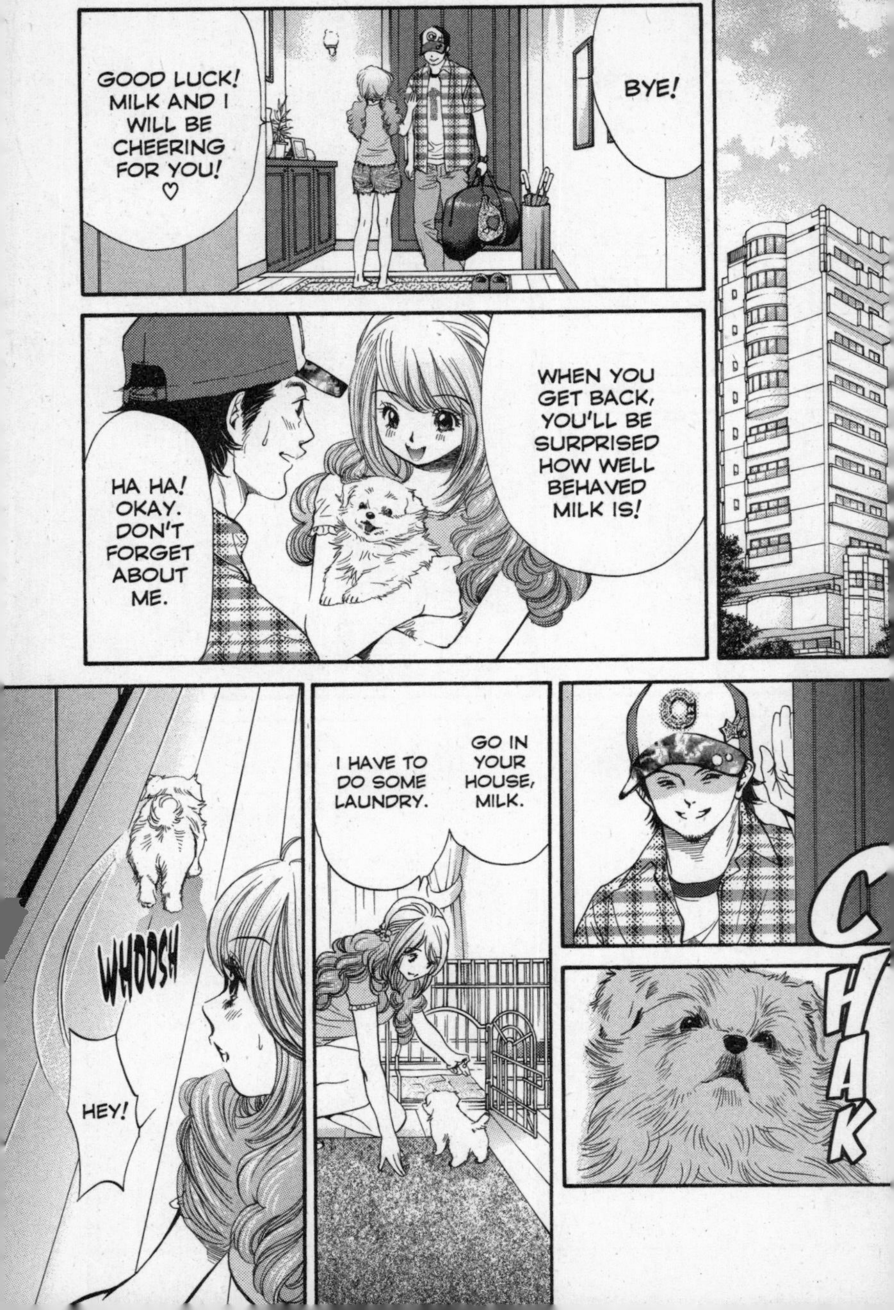
BYE!
GOOD LUCK! MILK AND I WILL BE CHEERING FOR YOU! ♡
WHEN YOU GET BACK, YOU'LL BE SURPRISED HOW WELL BEHAVED MILK IS!
HA HA! OKAY. DON'T FORGET ABOUT ME.
CHAK
GO IN YOUR HOUSE, MILK.
I HAVE TO DO SOME LAUNDRY.
WHOOSH
HEY!

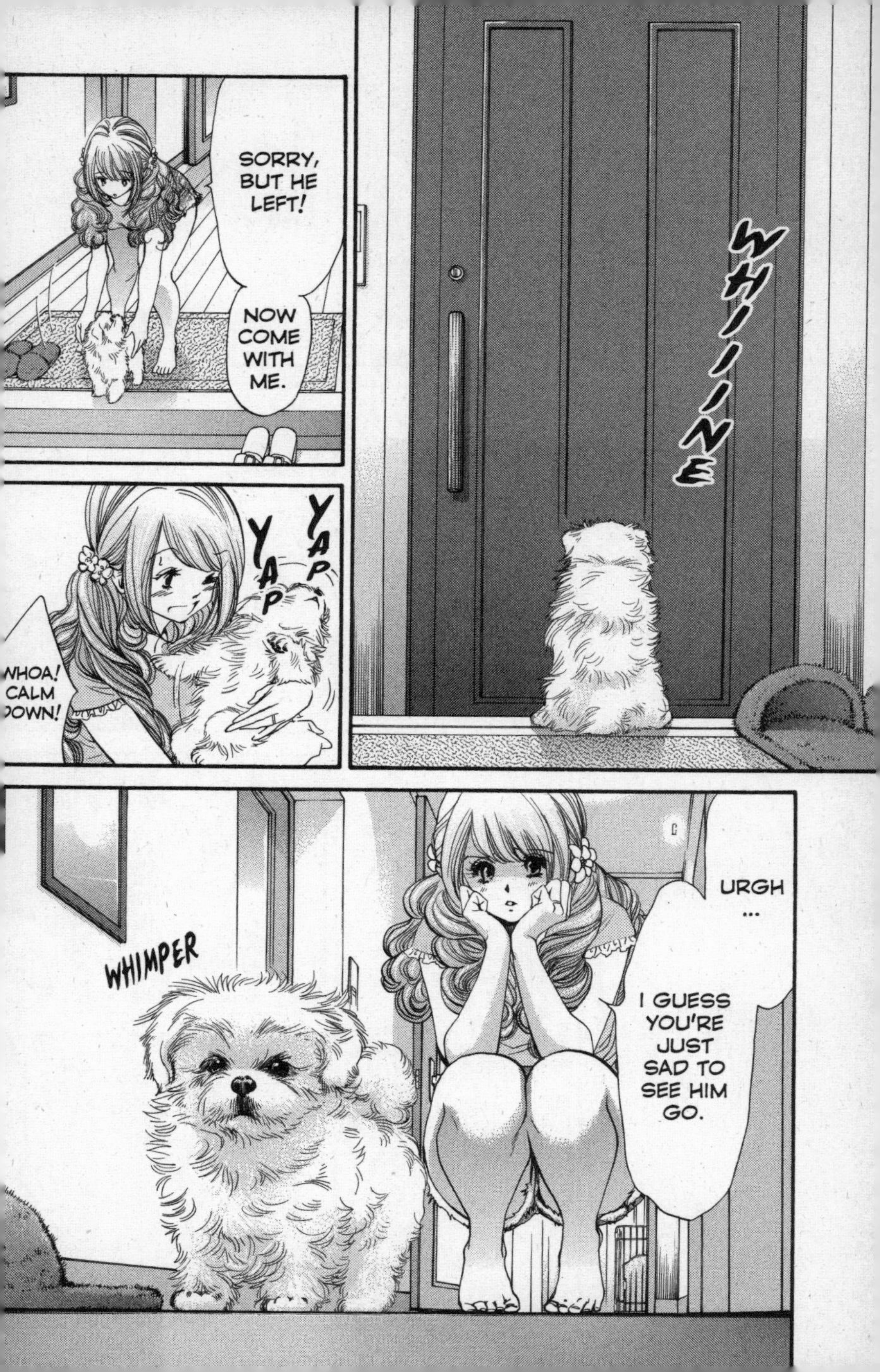
WHIIIINE
SORRY, BUT HE LEFT!
NOW COME WITH ME.
YAP YAP
YAP
WHOA! CALM DOWN!
URGH ...
I GUESS YOU'RE JUST SAD TO SEE HIM GO.
WHIMPER

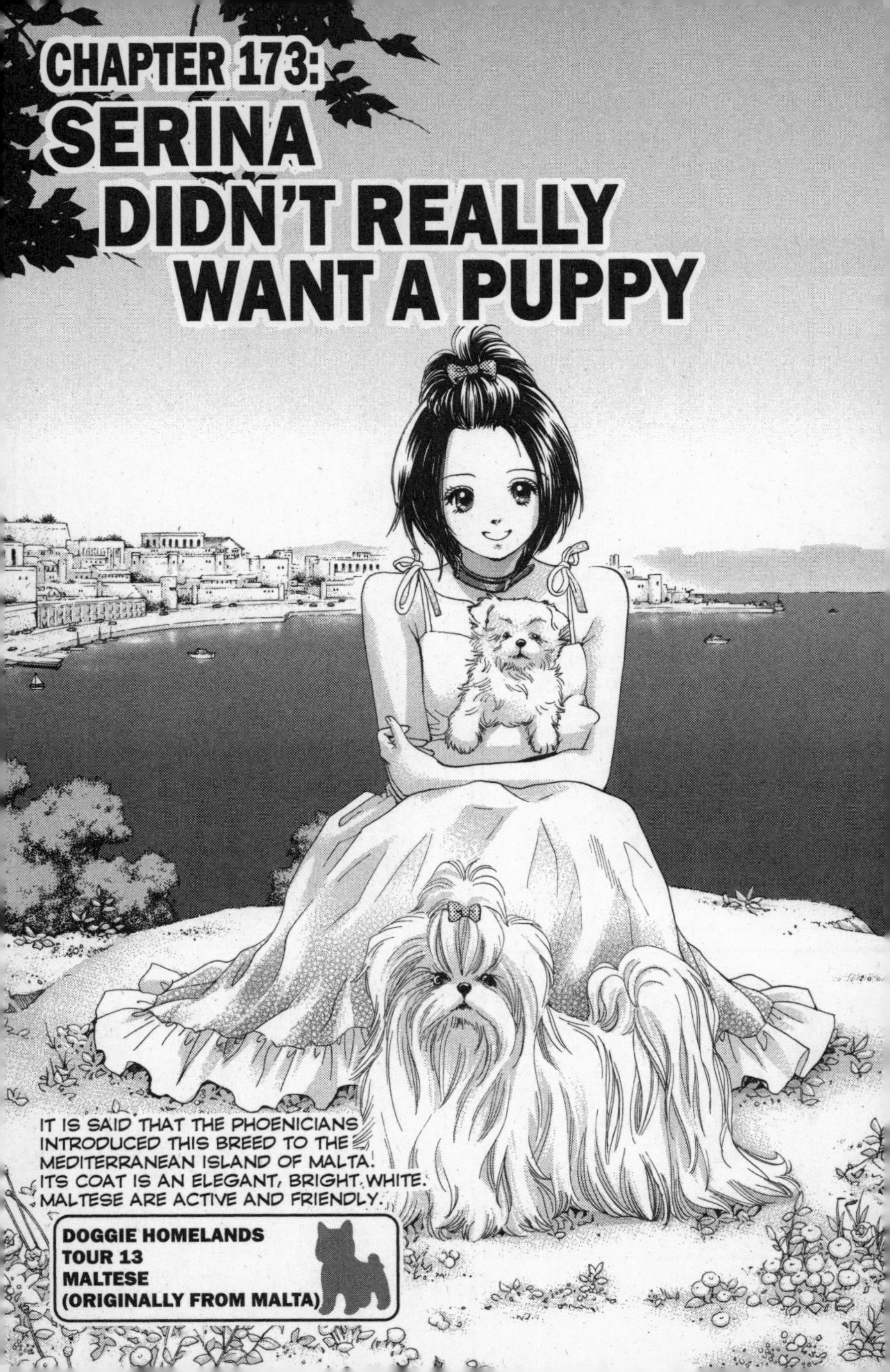
CHAPTER 173:
SERINA DIDN'T REALLY WANT A PUPPY
IT IS SAID THAT THE PHOENICIANS INTRODUCED THIS BREED TO THE MEDITERRANEAN ISLAND OF MALTA. ITS COAT IS AN ELEGANT, BRIGHT WHITE. MALTESE ARE ACTIVE AND FRIENDLY.
DOGGIE HOMELANDS TOUR 13
MALTESE
(ORIGINALLY FROM MALTA)

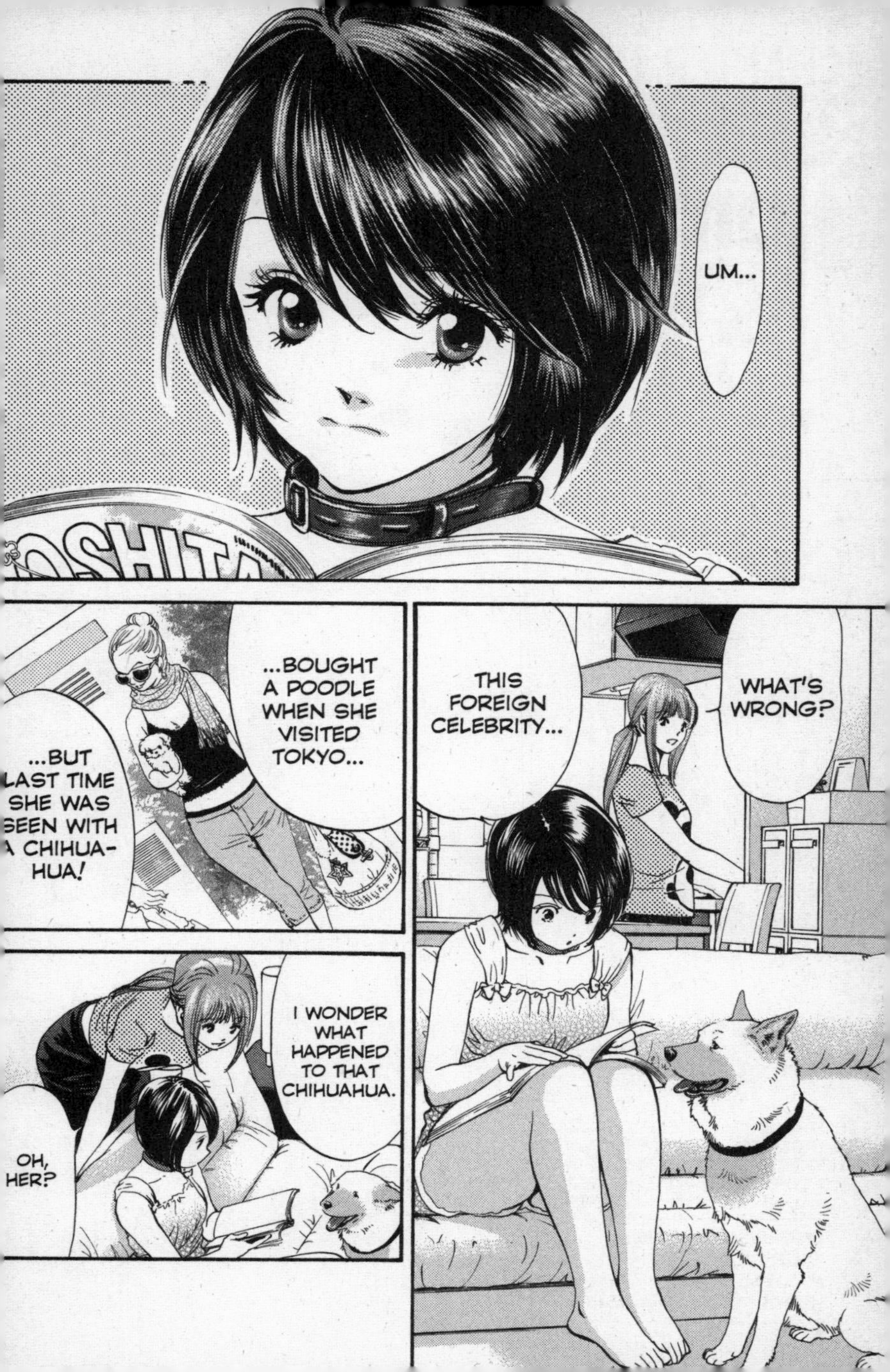
UM...
WHAT'S WRONG?
THIS FOREIGN CELEBRITY...
...BOUGHT A POODLE WHEN SHE VISITED TOKYO...
...BUT LAST TIME SHE WAS SEEN WITH A CHIHUA-HUA!
I WONDER WHAT HAPPENED TO THAT CHIHUAHUA.
OH, HER?

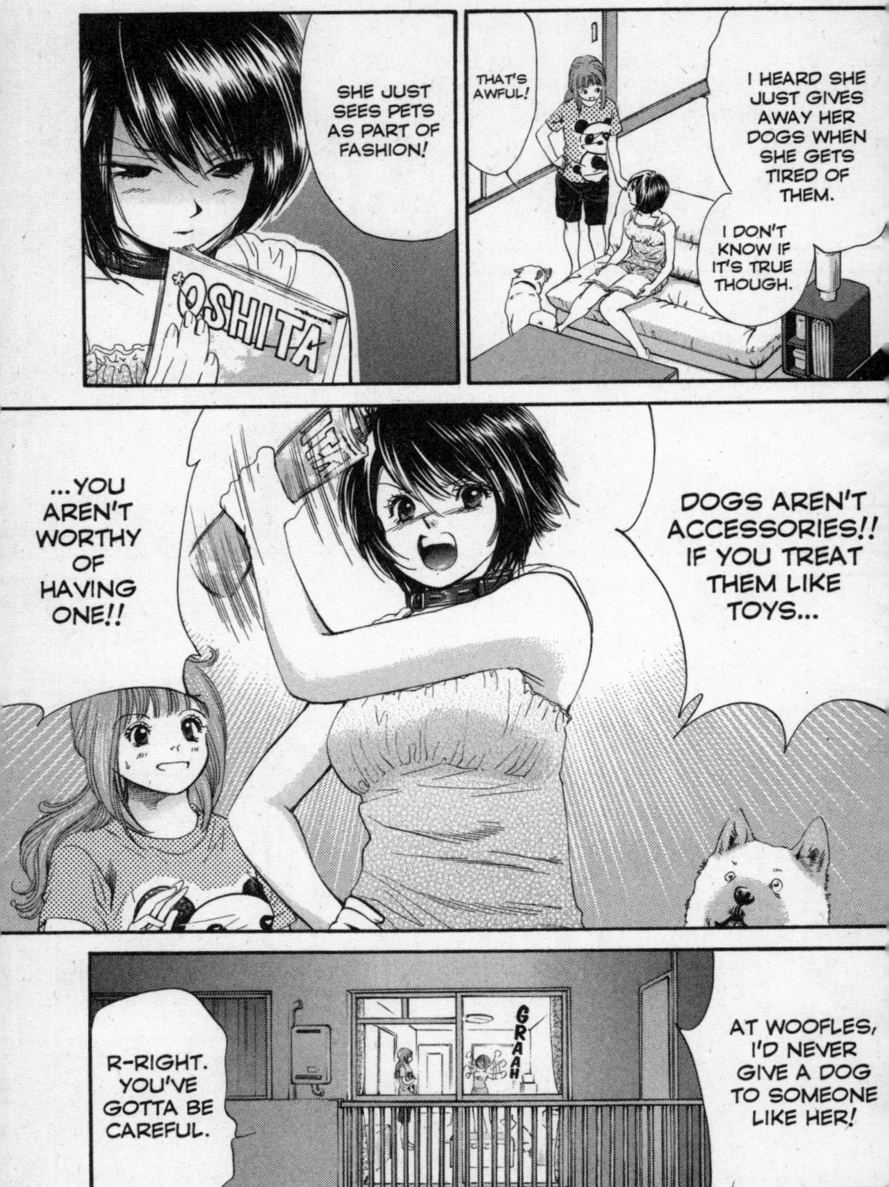
I HEARD SHE JUST GIVES AWAY HER DOGS WHEN SHE GETS TIRED OF THEM.
I DON'T KNOW IF IT'S TRUE THOUGH.
THAT'S AWFUL!
SHE JUST SEES PETS AS PART OF FASHION!
OSHITA
DOGS AREN'T ACCESSORIES!! IF YOU TREAT THEM LIKE TOYS...
...YOU AREN'T WORTHY OF HAVING ONE!!
AT WOOFLES, I'D NEVER GIVE A DOG TO SOMEONE LIKE HER!
GRAAAH
R-RIGHT. YOU'VE GOTTA BE CAREFUL.

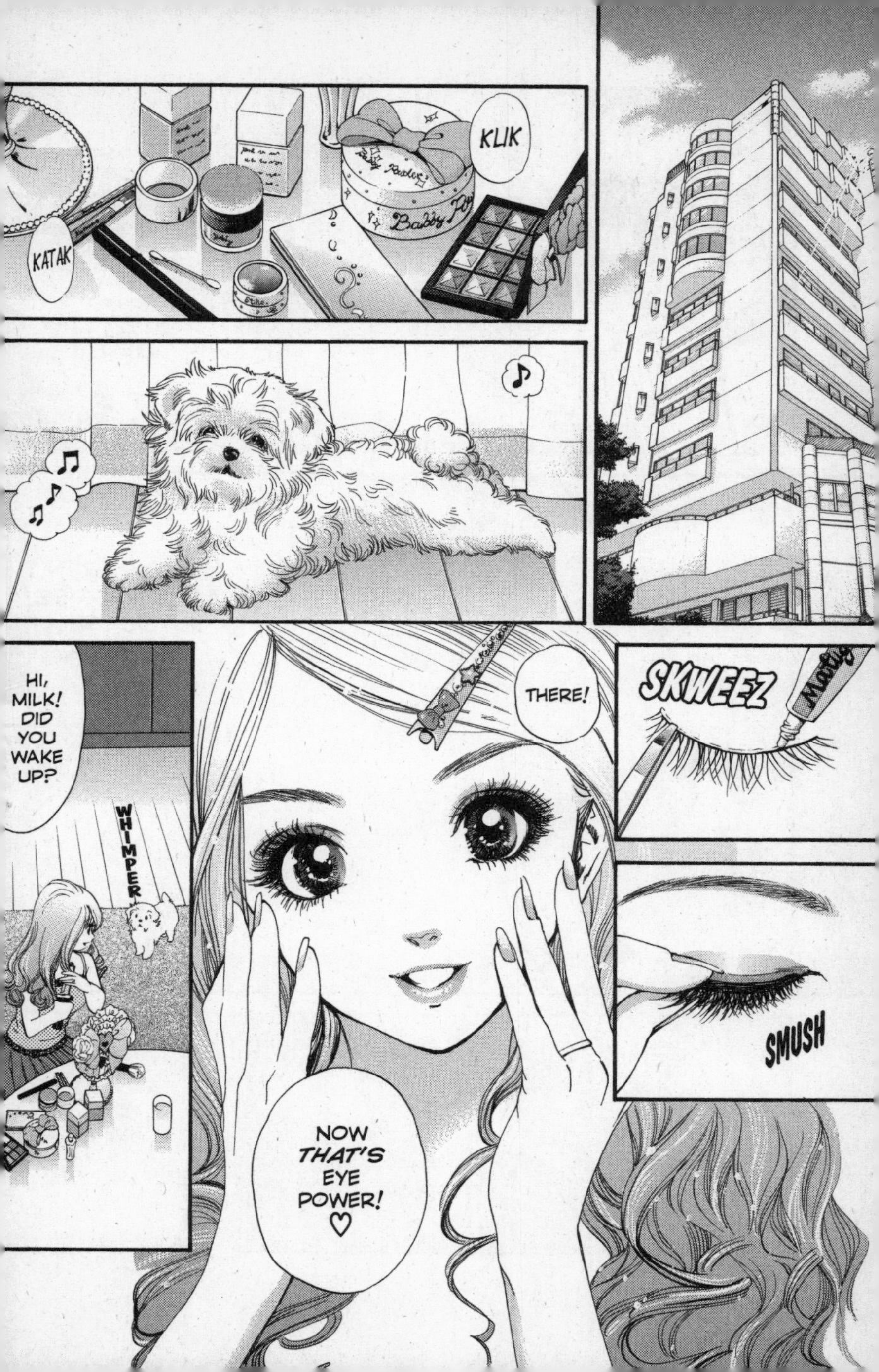
KLIK
KATAK
♪
♫ ♪ ♫
SKWEEZ
SMUSH
THERE!
NOW *THAT'S* EYE POWER! ♡
HI, MILK! DID YOU WAKE UP?
WHIMPER

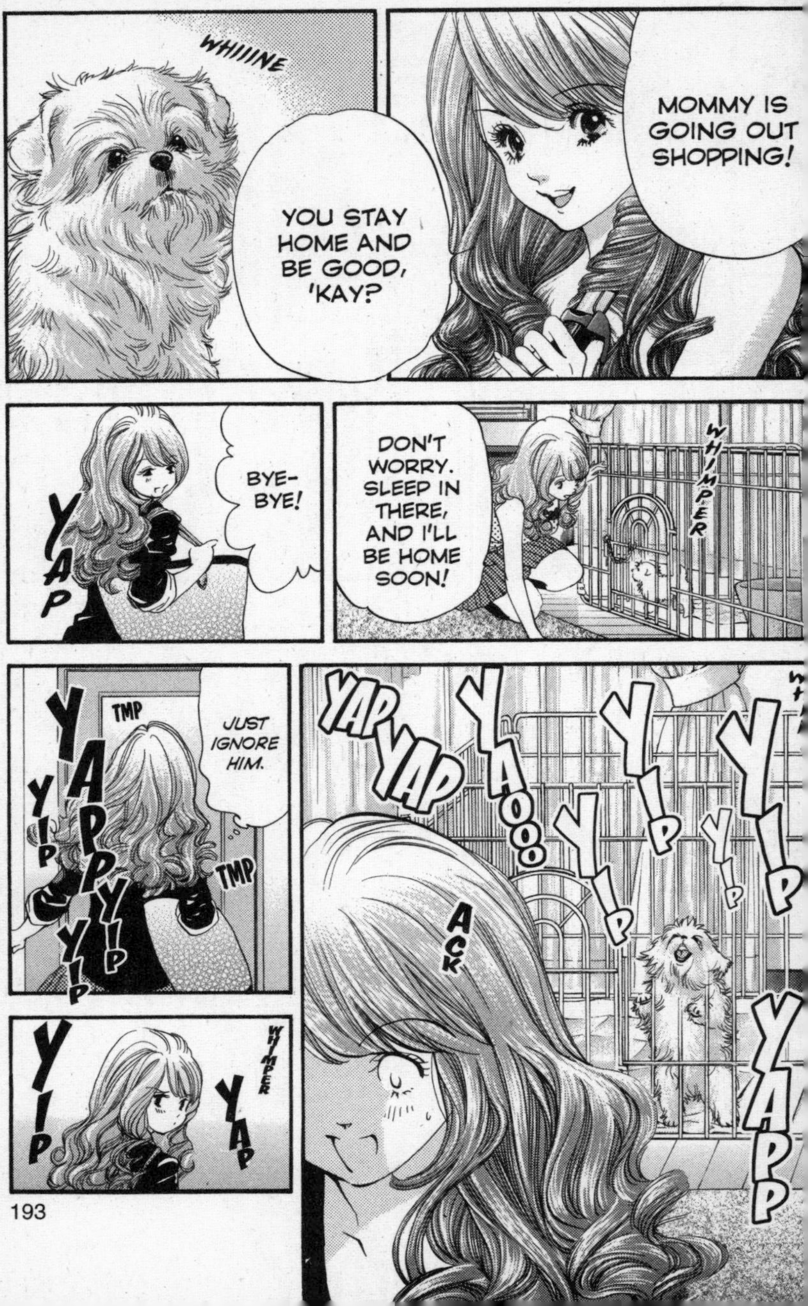

MOMMY IS GOING OUT SHOPPING!
YOU STAY HOME AND BE GOOD, 'KAY?
WHIIINE
WHIMPER
DON'T WORRY. SLEEP IN THERE, AND I'LL BE HOME SOON!
BYE-BYE!
YAP
YIP
YIP
YIP
YIP
YAOOO
YAP YAP
ACK
YAPP
JUST IGNORE HIM.
TMP
YAPPY
YIP
YIP
TMP
YIP
YIP
WHIMPER
YAP
YIP

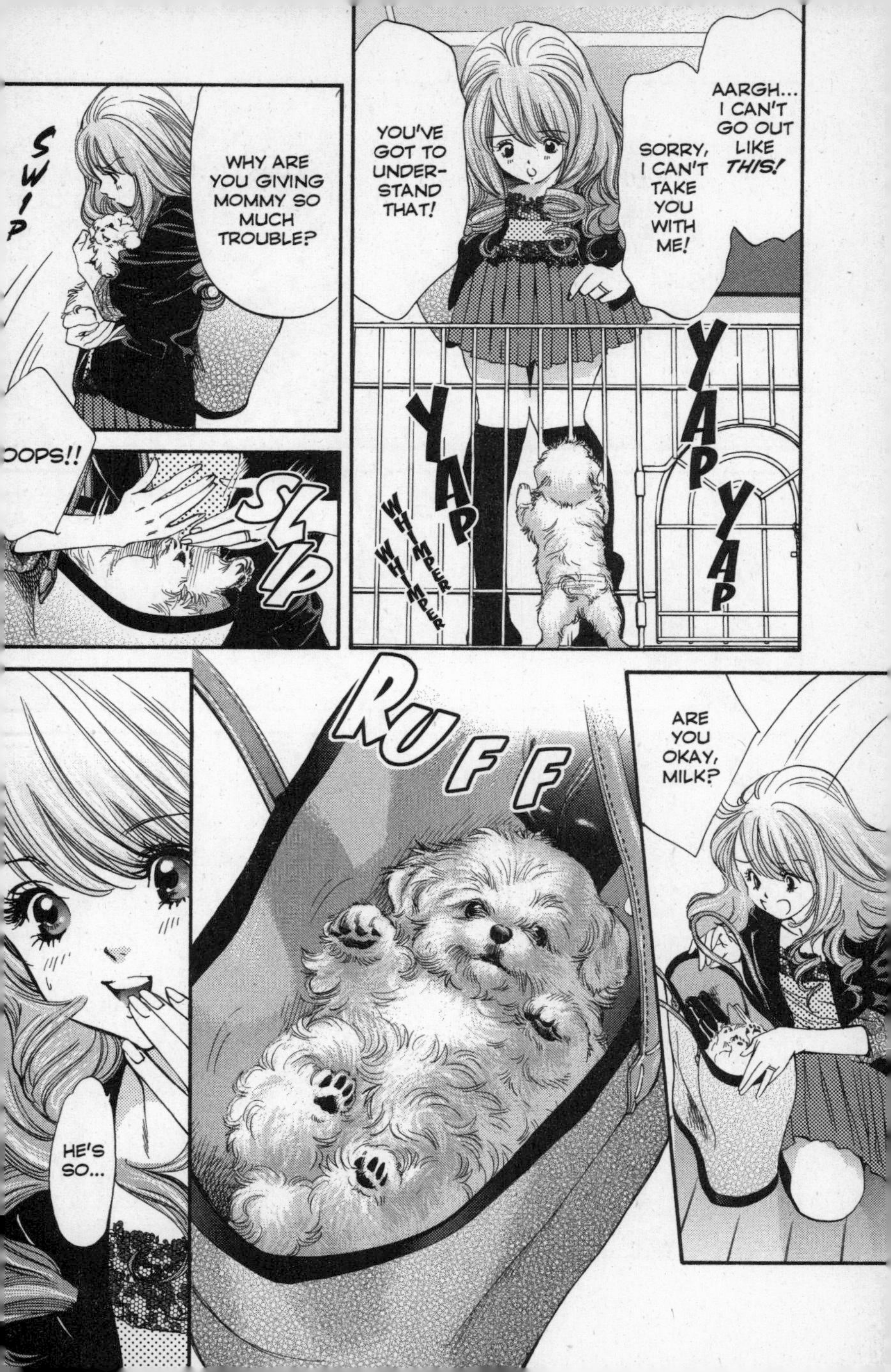
AARGH... I CAN'T GO OUT LIKE *THIS!*
SORRY, I CAN'T TAKE YOU WITH ME!
YOU'VE GOT TO UNDER-STAND THAT!
YAP YAP
YAP YAP
WHIMPER WHIMPER
WHY ARE YOU GIVING MOMMY SO MUCH TROUBLE?
SWIP
OOPS!!
SLIP
ARE YOU OKAY, MILK?
RUFF
HE'S SO...

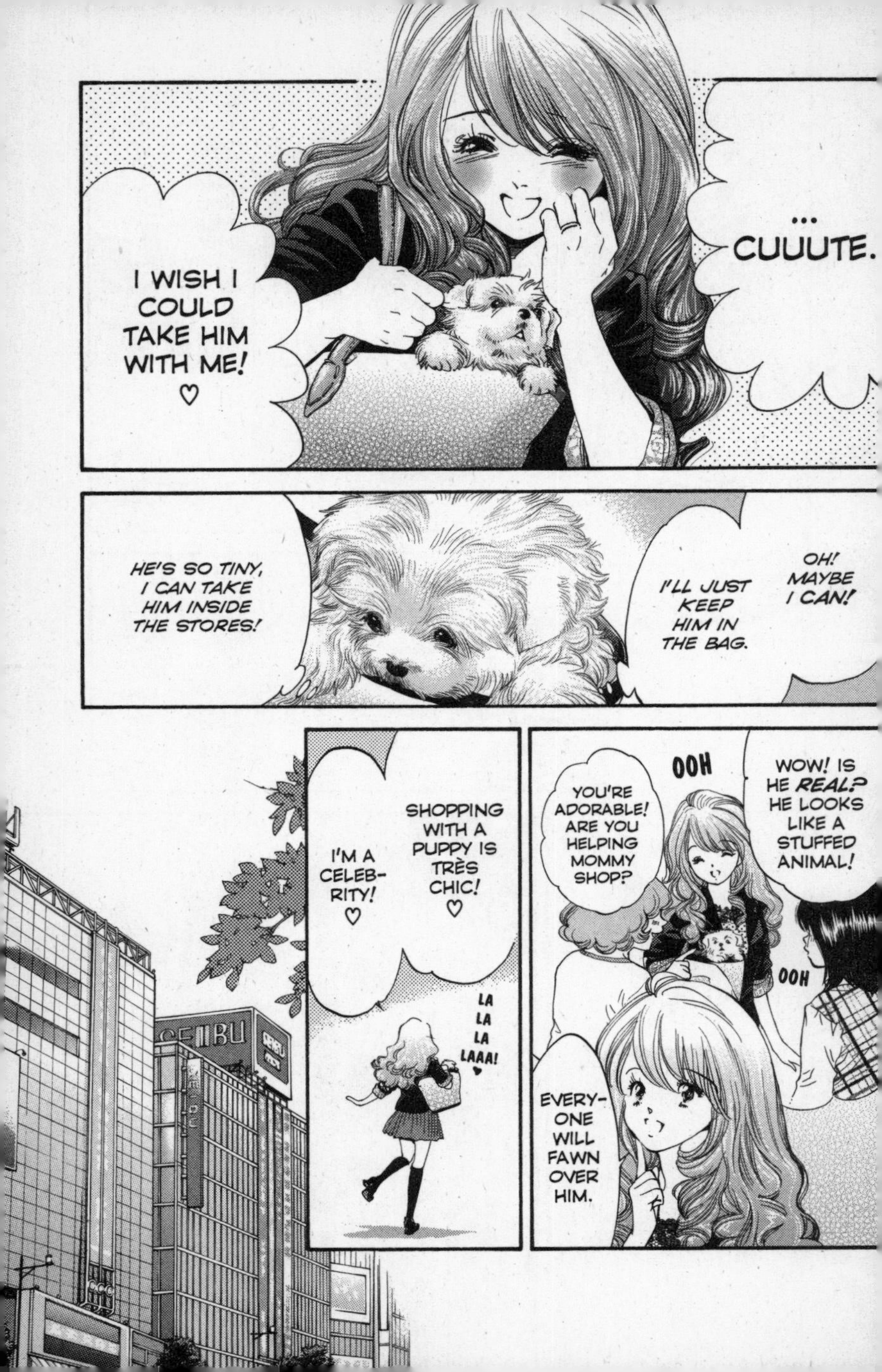
... CUUUTE.
I WISH I COULD TAKE HIM WITH ME! ♡
OH! MAYBE I CAN!
I'LL JUST KEEP HIM IN THE BAG.
HE'S SO TINY, I CAN TAKE HIM INSIDE THE STORES!
WOW! IS HE REAL? HE LOOKS LIKE A STUFFED ANIMAL!
OOH
YOU'RE ADORABLE! ARE YOU HELPING MOMMY SHOP?
OOH
EVERY-ONE WILL FAWN OVER HIM.
SHOPPING WITH A PUPPY IS TRÈS CHIC! ♡
I'M A CELEB-RITY! ♡
LA LA LA LAAA! ♥

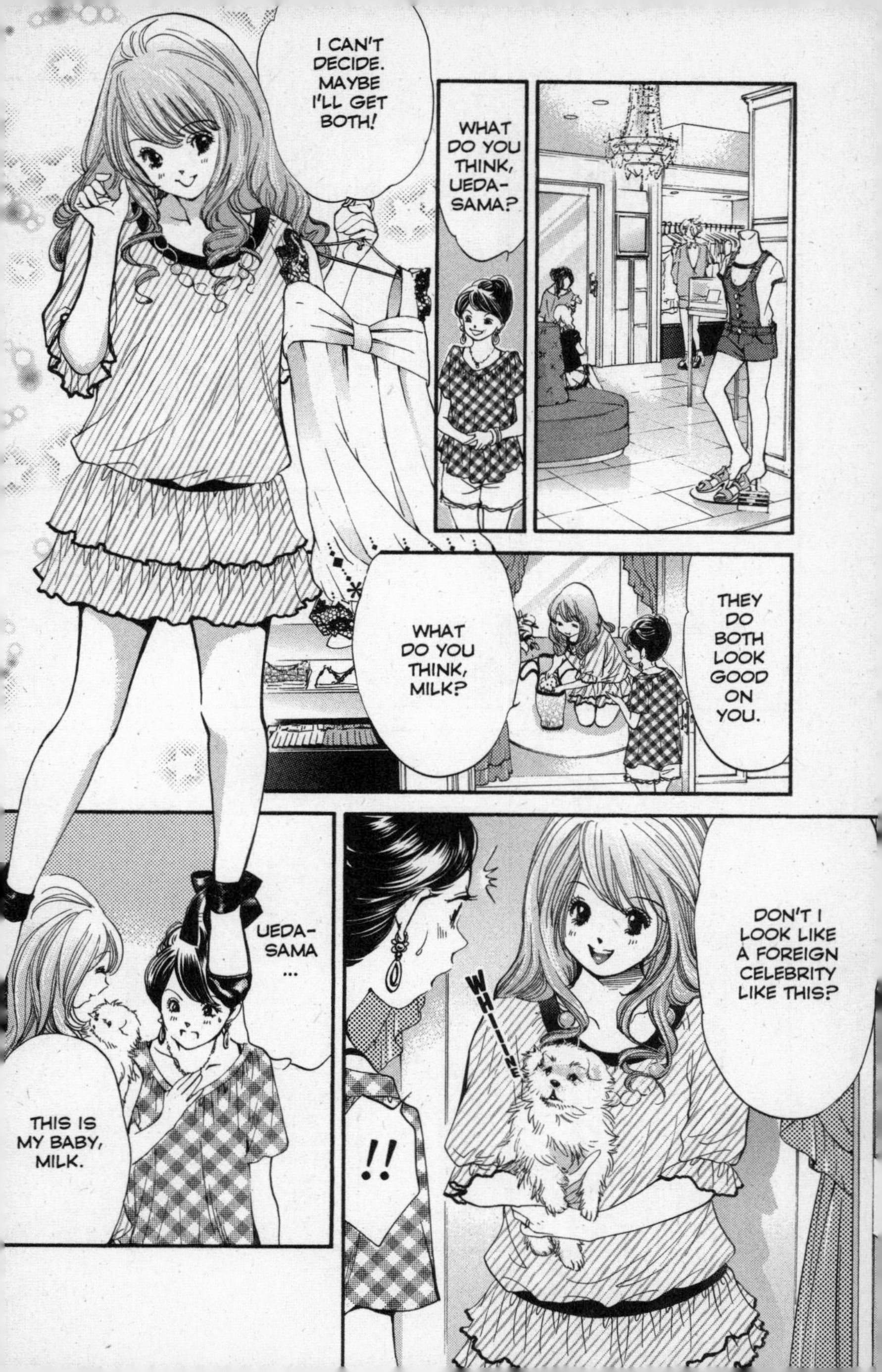
WHAT DO YOU THINK, UEDA-SAMA?
THEY DO BOTH LOOK GOOD ON YOU.
WHAT DO YOU THINK, MILK?
I CAN'T DECIDE. MAYBE I'LL GET BOTH!
DON'T I LOOK LIKE A FOREIGN CELEBRITY LIKE THIS?
WHIIINE
!!
UEDA-SAMA ...
THIS IS MY BABY, MILK.

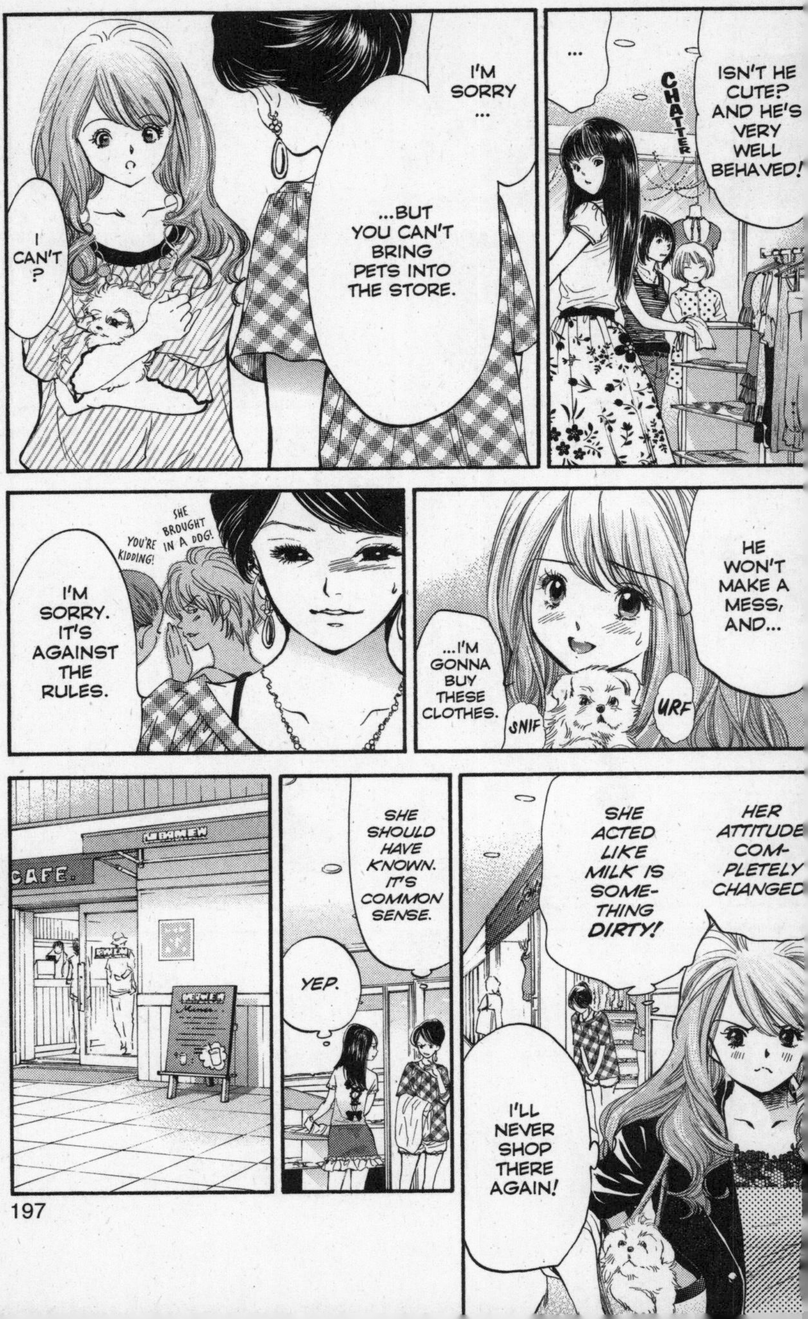
ISN'T HE CUTE? AND HE'S VERY WELL BEHAVED!
CHATTER
...
I'M SORRY ...
...BUT YOU CAN'T BRING PETS INTO THE STORE.
I CAN'T?
HE WON'T MAKE A MESS, AND...
URF
SNIF
...I'M GONNA BUY THESE CLOTHES.
SHE BROUGHT IN A DOG!
YOU'RE KIDDING!
I'M SORRY. IT'S AGAINST THE RULES.
HER ATTITUDE COMPLETELY CHANGED
SHE ACTED LIKE MILK IS SOMETHING DIRTY!
I'LL NEVER SHOP THERE AGAIN!
SHE SHOULD HAVE KNOWN. IT'S COMMON SENSE.
YEP.
CAFE.

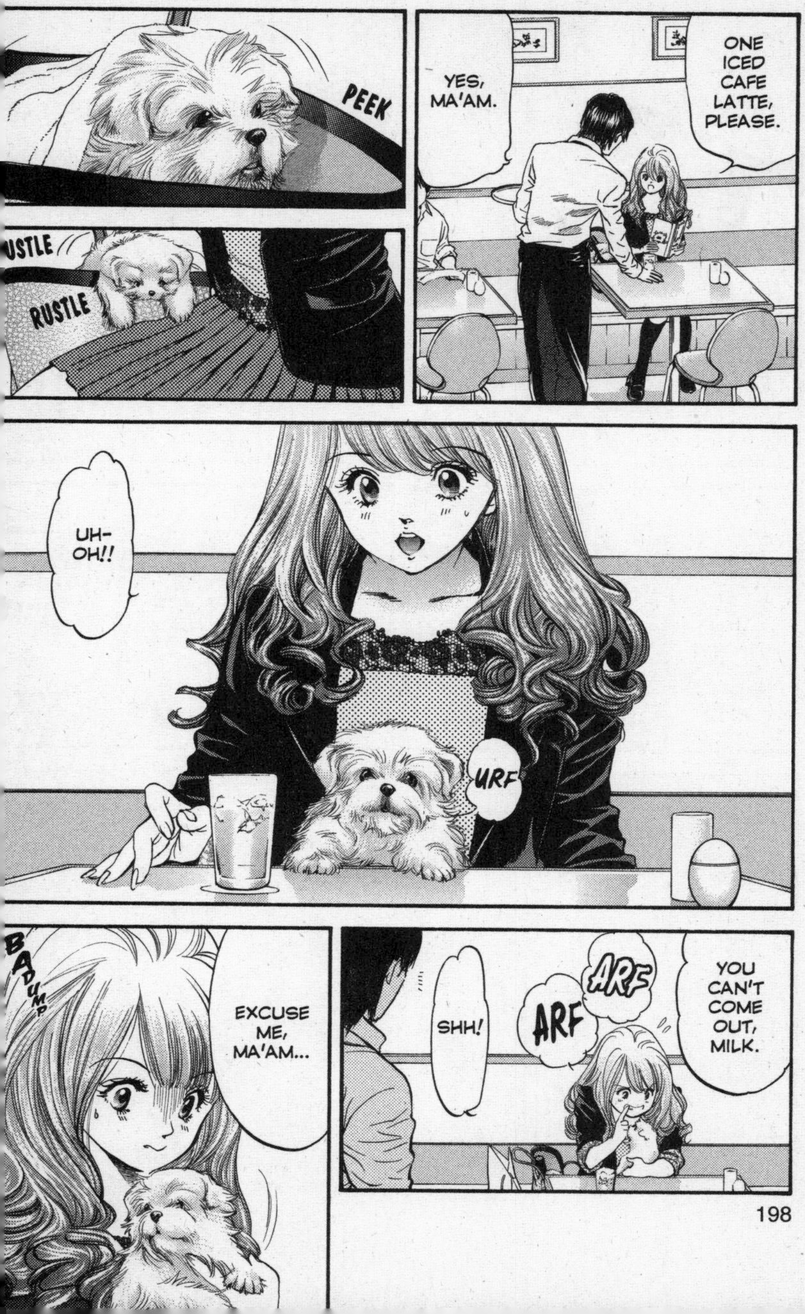
ONE ICED CAFE LATTE, PLEASE.
YES, MA'AM.
PEEK
RUSTLE
RUSTLE
URF
UH-OH!!
YOU CAN'T COME OUT, MILK.
ARF
ARF
SHH!
EXCUSE ME, MA'AM...
BADUMP

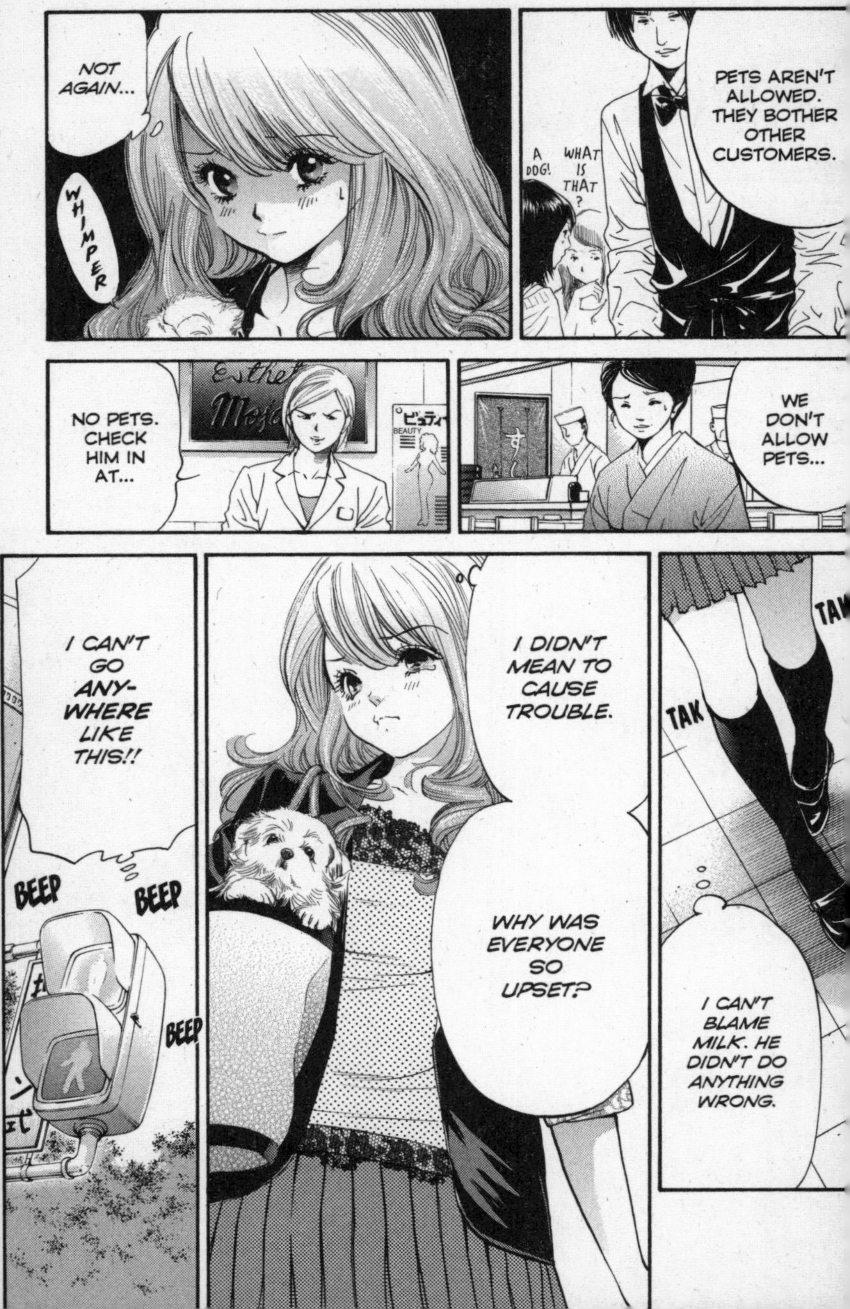
PETS AREN'T ALLOWED. THEY BOTHER OTHER CUSTOMERS.
WHAT IS THAT?
A DOG!
NOT AGAIN...
WHIMPER
WE DON'T ALLOW PETS...
BEAUTY
NO PETS. CHECK HIM IN AT...
TAK
I CAN'T BLAME MILK. HE DIDN'T DO ANYTHING WRONG.
I DIDN'T MEAN TO CAUSE TROUBLE.
WHY WAS EVERYONE SO UPSET?
I CAN'T GO ANYWHERE LIKE THIS!!
BEEP
BEEP
BEEP

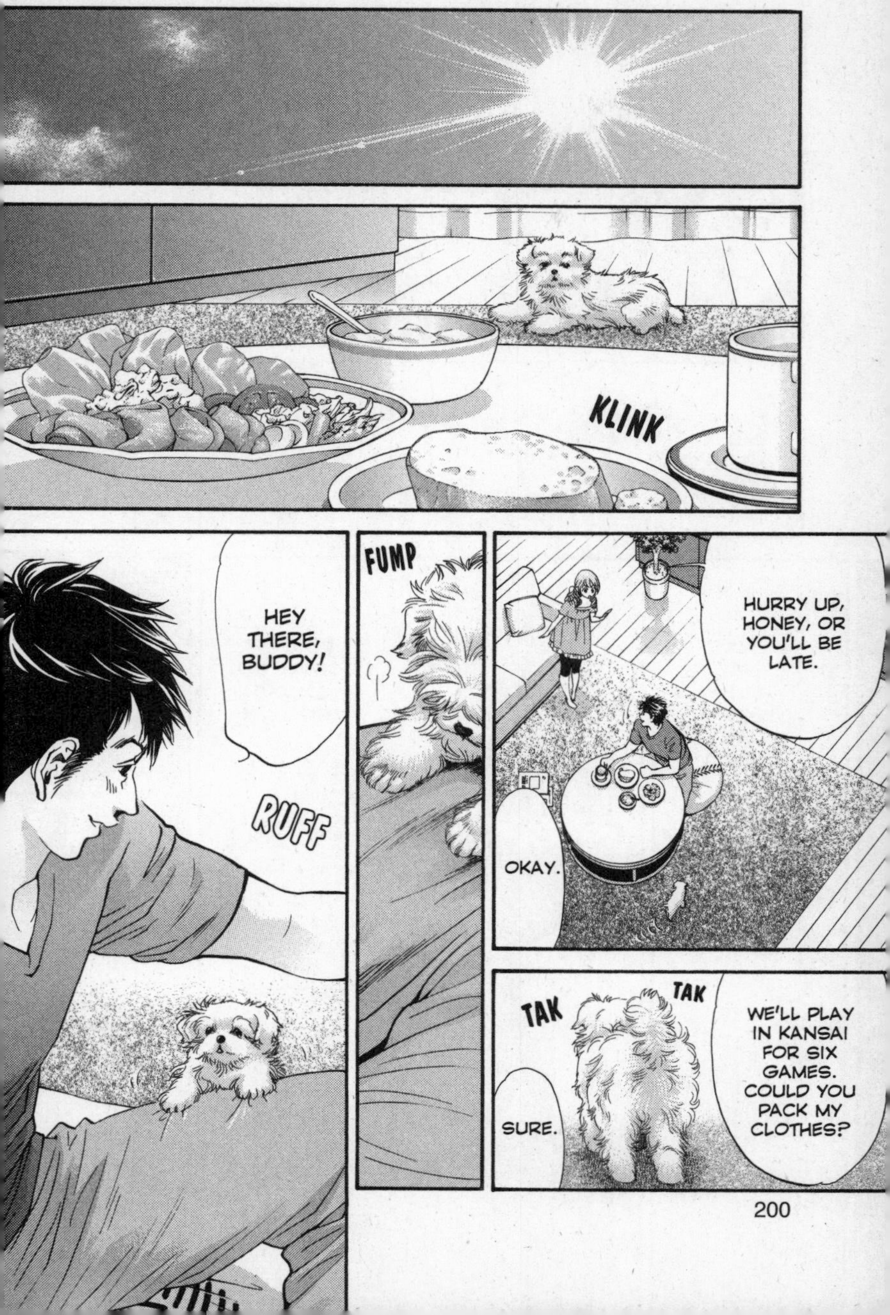
KLINK
HURRY UP, HONEY, OR YOU'LL BE LATE.
OKAY.
WE'LL PLAY IN KANSAI FOR SIX GAMES. COULD YOU PACK MY CLOTHES?
TAK
TAK
SURE.
FUMP
HEY THERE, BUDDY!
RUFF

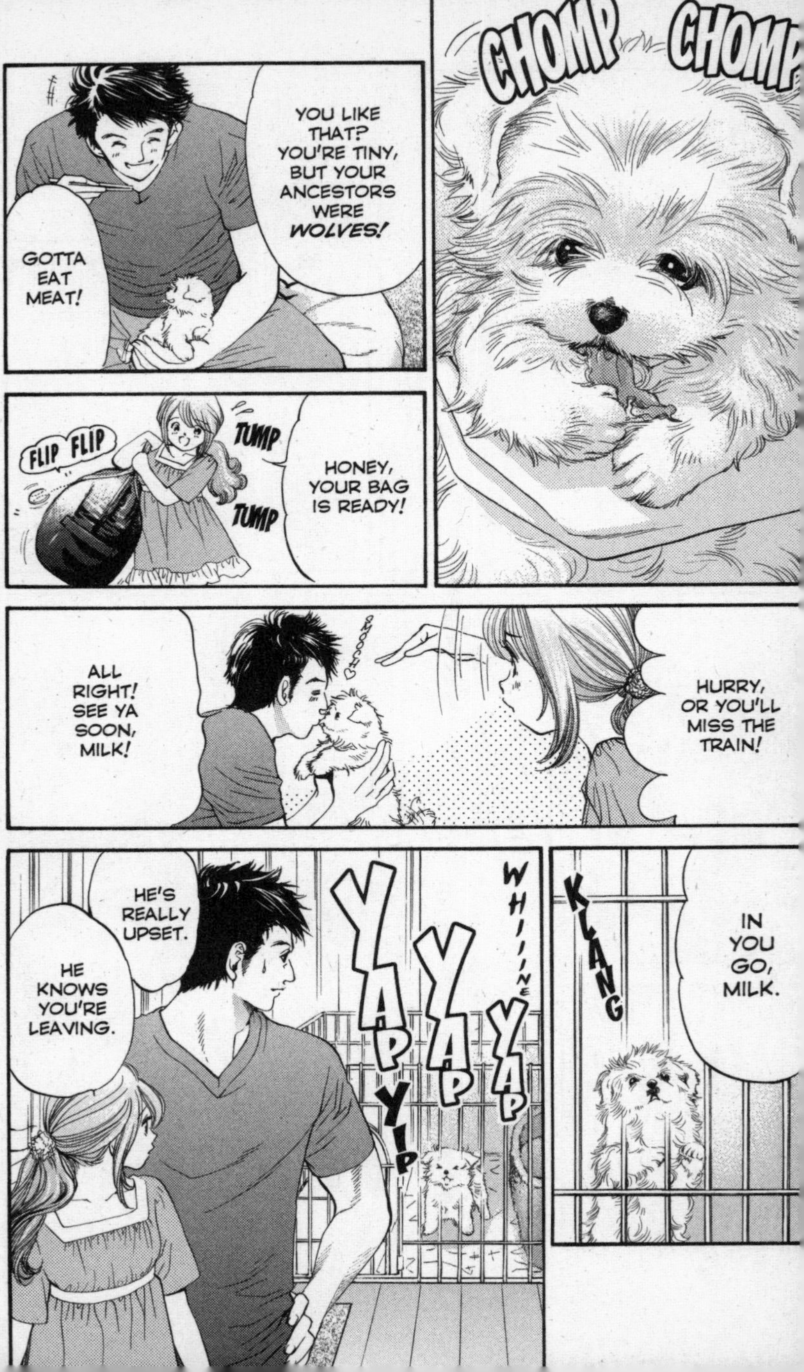
CHOMP CHOMP
YOU LIKE THAT? YOU'RE TINY, BUT YOUR ANCESTORS WERE *WOLVES!*
GOTTA EAT MEAT!
TUMP TUMP
HONEY, YOUR BAG IS READY!
FLIP FLIP
HURRY, OR YOU'LL MISS THE TRAIN!
SMOOCH
ALL RIGHT! SEE YA SOON, MILK!
IN YOU GO, MILK.
KLANG
WHIIINE
YAP YAP YAP YIP
HE'S REALLY UPSET.
HE KNOWS YOU'RE LEAVING.

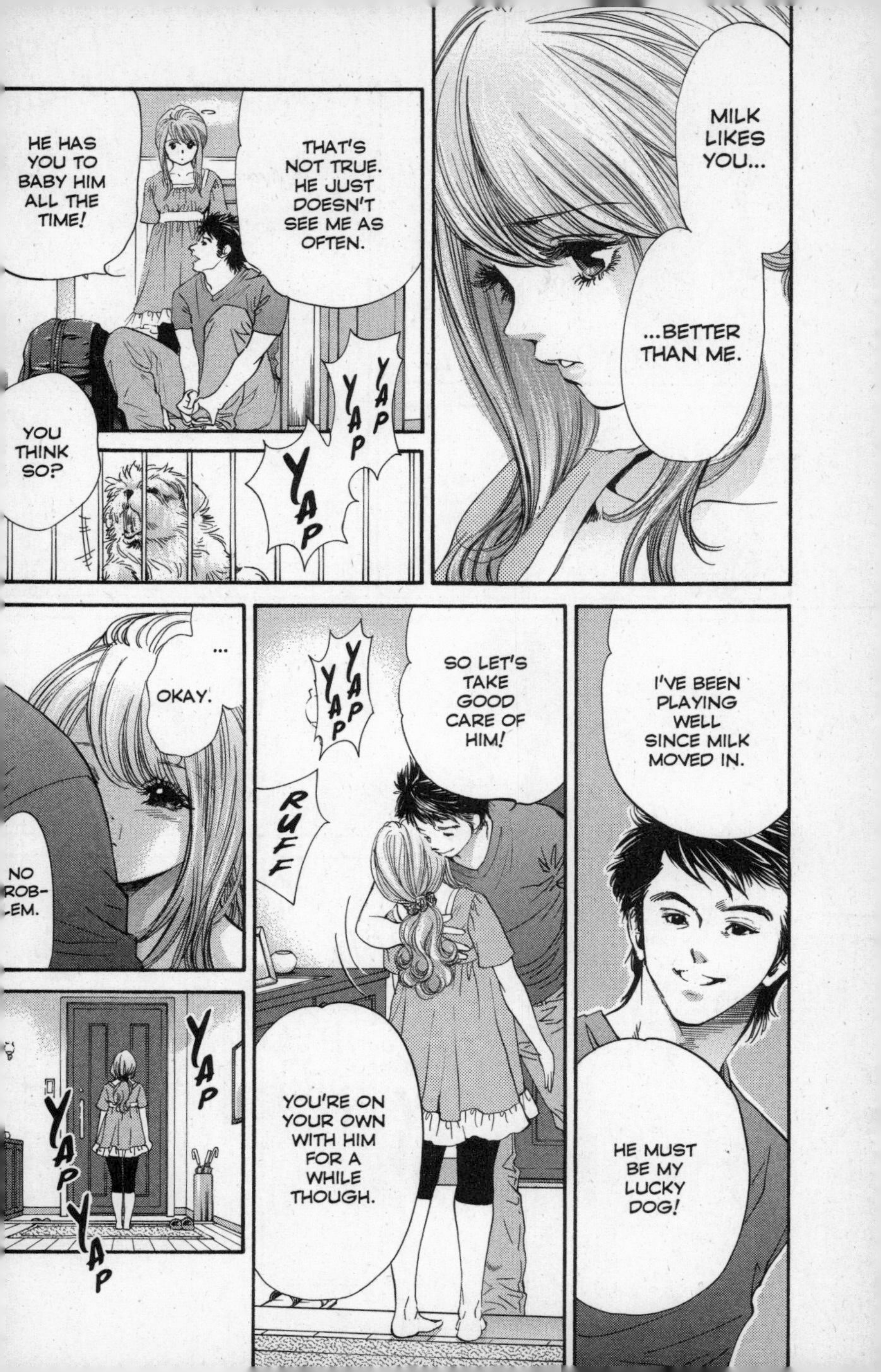
MILK LIKES YOU...
...BETTER THAN ME.
THAT'S NOT TRUE. HE JUST DOESN'T SEE ME AS OFTEN.
HE HAS YOU TO BABY HIM ALL THE TIME!
YAP YAP
YAP YAP
YOU THINK SO?
I'VE BEEN PLAYING WELL SINCE MILK MOVED IN.
HE MUST BE MY LUCKY DOG!
SO LET'S TAKE GOOD CARE OF HIM!
YAP YAP
RUFF
YOU'RE ON YOUR OWN WITH HIM FOR A WHILE THOUGH.
...
OKAY.
NO ROB- EM.
YAP
YAP YAP YAP

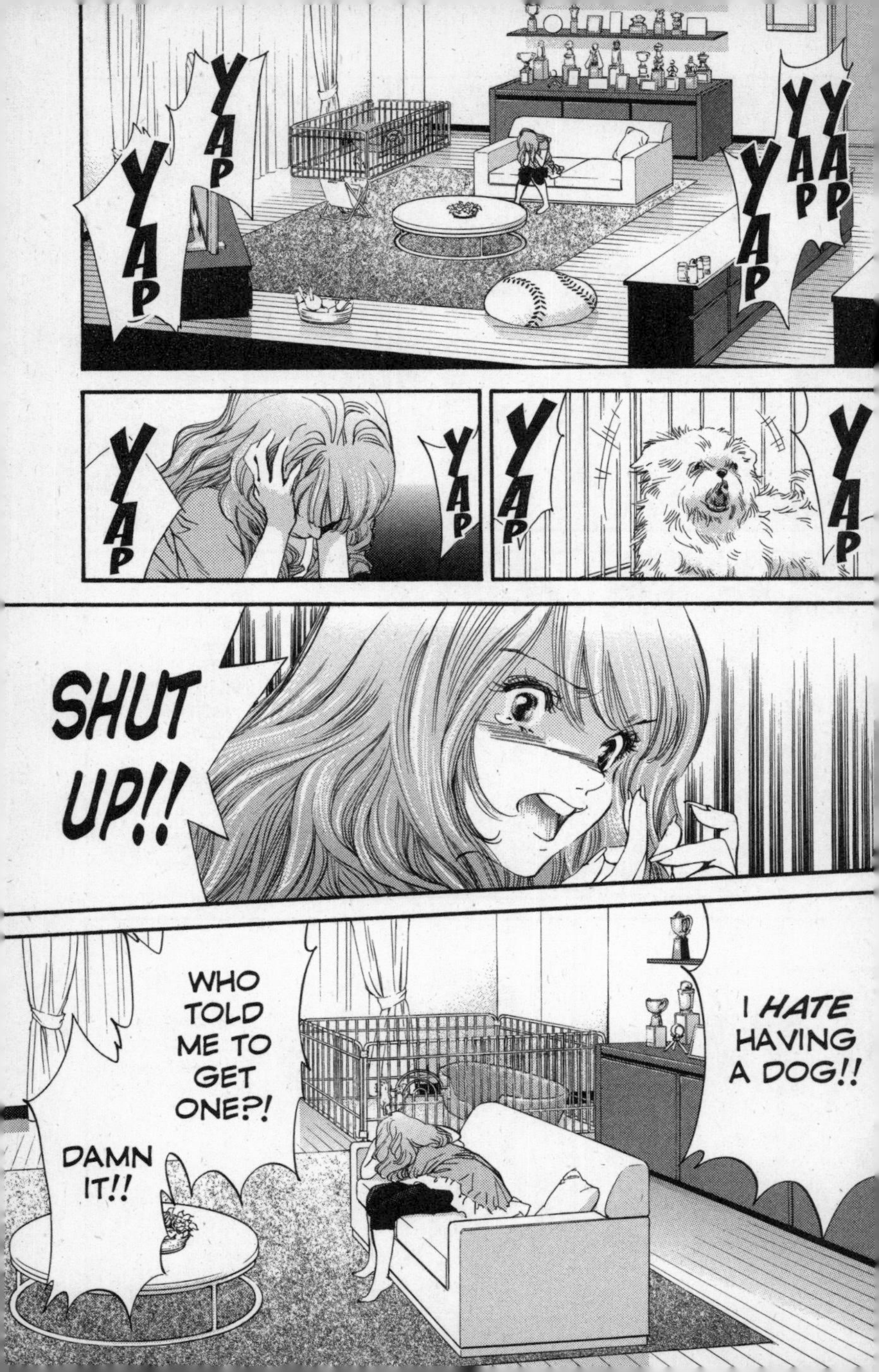
YAP
YAP
YAP
YAP
YAP
YAP
YAP
YAP
YAP
SHUT UP!!
I *HATE* HAVING A DOG!!
WHO TOLD ME TO GET ONE?!
DAMN IT!!

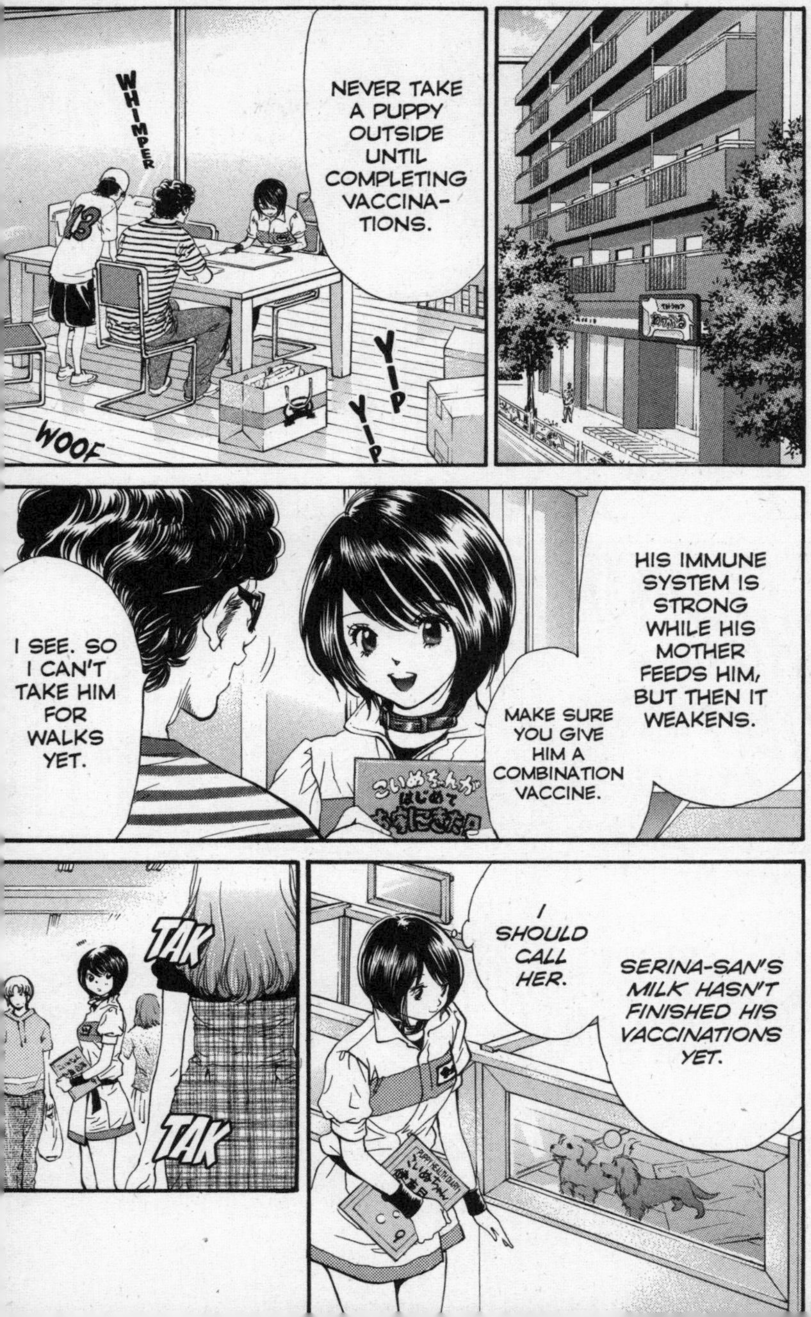
NEVER TAKE A PUPPY OUTSIDE UNTIL COMPLETING VACCINA-TIONS.
WHIMPER
YIP
YIP
WOOF
HIS IMMUNE SYSTEM IS STRONG WHILE HIS MOTHER FEEDS HIM, BUT THEN IT WEAKENS.
MAKE SURE YOU GIVE HIM A COMBINATION VACCINE.
I SEE. SO I CAN'T TAKE HIM FOR WALKS YET.
SERINA-SAN'S MILK HASN'T FINISHED HIS VACCINATIONS YET.
I SHOULD CALL HER.
TAK
TAK

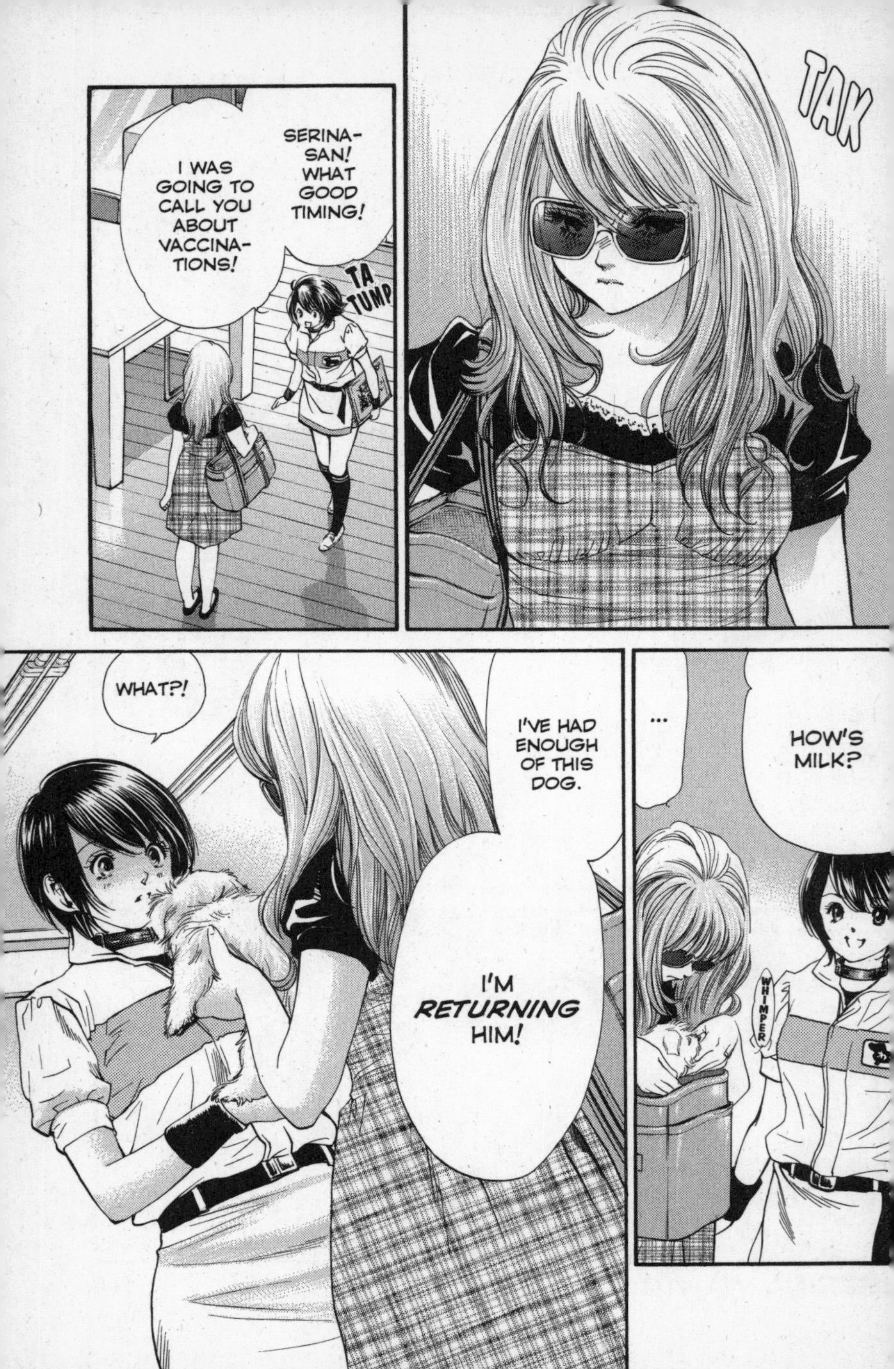
TAK
SERINA-SAN! WHAT GOOD TIMING!
I WAS GOING TO CALL YOU ABOUT VACCINATIONS!
TA TUMP
HOW'S MILK?
...
WHIMPER
I'VE HAD ENOUGH OF THIS DOG.
I'M *RETURNING* HIM!
WHAT?!

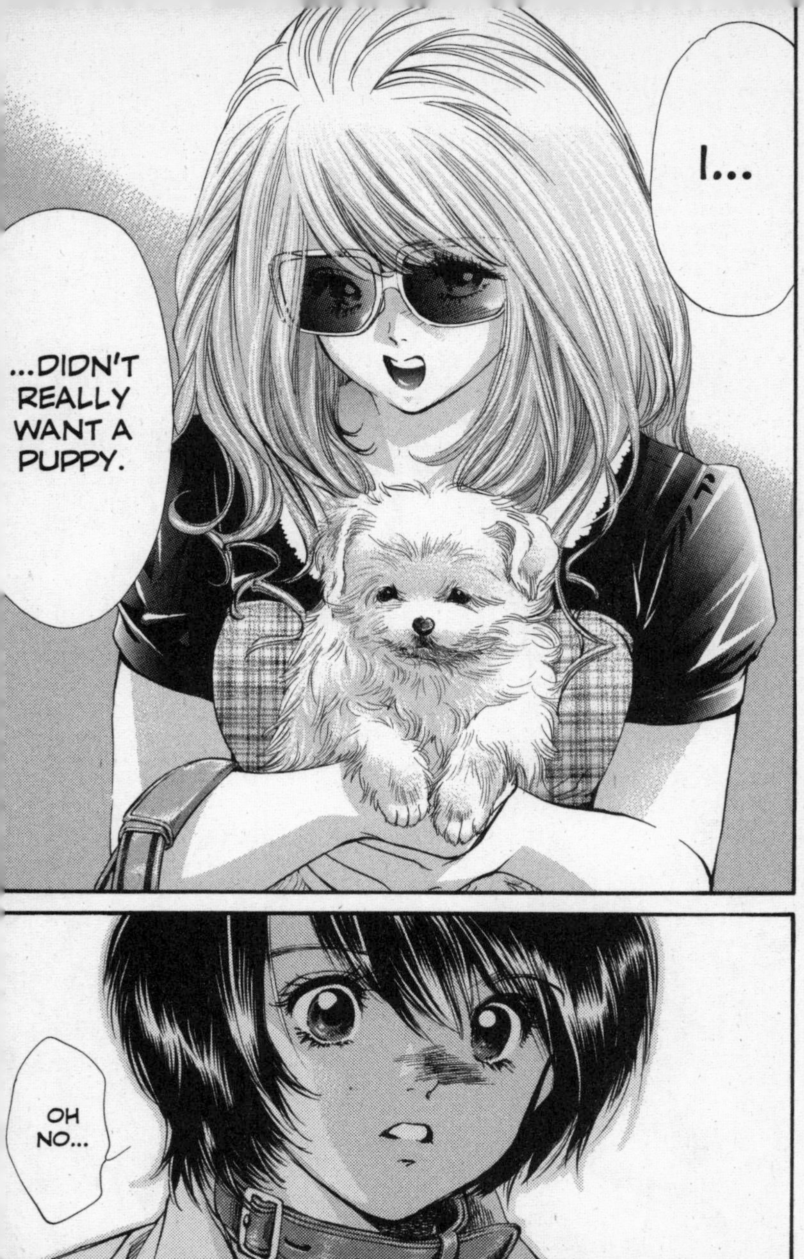
I...
...DIDN'T REALLY WANT A PUPPY.
OH NO...

SERINA WANTS A DOGGIE!/THE END

INUBA*KA

INUBAKA

Everybody's Crazy for Dogs!

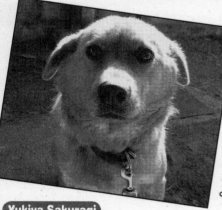

From Doihara-san in Hyogo Prefecture

🐾 Riku-chan (mutt)

When you say "Good morning," "Welcome home" and "Let's play," it's because you want to be together forever, right, Riku-chan? Let's play again today!★ Or, like in the picture, shall we just stare at each other?!

Yukiya Sakuragi

What sweet eyes! I've heard dogs understand what we say, so it's good to talk to them. Maybe the day isn't far away when we really will be able to converse with dogs.

From Kim-san in Kyoto Prefecture

🐾 (left & center) Bean-kun & Buffy-chan (basset hounds), (right) Aster-kun (English setter)

Bean-kun and Buffy-chan have been healthy ever since they were puppies. When they run, their big bodies shake, their ears swing and they step on them! They're bursting with cuteness! Although we got Aster-kun first, these two push him into a corner! Don't give in, Aster-kun!★

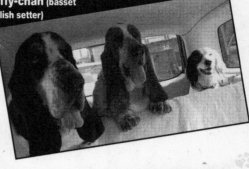

Yukiya Sakuragi

These dudes radiate dignity. Basset hounds sure do have long ears, don't they? Although they're huge and push Aster-kun into the corner, I'm sure they respect him as their brother… (lol)

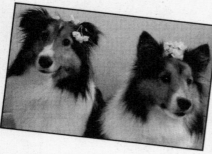

From Inubaka-san in Ibaraki Prefecture

🐾 **(left) Kyu-chan & (right) Rokka-chan (Shetland sheepdogs)**

With cherry blossoms in their hair, these two are the ultimate fashion icons! Kyu-chan, you always follow around your sister Rokka-chan because you want to play with her, right?

Yukiya Sakuragi

What pretty princesses!! What kind of princes will show up for these two tight-knit sisters, I wonder? (lol) Stay friends forever!

From Nakano-san in Hokkaido

🐾 **Bonta-kun (miniature schnauzer)**

Playful and friendly Bonta-kun isn't scared of anything! He's always fighting with bigger dogs! He's a little like Melon. Like Melon, he has a lot of friends he made at training class. Are you going to play with your friends again today?

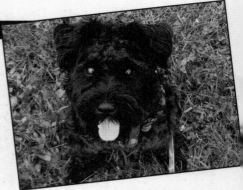

Yukiya Sakuragi

The Dog's Ten Commandments make me cry every time I read them. Dogs have to overcome a lot in order to get along harmoniously with people! But I believe a fuller and happier life awaits them if they do!

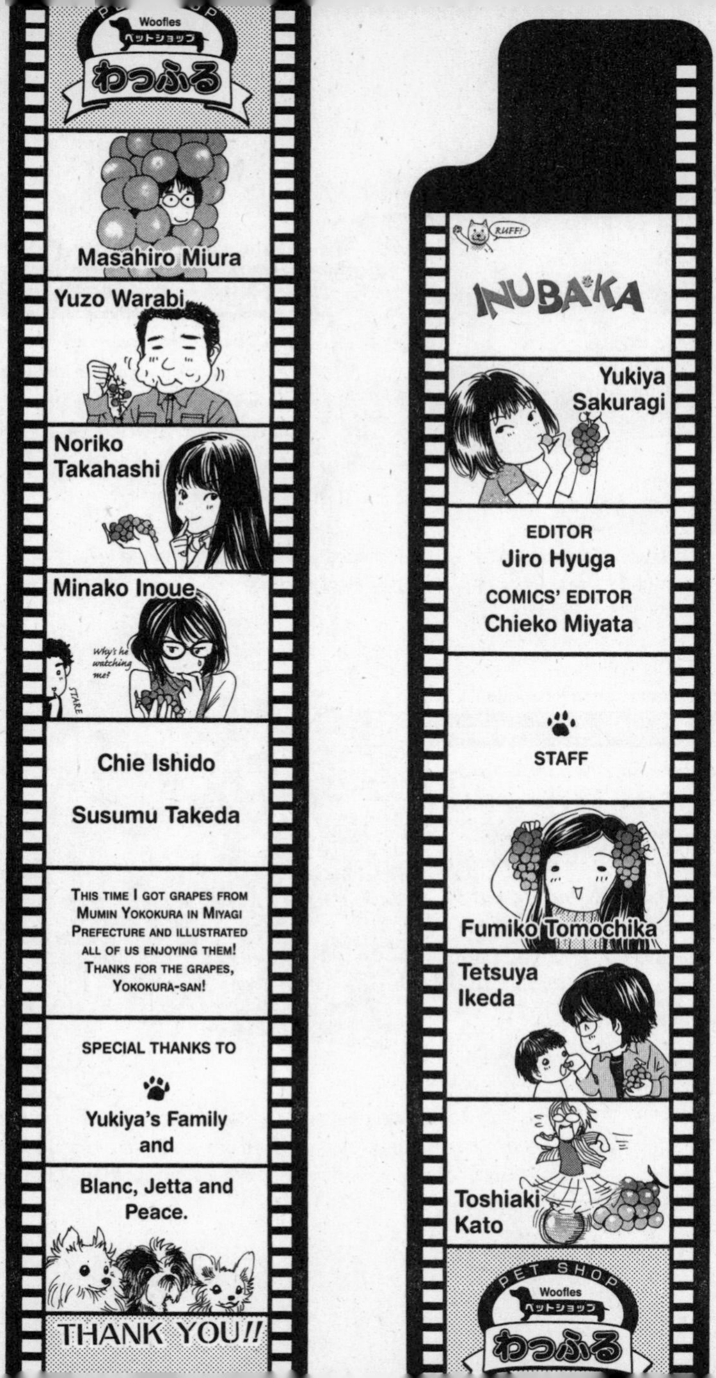
RUFF!
INUBAKA
Yukiya Sakuragi
EDITOR
Jiro Hyuga
COMICS' EDITOR
Chieko Miyata
STAFF
Fumiko Tomochika
Tetsuya Ikeda
Toshiaki Kato
PET SHOP
Woofles
ペットショップ
わっふる
PET SHOP
Woofles
ペットショップ
わっふる
Masahiro Miura
Yuzo Warabi
Noriko Takahashi
Minako Inoue
Why's he watching me?
STARE
Chie Ishido
Susumu Takeda
This time I got grapes from Mumin Yokokura in Miyagi Prefecture and illustrated all of us enjoying them! Thanks for the grapes, Yokokura-san!
SPECIAL THANKS TO
Yukiya's Family
and
Blanc, Jetta and Peace.
THANK YOU!!

Inubaka
Crazy for Dogs
Vol. #16
VIZ Media Edition

**Story and Art by
Yukiya Sakuragi**

Translation/Ari Yasuda, HC Language Solutions, Inc.
English Adaptation/John Werry, HC Language Solutions, Inc.
Touch-up Art & Lettering/Kelle Hahn
Cover & Interior Design/Hidemi Dunn
Editor/Carrie Shepherd

VP, Production/Alvin Lu
VP, Sales & Product Marketing/Gonzalo Ferreyra
VP, Creative/Linda Espinosa
Publisher/Hyoe Narita

Printed in Canada

Published by VIZ Media, LLC
P.O. Box 77010
San Francisco, CA 94107

10 9 8 7 6 5 4 3 2 1
First printing, July 2010

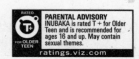
VIZ
media
www.viz.com

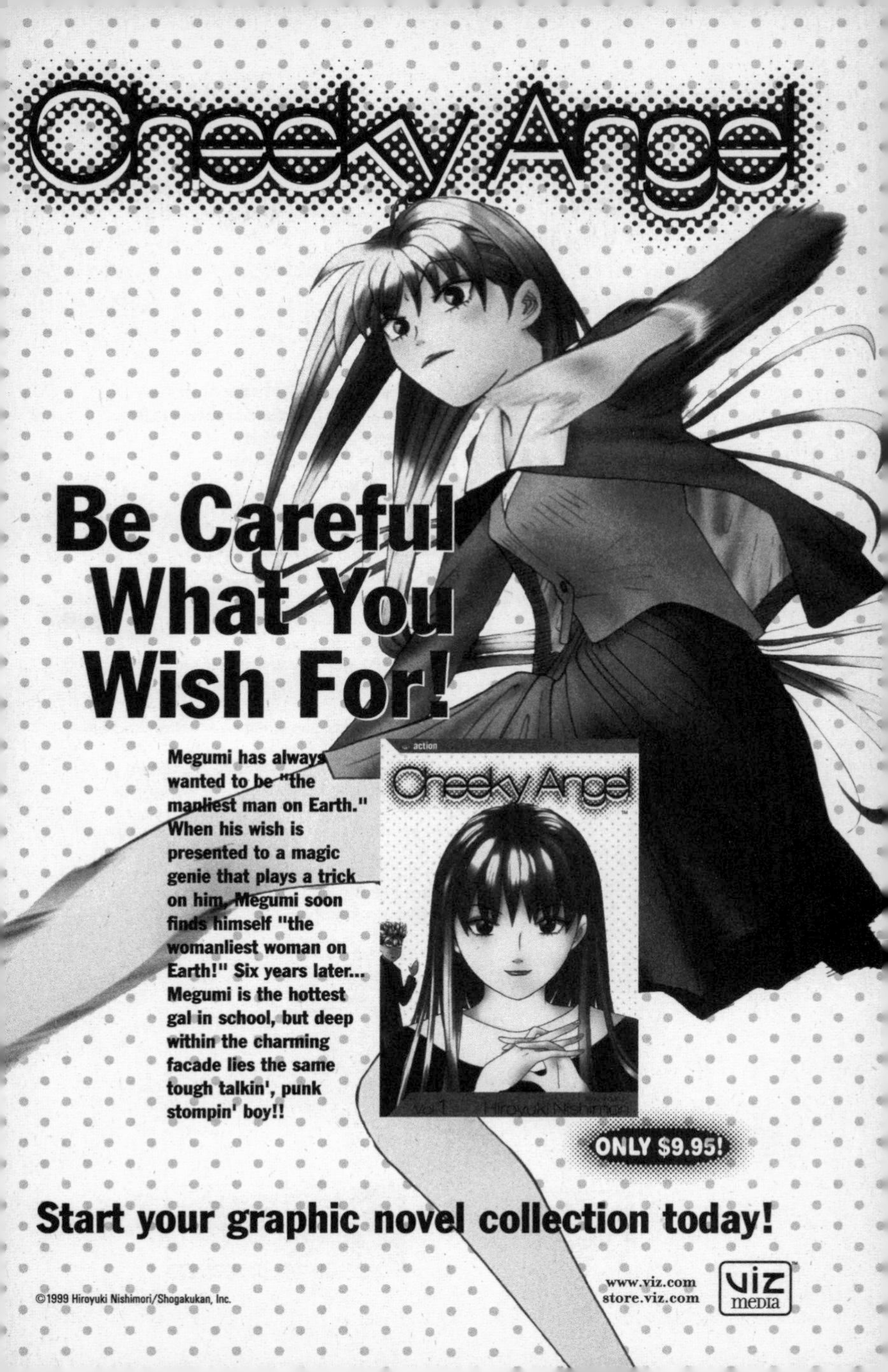
Cheeky Angel
Be Careful What You Wish For!
Megumi has always wanted to be "the manliest man on Earth." When his wish is presented to a magic genie that plays a trick on him, Megumi soon finds himself "the womanliest woman on Earth!" Six years later... Megumi is the hottest gal in school, but deep within the charming facade lies the same tough talkin', punk stompin' boy!!
action
Cheeky Angel
Vol. 1
Hiroyuki Nishimori
ONLY $9.95!
Start your graphic novel collection today!
©1999 Hiroyuki Nishimori/Shogakukan, Inc.
www.viz.com
store.viz.com
VIZ media

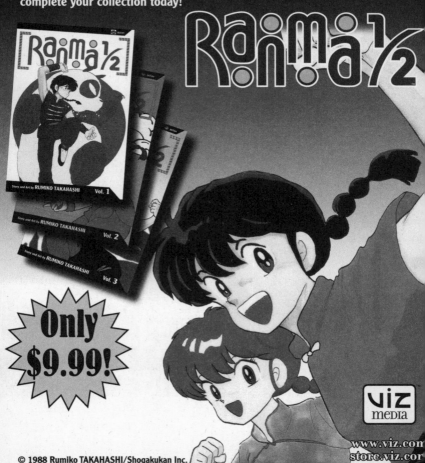

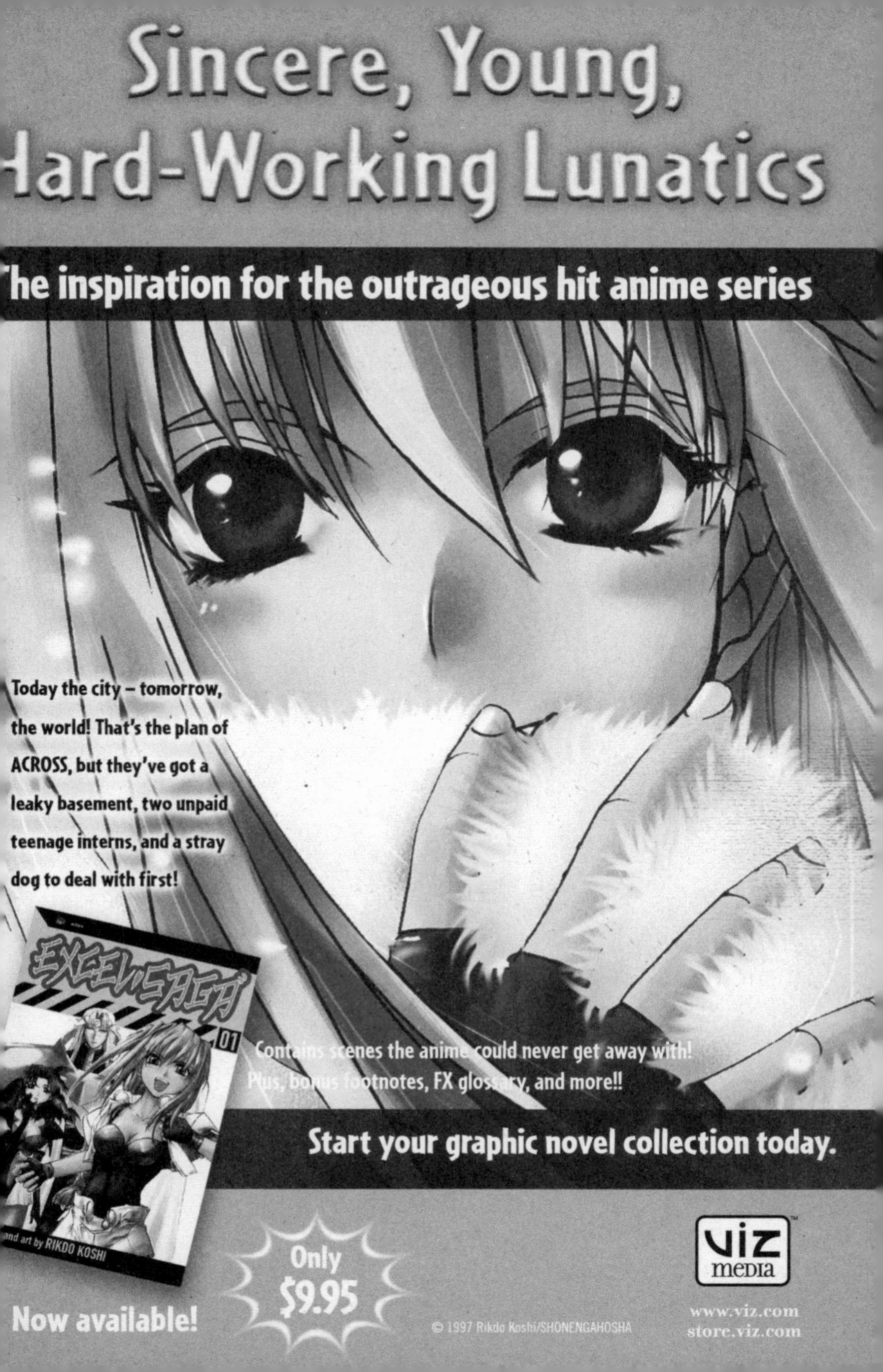
Sincere, Young,
Hard-Working Lunatics
The inspiration for the outrageous hit anime series
Today the city – tomorrow, the world! That's the plan of ACROSS, but they've got a leaky basement, two unpaid teenage interns, and a stray dog to deal with first!
EXCEL SAGA
01
and art by RIKDO KOSHI
Contains scenes the anime could never get away with!
Plus, bonus footnotes, FX glossary, and more!!
Start your graphic novel collection today.
Only $9.95
Now available!
© 1997 Rikdo Koshi/SHONENGAHOSHA
viz media
www.viz.com
store.viz.com

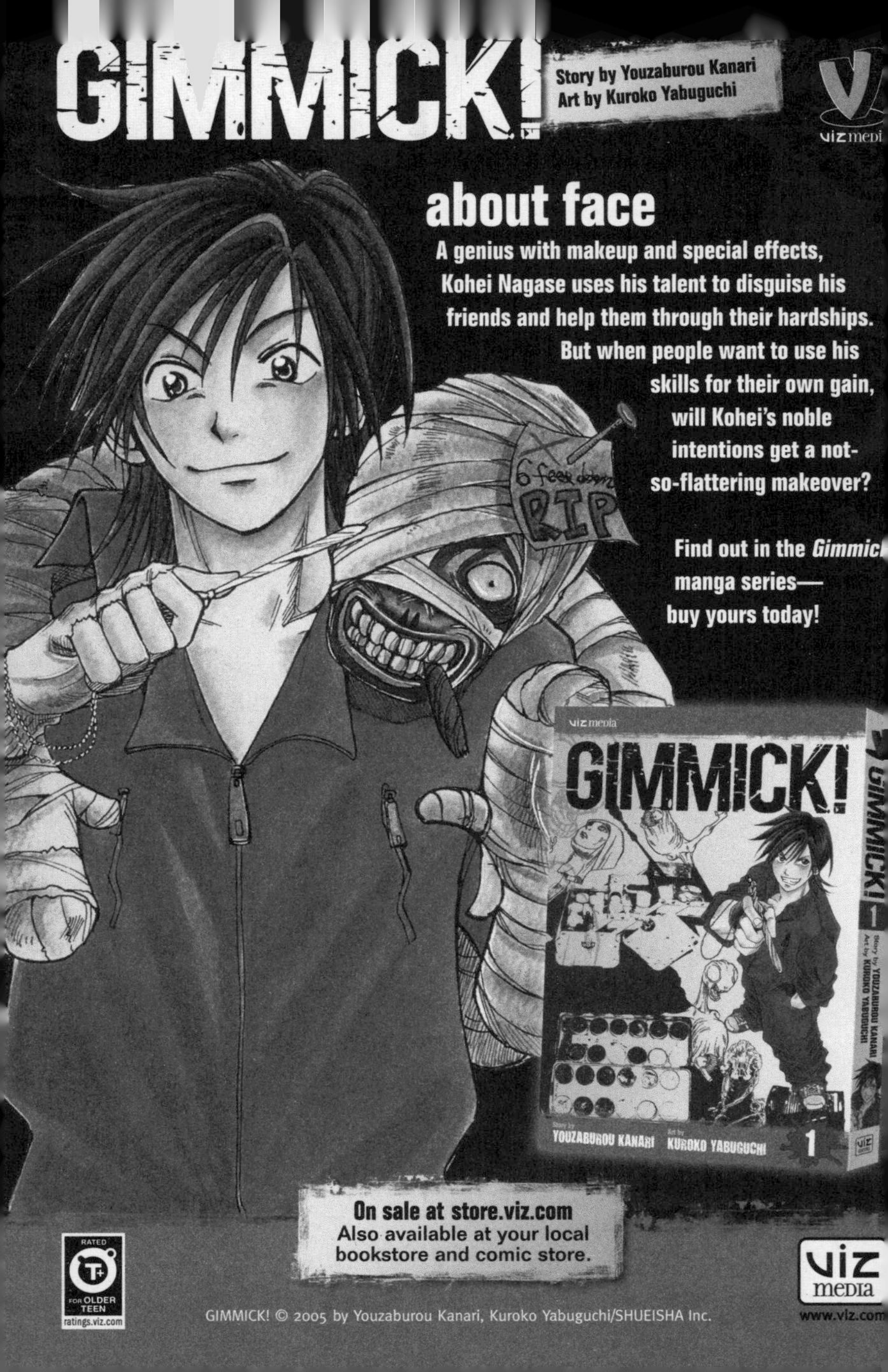
GIMMICK!
Story by Youzaburou Kanari
Art by Kuroko Yabuguchi
VIZ media
about face
A genius with makeup and special effects, Kohei Nagase uses his talent to disguise his friends and help them through their hardships. But when people want to use his skills for their own gain, will Kohei's noble intentions get a not-so-flattering makeover?
6 feet down
RIP
Find out in the Gimmick manga series—buy yours today!
VIZ media
GIMMICK!
GIMMICK! 1
Story by YOUZABUROU KANARI
Art by KUROKO YABUGUCHI
1
On sale at store.viz.com
Also available at your local bookstore and comic store.
RATED
T+
FOR OLDER TEEN
ratings.viz.com
VIZ MEDIA
www.viz.com
GIMMICK! © 2005 by Youzaburou Kanari, Kuroko Yabuguchi/SHUEISHA Inc.

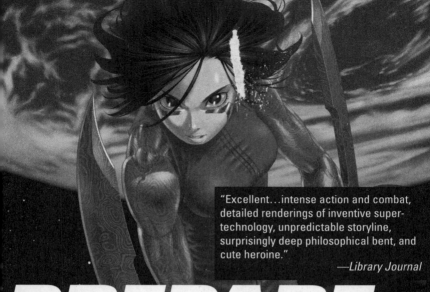
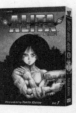
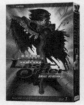

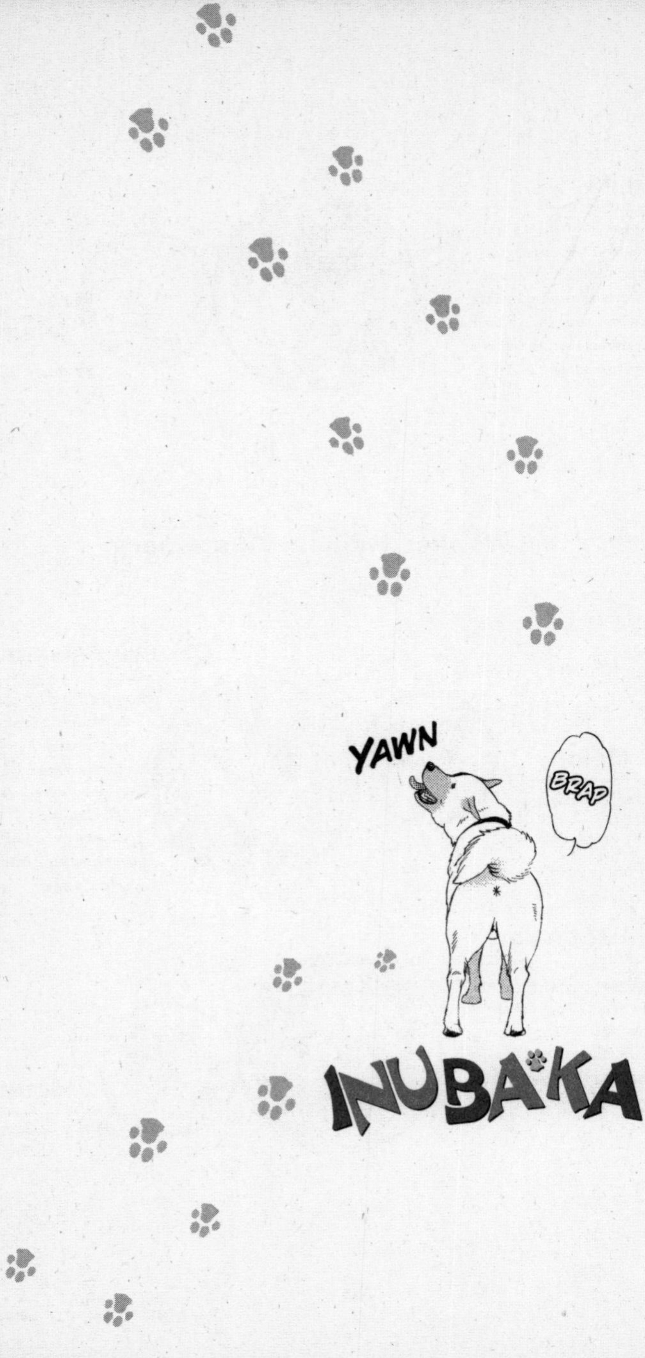
YAWN
BRAP
INUBAKA

Fujita

Owner of Lupin's sister Amuro. He kidnapped Suguri when she was a child, and when he found out she was in Tokyo, he followed her to Woofles. He is obsessed with Suguri.

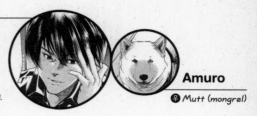

Amuro

♀ Mutt (mongrel)

Woofles Regular Customers

Chizuru Sawamura

Adopted a Chihuahua, Melon, after her longtime pet golden retriever, Ricky, alerted her that Melon was ill. She works at a hostess bar to repay Melon's medical fees.

Melon

♂ Chihuahua

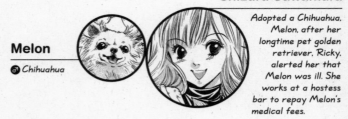

Hiroshi Akiba

Pop-idol otaku turned dog otaku. His dream is to publish a photo collection of his dog, Zidane. He is a government employee.

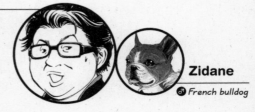

Zidane

♂ French bulldog

CHARACTERS

Suguri Miyauchi

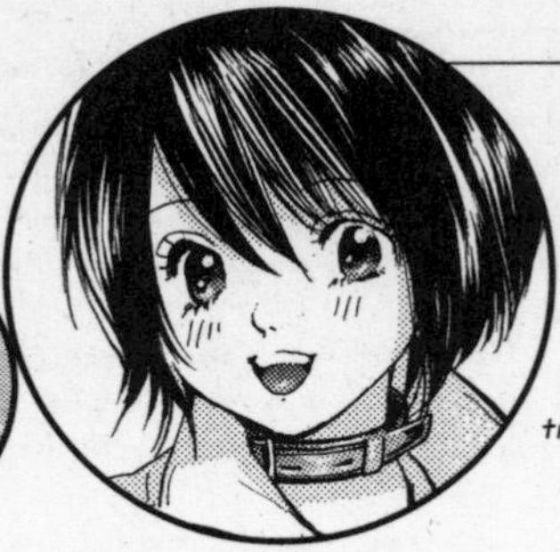

Seems to possess an almost supernatural connection with dogs. When she approaches them they often urinate with great excitement! She is crazy for dogs and can catch their droppings with her bare hands. She is currently a trainee at the Woofles Pet Shop.

Lupin

♂ Mutt (mongrel)

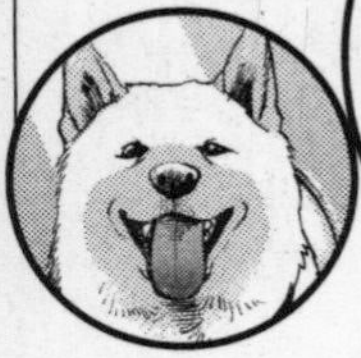

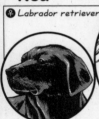

Teppei Iida

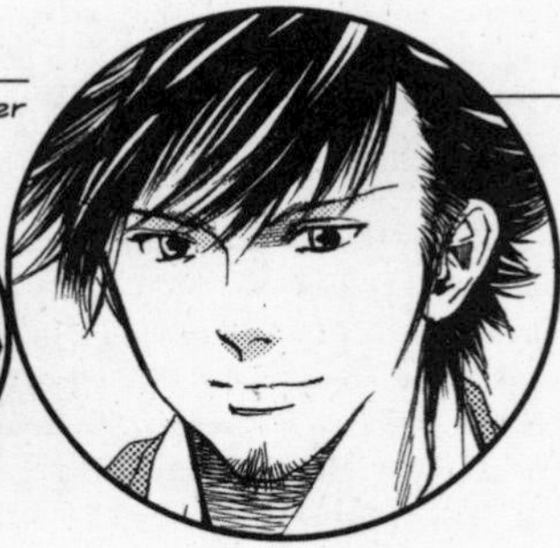

Manager of the recently opened pet shop Woofles. He is aware of Suguri's special ability and has hired her to work in his shop.

Noa

♀ Labrador retriever

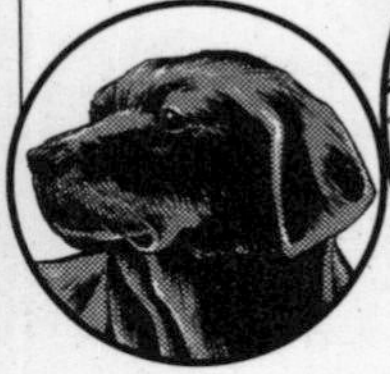

Momoko Takeuchi

The Woofles Pet Shop (second location) pet groomer. At first she had many problems and rarely smiled. But after meeting Suguri she's changed, and the two are now best friends.

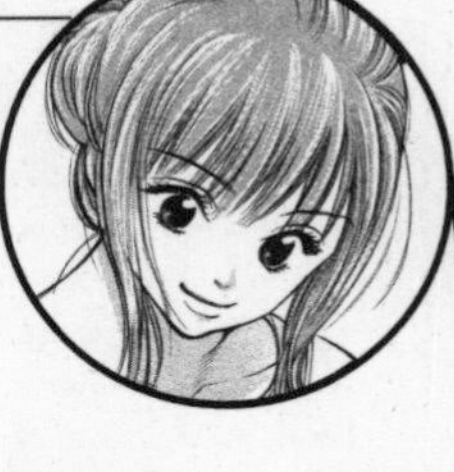

Mel

♀ Toy poodle

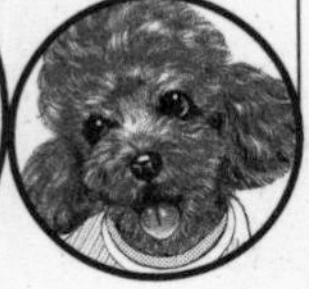

Kentaro Osada

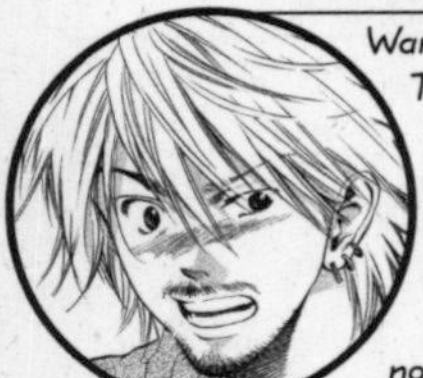

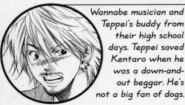

Wannabe musician and Teppei's buddy from their high school days. Teppei saved Kentaro when he was a down-and-out beggar. He's not a big fan of dogs.

Show Kaneko

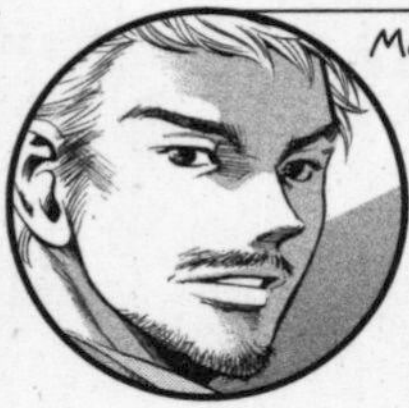

Manager of the main Woofles store and Teppei's boss. He is very passionate about the business and makes TV appearances from time to time.

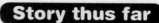

Story thus far

Teppei is the manager of the recently opened pet shop Woofles. He intended to breed his black Labrador Noa with a champion dog, but instead Noa was "taken advantage of" by an unknown and unfixed male dog!

The unknown dog's owner was Suguri Miyauchi, and her dog was a mutt named Lupin. Suguri is now working at Woofles to make up for her dog's actions.

Suguri's enthusiasm is more than a little unique. She has eaten dog food (and said it was tasty), caught dog poop with her bare hands and caused dogs to have "happy pee" in her presence. Teppei is starting to realize that Suguri is indeed a very special girl.

Suguri has now been working at Woofles for a year and has seen Noa bear a litter of puppies. Now Suguri wants Lupin to become a parent too! She goes back to her hometown to begin investigating Lupin's ancestry. During her search, she encounters a man named Fujita. He knows about the "great" Lupin (her dog's grandfather), who saved Suguri from a kidnapper when she was just a child.

However, it turns out that Fujita was the very man who kidnapped Suguri, and she decides never to see him again. After Fujita shows up at Woofles the next day, Suguri visits his apartment to tell him she doesn't want anything more to do with him. Fujita tells Suguri the truth about the kidnapping, but Suguri, frightened by Fujita's abnormal interest in her, runs away. Fujita follows her in his car, but Lupin's sister, Amuro, who was in the car with him, jumps out the window and is hit by a motorcycle...

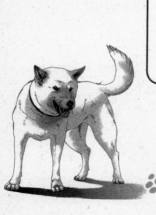

Contents

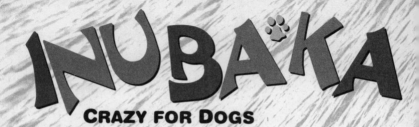

INUBAKA

CRAZY FOR DOGS

16

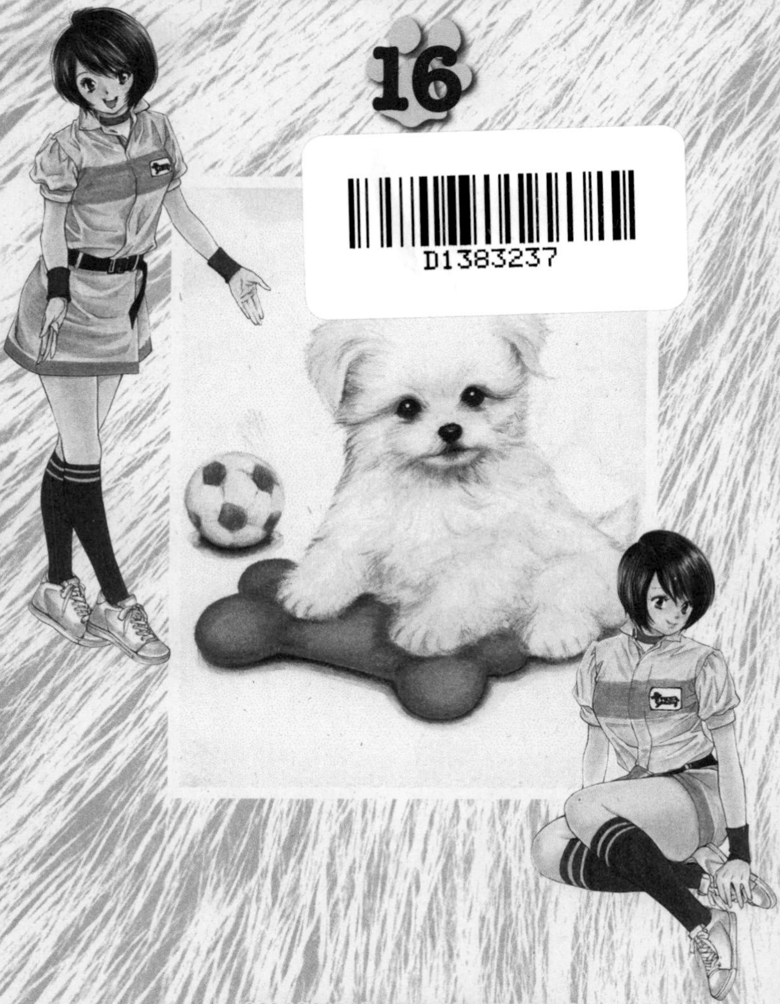

YUKIYA SAKURAGI